QUARTET

QUARTET

How Four Women Changed the Musical World

LEAH BROAD

faber

First published in the UK and USA in 2023
by Faber & Faber Ltd
The Bindery, 51 Hatton Garden
London ECIN 8HN

Typeset by Faber & Faber Ltd
Printed and bound in the UK by CPI Group (UK) Ltd, Croydon CRO 4YY

A CIP record for this book
is available from the British Library

ISBN 978–0–571–36610–1

Printed and bound in the UK on FSC® certified paper in line with our continuing
commitment to ethical business practices, sustainability and the environment.
For further information see faber.co.uk/environmental-policy

2 4 6 8 10 9 7 5 3

For my family

CONTENTS

PRELUDE

On a bleak day in March 1930, a crowd of smartly dressed women gathered outside London's parliamentary buildings. For many of the older women, it was not the first time that they had convened in the long shadow of Victoria Tower, its Gothic arches reaching up to the pale grey sky. As members of the Women's Social and Political Union, the militant suffrage organisation led by Emmeline Pankhurst, they had all marched on the House of Commons in support of women's right to vote. Now, their lapels bore medals reading 'For Valour', awarded to those suffragettes who had gone on hunger strike while imprisoned for the cause.

Others were far too young to have fought for suffrage themselves, but they still assembled to remember Emmeline Pankhurst, whose statue was being unveiled in a quiet corner of Victoria Tower Gardens. They felt that they owed Emmeline so much: those in their twenties had been able to cast their vote in a general election for the first time only a year before, thanks to the 1928 Equal Franchise Act that allowed women over twenty-one the same voting rights as men.

Equal suffrage was new enough to feel fresh, fragile and hard-won – and it had begun with Emmeline and her first arrest in 1908, just a few metres away in Victoria Street, while she was attempting to deliver a petition to the Prime Minister. Those new members of the British electorate who were unable to don a 'Valour' medal wore flashes of WSPU colours – green, white and purple – in memory of the liberator they had never met, matching the fabrics that covered Emmeline's statue.

As rain threatened to mizzle through the park, an elderly woman stepped forward, clad in a fine silk doctoral robe and cap. This, in itself, was a symbol of women's changing status: women had only begun to be awarded British degrees from 1878, and in 1910 this lady became one of just three women in England to hold a music doctorate. Brandishing a conductor's baton, she exuded an air of 'enormous eagerness', still 'indomitable & persistent' in her seventies, with blue eyes that 'positively glitter' under untameable wisps of grey hair.

Her presence immediately brought an energy and vigour to the proceedings, the women cheering visibly as she led the Metropolitan Police Band in a rousing rendition of *The March of the Women*, the suffrage anthem she had composed herself in 1910. All suffragettes knew the *March* by heart – it had been sung at rallies, in prisons and at meetings – and now it brought tears to the eyes of the older women to hear their battle song again, played by the very men who had once arrested them.

Ethel Smyth conducting the Metropolitan Police Band.

The woman was Dame Ethel Smyth, 'the greatest woman composer in the world', as one newspaper called her, numbering her 'among the most "militant" of the Suffragettes'. Never one to suffer fools gladly, she had been jailed for bricking the windows of a politician who made 'the most objectionable remark about Women's Suffrage she had ever heard'. Ethel was certainly among the women in the crowd for whom this event was especially moving – not only had she fought alongside Emmeline and been imprisoned with her, but she had been her closest friend and possibly her lover. The composer was always circumspect about revealing the intimate details of her relationships, but one of her later passions, the writer Virginia Woolf, revealed that 'Ethel used to love Emmeline – they shared a bed'. It must have been a poignant moment for Ethel, seeing Emmeline's familiar features revealed, now cast in bronze, caught forever as Ethel remembered her best, mid-speech with hands held aloft, convincing her listeners of the importance of her cause.

Among the pieces Ethel conducted was a Minuet by her younger contemporary, thirty-two-year-old Dorothy Howell. When Ethel and Emmeline were incarcerated in Holloway, Dorothy had still been in school, only just beginning to follow in Ethel's footsteps by taking private composition lessons. A quiet, unassuming woman, Dorothy led a far less unorthodox life than Ethel's – the two women could not have been more different if they had tried. While Ethel had numerous love affairs with both men and women, Dorothy remained resolutely single; Dorothy was Catholic, but Ethel could never quite embrace Catholicism.

And yet they were bound together by music. Ethel staunchly supported Dorothy's compositions, insisting that her music be heard at the unveiling even when Dorothy modestly worried that her contribution might 'let women down'. Despite their differences of age and outlook, they became threads in the rich tapestry of each other's lives. It was almost inevitable that their paths would cross at some point. Women composers were a rarity in England, and were often grouped together by programmers.

Throughout the nineteenth and twentieth centuries, Britain's musical gods were all male. When Ethel picked up her piano scores and songbooks as a child, it was Bach, Beethoven, Mozart, Schubert and Brahms whose names adorned the covers. Beyond this, it was thought not just unlikely but a biological impossibility for women to manage the kind of abstract thought associated with composition. It was begrudgingly accepted that women could write and paint because, as one author put it, these art forms 'all have a basis of imitation'. But music was different. Creating music required the ability to think both logically and emotionally, and involved no imitation of nature whatsoever. It was a talent considered beyond women's reach.

In this world Ethel would be the first woman to receive a damehood for composition, the first woman to have her work performed at New York's Metropolitan Opera (and, indeed, she remained the only woman to have an opera performed there until 2016), and the first woman to publicly and aggressively confront gender prejudices in British musical institutions. She composed a vast body of works including string quartets, sonatas, songs, orchestral pieces – and six operas, all of which were staged. Reviewing Ethel's legacy, one astonished critic named her greatest achievement as blowing 'to blazes' the idea that women couldn't compose. 'She strode through the masculine "closed shop" of the composers' world without a thought for feminine propriety.'

Yet Ethel, and later Dorothy, were not lone female voices in Britain's male-dominated compositional world. On the same day that their music boomed through Victoria Tower Gardens, just a few miles away in Highbury the composer Rebecca Clarke was giving a concert with the English Ensemble, a critically acclaimed, all-woman group that she had formed in 1927. And in Buckinghamshire, seven-year-old Doreen Carwithen, one of a new generation of composers, was practising at her family piano, starting the lessons that would eventually make her one of Britain's first women film composers.

o   o   o   o

Between them, these four women redefined who musicians could be and what they could do. They were all trailblazers in their way. Suffragette, pioneer and activist Ethel Smyth (1858–1944) is the grande dame of *Quartet*. Women had been composing before her, but she was the first to really force musical institutions to confront their gender problem. She demanded to be given the same rights as men and to be treated equally, and for her compositions not to be judged by a different standard because of her gender. Rather than remain content with being a teacher or domestic music-maker, Ethel rebelled against the roles that had been carved out for musical women in Victorian society. On the golf course opposite her cottage in Surrey, she taught Emmeline Pankhurst to throw stones to hit a target, and when the two suffragettes were later arrested for property damage they were jailed in cells next to one another. In true Ethel style, she responded to her incarceration by rousing choruses of imprisoned women to sing *The March of the Women* in jail, conducting from her cell window with a toothbrush.

Ethel was truly unusual for her time. Her life is completely unrepresentative of the experience of most women composers in the late nineteenth and early twentieth centuries. Indeed, she was lucky she was embraced as an eccentric and not institutionalised as a lunatic. Few could lead a life as bold as hers. Few, perhaps, would want to.

Rebecca Clarke (1886–1979) was one such composer who came of age in Ethel's wake. Like Ethel she was outgoing, fun, and had a wicked sense of humour. But in most ways she was Ethel's opposite. Rebecca was elegant and stylish, always dressed in the latest fashions. With her long dark hair and tall, slender figure, she wouldn't have looked out of place in a Pre-Raphaelite painting. She hated being at the centre of a scandal. Nor did she want to be seen as a 'woman composer'. Rebecca was born nearly three decades after Ethel, and by the time she was premiering her first works it was far more normal for women to be successful musicians. Few were composers – that would remain rare throughout the twentieth century – but her closest friends were some of the most celebrated musicians of their day. Where Ethel had been forced to foreground the fact that she was a woman, demanding equal treatment with men, Rebecca preferred to say that gender was irrelevant. In private she may have been outspoken on the issue, but her hatred of being pigeonholed as a 'woman composer' meant that she rarely expressed forthright support for women's causes.

Rebecca's feelings about feminism were also shaped by the fact she split her career between the UK and the USA, where attitudes towards women composers were sometimes more accommodating than in Britain. Rebecca's career was a whirlwind of triumphs and breakthroughs. A talented violist, she made history in 1913 by becoming one of the first six women in the world to be hired by a professional orchestra. With her best friend, cellist May Mukle, she toured not only America, but went as far afield as Singapore and China. And, confident in the quality of her music, she was not one to hide her light under a bushel. Rebecca began composing while figures like Ralph Vaughan Williams, now most famous as the composer of *The Lark Ascending*, dominated the UK scene. She worked alongside them very much as their equal, and was taken seriously by critics as an important modern composer.

Dorothy Howell (1898–1982) was far less outlandish and altogether more reserved than either Ethel or Rebecca. She was unfailingly modest, and knew her own mind. Billed by the press as a child prodigy when, aged twenty-one, she had a major success with an orchestral work called *Lamia*, she nonetheless seems to have been unaffected by the media frenzy that surrounded her. She delighted in writing whimsical pieces with titles like 'Tortoiseshell Cat', 'If You Meet a Fairy' and 'Puddle Duck (with apologies to Beatrix Potter)'.

Drama didn't follow Dorothy as it did Ethel. She was warm and gentle and generous, and remembered fondly by those who knew her. Like Rebecca she loved fashion, and was constantly going on shopping trips to buy new concert dresses, hats and shoes. But she didn't seek to stand out from the crowd. Dorothy had conservative tastes – her dresses were demure, and she kept her hair short and simply cut. As in clothing, so too in her lifestyle and in her music. When she first heard the dissonant, jarring sounds that would come to dominate 'modern' twentieth-century music, she reacted not with horror or panic, as many musicians did, but with amusement. Unfazed by modern trends, she always wrote melodious music that she felt was true to her, and she found a supportive home for her work within the Catholic Church.

The last of the quartet, Doreen Carwithen (1922–2003), led a life completely out of the limelight. Of all the personalities in this book, Doreen is perhaps the most complex. She looks so approachable in photographs, with her curly hair and endearingly lopsided smile that could blossom into the most candid grin when she found something genuinely funny. And yet she's something of an enigma. In her early diaries and letters she comes across as a hard-working, earnest woman. She needed her own space – she frequently wrote about needing to find time away from her boisterous and noisy family members – but she had plenty of friends and a packed social schedule. And yet those who knew her at the end of her life describe her as difficult, belligerent and exacting. She had very few friends at the time of her death, having pushed away many of those close to her.

Her career follows a similarly perplexing trajectory. In her early years she was one of the stars of the Royal Academy of Music where, like Dorothy, she studied piano and composition. She was one of the first students to be accepted on to a scholarship programme to score films, and was the only woman in her cohort. She would become one of the first British women to work predominantly as a film composer. And yet by the 1960s Doreen's name had all but vanished from concert programmes, and by the 1970s she had stopped composing altogether. What happened?

The answer is at least partly tied up in Doreen's relationship with the composer William Alwyn. The pair fell in love when she was studying at the Royal Academy, and William, married and seventeen years her senior, was her composition tutor. From the moment their relationship began – probably some time in 1944, when Doreen was twenty-two – it dominated her life. She spent the next twenty years conducting a passionate affair with him.

Doreen with her cat Aethelfirth in the 1940s.

This relationship was a huge risk for Doreen. Living in fear of discovery and the inevitable judgement and ostracisation that would follow, she kept William entirely secret. Her own family didn't know about the affair until the couple finally eloped in 1961, after which Doreen gave up her career to promote William's music. The story of artistic women either putting aside their own ambitions for domineering men, or having their achievements ignored by historians who are focused on their partners, is such a familiar one. In a more extreme case, composer Gustav Mahler forced Alma Schindler to choose between marrying him and continuing to compose – she chose him, stopped writing, and is now remembered as Alma Mahler, serial adulteress and mistress of famous men, rather than as Alma Schindler, composer. Similarly, Doreen the composer disappeared entirely into William's shadow. Like Dorothy and Rebecca before her, when Doreen died, very few people knew that she had ever composed at all.

o   o   o   o

History is full of women like these, who were famous in their lifetimes but have since become ghosts who haunt the pages of books dedicated to the men they worked with, talked with, and sometimes loved – men like Ralph Vaughan Williams and Benjamin Britten, who are today considered indispensable to the story of British music in the twentieth century. *Quartet* makes an unapologetic case for the importance of women in music history, and analyses both the obstacles that women faced, and the ways that they found to overcome them and assert their agency in a world where the odds were stacked against their success.

But this book does not 'rewrite' history. It relates a history that has always been there, waiting to be told. Nor do I want to mythologise these women. This is not a hagiography. The women in this book were all very real and relatable people with fears, anxieties and shortcomings. Between them they had some exceptional and admirable qualities, but as much as anyone else they acted out of jealousy, held petty grudges, and could be difficult or unthinking towards their peers. And this is, for me, what makes them interesting. I have not tried to airbrush their shortcomings for, as Ethel put it, 'the faults of people you are fond of are as precious as their virtues.' And sometimes these faults were born of necessity – Ethel gained a reputation as a 'difficult' woman, but without her belligerence she would never have even studied music, let alone built a career from it.

I have chosen the four women in *Quartet* for a number of reasons. First, they all wrote exquisite, breathtaking music. Second, they all achieved things that are still considered 'extraordinary' for women, even today. By the middle of the twentieth century there were sufficiently large numbers of women working as composers that it was far more difficult to choose who to include than who to leave out – but Doreen stands out for her under-appreciated music, her fascinating private life, and her career being mainly in film music. Even in 2018, only 6 per cent of the highest-grossing films were scored by a woman. Similarly, Ethel was best known as a composer of operas, and yet 2019 was the first year that the Vienna State Opera performed a work by a woman.

There were many important ways, though, in which the women in this book were *not* 'the first' or 'the only'. Although Ethel was often hailed as 'the first woman to write an opera', that accolade in fact went to Francesca Caccini, whose opera *La liberazione di Ruggiero dall'isola di Alcina* was performed in Florence in 1625. Rebecca was one of the first professional orchestral string players, but Catherine Plunkett had appeared on London stages as a violin soloist as early as the 1740s. French composer Germaine Tailleferre was scoring films in the 1920s and 1930s when Doreen was still a child, and the abbess Hildegard von Bingen had composed sacred music in the twelfth century, long before Dorothy began writing Catholic music. Ethel, Rebecca, Dorothy and Doreen all had precedents and contemporaries, and their successes built on other women's work.

Crucially, though, none of the women in *Quartet* could have been strongly aware of their predecessors because history books of their period simply didn't include them. Historical forgetting is such a powerful form of erasure. It robs women of role models, and leaves them going in circles, repeating the same 'breakthroughs', diverting valuable energy and resources from real progress. It's because of this historical tendency to forget and isolate women that *Quartet* is a group biography. It could have been the story of just one woman:

any one of them could (and hopefully will) be the subject of count-less volumes of books. But it is important that each of these women is not 'the only' today, any more than in their own lifetimes. While male critics could bluster all they liked, music just wasn't as much of a man's world as they tried to suggest. Professional musical women may have been in a minority in the early 1900s, but they were there and they were often extremely successful.

Accordingly, one thing that unites all four women is how import-ant networks were for building their careers. And these were often networks made up mostly of women. When musical women found doors closed to them, they turned to one another for support. Sometimes this meant performing each other's music – Doreen's best friend Violet Graham premiered her Piano Sonatina, while Rebecca played in various chamber groups with some of her closest friends – and sometimes they gave help in financial form. Being a composer was an expensive business, especially if you were a woman. If Ethel wanted one of her orchestral works performed, she had two options. First, she could wait for an interested conductor to take up the work – but as she repeatedly pointed out, conductors were extremely unlikely to perform music by women. The second option was to hire the venue and players herself, and try to cover costs with ticket sales.

Faced with this ongoing problem and finding herself locked out of the 'Old Boys' network that played each other's works at festivals – whom she called the 'Machine' – Ethel built herself an 'Old Girls' network of wealthy and famous women patrons who supported her unfailingly. In her lifetime Ethel was criticised for her dense thicket of friendships, accused of letting them distract her from her work. She replied cuttingly that 'if the world is inclined to scoff or speak ill of women's friendships, this is one of those cheap generalities which will pass muster only as long as women let men do their thinking for them'. As far as she was concerned, her many relationships with women were the 'shining threads in my life'. Without them, she would not have had a career at all.

The sheer number of financial and social barriers to becoming a composer meant that the profession all but excluded working-class women. It's no coincidence that all the women in *Quartet* were middle class – whether upper middle class like Ethel, or moving between the lower middle and middle middle classes like Rebecca. It wasn't impossible for women in either the upper or working classes to have musical careers, but the upper classes were heavily restricted by social expectations, while the sheer cost of musical tuition was out of reach for the majority of working-class women – to say nothing of the later costs of staging concerts or the advantages of having wealthy social connections. Although the composers in *Quartet* faced a plethora of obstacles and were disadvantaged by their gender, their class and race also gave them positions of relative power and privilege. Focusing only on the difficulties that women faced risks presenting them as victims, and the reality is far more nuanced than that. These women had individual agency, and used what structural advantages they had to effect change for themselves and for others, finding inventive ways around prejudice to forge careers against all the odds. Their stories are as much about empowerment and self-determination as they are about setback and limitation.

o   o   o   o

When Ethel came to compose her fourth opera, *The Boatswain's Mate*, in 1913, she used her own life as inspiration. At the height of the fight for women's suffrage, Ethel conjured up a subversive comedy about women's rights, making policemen figures of fun and secretly casting Emmeline as the heroine. Her opera took shape as she wrote articles supporting the suffragette destruction of Velázquez's sensual and erotic painting *The Toilet of Venus*. 'If nothing but the loss of the irreplaceable can put a stop to this wickedness of forcible feeding, frighten the country out of connivance at injustice and cruelty, and make it set free its women,' she wrote, 'then let one masterpiece after another go.' She bounced between notepaper and manuscript: between the final flourishes on angry letters, she was penning her own masterpiece, weaving themes from her suffrage anthem into the *Boatswain's* Overture.

As Ethel shows, all the women of *Quartet* are interwoven with the context of their time, as are the pieces they composed and the responses to them. Their remarkable and often radical lives – full of excitement, hope and heartbreak – spanned two world wars, the campaign for equal pay, and the cultural upheaval caused by women in numerous art forms trying to establish professional identities for themselves across multiple continents. So while this is a history of four women, it is also an alternative social history of nineteenth- and twentieth-century Britain, seen through a musical lens.

The majority of Ethel's life was lived during the height of the British Empire, as were Rebecca and Dorothy's early years, and inevitably this shaped their outlooks and experiences. Ethel and her social circle were children of empire, and thought the British Empire was 'the best civilizing force in the world', bringing moral and intellectual enlightenment to colonised peoples. This assumption even underpinned the rhetoric of the suffrage campaign. The fight for women's rights was frequently framed as being important 'not just for English women alone, but for all the women, degraded, miserable, unheard of, for whose life and happiness England has daily to answer to God'. Rooted in Victorian racial ideology, imperial feminism cast white middle-class British – and especially English – women as the potential saviours of their counterparts in colonised countries.

This is reflected in Ethel's views about race. Ethel composed *Boatswain* while staying in Egypt, and alongside her discussions about suffrage she frequently espoused racist sentiments in her letters to Emmeline – which Emmeline never seems to have objected to or disagreed with. Ethel was a flawed, complex and very real human being. Without acknowledging this we end up with a strange, whitewashed view of history, with our predecessors painted as heroes seen through twenty-first-century eyes – history as we want it, not as it was.

Born a generation later, Rebecca and Dorothy never held such inflammatory opinions. But politics similarly shaped their world. It was British imperial politics that made Rebecca's performance tours to Asia possible, involving travels across India, Japan and Myanmar. And Dorothy might have been too young to join Ethel in the suffrage campaign, but the subsequent changing views about women and laws concerning their right to work affected her as much as Ethel or Rebecca. So, too, would later feminist movements impact on the fate of Ethel's music long after her death, just as much as they shaped the reception of Doreen, Dorothy and Rebecca's work.

These composers were responding to similar musical and cultural trends, working with the same people, and their music was often played on the same concert programmes. So the book is structured chronologically, weaving together the overlapping lives of all four women. They met, however, much less often than one might think, given how rare it was for women to work as composers. Because they had to fight so hard for their own credibility and to secure performances, they often did not have the time or the energy to form musical communities with other composers that might ultimately have helped them to be considered less unusual. And even when they did meet there was no guarantee they would get along. Ethel, Dorothy and Rebecca met on a couple of occasions, and Rebecca and Ethel struck up a polite acquaintance, but they were never close friends. Late in her life, Rebecca recalled being appalled by Ethel's suggestion that her good looks might have had something to do with her success. She took this as an insinuation that she had slept her way to fame. (It's much more likely that Ethel was trying to flirt with her, in her brusque, forward way.)

Rebecca Clarke, *c*.1922.

o   o   o   o

Piecing together these women's lives is a lot like being a musical detective. As for so many women whose voices have been excised from the historical record, trying to locate the traces of their lives means encountering dead ends, silences and lost documents. The first time I visited Dorothy's niece and nephew, Merryn and Columb Howell, there was a manuscript score drying on a rack by the roaring fire. 'Oh, that's one of Aunt Dorothy's pieces,' Merryn informed me. 'It was found in a barn. We're just trying to get rid of the mould.' It took a while for anything to become legible through the damp – it turned out to be a violin work, Dorothy's clear, neat handwriting emerging through the stains. Articles about her career covered the entirety of the table in the middle of the room, spilling over into boxes perched on the chairs. Dorothy's young face gazed hopefully from pages that are now a century old. I'm glad she couldn't see into her future, where I was witnessing her niece and nephew desperately trying to save her scores from disintegrating and disappearing completely. It's only thanks to them that any of Dorothy's music survives at all. In her final years she became so depressed about the neglect of her music that she tried to burn the lot, and it was only Merryn's quick thinking that saved Dorothy's musical legacy from the flames.

The cardboard boxes holding Dorothy's music are tattered, flimsy; sometimes I worry that they will simply fall apart in my hands. Big orchestral pieces are separated using plastic filing sleeves labelled with stickers. The rest are stacked precariously, nestled alongside chocolate boxes full of family photographs, and shoeboxes containing decades of diaries. On one occasion I notice that an apple box looks deeper than the base suggests. I remove the bottom panel, and underneath lie reams of student works, some thought lost, others not known to exist at all. Among these is a scene from an opera, *Perdita*, that Dorothy composed when she was just nineteen. The fire crackles, rain lashes the windows and skylight, and Merryn offers me another cup of tea as we turn to Dorothy's travel box, which still contains the prayer book she inherited from her grandmother. This book went with Dorothy to her convent school in Belgium, and to the convent in Harrow where she would have composed *Perdita*. And it is beautiful. An exquisitely carved madonna stands in the back panel, gazing down on the Latin words covering the fragile, thin pages. Dorothy must have handled this old book with great care to leave it in such a pristine condition; it has certainly fared better than many of her scores.

Dorothy Howell in 1919.

The physical, tangible, tactile remnants of these women's lives speak volumes about their personalities, and have inevitably shaped how I have written about them. So, too, has the vast imbalance in sources available about each woman. Dorothy left few formal writings: no memoirs or books about her life and times. The closest she got to this was writing obituaries for her friends. There is no formal archive of Dorothy's possessions. But there is more haphazard, informal, uncatalogued information about Dorothy than about any other woman in *Quartet*. She was a precise woman who liked things to be proper and orderly – but she also kept *everything*. What others might have viewed as clutter she felt was cosy. Her perfectly preserved handwritten recipe books lie alongside the reviews of her major works, concert programmes with hastily scribbled thoughts about the performances next to letters offering her prestigious commissions. Dorothy was not somebody who tried to shape her legacy or image. Family was of paramount importance to her, and accordingly all her possessions were left to, and remain with, her surviving family members.

Rebecca, by contrast, curated her work much more carefully. Again, she left her belongings to family, but her scores were neat and well ordered. They were supplemented by a memoir that she wrote in her eighties, and a few choice ornaments and pieces of furniture either inherited or purchased on her many international performance tours. Rebecca's belongings suggest a much more elegant, worldly woman than Dorothy – and also someone who was reserved, a little guarded, careful and thoughtful about what she revealed of herself to the world.

The only composer whose material all resides within a single archive is Doreen – and that archive is named after William Alwyn. This was entirely Doreen's choice. She seems to have kept her music and possessions insofar as she thought them useful for telling William's story. Her compositions only resurfaced in the 1990s, long after William's death, and after scholars had been studying William's music for decades. Thanks to the care of archivists at Cambridge University Library, nearly all of Doreen's scores are now neatly catalogued and preserved. Even so, we still turned up pieces by Doreen in the process of writing this book that are not in her official works list. And the archive reveals how persistently Doreen's life revolved around William and William alone. At the heart of the collection are the bundles of letters that the couple sent each other throughout their twenty years apart, Doreen's always longer and more tender than William's, reassuring him that she was 'ready to come with you to the end of the earth', and that 'life without you would be quite impossible'.

As for Ethel, her voluminous letters, diaries and manuscripts are flung far across the world, often residing in archive collections dedicated to friends who have become far more famous than she is. Tracking down Ethel's documents is like tracing a who's who of the early twentieth century; we find her letters to Virginia Woolf in New York, correspondence with Emmeline Pankhurst in North Carolina, and hundreds of letters to and from the Irish author Edith Somerville in Belfast – and Ethel crops up again in the papers of the patron and heiress Princesse Winnaretta de Polignac in Paris. Given how important these relationships were to Ethel, it feels appropriate that little pieces of her history are tucked into these varied collections scattered across the globe. And yet it simultaneously reinforces a narrative about Ethel that dogged her during and after her life: that she was famous by association, far more interesting for who she knew than for anything she achieved herself. She was always a cameo – often a comic one – never the protagonist. Here, I have tried to show how Ethel's relationships sustained and influenced her not just personally but also artistically. Ethel needed her muses.

Of all the women in this book, the most has been written by and about Ethel. She is both a biographer's dream and nightmare. Unlike Dorothy, she certainly had an eye for posterity. She penned eleven books herself, the majority of which were autobiographical. Truthfully, even those that purport to be about somebody else are mostly about Ethel. She quipped that 'my mother had told me often it was bad manners to talk so much of myself, but I found the subject so absorbing that I never cultivated the opposite art'. Thousands of articles were written about Ethel when she was alive; she inspired characters in satirical novels and plays, and she appeared in an extraordinary number of aristocratic and artistic memoirs. So many stories surround Ethel that writing about her can sometimes feel like attempting to glimpse the truth through a smokescreen. She may have started her diary as something private, but she later went back and edited her entries, carefully curating her image for history.

And while she was, in some ways, remarkably truthful in her auto-biographies, she also kept much hidden that she worried might damage her musical reputation.

One of the many areas where Ethel's seeming candour obscured a more complex reality was her relationships and sexuality. She has sometimes been dubbed a 'lesbian composer' because the majority of her significant romantic relationships were with women, but Ethel herself never used this description. Indeed, one of her most significant relationships was with a man, Henry Brewster. He was, however, the exception rather than the rule. 'I wonder why it is so much easier for me, and I believe for a great many English women, to love my own sex passionately rather than yours?' she wrote to him in 1892. 'I can't make it out for I think I am a very healthy-minded person and it is an everlasting puzzle.'

Ethel was inexact about her own sexuality and avoided labelling herself. Nor did she talk openly about her sexual experiences, even when encouraged to by Virginia Woolf, with whom she evidently discussed the details of her relationships with other women. In 1930, talking about Ethel's writing, Virginia prompted: 'Lesbianism? Thats your theme; I await illumination anxiously', and a decade later when Ethel was preparing another autobiography, Virginia demanded that the book include 'an analysis of your sex life'. In both instances, Ethel declined.

Just as with politics, the context for Ethel's relationships was very different to today. In the Victorian era, female relationships took an astonishing array of forms. 'Romantic friendships' were a socially accepted form of intimacy between women, and while these were not necessarily sexual, the acceptance around romantic friendships allowed same-sex sexual relationships to hide in plain sight, sometimes coexisting with heterosexual relationships and marriages. And even if a relationship was not physical it did not equate to a lack of sexual desire. As historian Martha Vicinus points out, 'a sexual love might not achieve physical consummation for a variety of reasons, including social circumstances, religious scruples, a belief in the superiority of nonfulfillment, or a preference for the erotic pleasure of unfulfilled, idealized love.'

Many of Ethel's relationships with women were physically affectionate; some may have been more than that. But focusing on physicality risks obscuring a broader truth – that for Ethel, whether or not her relationships with women were physical, they were romantic, erotic, passionate, all-consuming and deeply important to her. For these reasons I have not labelled her sexuality. Instead, I have tried to use her own language where possible. She referred to significant women as her 'passions', and in both her public and private writing she spoke about her love for them, so I have used these words to describe Ethel's relationships in terms she understood.

Explaining why she wrote so many autobiographies, Ethel wrote that 'I very definitely desire that women shall know how it was with me', to reassure others that they 'are not as alone as they perhaps believe; that we women have all travelled that road and are helping where we can'. Despite her best efforts, over the years even her indomitable voice has been suppressed and silenced, falling victim to what she called the 'temptation to pretend that women are nonexistent musically, to ignore or damp down our poor little triumphs such as they are'.

The lives of the women in *Quartet* are important. They show us that music is not and has never been exclusively a man's world. I hope that discovering these women's stories will make you fall in love with them as much as I have, but most of all I hope that this book leads you to their music. Each wrote astonishing music that has, until relatively recently, been heard far too little. New recordings and performances of their pieces are showing us just how much incredible music is out there – and how very, very limited our stories have been. If we choose it, music histories could be filled with the notes of surprising, exciting and delightfully difficult women. It's time their stories were told.

ETHEL

It was on 22 April 1858 that Ethel Mary Smyth was brought forth screaming into this world. Later in life, she would maintain that she had been born on the 23rd. After all, being both a patriot and a woman of talent – no, genius – she felt it far more appropriate to share a birthday with Shakespeare, on St George's Day. It was neither the first nor the only time that Ethel would tweak the facts of her life to better reveal what she knew to be the underlying reality: that she was exceptional.

Ethel wove a web of legends around herself all her life – without a little self-mythologising she might never have achieved the things that she did. And like all the best stories, her tales were based in truth. Ethel was born a military daughter, fourth of the eight children in Colonel John Hall Smyth and Emma Struth's large and boisterous family. John came from a long and illustrious line of perfectly ordinary bankers, clergymen and army officers, and he meant to follow their example by living according to a code of honour and duty. He loved his family, country, God and his monarch. If he felt any one of them had been threatened or insulted, his handlebar moustache would bristle with indignation. His formidable stature was somewhat undermined, however, by his unlucky habit of mixing up his words when annoyed. His attempts to reprimand his wayward children more often ended in laughter than repentance after he had commanded the dog to stop making his son bark, or some other unfortunate slip of the tongue.

If Ethel's musicality came from either parent, it was certainly her mother. Emma – or 'Nina', as she was known – had a singing voice that 'would have melted a stone', and Ethel especially delighted in her rambunctious renditions of dance tunes, thundered out on the family piano while her children whirled around the room. Nina was the paragon of a society lady. Not only was she a consummate pianist and singer, but she was also quick-witted, spoke multiple languages and always dressed tastefully in the latest fashions. As a family friend remarked to Ethel, if Nina had married a diplomat instead of a colonel, she and her dark brown eyes and thick black hair 'would have been known and acclaimed all over Europe'. In short, she was beautiful, bright and, by the time Ethel was growing up, desperately, desperately bored. If Nina had been born a few decades later she would surely have pursued a professional career. As it was, her intelligence and personality were much larger than the world in which they were contained. This mismatch made her seem like 'a tragic figure' to Ethel. Occasionally, Nina's most melancholy moments would erupt into explosive rows with her daughter, who was nicknamed the 'Stormy Petrel' on account of being just as fiery and fiercely passionate as her mother. During these episodes Ethel admitted that not even their imposing home was 'large enough to hold her and me'.

When Ethel was born her family lived at Bourne House in Bexley, but the first house that she remembered with any clarity was Sidcup Place. It was a large, sprawling building, separated from the rest of the world by high brick walls enveloped in ivy, and it provided the perfect space for increasing numbers of children to let themselves and their imaginations run wild. Ethel's fondest childhood memories involved afternoons spent chasing her older siblings Johnny, Mary and Alice through the gardens. They tore through the shrubbery that smelled of the cool dampness of spring, with bracken and leaves still crisp from winter crackling underfoot; played croquet under the never-ending shade of the acacia that seemed to bloom yellow-bright as the sun all year round; broke into the kitchen garden to steal the enticingly fragrant fruits and herbs kept behind its walls, gleefully bearing their contraband to the safety of a tree house they built in an elm tree by the duck pond. The Smyths believed fervently in the importance of outdoor life, and Ethel's carefree childhood instilled in her a lifelong, unladylike passion for all kinds of sports, from riding and hiking to lawn tennis and golf – the only pursuits that would stand equal to her love of music.

Exploration inevitably entailed a little rule-breaking. The family pigs fascinated Ethel: if she wasn't riding them round the courtyard and being thrown unceremoniously into a manure heap, then she was bribing the farm hands to let her watch them be slaughtered. Such antics deeply upset Johnny, who had much more conservative opinions about the way his sisters should behave than they did. When Mary and Ethel were busily engaged in vicious brawls that (allegedly) involved embedding kitchen cutlery in each other's faces, Johnny retreated under the nearest available table. Later, Ethel was followed by three more sisters and a brother: Nina, Violet, Nelly and Bob. Faced eventually with six strong-willed sisters, Johnny admitted defeat. Women ruled the Smyth household.

When they tired of the gardens, Ethel and her band of miscreants would storm indoors, transforming various rooms into battlegrounds for their imagined wars. The gallery was a favoured venue, long enough to get up speed skidding along the floor screaming, but when more privacy was needed the group headed upstairs to the attic. This was a den of treasures. Here Ethel smoked her first furtive cigarettes (a habit that she would only kick much later in life), and discovered her father's collection of swords and pistols that he had brought back from India.

To Ethel these weapons were just an exciting addition to their war games, but it was through her father and objects like these that she got her first introduction to imperial politics. As a military daughter, imperialism was part of the fabric of her upbringing. John had been sent to India when he was fifteen, and when he and Nina married in 1849 he was serving in the Bengal Artillery. They initially set up their family home in Bengal, moving back to England just before Ethel was born. John worked his way up the military ranks, was promoted to Lieutenant Colonel in 1858, and decorated in 1861 for his role in suppressing the 1857 Indian Rebellion, when Indian soldiers rose up against the British East India Company's rule. This was a formative environment for Ethel, shaping the woman she would become. She inherited her family's conservative political views and would forever be a staunch supporter of the military.

o   o   o   o

To accommodate their growing family, when Ethel was nine the Smyths moved west to take up an even larger house, Frimhurst, near the military town of Aldershot. Still standing today, Frimhurst was an enormous building sat between Basingstoke Canal and the railway, which provided Ethel with a favourite pastime of lobbing stones at passing trains. The orchards and expansive fields could have provided as exciting a space for childhood games as Sidcup Place, but Ethel was growing out of the reckless days of her early youth. Frimhurst marked the beginning of her passage towards adulthood and all of its complexities.

A major difficulty Ethel had to face was matrimony. The Smyths' main hope for their six daughters was a good marriage, but Ethel never shared this vision for her future. She preferred to leave wedded bliss to her older siblings. She viewed the eldest Smyth, Alice, as a Regency relic, and mocked her mercilessly for falling into a Jane Austen-esque swoon after the first of her many proposals. And she didn't mind when her own suitors drifted off to woo Mary instead, after they grew tired of her beating them at sports. Alice and Mary were inadvertent protectors; being the third daughter allowed Ethel more freedom than she would have had without older sisters to fulfil her parents' marital ambitions. She showed a wild disinterest in anything that involved a maternal instinct. Dolls were her most despised toys, and she and Mary bestowed a series of increasingly severe illnesses upon them, maintaining that they needed to remain in quarantine lest their fatal diseases spread. Animals were Ethel's preferred company. She became a formidable horsewoman, going hunting during the time that other women spent developing their needlework and building up the skills that would help them on the marriage market.

Ethel saw marriage as a restriction of her freedom. She never expressed any desire to become a mother. And beyond this, she was more interested in women than in men. The boys who tried to capture her heart aroused very little emotion on her part at all. The closest she came to marriage was a whirlwind romance with William Wilde, Oscar Wilde's shorter-haired, bearded brother, whom she met on a trip to Ireland. Ethel was attracted to his intellectual enthusiasm, and they bonded over a shared love of poetry, philosophy, music and lawn tennis. On the ship back to England the two sat under the stars wrapped up in a blanket, debating philosophers' relative merits, shivering slightly as they tasted the salt lingering on their lips, carried by the cold sea air. The romantic mood was broken only briefly by a seasick Ethel vomiting on William. But he was undeterred, and by the end of the voyage the two were engaged, the result of an impulsive proposal made atop a collapsing biscuit tin.

William was hopelessly in love with Ethel – but she was not with him. From her perspective, it was all a great game. The main excitement of the proposal was being able to trump her sisters by having got engaged before she appeared as a debutante. She was most disgruntled, therefore, when William asked her to keep the engagement secret for a while. For Ethel, secrecy defeated the point of the whole endeavour. His earnest love letters were the final straw, and after just three weeks she admitted to herself that she had accepted William only from 'flattered vanity, light-heartedness, adventurousness, anything you please except love', and broke off the engagement.

Ethel's heart lay elsewhere. Her attention was devoted almost exclusively to women, and she was smitten with countless ladies including her governess, family friends and classmates at her boarding school in Putney. She kept track of these 'passions', as she called them, by compiling an ever-growing list of women 'to whom, had I been a man, I should have proposed'. Whether Ethel's ardour was reciprocated was another matter. Many learned to love her uncompromising attitude, but even then she could be overwhelming. When she loved she loved intensely and completely. She exuded warmth, spoke truthfully and judged fairly, which meant she gained affection as easily as she gave it. But her friendships were often tempestuous. To Ethel, heated disagreements were only proof of how much she cared. Reconciliations were as unrestrained as the flare-ups that caused them. Her tendency to fly into a blaze at the slightest provocation earned her the nickname the 'uncastrated cat' from Virginia Woolf, Ethel's last great passion, who compared being the object of her affections to 'being caught by a giant crab'. And yet, despite Virginia's protestations, she cared deeply about Ethel. They remained close until the writer's death.

Ethel's passions also provided her with artistic inspiration. For some composers, the relationship between their life and works can be oblique, making it difficult to draw links between events and compositions with any certainty. But Ethel had a distinctly autobiographical tendency, and many of her finest pieces were inspired by and tangibly related to people she knew. When composing under the immediate influence of a muse, Ethel could write music that was both bold and intimate, sprightly and humorous, and always with a driving energy that stunned her listeners.

This autobiographical approach to composition began with her earliest, adolescent attempts to write music. Ethel was brought up as an Anglican, so her first experiences of music were the stirring but often quite uninventive hymns she sang on Sundays. For teenage Ethel, music was a way of expressing devotion. Accordingly, her earliest compositions were short religious pieces, each of which was dedicated to a different woman on her list of passions. She had an exceptional flair for melodrama, and from a very early age found that both music and literature provided her with an outlet for her more turbulent emotions. Perhaps realising the futility of her amorous attachments to much older women, or to protect herself against the pain of an unrequited love, she would frequently imagine death and disaster upon her passions, then commit herself fully to the 'agony of love' that this motivated, writing short choral pieces on texts like 'Come sweet death', or 'O darkest woe, O heart's pain'. Young Ethel relished the anguish of being lovestruck and heart-worn in an almost chivalric way, which inspired an outpouring of poems about her 'shallow heart within its cage', short plays, and musical miniatures that would be a great source of entertainment for older Ethel.

Alongside her distinctly overdramatic poetry, from the age of eleven Ethel began to take a serious interest in music. Like all Victorian girls of her class, she had singing and piano lessons, and she made her first informal public outing as a singer duetting with Mary, then thirteen, with mother Nina accompanying them at the piano. The pieces they sang were short – sometimes quirky and jovial, often featuring a young woman longing for love – and always saccharine. Such performances were commonplace, advertising girls' eligibility to the local gentry. But Ethel attacked her musical studies with an uncommon seriousness. A turning point came with the arrival of a new governess when Ethel was twelve. The governess had studied at the Leipzig Conservatoire, which was at the time the most prestigious musical institution in Europe, and she introduced Ethel to the 'classical' music that was taught there.

This was the moment when, as Ethel later recalled, 'a new world opened up before me.' She enjoyed the popular ballads that she sang at home, but the piano sonatas that her governess played invoked new depths of feeling. Unlike the dances and songs that Ethel was used to, sonatas weren't designed for communal music-making. They were written to be listened to intently, in silence. Gone were the romping oom-pah-pah bass lines she knew from popular songs, replaced by delicate melodies and thundering chords, whole worlds of contrast that unfolded in the most surprising ways. When Ethel heard these pieces she felt sorrow, fear, pity and an elation that she had never experienced before. She began learning Beethoven's piano sonatas, devouring any scores she could lay her hands on. This new governess had given Ethel a purpose. She decided that from hereon in, she would devote her considerable energies to music, and go to study in Leipzig.

o o o o

There was only one problem with Ethel's plan. There was no way her father would allow it. In the Britain that John had been brought up in, music was simply not a reputable career for either women or men. It was seen as a frivolous, effeminate pastime suitable only for the drawing room. Levels of musical professionalism in England were woeful. Music, as far as the English were concerned, was foreign. Nobody was prepared to lavish more money on going to concerts than the English, but the high-earning stars that audiences paid to see usually came from abroad. And English composers were even more rare than English virtuosi.

But in the fifty years between John's birth and his daughter setting her sights on Leipzig, the status of music in Victorian England had changed significantly. In an era when England's national narratives maintained its superiority in all things, the lamentable state of English music-making had become a source of considerable insecurity. Particularly embarrassing was the fact that England had no equivalent of Beethoven or Mozart. Instrumental music on English programmes was written by Germans, and opera by Italians. While this was only a minor issue in the early nineteenth century, when Germany and Italy became unified countries in 1871 and seemed to present serious military threats to Britain, their cultural dominance became increasingly unpalatable. English music needed a champion.

In a society obsessed with the idea of progress and individual improvement, music needed to be reimagined as something useful in order to be taken seriously. This happened slowly, as the result of various colliding forces with mutual interests. As the price of printing went down and relatively cheap newspapers like the *Daily Telegraph* became available to a wide public, the musical press grew at an astonishing rate. Journalists who saw themselves as public educators created a discussion about what 'good' music was and should be, and their reviews helped to build (or break) the reputations of emerging musicians. Audiences relied on journalists to guide them through the bewildering array of concert options that became available from the 1870s onwards, as supply grew to meet demand. Where concerts had previously been available only to the upper classes, the standardisation of working hours and rise in average earnings meant that there was a potentially much larger, middle-class public wanting to spend money on concerts. And these prospective audiences were willing to pay for music in their own homes as well. Industrialisation made mass-produced pianos available to the middle classes, and the number of copyrighted editions of music published per year rose by over an astonishing 5,000 per cent between 1835 and 1901.

Perhaps most important of all was the realisation that if music could corrupt, it might also be used for positive change. In 1871 the Reverend Hugh Reginald Haweis published a hugely popular book called *Music and Morals*, which argued that music had the potential to be a morally improving force. But – and this was a big 'but' – only under certain conditions. Good music needed to improve the 'moral health of society', and to do so it had to contain a carefully controlled combination of emotion with elevated philosophical thought.

The idea that 'good' music engaged both the intellect and the emotions was not new, but the Victorians embraced it with an unparalleled fervour. Religious music blossomed, particularly choral pieces like Handel's *Messiah*. With its rousing choruses proclaiming the glory of God, the *Messiah* became a staple of Victorian music-making. Performances were extravagant and often enormous – an 1857 rendition at the Crystal Palace featured more than two thousand singers. This focus on morality widened the gap between what was applauded as serious and moral music, and what was denounced as frivolous, sentimental and immoral. Traces of these ideas still linger around classical music today, in its associations with difficulty, complexity and elite social status – but also with transcendence, greatness and cultural worth.

Believing wholeheartedly in this idea of what classical music was and could be, seventeen-year-old Ethel desperately wanted to be part of this musical world. She wasn't the only woman of her generation to have this aspiration. Middle-class British women of the 1870s were demanding – and getting – increased legal and social autonomy. In 1870, the Married Women's Property Act granted married women the right to inherit property and own any money they earned, and this would be extended in 1882 to allow a woman the right to buy and sell her own property independent of her husband. The University of London began accepting a small number of women in the 1860s, and the founding of all-women Cambridge colleges Girton and Newnham, in 1869 and 1871 respectively, opened up educational opportunities that could only be dreamed of by early Victorian women.

Late Victorian women's movements tackled a whole host of different issues to try to improve women's lives, from providing trade union support for women to reforming divorce laws. And the campaign for the vote was well underway. The National Society for Women's Suffrage had been established in 1867 to help women to gain the vote peacefully, by constitutional means. The momentum behind this campaign would grow over the rest of the century, but it remained resolutely peaceful, with petitions as a primary weapon of choice until 1903, when the Pankhurst family set up the Women's Social and Political Union under the slogan 'Deeds not Words'. Emmeline and her daughters Christabel and Sylvia instigated a policy of militancy, strategically seeking high-profile arrests. Christabel Pankhurst was first jailed in 1905 for spitting at a policeman after she disrupted a political meeting, and by the end of the decade, hundreds of women had been imprisoned for demanding that their voices be heard. The images of women clad in flashes of white, green and purple being dragged away by policemen have since become synonymous with the suffrage campaign in Britain, but the Pankhursts were building on decades of work by Victorians who opened up education, politics and workplaces to the women who would come after them.

As women's social freedom grew and music became more respectable, increasing numbers of British women turned to professional composition, performance and teaching. Most received their musical education in England, either through governesses and private tutors, or at the Royal Academy of Music, which had been co-educational since its inception in 1822. Many of Ethel's compositional contemporaries studied at the Academy, such as Rosalind Ellicott (born 1857) and Dora Bright (born 1862) who, like Ethel, composed large-scale works and had orchestral works performed at important venues.

By the 1870s the Royal Academy had a mixed reputation, partly because of its varying teaching standards, but also partly because women were educated there. And as Ethel saw it, the rising numbers of English women composers presented her with a problem. She didn't want to be associated with them. Critics declared that women who composed with 'the mystery of grace and enchantment' innate to female nature were to be applauded – but the woman who transgressed 'the limits God has imposed upon her' by writing 'manly' and 'powerful' music was 'a monster who excites disgust and repulsion'. So Ethel wanted to be seen as an honorary man. Her decision to go to Leipzig was a way of distancing herself from women like Dora and Rosalind. *Because* Germany was in many ways less hospitable to women composers (some institutions barred women from composition classes altogether) and because it was considered Europe's musical capital, Ethel felt she would be taken more seriously if she could succeed there.

So she set about single-mindedly making her way into the male-dominated world of (German) classical music. She practised diligently and kept writing her songs and chorales, but she desperately needed to find a competent composition teacher – no easy task in rural Surrey. However, by a stroke of good luck that must have seemed to Ethel like divine intervention, an officer called Alexander Ewing arrived in their lives after he was posted at Aldershot. Although a military man, he had studied music in Germany and subsequently composed a popular hymn tune called 'Jerusalem the Golden', which practically made him musical royalty in Ethel's book. Encouraged by Alexander's wife who, being a popular children's author herself, supported Ethel's musical ambitions, Ethel showed Alexander her short compositions. He declared her an extraordinary talent, and offered to teach her harmony. John finally gave in to the combined protestations of Ethel and her advocates, and grumblingly consented.

This was the breakthrough that Ethel needed. Twice a week she made her way to the Ewings', where for two hours before lunch she would sit with Alexander to analyse her compositions, practise harmony exercises, and explore the latest scores by modern composers. Alexander introduced her to the music of Johannes Brahms, Franz Liszt, Hector Berlioz, Richard Wagner and Robert Schumann. Brahms's music was complex, tense and densely wrought, teaching Ethel how to build whole pieces from the smallest of ideas, sometimes just three notes. From Schumann she learned how to create subtle, chimerical harmonies that exploded like fireworks in any number of unexpected directions. And from Liszt came sheer joy in virtuosic, dazzling writing that challenged the performer and astonished and delighted the listener. 'These expeditions were', Ethel later recalled, 'the delight of my life.' As in all things, Ethel attacked her studies with an enthusiasm that was so effervescent that those around her couldn't help but be swept up by it. Alexander found himself wanting to compose again, so the two worked side by side, Ethel feeling as though she was at the very frontiers of new music.

Of course, such an idyll could not last. John truly believed that he knew what was best for his daughter, and kept watch for any excuse to stop Ethel's lessons. Before long he got the ammunition he needed. Rifling through Ethel's post, John found a letter from Alexander which he deemed highly inappropriate. He convinced himself that Alexander was intent on pursuing Ethel romantically. John wasn't just being difficult – it was not unheard of for tutors to instigate relationships with their unmarried students. If he wanted to protect Ethel, it wasn't unreasonable to clamp down on any whiff of impropriety. Despite Ethel's vehement objections, John put an immediate end to her lessons.

Alexander's dismissal was just the first in an escalating series of spats between Ethel and John. He had hoped that studying in Leipzig was just a childhood dream that his daughter would grow out of, turning her thoughts instead to marriage and starting a family. By the time she turned eighteen Ethel was 'exceedingly fair, tall, and good-looking, the merry twinkle in her eyes betokening an inexhaustible fund of humour', and had a formidable personality that attracted as many men as it repelled. Many were completely disarmed by her unpredictability, self-confidence and determination to speak her mind. John watched in dismay as Ethel rejected suitor after suitor, and when she announced her intention to leave for Leipzig within the year, his patience finally ran out. Declaring that he would sooner see her 'under the sod' than in Leipzig, John banned her from leaving.

So began a prolonged battle of wills, with each proving a more determined adversary than the other had bargained for. Protectiveness certainly came into John's thinking, not just anger at Ethel's wilful defiance of his wishes. The whole family was still grieving for Johnny, who had died in 1875 when Ethel was seventeen, from injuries sustained in a riding accident. Nina was left utterly heartbroken. With his death 'most of the sunshine went out of her life'. Ethel, too, was profoundly affected. She took to using Johnny's violin, feeling that the instrument kept her close to him. And just a few days before Johnny died, both Alice and Mary had got married, leaving the family home shortly after his funeral. Ethel, then, was the eldest child still left in the Smyth household. Understandably, this might have made John more keen for her to pursue a conventional path that he felt would keep her safe and close to home.

Whatever John's reasoning, Ethel was having none of it. She resolved to make life at home completely unliveable. She refused to leave her room for days on end (prompting John to nearly kick down her door) and started fights. Some days she managed to sneak out of the house, and borrow enough money from tradesmen to get herself a third-class omnibus ticket to London so she could go to concerts – unchaperoned. Ethel got a particular pleasure from the chaos of rattling around on the wooden benches that lined the inside of the omnibus, jostling her fellow passengers as the horses rumbled slowly towards London, making her way through the dirty, busy, noisy streets that smelled of manure and oil and thrummed with the noise of carriages, bells, dogs, shouts, street musicians – and then finally retreating into the quiet entrance foyer of St James's Hall in Piccadilly, then London's premier concert venue. It felt like a temple. Under a vaulted ceiling with gilded angels bearing scrolls inscribed with the names of her musical idols, in the dim, cloying gaslight, Ethel experienced 'the revelation' of hearing some of the finest musicians of her time play the serene music of Schubert, a composer 'nearer my heart than any other'.

However furious John was upon her return, these trips sustained Ethel, emboldening her acts of domestic guerrilla warfare. She enlisted a number of women in the family's social circle to try to persuade John to change his mind, and boycotted everything from dinner parties to church, finally refusing to speak to anyone at all.

Ethel was playing a dangerous game. She was lucky that no matter how exasperating her family found her, they ultimately loved her and wanted the best for her. Less sympathetic parents might have viewed her actions as manifestations of mental breakdown and called in a psychiatrist. Accusations of insanity and the threat of the asylum loomed over all Victorian women who rebelled against the expectations placed upon their gender – particularly unmarried women, who were 'widely considered a social problem'. Fortunately for Ethel, however, it was John who eventually conceded defeat. Finally persuaded – or perhaps just worn down – by his daughter's determination, John gave his blessing for Ethel to go to Leipzig. Chaperoned by Alice's husband, Harry Davidson, nineteen-year-old Ethel set out to fulfil her childhood dream in July 1877.

o o o o

'LEIPZIG!!' Ethel wrote to her mother the moment she got to the city: 'Here I am!!' She was overwhelmed walking down the same tree-lined avenues that Mozart had, treading the same worn pavements as Bach. For Ethel, wandering among the terracotta roofs and smooth white walls of Leipzig was like stepping into a fantasy world. She made her way straight to the Gewandhaus – Leipzig's concert hall that had housed performances by Mozart, Beethoven, Mendelssohn, Schumann, Wagner and Brahms – and to the Conservatoire. She felt she was where she was meant to be, composing herself into history at the heart of Europe's most musical country.

Ethel's new existence was a blaze of independence and freedom. She had her own space – a light, airy, whitewashed room with large windows and stained wood floors – and she hired a piano so she could compose whenever inspiration struck her. In Leipzig, Ethel could just wander to concerts at her leisure. True, she still needed a chaperone. But she could find ways around that. She once disguised herself as an old lady, indulging her love of the dramatic with padded-out clothes, powdered hair and wrinkles pencilled on to her face. In her first few months, Ethel got to hear more music than she had in her whole lifetime so far, played by some of the most eminent performers of the day.

Ethel was in her element. Having worked towards this moment for the last eight years, she was determined to make the most of it. Her days were packed with composition, piano, singing, choir, harmony and ensemble performance classes. Evenings were filled with concerts or plays. She threw herself into her studies with gusto, subjecting her work to ruthless self-criticism and then devoting herself single-mindedly to improving the areas where she felt she was weakest – even when that meant swearing off composition for a few months to dedicate herself to piano practice. As her tutors pointed out to her, a composer who couldn't sing and play the piano was their own worst enemy. Composers needed to be their own advocates, and if they couldn't play their own works to prospective conductors, their music would not get performed. This was *especially* true if they were a woman. Not only were women's works less likely to be published in the first place, but women also had to overcome the scepticism of conductors who believed that they simply couldn't compose at all.

So Ethel practised. Five hours a day she sat at her piano, working through technical exercises until she was capable of playing the most challenging of her own works. And these were, by this point, getting extremely complex. She had moved on from the songs she had written in England, and was now also composing challenging sonatas – solo instrumental pieces with multiple movements. Her Piano Sonata No. 1 was heavily influenced by Beethoven's drama, Mozart's clean lines and melodies, and the intensity that Ethel loved so much in Brahms's music. Nonetheless, this sonata also has many of the hallmarks of Ethel's compositional style. The first movement is strident and gripping, with sudden turns and changes that give the music a decidedly theatrical feel, as though there has been a sudden plot twist. Contrasted with this outgoing, effusive music are moments of exquisite tenderness and interiority. They are never sentimental but are curiously ambiguous, seeming to hint at something just beyond the listener's reach. It's this combination of power and vulnerability that makes Ethel's music so compelling. She dedicated the sonata to her mother, and tried not to burst with self-satisfaction when a fellow composer and violinist declared one of her themes to be 'so pure and fresh, that I could almost swear it was Mozart'.

Ethel's pieces received admiration from everybody in her musical circle. She was soon promoted within the Conservatoire cohort to study with Carl Reinecke, the most sought-after composition tutor in the city. Ethel recorded every accolade and commendation, and relayed them verbatim in her letters home. The sense of relief in these letters is overwhelming. For all her bluster and bombast, Ethel was well aware of the risk she had taken in going to Leipzig. Although she was considered talented by her family friends in England, this did not necessarily mean that professionals would think the same. She had set aside marriage, courted scandal and enraged her family on a hope. 'I sometimes doubted whether it was only for a woman & an Englishwoman [. . .] that I was anything particular in music,' she admitted to her mother, not knowing whether 'such talent as I have deserved to have everything else put aside for it!' And now here she was, praised by musicians who played in the world's best-known orchestras, and who counted famous composers like Brahms among their friends.

Ethel was practical. She knew that talent alone was not enough to build a career. It would take years of dedicated hard work and humility. Hard work was possible; humility she would find a little more difficult. But the affirmation that she did at least have talent made her more determined than ever, and even more resolute in her decision not to marry. 'Every day I become more & more convinced of the truth of my old axiom – that why no women have become composers is because <u>they have married</u> – & then very properly made their husband & children the first consideration,' she mused to her mother. She reassured her family that they need not fear a scandal while she was living in Leipzig. Even if Brahms himself were to propose to her, she would decline him. Ethel considered herself married to her music and saw her compositions as her children. In one of her rare vulnerable, tender moments, Ethel thanked her mother for supporting the aspirations of her 'sole unmarried daughter'. How many daughters, she pondered, were blessed with a mother who had the 'understanding-ness & unselfishness' that Nina did?

Nina's continued support was all the more valuable because for the first time Ethel was starting to come up against the consequences of direct prejudice against women composers. She was prepared for some initial hostility, but she expected to get her way eventually, as she had with her father. The realities of negotiating the musical world as a woman were tougher than she expected, however.

She first approached a publisher, Breitkopf & Härtel, with a set of songs. Publication was an absolute necessity for a composing career because without it, performances could not follow. As Ethel put it, 'a nun walled up alive in her convent would have a better chance of exercising influence than manuscripts in a cupboard.' In Ethel's gendered musical world, it was considered perfectly acceptable for women to write songs because they were short and associated with the expression of emotion, and because they had texts – the theory being that texted works were easier to write because the composer could follow the sentiment of the words rather than having to think abstractly. Song was one of the few genres in which women were admitted as composers, and some of the most successful songwriters of the nineteenth and twentieth centuries were women.

Ethel's English contemporaries Maude Valerie White and Liza Lehmann were household names as song composers, and the older Clara Schumann and Fanny Mendelssohn had also published songs in Germany. But this reputation could also be limiting. Fanny's family supported her brother, Felix, to become one of the most celebrated composers of the nineteenth century. For Fanny, however, her father believed that music must 'always remain but an ornament; never can and should it become the foundation of your existence and daily life'. Although Fanny composed more than four hundred pieces ranging from choral works to chamber pieces, only a tiny proportion of songs and piano works was published during her lifetime. She withheld much of the rest from publication for fear of bringing her family into disrepute, confiding to Felix that she hoped she wouldn't 'disgrace all of you through my publishing, as I'm no *femme libre*'.

With the stereotype of women as song composers in mind, Ethel hoped to come away from Breitkopf with a fee that would at least cover one of her dress bills. After all, she knew the editor who would be considering her pieces, and she was writing the kind of songs with German texts that were extremely popular at the time. He had heard her play them, and knew they got a good reception. But when the time came, he politely informed her that although the songs were good enough that he was prepared to publish them, music by women simply did not sell. Clara and Fanny were the exceptions, partly because they were married or related to male composers, and because Clara was already celebrated as one of the world's most famous concert pianists. As an unknown name, Ethel left with a contract but no fee.

Ethel remained undeterred. Publication was the first really significant hurdle for any aspiring composer, and she had cleared it in a useful learning curve. She knew what to expect the next time she approached a publisher, and wouldn't enter into a negotiation so naively again. Next time, she wanted to offer something more substantial than songs. Even though songs had a large market and were the most likely pieces to get good sales, Ethel knew it would be larger works that would make her name. She had no intention of falling into the trap of being dismissed alongside her female contemporaries as 'merely' a song composer. She continued to work on her sonatas and fugues, and, eventually, her first string quartet.

In the hierarchy of chamber music genres, the string quartet stood right at the top: Ethel likened it to 'an exquisite omelette', compared to orchestral works that have 'so many ingredients that a rotten egg can pass undetected'. Every note had to be honed and perfected. It was the genre she was most determined to conquer. Her student sketchbooks were filled with quartets that she finished but never felt confident enough to release to the public.

Working continuously and powering through her whirlwind schedule on caffeine and exhilaration, Ethel soon found herself feeling distinctly under the weather. Ill health would trouble her all her life, and this time the doctor diagnosed a case of the 'nerves' brought about by 'cerebral excitement', expressing extreme displeasure that she had been practising piano for five hours a day. When Ethel pointed out that men practised the same hours as she did, the baffled doctor informed her that the situation for men was quite different. He banned Ethel from concerts, the theatre and anything more than two hours' work – practice *or* composition – per day. For several weeks she stuck to his prescribed schedule, spending much longer than she really needed away from work and from her professional community.

o   o   o   o

As soon as she was feeling well enough to defy her doctor, Ethel resumed her schedule of evening performances, immersing herself in the very best drama that Leipzig had to offer. Her brother Johnny had introduced her to Shakespeare, and the playwright would remain one of Ethel's lifelong loves. Not only did she adore the pathos, tragedy and humour of Shakespeare's plays, but his status as a national icon also made up for England's lack of famous composers. Even in Leipzig, Shakespeare was admired as a cultural figure. So night after night, Ethel went to see German productions, introducing herself to the classics of European drama as well.

Literature was an enduring source of fascination and inspiration for her, but in Leipzig there was an additional, amorous motivation for her theatrical enthusiasm – the actress Marie Geistinger, with whom Ethel was completely smitten. Of course Marie was pretty, but it was her voice that Ethel found most captivating; the voice was the feature that, for her, had the most powerful sensual potential. Marie's voice was 'deep & thrilling', stirring Ethel to such an extent that she took to hovering around the stage door after Marie's productions with a posy of violets or roses, hoping to catch a glimpse of her new idol.

After she received several impassioned letters of admiration, Marie arranged for Ethel to call at her dressing room. The experience made such an impression on Ethel that she felt compelled to put it into musical form. 'I came home, felt another creature, and forthwith composed the best thing I have yet done,' she confessed to her mother (neglecting to mention the emotional 'commotion' caused by the sight of Marie in 'a tight-fitting blue satin bodice covered with spangles').

Ethel wasn't wrong about it being her best work: the piece would become her Piano Sonata No. 2, and it was a considerable advance on her first. This time the dramatic contrasts were more coherent, the key changes less forced, the slow movement lyrical and vulnerable. The whole scale of the piece was more ambitious. Partly this was down to increased experience, but now Ethel also had a muse. She composed into the first movement all the events of her first meeting with Marie – not that her listeners would know about it. But that was part of the thrill. Ethel's works were often clandestine declarations of adoration: the Piano Sonata No. 2 was truly decipherable perhaps only to Ethel and Marie themselves.

For a while the two artists maintained a friendship, but once the lustre of the stage was stripped away, Ethel decreed that Marie was lamentably dull. Besides, Ethel's circle of friends in Leipzig was widening, and some of her acquaintances informed Ethel that because Marie had been married multiple times, she was an unsuitable friend for a young, unmarried woman. So Ethel summarily dispensed with Marie via letter, informing her that 'if she reflected on her past life she would understand why'. Even by Ethel's somewhat tactless standards, ending a months-long friendship in such a way was unusually cruel. Years later she would look back on this episode with deep regret, admitting that her actions were both 'odious' and 'cowardly'. Nonetheless, this wouldn't be the only time that Ethel would do something unkind motivated largely by self-interest, seemingly oblivious to (or unperturbed by) the potential consequences of her actions.

Ethel had learned just how important a network of friends and supporters would be for her career, and she wasn't prepared to risk her blossoming reputation to stand up for Marie. She was becoming widely known as a composer in Leipzig, and frequently performed at the salons and musical gatherings of the city's musical elite. In the intimate candlelight of her friends' homes Ethel played her pieces 'with a storm of passion, a convincing strength, a compelling fury beyond compare'. Bowled over by the force of her playing that seemed to burst through the wood-panelled walls of their dark music rooms, Ethel's audiences sat spellbound. Her music and personality brought her fame throughout the small city. One admirer recalled how 'our little circle was suddenly brightened by the meteor-like appearance among us of a young and most attractive girl'. 'None of us knew what in her to admire most: her wonderful musical talent [. . .] or her astonishing prowess in athletic feats of agility and strength.' Her effect was 'altogether electrifying'.

One of the people whom Ethel was proudest to count among her supporters was the composer Johannes Brahms, who was broadly recognised as one of the most important composers alive and who had just premiered his impressive Second Symphony. Ethel was introduced to him at a party but, as always when she met one of her idols, she was initially starstruck and could think of little to say, especially when faced with Brahms's brusque and dismissive manner. Over time, though, they developed something like a jovial mutual respect, and Brahms even passed on the occasional compliment about her music (when he didn't realise she was the composer). Once Ethel had recovered from her initial awe, she objected to his attitude towards women – either ridiculing them, or 'staring at them as a greedy boy stares at jam-tartlets'. But Brahms took her chastisements in good humour, and she appreciated the fact that he never courted celebrity. Such was his dislike of dinners and parties held in his honour that on one occasion he took great delight in showing an insulting poem that Ethel had written about him to nearly every guest.

o   o   o   o

Having finally reached the hallowed Conservatoire, after just a few months Ethel declared it inadequate. The classes were too big for her to get the kind of detailed, personalised feedback she needed to really progress at composition. So she quit, seeking private tuition instead. Luckily for Ethel, Heinrich von Herzogenberg, a composer and the conductor of Leipzig's celebrated Bach Society, took a shine to her. He made her an exception to his rule of not accepting students. Predictably, twenty-year-old Ethel threw herself into Heinrich's lessons with such aplomb that it wasn't long before she was once again feeling quite poorly. She got herself into a lifelong boom and bust pattern, with periods of excessive and enthusiastic overwork followed by days – sometimes weeks – of illness ranging from fatigue to fevers. As spring blossomed into summer, Ethel experienced increasing fits of dizziness and heart palpitations which she was determined to ignore, until one day in May 1878 she collapsed on the floor at a friend's birthday party, her heart seeming to have given up under the stress and strain of her hectic schedule.

Dizzy and disorientated, Ethel was swept away from the party by a woman whose 'dear face, framed in a haze of golden hair' gave her a celestial aura – or so it seemed in her delirious state. Together the two women slowly climbed the stairs at Ethel's lodgings, the elder supporting the younger, murmuring gentle encouragements until they reached the cool quiet of Ethel's attic room. Ethel was put to bed and the doctor called, who delivered a grim diagnosis: he feared her heart was permanently damaged. He prescribed imme-diate bed rest, with no physical exercise or any of the cake and ale indulgences of which she was so fond. Devastated by the prospect of an enduring frailty that would rob her of her greatest pleasures, Ethel allowed herself to be tucked in and soothed by her new-found guardian angel, who took up a daytime vigil at her bedside.

Ethel's saviour was Heinrich's wife, Elisabeth – or Lisl to friends. The two women had paid little attention to each other while Ethel was at the Herzogenbergs' house, even though they sometimes studied alongside one another. Lisl was a naturally reserved person, and Ethel's robust personality did little to immediately endear her. It wasn't until Lisl encountered Ethel in a moment of vulnerabil-ity that the older woman truly opened up her heart to her. With Ethel in her weakened state, the two women complemented each other perfectly. Even though there were only nine years between them, Lisl saw in Ethel a respite from the misery of childlessness, despite years of trying and praying. On Ethel's part, she always had a soft spot for maternal women; she enjoyed being looked after and offered guidance, and never more so than when she was ill. And so Lisl perched by Ethel's bed on a rickety wooden chair, reading aloud with a book in one hand and Ethel's hand grasped in the other, until Ethel fell asleep.

For weeks Ethel stayed in her bed, lying under the sloping roof of the attic, the windows kept ajar to protect her from the rising summer heat. With every meal that Lisl brought and book that she read the two grew a little closer. Ethel adored the way that Lisl had an 'aethereal quality' that was uniquely combined with a definite 'homeliness' and a phenomenal sense of humour. She was 'better than beautiful, at once dazzling and bewitching; the fairest of skins, fine-spun, wavy golden hair, curious arresting greenish-brown eyes, and a very noble rather low forehead'. Ethel willingly accepted Lisl's attentions, allowing her to wash her, clothe her and brush her hair before she went to sleep. Ethel loved her 'as no one can ever have loved anyone..yes..from the very first moment, swept away, drowned, burning'. She believed this was 'the very tenderest relation that can ever have sprung up between a woman and one who, in spite of her years, was little better than a child'.

Under Lisl's care, Ethel's health slowly improved. Contrary to the doctor's fears, her heart was not permanently damaged, and as she recovered her strength Lisl started reintroducing music back into Ethel's life. She played Bach and Brahms on Ethel's piano, even sharing some of her own compositions. Lisl was a gifted musician with a formidable reputation in Leipzig, but she had once hoped for a more exceptional and public career than the private roles she eventually had, advising both her husband and Brahms, who was a close personal friend. Lisl's unrealised musical ambitions would cause one of the more noticeable tensions in her relations with Ethel. She wanted to nurture and protect Ethel, but like many mothers, whether consciously or not, she also tried to realise her dreams vicariously through her newly adopted daughter. She would regularly reproach Ethel for spending time away from her music, adding bitterly that 'I often could weep to think of the time I have lost, how badly I have husbanded my little talent'. Lisl saw it as her duty to guide Ethel to success where she herself had failed.

By the time Ethel was well enough to look after herself the two women were inseparable. Lisl would be Ethel's guide, her confidante, her muse – and they would cause each other more pain than they had thought possible to bear from someone they loved.

SERENADE

As her twenty-fourth birthday approached, Ethel began to feel restless. She had been living in Leipzig for five years, and the once exciting city was now feeling small and provincial. She had settled into something like a family life with the Herzogenbergs, becoming such a permanent fixture that Heinrich began to resent her constant presence. This would be a recurring issue among the families of Ethel's passions. Family members inevitably had to cede ground to accommodate Ethel, and quite understandably felt as though their homes were under invasion.

Luckily for Heinrich, Ethel desired 'contact with other forms of beauty than music'. She determined that the only answer was to head to Italy, the country of Michelangelo and Da Vinci. Lisl was, of course, against the plan, because it would both take Ethel away from her and distract her from devoted musical study. Once Ethel had decided on a course of action, though, there was very little that could change her mind. So Lisl begrudgingly gave her blessing, deciding that it would be best for her to stay with watchful friends and relatives. In the summer of 1882 Ethel set off for Italy, armed with her mountaineering equipment and letters of recommendation from Lisl, bound for the homes of Lisl's friends the Hildebrands, and of her sister, Julia Brewster.

Shrouded by cypresses, the cream walls of the sixteenth-century convent at San Francesco di Paola stand cool against the heat of the Florentine sun. The convent was built at the foot of a small hill, and its top floor overlooked Florence's masses of trees that, by the time Ethel arrived, were flickering autumnal golds and greens over the city's red rooftops. Every cobble and flagstone was saturated with art history. Here, Da Vinci had painted *The Adoration of the Magi*, and now, years later, the convent walls were decked in frescoes by the sculptor Adolf von Hildebrand, who had made the ancient building his home. Ethel was immediately welcomed by Adolf and his wife, Irene. She rented a nearby room, bright and uncluttered, with a small charcoal fire for cooking, and settled herself into Italian living.

It wasn't long before she had managed to stir up trouble. Adolf immediately took to Ethel and her striking profile. He asked her to sit for a bust which he worked on daily in his studio from early morning until lunchtime, at which point he would ask his model to join the family for a meal. There was just the small matter of negotiating the stairs. Ethel had hurt her knee badly in a mountaineering accident, and the Hildebrands' home was on the first floor. Irene, therefore, opened the door every day to the sight of her husband carrying the composer up the stairs, and then had to sit and listen to her tales of bravado and adventure over lunch. Because Ethel had no designs on Adolf, it didn't occur to her that Irene might disapprove of this behaviour. Nonetheless Irene grew so tired of the stairs charade that she eventually destroyed the nearly-complete bust of Ethel. The modelling stopped.

More intriguing than the Hildebrands, however, were the family living nearby who would change the course of Ethel's life: Julia and her husband, the writer Henry 'Harry' Brewster, and their children. Julia came with quite a reputation. Lisl was devoted to her sister, and often spoke about her to Ethel. The image Lisl painted was a peculiar one: of a woman with an almost otherworldly quality. 'What a poor earthly, dusty creature I feel near her,' Lisl wrote. 'She flies the company of others rather than seeks it. Both of them wish to live for themselves and the family only, and when they do associate with other people, it never gets beyond intellectual relations.' Even more intriguing, according to Lisl they had the most 'extraordinary views on marriage'. As Ethel understood it, Julia and Harry had agreed that 'if either of the couple should weary of married life, or care for someone else, it was understood that the bond was dissoluble'.

Ethel's opinions about marriage and relationships were equally unconventional for her time, so it's unsurprising she was drawn to Lisl's description of her saint-like, hermit sister.

The reality was even more exciting than Ethel had imagined. 'Julia was the strangest human being, if human she was, that I or anyone else ever came across, fascinating, enigmatic, unapproachable, with a Schiller-like profile and pale yellow hair.' Ethel was so taken with her that she barely even noticed Harry. She found him to be the far less interesting of the pair, and although he gave the impression that he had 'read all books' and 'thought all thoughts', she remained deeply unimpressed by his dismissal of her beloved Shakespeare. When Harry disappeared to Algeria a few weeks after Ethel's arrival she was secretly delighted, hoping it would give her the opportunity to get to know Julia better.

Julia proved to be a difficult woman to pursue. She limited Ethel to one visit a fortnight, remarking to her that 'one must be *very well* to enjoy you'. But this was hardly a deterrent. Ethel found plenty to do while waiting for her fortnightly ration, delighting in exploring Florentine churches – carried up the steep church steps by either a painter or the amateur champion heavyweight boxer of England, both of whom fell head over heels in love with her. Julia lost none of her allure. Ethel found her more perplexing with every visit that passed. Talking to Julia was like having a tutorial on metaphysics or poetry, earning the Brewster household the nickname 'Ivory Tower'.

Delighted by her new companion, Ethel wrote excitedly to Lisl about her admiration for Julia and her way of life. This was not one of her more tactful moves. Ethel felt that her relationships comprised three phases: in the first, passion-struck, she was constantly at the side of her new-found love (what one of her later passions called the 'My God, what a woman!' phase). This would then calm into a more manageable affection, which lasted until phase three, where she would practically vanish entirely, because she had embarked upon another 'My God, what a woman!' phase with somebody new.

Having accustomed herself to phase one, Lisl was not impressed by any move towards phases two or three – and certainly not when the other woman was her sister. 'I sometimes feel that I am of no real use to you at all – merely the dumping-ground you need,' she rebuked Ethel. It didn't help that although Lisl doted on Julia, she was also quite jealous of her, and particularly of her two children. She felt 'a kind of bitterness' that Ethel was so easily impressed by Julia, reminding her that it was she, Lisl, who loved her 'from the deepest depths' of her being.

Ethel would always apologise, and Lisl couldn't stay angry for long. Besides, Ethel had other matters drawing her attention. After a few months of lion-hunting, Harry had returned to Florence in early 1883, and on getting reacquainted she found she had more in common with him than she'd previously thought. She loved anything that expanded her intellectual horizons in a way that excited her, and Harry – or H. B., as Ethel referred to him in her letters – sparked a lifelong love for French writers like Flaubert and Baudelaire. He challenged her. They would sit for hours in the shade of the cypresses talking about history, music, morality and the nature of love. Over the coming year Ethel slowly came to think that H. B. had 'the gentlest, kindest, most courteous manner imaginable'. And she thought him 'extremely good-looking', with his 'perfect nose and brow, brown eyes set curiously far apart, and fair fluffy hair'. Without meaning to, Ethel began loving H. B. 'Our roots were in the same soil,' she mused many years later. 'This I think is the real meaning of the phrase "to complete one another".'

What Ethel hadn't realised, however, was that H. B. had fallen for her almost immediately when they first met. While she had been blithely traipsing round Florence, a whole family melodrama had been playing out under her nose. Julia and H. B. had already been experiencing problems in their marriage – they had a gentle and caring relationship but it lacked sensuality. They were physically awkward in each other's company, and H. B. felt constrained by their isolated lifestyle. Ethel's arrival had been like a tornado, as she tore through the convent's quiet domestic existence, hitching up her skirts to go hiking armed with little else but a knapsack and revolver, all the while writing music as characterful as she was. Ethel loved to treat the Brewsters to evening performances, often singing songs that she had written in Leipzig, ranging from plaintive waltzes to jaunty ballads.

Ethel was everything Julia wasn't, and H. B. was entranced. His swift departure had been no flight of fancy, but an attempt to clear his head. He hadn't tried to hide his feelings from Julia. They discussed his affection for Ethel at length, Julia maintaining that it would amount to nothing more than a passing fancy. She must have felt extremely secure in her relationship with H. B. to have allowed Ethel to stay with them for a full seven months over the winter of 1883. Or perhaps she felt that it was relatively immaterial, because Ethel's attentions were directed towards her. Julia misjudged. By May 1884 she found herself debating the future of her relationships with both her husband, and with Ethel.

Together, the three of them tried to reach an amicable solution. Ethel still adored Julia, and H. B. had no intention of leaving her. Instead, he wanted to abide by the conditions of their original marriage agreement, and to expand the marriage to include Ethel. To H. B., the situation was perfect – Ethel loved both him and Julia, and Julia cared for both of them. 'I will do nothing that diminishes us,' he reassured his wife. The trouble was, H. B. and Ethel were polyamorous, and Julia was not. She may have originally thought that she could handle an open marriage, but faced with the reality eleven years later, Julia was not prepared to share her husband.

If H. B. thought he would be able to quietly incorporate Ethel into their lives, he was sorely mistaken. Julia resisted in the strongest terms, insisting that his feelings for Ethel would fade. She refused to countenance his vision of an equal, three-way relationship between the three of them. 'You know and must feel that I appreciate you,' she wrote to Ethel, 'but I feel it as one of the necessary conditions of my future life to defend my sincerity on this occasion inwardly and outwardly.' She made her position extremely clear. As far as Julia was concerned, H. B. pursuing a relationship with Ethel would be adultery. She suggested that all parties cease correspondence, to allow H. B. and Ethel time and space to forget one another. Faced with Julia's unexpected and unequivocal opposition, Ethel backed down, and left Italy for Frimhurst. 'Your strength gives me strength,' she told Julia, agreeing to her terms. 'You are my best light.'

H. B., however, was less willing to let go of Ethel. Her arrival had allowed him to cast himself as the protagonist in an epic drama, and he had no intention of letting Julia write his ending. 'The poem would lack tragic dignity if all went on smoothly,' he explained to Ethel. 'But certainly the softness of poetry will come over the tragedy because we all three of us have got the right music in us.' When Ethel tried to cut ties, H. B. persisted in sending her long love letters, begging her to ignore his wife's wishes, assuring Ethel that Julia did not know what was best for her. And when that didn't work, he resorted to an ultimatum. 'If I have to give you up I give her up also. What will you have gained then? you will have made us all three miserable and brought everything to a complete smash.'

Ethel was beside herself, torn between two people she loved deeply. 'I never cared even foolishly before, & half of me lives now for the first time – & only for you,' she wept to H. B. But her feelings were complicated. 'My love for Julia is one of the deepest richest experiences of my life,' she explained to him. 'It comes next after my love for you & is so mixed up [. . .] that I can't separate the two.' Ethel empathised with Julia's position more than H. B. did, subtly reprimanding him with the reminder that 'not even you can tell how she will bear this'. In the face of Ethel's reservations, H. B. remained stoical. The scenario was, as he portrayed it, a philosophical puzzle, a conundrum to which he had the best solution.

They were 'three civilizations at war', and 'my form of civilization is higher and must prevail against both of you for the common good of all three, at any cost.'

Perhaps Ethel should just have walked away, especially when faced with H. B.'s cavalier attitude towards Julia. But the truth was that H. B. and Ethel were peculiarly well suited. They were in agreement in their views on love and marriage: both felt trapped within a society whose norms were monogamous and heteronormative. Ethel could discuss her sexuality honestly with H. B., openly and freely, without fear of judgement, and he encouraged her to see other women. His words about free love and emancipation inspired her to set them to music. Spiritually, intellectually and emotionally, Ethel was consumed by H. B. But she couldn't bring herself to betray Julia. 'I mean to try & bear to give you up "bravely",' she informed him, and resolved to remove herself completely from his life.

o   o   o   o

Heartbroken and melancholy, Ethel returned to Leipzig and to Lisl, who welcomed her with open arms. The obvious rift between Julia and Ethel meant that Lisl forgave and forgot all tensions. Ethel was relieved to find 'blame neither attached to me nor was laid at my door'. Lisl only sought to support her friend through the miserable situation. She tried to coax her to focus on composing, but it proved a difficult task. Ethel's imagination was fired by strong emotions that made her feel loved and supported. Isolation and despair, however, were far too distracting for serious work. Nonetheless, the publication of her String Quintet in E major op. 1 provided a little solace, especially because this was a piece that held a particular significance for Lisl. When Lisl heard the Adagio, she confessed that it 'felt as if you were undressing before the horrid Leipzig public! But luckily they know nothing about what that piece might tell them!' It remains a mystery what meaning Lisl heard in the Quintet. Ethel dedicated the work to the memory of one of her dear friends, Rhoda Garrett, who had died in 1882, so possibly the Adagio was an elegy for her. Or perhaps the movement's searing melodies and tense, dissonant, awkward bass lines encoded something of Ethel's relationship with Lisl, or with Julia, her music giving her a way to bare her soul to those listeners who wanted to hear.

Henry Brewster as Ethel knew him.

To Ethel, now twenty-six, it seemed as though Lisl was the only thing keeping her afloat in a sea of woes. When Ethel was in England they exchanged letters at an astonishing rate, and when in Leipzig the two women would sit together, Ethel's head on Lisl's knee, Lisl gently stroking Ethel's hair as she unburdened herself of all her troubles. Ethel made sure that 'Every turn in the situation, every action, every thought of my heart was known to her', making the two of them 'more closely if more tragically knit than ever'. Lisl showed remarkable patience with her friend, believing that she had the best of intentions in an impossible situation.

H. B., however, was still determined that his *ménage à trois* would come to fruition. He continued to write to Ethel, announcing that he would 'fight for you as for sweet life', even when she begged him not to. 'It is all wrong,' she told him, and her composition was suffering. 'For the sake of my work which is drowned in longing for you – for the sake of everything and because you love me, give me no further sign of your existence.' On a couple of occasions H. B. even showed up in Leipzig, demanding to see her, and they stood fighting in the snow and ice in the courtyard outside her rooms, only parting ways in the early hours of the morning, still no closer to a solution. In the face of H. B.'s persistence, Ethel succumbed. 'I do not know which way to turn – I want you so terribly,' she admitted to him. She allowed herself to be drawn into a correspondence, reneging on her promises to both Julia and Lisl that she would leave H. B. for good.

This put Lisl in a distinctly awkward position. She loved Ethel dearly, but she could not ignore the devastation that her actions were causing her sister. Julia was becoming quite ill from the stress of her marriage breaking down. Even as he watched his wife getting sicker, H. B. refused to relent, and Ethel's inability to completely disassociate from him made her complicit in his actions, as far as Lisl could see. She tried as hard as she could to dissuade Ethel from continuing her relationship with H. B. but Ethel kept wavering, hoping that Julia would eventually change her mind. After months of pleading and persuasion, Lisl gave up. In June 1885, a farewell letter landed on Ethel's doorstep. Lisl couldn't reconcile herself to staying friends with someone who could cause her sister so much pain, and told Ethel that she no longer considered her part of her life.

Ethel never recovered from the pain of this separation. 'My mistaken reading of Julia's soul was honest,' she lamented. Even decades later, she maintained that 'if that time were to be lived through again, I believe [. . .] that I should act as I did then'. She simply failed to appreciate how much damage she had caused to Lisl, and to Julia and her children. Ethel was never one for subtleties, and was particularly aggrieved that Lisl had moved straight to excommunication without offering her an ultimatum – not realising that from her friend's perspective, the months of negotiating had been precisely that. Perhaps this lack of bluntness was a mistake on Lisl's part, especially if she wanted the eventual outcome to be that H. B. returned to Julia. Forced to choose between Lisl and H. B., Ethel might well have picked the former. As it was, H. B. felt that an injustice had been done to Ethel. By November 1885, he had negotiated a separation from Julia. He wrote to Ethel immediately, but being exiled from Lisl had affected her profoundly. 'No – it cannot be – can never be,' she told him. 'I have been too mistaken – have sinned too deeply. By all you feel for me I entreat you not to answer this – never write to me again – nor try to see me.' Finally, disbelievingly, H. B. accepted Ethel's rejection. The following month he left for America. They would not speak again – for now, at least.

H. B. and Ethel's love had inflicted chaos on their lives, and on those around them. There was nothing for Ethel to do but try to find comfort in her composition, and build new relationships to help her nurse the shattered fragments of her heart. Chief among her new friends was an enormous half-St Bernard dog called Marco. Ethel always maintained that 'nothing is more natural than that in a certain sense a dog should be more than all the world to you, particularly if you live alone'. So it was with lumbering, gentle Marco, who never left Ethel's side. He even attended rehearsals (on his best behaviour).

Ethel was excellent at maintaining a public facade of joviality, and to those oblivious to her domestic dramas, she seemed to be enjoying success after success. She was having works performed and published, her reputation was growing, and her musical network was widening. At one particularly lively Christmas party Ethel and Marco made quite an impression on the composer Pyotr Ilyich Tchaikovsky, getting into a spirited debate about the merits of Brahms's music.

Ethel Smyth with her dog Marco, *c.*1891.

Delighted by Ethel's forthrightness, Tchaikovsky took the young woman under his wing, and opened her ears to the importance of orchestration. Ethel had tried her hand at some orchestral pieces before, but they had never come to life in the way she wanted. Tchaikovsky taught her how to make her orchestral music speak. He told her to imagine orchestral instruments like voices, and this was the prompt that she needed. She began seriously studying other composers' scores to understand the alchemy of orchestration, learning how to hold the audience in 'spasm upon spasm of physical delight' through unique combinations of sound. Despite his personal ambivalence towards dogs, Tchaikovsky grew particularly attached to Ethel and Marco, seeing him as one of the 'originalities and eccentricities' of this 'lonely woman'. A 'lonely' woman – an unusual characterisation of Ethel, but an astute one. Tchaikovsky saw past the bluster and bombast. For though Ethel was always surrounded by friends, she had set out to be a trailblazer – and that is a lonely path indeed. And now, without Lisl or H. B., she was more alone than ever.

o   o   o   o

In an attempt to banish Lisl, H. B. and Julia from her mind, Ethel filled her days with endless concerts. She moved from Leipzig to Munich, hoping to expand her address book and find new opportunities for her work to be performed. One of her most fervent admirers was Hermann Levi, conductor at the Bavarian State Opera, who reserved her free seats in the plush, gilt-covered venue. Ethel had always had a flair for the dramatic, and with the benefit of Tchaikovsky's guidance on orchestration, she was seriously turning her thoughts towards writing a large vocal work.

Levi's speciality was Wagner – not Ethel's favourite composer, but one she knew could teach her a great deal about the art of operatic composition. Night after night she went to the opera, score in hand, following the drama on the page to learn how Wagner built his sound world. On one evening in the theatre's dim half-light she noticed the Trevelyan family, old acquaintances from England, in one of the boxes below her. The first few times she'd met them, Ethel hadn't paid much attention. Even among her exclusive social circle, the Trevelyans stood out as aloof. Sir Alfred was the seventh Trevelyan baronet, and the whole family was deeply enmeshed in the upper echelons of British politics, wearing their privilege easily. They cared, as Ethel put it, not 'two straws about society'. But in the wilderness of exile from Lisl, Ethel craved any connection to home, so she ingratiated herself with the Trevelyans, and especially their daughter Pauline. Ethel observed that there was 'something in her face (I did not feel it at first) that fills me with infinite longing and love'. And Pauline loved music. 'By one short phrase in music, by a note sometimes, you can convey more to a fellow musician than by endless words,' Ethel thought. Her ability to communicate musically with Pauline lifted their friendship 'high above rocks and brambles into hitherto unexplored regions of serenity'.

Not only was Pauline musical, but she was also Catholic, providing spiritual direction at the time when Ethel needed it most. She couldn't help feeling wracked with guilt, and tormented by the reality that loving H. B. was impossible, however much that hurt her. Ethel had never been more unsure of herself. There were times, she confessed, when she felt that were it not for Marco and her friends, she could not carry on. She reached a crisis point in December 1889. In her cold, bare lodgings, delirious from a winter fever, Ethel prayed for a sign – and a letter from Pauline arrived asking if Ethel could return her copy of *The Imitation of Christ*, a devotional book by Thomas à Kempis.

Ethel began reading the *Imitation* in a frenzy, pausing for neither sleep nor food. It was a moment of epiphany. 'Now all was clear to me,' she realised. Her problems were caused by the fact that 'I had always thought of myself, and of nothing else [...] No wonder I had failed; no wonder all I had touched, no matter with what excellent intentions, had turned to dust and ashes.' Ethel knew what she had to do. Still shaking and nauseous from the flu, she dragged herself to a boat and booked a passage to England, desperate to get back to Frimhurst so she could nurse her elderly parents. She had to look to others, and to God. She couldn't quite reconcile herself to Catholicism, instead falling into the Anglican practices of her childhood. Nonetheless, she let herself be guided by Pauline, who 'burned like a steady light beside me, warm and quiet, helpful and practical'.

Ethel slowly started to piece her life back together. Back in England on a more long-term basis, she could cultivate a circle of friends to bring her the stability and support she so desperately craved. Ethel needed a varied constellation of friends around her. She thrived on personal drama, loved a good fight and adored being the centre of attention – but she also wanted friends who could provide calm and stability through her more volatile episodes. She split most of her time between her family at Frimhurst and the Trevelyan estate on Exmoor. When she wasn't there, she was being entertained by Eugénie, the last Empress of the French, who had settled in England after France was defeated in the 1870–1 Franco-Prussian War. She regularly invited the Smyth family to tea at her mansion, Farnborough Hill. Or, occasionally, Ethel went to Lambeth Palace to see Mary Benson, wife of the Archbishop of Canterbury.

Mary was as religious as Pauline, and remained one of Ethel's closest confidantes throughout her separation from H. B. Like Ethel, Mary had a complex romantic life. She had been prepared for marriage to Edward Benson since she was eleven, and they wed when she was just eighteen. But Mary was a lesbian. She did not and could not love Edward. Yet she struggled to reconcile her sexuality with her religious beliefs, and with her lived reality. After bearing Edward six children she suffered a mental breakdown. The couple agreed that Mary should be Edward's wife in name only: she would support his career, and in return she could bring her female lovers to live at Lambeth. Throughout Ethel and Mary's friendship, Mary was involved with a woman called Lucy Tait. They went on to live together after Edward's death in 1896, and stayed in a relationship until Mary died. Even with this acceptance from her family, Mary was still troubled by her feelings for women. She poured out her soul to her diary, praying that 'all carnal affections may die in me'.

Mary was, therefore, able to provide a sympathetic counsel that Ethel greatly valued. And she adored looking after lost souls. Her patience and empathy meant that she effectively acted as an unofficial therapist for multiple women – which Ethel always slightly resented, because she felt that her troubles were far more pressing than anybody else's. Ethel told her that she was not content with the role of 'outside patient' because, put simply, 'I wanted you.' And Mary's family certainly bore the consequences of Ethel's belief that she was entitled to Mary's time. She was a relatively omnipresent figure at Lambeth, whether she was out on the sweeping gravel drive teaching the Dean of Windsor to ride a bicycle, or collecting one of Mary's daughters for a game of cricket or golf. Edward got so sick of Ethel that he eventually banned her from his sight. (She placed the blame at least partly at Mary's door, telling her that 'if the men of the family are insupportable it is generally the fault of the women for not standing up to them'!)

Ethel's visits to Farnborough were far less inflammatory. Empress Eugénie had no family to feel displaced, and she was grateful for the company of a personality so buoyant that it made her cavernous home feel less empty. Short, pale Eugénie had 'an unquenchable fire within' coupled with a generous sense of humour, and she carried herself in 'the easiest, most graceful style'. Unlike Pauline, she was profoundly unartistic. In general Ethel and Eugénie steered clear of musical matters, the exception being Ethel's own career. Eugénie was a staunch supporter of suffrage and of women's right to work, and accordingly took a keen interest in Ethel's music from the outset – whether she enjoyed listening to her compositions in the drawing room or not. Ethel was deeply grateful for the Empress's support, considering her 'the kindest person I have ever met'.

With a new group of friends and H. B. receding into the distance, Ethel could turn her thoughts to work again. She had been composing sporadically since her break with Lisl, producing the Violin Sonata op. 7, which premiered in November 1887. She sent this and a couple of other scores to the famous violinist Joseph Joachim in the hope that he would take them into his repertoire. To have a soloist like Joachim take on a piece was every composer's dream; star performers wielded an enormous amount of power to make or break composers' careers. But he wrote to her condescendingly, saying that although the pieces had 'many a clever turn, and a certain facility', they were nonetheless 'failures'.

It was an unnecessarily harsh judgement. The Sonata may have been excessively influenced by Brahms, but it was still a captivating and passionate work. Ethel thought she detected a whiff of misogyny around Joachim's decision, perhaps prompted by the fact that reviewers at the premiere had declared the Sonata 'devoid of feminine charm and therefore unworthy a woman'. Riled, instead of swallowing the criticism she accused Joachim of performing plenty of 'deadly dull' pieces when the composer's 'mama was a giver of smart musical parties'.

Needless to say, Joachim didn't reply. A more conciliatory tone could have kept open the possibility that he might perform a future work. But Ethel didn't just burn her bridges. She left them charred heaps of ash. This kind of exchange became a pattern throughout her career, sometimes causing her to miss out on opportunities and commissions. As a friend astutely observed, 'the tremendous *attack*' and 'West-wind "sausing and brausing"' of Ethel's personality could 'sometimes scatter people's feeble wits'. But Ethel was in a difficult position. Without this determination she might not succeed at all.

Ethel's opera trips and orchestration studies, at least, were beginning to bear fruit. In 1888 she tried her hand at a cantata, a religious work for choir and orchestra, with the text taken from the

Song of Songs. Ethel's pain and anguish over H. B. and Julia was poured into every note of this piece, *Song of Love* op. 8. She chose passages that focus on love and separation. 'I could not find him, I call'd him but he gave me no answer,' the singer laments. 'I will seek him whom my soul loveth.' Even though the final line declares that 'Love is as strong as death', it's hardly convincing: the music fades away on to one quiet, quiet chord. It's more of a hope than a statement of fact.

The enduring appeal of Handel's *Messiah* meant that large choral works were extremely popular in England, so Ethel hoped that *Song of Love* would find a ready audience among the many choral societies across the country. She was sorely disappointed. As she was an unknown composer, and a woman at that, choirs, conductors and the Royal Philharmonic Society paid no attention to her enthusiastic letters. Discouraged, Ethel dismissed the cantata as 'an amusing first attempt', and it has yet to receive its world premiere. Nonetheless, it paved the way for an orchestral work: her four-movement Serenade in D major for orchestra. During her time in Munich she had befriended the conductor August Manns, who directed the orchestra at the Crystal Palace in London. He was so impressed by one of Ethel's string quartets that he offered to conduct any orchestral work of hers that reached him before 1 January 1890. Clearly she had found her orchestral 'voice', because Manns immediately scheduled the premiere for April. Just after Ethel's thirty-second birthday, her music would be heard publicly in England for the first time, at one of the biggest venues in London.

o   o   o   o

Five storeys high and built from 1,650,000 square feet of glass, the Crystal Palace stood shining in the centre of Sydenham. Few buildings were as iconic in Victorian Britain; it was a monument to the ideal of combining pleasure and education, encased in a 'hard modern twinkle'. Visitors to the site could wander through courts dedicated to art from across the Empire or watch circus acts in the Centre Transept, before heading out into the gardens to enjoy the cooling spray from the enormous fountains and marvel at the life-sized models of dinosaurs that roamed the park. And on Saturdays there was the option of a concert, held in the enormous Concert Room, which regularly attracted considerable crowds. While Ethel was away in Leipzig, English music had been undergoing an impressive transformation. Frustrated by the predominance of foreign composers in English concert halls, some critics and performers had been championing a new generation of English composers – Hubert Parry, Charles Villiers Stanford and Arthur Sullivan – who were writing so prolifically that one critic declared in 1882 that 'English music has arrived at a renaissance period'.

At the heart of this 'renaissance' had been Manns and his orchestra at the Crystal Palace. He had made a point of premiering new works by English composers since the establishment of the Palace concerts in the 1850s, earning a reputation for introducing audiences to the newest and most exciting English music. The inclusion of Ethel's substantial four-movement Serenade in the 1890 concert, therefore, signalled her as an upcoming talent to be taken seriously. And it wasn't just any concert. It was the last of the season, which guaranteed an even larger audience than usual. Ethel's Serenade was placed alongside two new songs by Parry, and Tchaikovsky's Second Piano Concerto – only the second time the concerto had been heard in England. It was an astounding vote of confidence in her.

As anticipated the Concert Hall was full to bursting, packed with enthusiastic listeners – not least Ethel's parents, beaming with pride. Despite John's initial resistance to Ethel's musical ambitions, he had at last come round to the idea, and resolved to support his daughter in any way he could. He broke his lifelong habit of not attending orchestral concerts for Ethel's premiere, and pre-prepared a telegram to send off to Bob, Ethel's brother in India, to tell him the work had been a 'great success'. He was so anxious to send it that between every movement he tried bouncing out of his seat, only kept in place by the more patient Nina. And indeed the audience welcomed Ethel's sprightly piece warmly – with good reason. As orchestral debuts go, Ethel's Serenade was extraordinarily self-assured, full of energy and humour that gives the impression she is letting you in on a personal joke.

Even the critics, sometimes lukewarm about premieres, hailed the Serenade as a triumph, particularly because Ethel was a woman. *The Times* declared it had 'a vigour and certainty that are most rarely found in works by female hands in any branch of art'. Another observed that while it was unremarkable that the Serenade was full of 'grace', because this was to be 'anticipated in a work from a feminine pen', they nonetheless found themselves pleasantly surprised by 'the skill, the finish, and the resource shown in the orchestration', which were 'less expected' from a woman composer.

These kinds of vague generalisations about what women were and were not expected to be able to produce were commonplace in nineteenth-century criticism, but Ethel's fiery writing style at least meant she avoided the usual judgement of women's work being too 'feminine'. She was not the first British woman to have orchestral music performed: among others, a woman called Alice Mary Smith had been composing symphonies and other orchestral works since the 1860s. Many of these were premiered at reputable London venues, and the critics had declared themselves astonished that her First Symphony could have come 'from the pen of a young lady'. But critical memories were short. Thirty years later, reviewers were still framing it as unusual and surprising for women to compose in these genres. It was a refrain that Ethel would hear all her life.

Whether the Serenade was good or only good for a woman, the audience loved it. Stamping and clapping, they called the composer to the stage. Ethel had chosen to sign her name 'E. M. Smyth' on the programme to avoid any gender prejudice, and the roar of applause grew even louder when a woman stepped out to receive her ovation. Ethel couldn't have hoped for a better introduction to English musical society. As she stood taking her bows, she tried to find her family in the audience to catch their eyes – and then to her astonishment, sitting behind Nina, she spotted a figure whose searing gaze she would recognise anywhere. It was H. B. Back from America, he was passing through London on his way to Liverpool, and had made a detour to witness the debut of the woman he still loved, despite everything. Ethel hurried off the stage, longing impatiently for the end of the concert so that she could go to him, scared he might leave without speaking to her. She needn't have worried. H. B. whisked her off to a nearby tea shop for a celebratory brew and cakes.

Years of fighting with Julia had taken their toll on H. B., who was now sporting a shaggy beard which Ethel hated. He was quieter, more reflective and more sure than ever that he loved Ethel. And for her part, separation had done nothing to quell her ardour. Keeping apart from H. B. had been agony for her. Even though she had Mary Benson and Pauline, when Ethel found herself in a dilemma she still caught herself wondering what H. B. would say or do. When she finished a book, she longed to discuss it with him, missing their long conversations with her tucked up in an armchair, H. B. sprawled on the carpet. Now he had walked back into her life, she would not let him go again. They agreed that it was pointless to deny their feelings for each other. They would resume their relationship, with or without Julia's consent. Ethel left the tea shop with a light heart, happy to put H. B. on his boat from Liverpool in the knowledge that this time, he would eventually be sailing back to her.

Ethel's friends were less happy about her decision, especially Mary Benson. For all the difficulties in her own marriage Mary still viewed it as a state of union sanctified by God, and could not condone Ethel's disregard for Julia and H. B.'s vows. But Ethel maintained that she was doing nothing wrong. Between H. B. and Pauline, Ethel had the love and stability she needed to work, and music was flooding back into her again. This time, it was to be a sacred work – a choral Mass. Influenced by Pauline, Ethel was still in the throes of religious fervour, and the Mass would be her offering both to God and to the woman who inspired her.

REBECCA

A comfortable stillness falls over Harrow on the Hill, basking in the warm glow of the August sun. Geese patter along the roads, weaving in and out of the dappled shadows cast by the thick red and white blossoms on the chestnut trees reaching their protecting arms over tired travellers. The air is thick with clover. From the very top of the hill the bustle of London is just visible in the far distance, but it lies beyond fields glimmering with yellow buttercups and clouds of daisies. Occasionally the delicate peals of the muffin-man's bell and murmurs from the ducks add to the hazy quiet.

Rebecca Helferich Clarke was born on a day like this, on 27 August 1886 in Clematis Cottage on College Road. On warm afternoons Rebecca's mother, Agnes, would walk her dark-haired, wide-eyed baby in a pram along Harrow's narrow roads, her long skirts brushing through the 'rivers of coloured leaves' that fell outside their door in the autumn. Few of the neighbours noticed Agnes as she passed. She was quiet and unobtrusive, with 'truthful, affectionate eyes', and a gentle, unassuming manner that gave the impression of 'something eager and innocent about her', usually wearing dark and practical clothes that allowed her to manage the gardening.

Her husband, Joseph, was quite a different matter. The two could not have been less alike in appearance, personality and outlook. Joseph had 'striking [. . .] features, set off by blue-black hair and a beard and mustache that were auburn', all of which made him, as Rebecca observed, 'extremely attractive to women'. He saw himself as a Byronesque figure: a traveller, inventor and thinker, who swept Agnes up into his story. They met in Munich, where Agnes's father was a professor at the University and Joseph a student, having moved from Boston to Germany with his mother. Teenage Joseph was far more concerned with exploring the world than with studious endeavour. In 1874, aged eighteen, he cycled round Europe with a friend on newly invented 'boneshaker' bicycles, and no sooner had he returned than he set off to join an archaeological dig at Assos in Turkey. Of course, he wasn't going to miss the opportunity to sail there. He bought a little single-mast boat, named it the *Dorian*, and sailed it with a fellow archaeologist along the Danube to the Black Sea. It gave them 'an exhilarating sense of adventure' to be casting out on their own, sleeping under the stars, sometimes getting caught in the crossfire of battles that were raging across the Ottoman Empire. Despite their perilous escapades they reached Assos unscathed, where Joseph found mosaics that were sent off to a museum in Massachusetts, and got his name into the *Encyclopaedia Britannica* for swimming across the Dardanelles.

'Can it be wondered at', Rebecca mused, 'that Mama, growing up in her quiet home in Germany, followed everything he did – and thought it all extremely romantic?' Whenever Joseph returned to Germany he would enthral Agnes with his tales. She, who had barely travelled at all, was charmed by this handsome man who had seen the entire world (or so it seemed to her), and yet somehow still found her exciting. It wasn't long before the two were married, and Joseph whisked her away to England to set up home in the small semi-detached house festooned with clematis on College Road. But the domesticity of Harrow was a far cry from Joseph's globetrotting days. Although he was content to settle with Agnes and explore the new adventure of being a husband and father, he was always restless, agitated, looking for something new to spark his interest.

Mostly, Joseph found the sense of uncertainty he craved through his job – or lack thereof. Finances were precarious during the first months of their marriage, because he never seemed to be in clear, full-time employment. Money simply slipped through his fingers. On one occasion Agnes 'cried with disappointment and vexation' when she finally consented to pawning some of their belongings, and Joseph returned not with money, but with a lizard-shaped paper-weight and a guilty expression. Eventually, Joseph was persuaded to take a job as European patent expert at the camera company Kodak. It suited him perfectly. He got to travel, and it left him with enough free time to explore anything else that caught his fancy.

Joseph could, at times, be a devoted father. He loved playing games with his children, and enjoyed delighting them with stories of his youthful adventures. He had a wonderful ability to 'stimulate our imaginations as no one else could', and his brief astronomy lessons left Rebecca with a 'sense of Mystery' that 'remained with me all my life'. But he could also be cruel and manipulative. When they played, Rebecca sometimes got 'an uneasy feeling [. . .] that he might at any moment start some little teasing game that would turn out to be frightening'. He had an unpredictable temper, and when he was in a mood everyone had to tiptoe around him, unsure if they were about to commit a perceived indiscretion that might start an almighty row. Rebecca was born into a fight – Joseph was vehemently atheist, Agnes Lutheran, and Joseph's solution to this was to read through the entire Bible with her, pointing out contradictions. Hoping to erode Agnes's faith through either logic or sheer fatigue, Joseph hauled his pregnant wife through the book page by page. Rebecca maintained that she was 'by far the most stormy and difficult and temperamental' of all her siblings, and Agnes always put this down to her arriving amid 'all those discussions about religion'.

When Joseph wasn't warmongering, Rebecca's home could be delightful. She was devoted to her mother, feeling that 'all warmth and comfort and safety came from Mama, the centre of my universe'. Christmas was a particular joy. Agnes's baking filled the little house with the smell of cinnamon and cloves and tangerines, and she sat with Rebecca – and, later, Rebecca's brothers Hans and Eric, born in 1887 and 1890 – gumming together brightly coloured paper chains. Of an evening the family enjoyed the peaceful, flickering light of the Advent candles, cocooned in the scent of cake and wax and pine needles, listening out for passing carol singers. Sometimes they joined in, Agnes at the piano that took up their entire sitting room, filling the house with the sound of their 'pleasant untrained voices'. One of the things that united Agnes and Joseph was a shared love of music, and Rebecca often heard them singing together, with Agnes sight-reading the accompaniments.

When Rebecca was four, the family moved to a slightly larger terraced house near Harrow station, with a long garden that stretched down to the railway. The children loved the freedom of the garden, clambering up the fruit trees to eat cherries and watch trains. Joseph similarly enjoyed the large lawn, because it provided him with a range to use stray cats – or his children's legs – as target practice for his new airgun. Rebecca trusted that 'It was not by way of punishment, and he bore us no malice', but nonetheless 'Our legs, when we took off our stockings at night, were often pocked with blue bullet marks.'

Although this might have been a game to Joseph, the punishments he doled out to his children certainly were not. He was a strict disciplinarian who believed in corporal punishment, and he beat all his children, 'sometimes really painfully'. Rebecca was 'the naughtiest' of her siblings (although usually her misdemeanours were as insignificant as biting her nails), and so received the majority of the whippings 'while Mama waited helplessly outside the door and cried'. These moments stayed with Rebecca her whole life, and though she maintained that her father had 'persuaded himself that he was doing the right thing by us', she never forgot or forgave the 'despotism' that came from his views about 'male dominance'.

As Rebecca grew, her school friends gave her a little independence from her family. She was sent to Miss Turner's day school – the result of another row, this time won by Agnes. Joseph had wanted Rebecca to attend the free board school alongside children from poorer families, because it 'appealed to his Socialistic ideas, as well as being cheaper'. Agnes, however, was acutely aware of the multiple ways the English found to discriminate against those they perceived as being either foreign or lower class. She was concerned that her half-German, half-American children should go to schools where they would pick up middle-class accents. So Miss Turner's it was, where 'Great emphasis was placed on behaving like a little lady.' Agnes would bake cakes and desserts for her daughter to host tea parties, a repeated highlight being an attractive chessboard 'made out of squares of vanilla and chocolate blancmange'. Agnes absolutely adored being able to entertain her children's friends, and when they played blind man's buff 'her grey eyes would shine and her cheeks become pink, while little soft untidy wisps of hair escaped onto the back of her collar, as always when she was active.' These were days that Rebecca treasured. Her house was always a home, because 'Mama was there'.

It was also Agnes who first introduced her children to the excitement of London life. Just a few miles north of the Crystal Palace where Ethel's music was being played, five-year-old Rebecca was stepping into central London from the quiet of Harrow, which felt like entering into a different, magical world. The fog was sometimes so thick that day transformed into night, and she would watch in astonishment as 'a dark blob would loom up in the street, presently revealing itself as a horse's nose; and bit by bit the rest of the horse emerged, gradually followed by a spectral cart.'

Agnes shepherded Rebecca and Hans through the fog to all of London's most famous monuments, teaching them the history of statues and buildings. But Rebecca's mind wandered elsewhere. She was more captivated by 'the special London smell of smoke, leather, half-frozen horse droppings and mud' and the sounds of 'carriage wheels, cracking of whips, jingling harness and perpetual clip-clop of hoofs on slushy slippery streets', and nowhere was noisier and smellier than the markets. Gripping tightly to Agnes's hand, she stared wide-eyed at the flower stalls that seemed like fountains of bright, glorious colour, inhaling the scents of the new-cut blooms that stood next to boxes of oranges, apples and every kind of berry she could imagine. 'I was in heaven.'

London was a fleeting heaven, though. Eventually Rebecca would always have to return to sleepy Harrow, and the misery of violin lessons. Joseph was a keen cellist of dubious ability who harboured dreams of being able to play chamber music with his family, so Rebecca's introduction to performance at seven years old came about because of one of his whims.

When Rebecca first started learning an instrument, there were certainly no indications that music would eventually become her all-consuming passion. Being 'only a girl', she was not granted her own tuition, but was instead sent along to Hans's violin lessons to 'pick up anything I could'. And while she *could* play the violin, she absolutely hated it. Agnes had to coax her into doing just a few minutes of daily practice. Rebecca would saw away at the instrument in floods of tears, her dark hair becoming increasingly unkempt as she screwed up her large eyes in anguish, with her nose dribbling freely. She hated the scratching squeaks and the uncomfortable position she had to contort herself in to get any sound out at all. It was not an auspicious start.

As Joseph became more established in his Kodak job the family finances improved significantly, but Agnes never spent money on herself. Instead, she worked on her latest dress for Rebecca or jumper for Hans, letting her daughter sit at her feet and play with a bag of fabric scraps, revelling in the novelty of the different textures. But Joseph's unpredictable presence meant that life at College Road 'was like living on the edge of a volcano'. And his aggressive atheism caused no end of trouble for the family. The local community noticed that they were never at church on Sundays, and successive maids tried to impress upon the children 'the eternal torture' that awaited them in hell should they follow their father's path. Although atheism was more prevalent in Britain than ever before, church attendance was still associated with social respectability, especially outside of large cities. Particularly because Agnes chose to employ religious staff and send her children to schools that valued the church, the hard-line stance that Joseph imparted to his children made Rebecca feel as though 'we were outcasts'. It was an experience that she would have to get used to.

o   o   o   o

At Frimhurst, only a couple of hours' travel from Harrow, on 'a bitter starlit night' in January 1891 Ethel's mother died quietly in her sleep, with Ethel at her bedside. Nina had been Ethel's most unwavering supporter; even in her final days she was still cutting out all of her daughter's press notices to send to Bob in India. Yet Ethel couldn't help but feel 'a deep sense of relief [. . .] mingled with my sorrow'. She adored her mother, but it was from Nina that she had inherited her argumentativeness, and their relationship had always been tense. She consoled herself with the comfort that she had come back to England to nurse her mother in her twilight years, and that the last months they spent together, at least, were free from fights. An illumination Ethel made saying 'Let not your heart be troubled' had hung over Nina's bed, bringing her solace every evening, and Ethel now slipped it into her coffin. They buried Nina next to Johnny, in the graveyard of St Peter's Church in Frimley.

Concerned by Ethel's unhealthily long work hours, sadness over Nina and escalating anxiety over the situation with Julia and H. B., her sister Mary whisked her off on holiday to Algiers in February 1891. What they both needed, Mary decreed, was a change of scene to give a sense of perspective. By the 1890s, holidays to Algeria and the Middle East were very much part of the lifestyle of upper-middle-class women – among whom Mary, wife of a mining heir and close friend to artists including John Singer Sargent, was building quite a reputation as a fashionable hostess. Her hunch that Ethel would be revived by a new environment proved correct. By April, when

Ethel set off from Algiers for Cape Martin to holiday with Empress Eugénie, she was ready to begin composing again.

Eugénie was quite content to structure their holiday-making around Ethel's compositional bursts. The stunning seaside views and distance from her troubles gave Ethel the courage she needed to begin her most ambitious project yet. Starting a new work was never anything less than a Herculean effort, especially when it involved something as daunting as a full Mass for choir, soloists and orchestra. She would sometimes procrastinate for months on end before she could shake her 'leaden reluctance' to face the blank manuscript. But when she finally put pen to paper she composed continuously, taking few breaks, immersing herself in the work completely.

As she gazed out over the sea Ethel thought of Pauline, and put into the Mass all the religious devotion that this 'unearthly' woman inspired. Ethel always felt that a shroud of mystery hung about Pauline, giving the impression that she was 'a visitant from another planet lent to this world for the time being', and this otherworldly quality shaped Ethel's Mass. The Kyrie – the opening prayer – opens with a ghostly murmur from the basses, their lament spreading upwards through the choir, like a thin tendril of smoke slowly fanned into an inferno as the whole choir call out as one: 'Lord, have mercy'. The Benedictus became one of the most profoundly moving pieces that Ethel ever composed. It's a soaring, sweeping prayer of hope, written with such sincerity that it feels as though the singer is bestowing a blessing upon the listeners. Perhaps the Mass was also Ethel's way of bidding farewell to her mother.

Ethel kept composing throughout the summer as she toured the Adriatic with Eugénie on her yacht, the villas of Trieste and vibrant colours of Corfu suggesting phrases and chords. She completed the framework of the Mass by autumn, and began orchestrating. Crucially, though, she needed to find both a publisher and a choir willing to perform it. This was no easy task. Her friend Hermann Levi from the Munich Opera wrote her a letter of recommendation stating that the Mass was 'the strongest and most original work that had come out of England since Purcell's time', but other conductors were hesitant to take up the piece. They were sceptical about Levi's support for Ethel, insinuating that he was not influenced purely by musical considerations. Ethel learned to confront this hurdle head on – when she turned up to one journalist's office, having been told to stay away so he could judge her music on its merit and not be swayed by her 'sex appeal', she bounded into the room warning him 'You won't really fall in love with me, will you? There is no danger of that,' before launching into a rendition of the work.

When Ethel could not take this forthright approach, it proved harder to convince conductors to take up the Mass. Performance and publication were a vicious circle: choirs wouldn't perform it unless it had been published, and publishers wouldn't accept it until it had been performed. Seeing the impossibility of Ethel's situation, Eugénie came to her rescue. When Novello agreed to publish the Mass on the conditions that it be performed before royalty, and that Ethel cover half the publication costs, Eugénie promised both to attend the premiere, and provide the necessary £100 for printing. Royal patronage of any kind was still worth a great deal in the 1890s. Having royals attend a performance did not guarantee the popularity of a work, but it vastly increased the likelihood of repeat performances and therefore sales of scores. The ultimate coup was to have Queen Victoria attend, so Eugénie took it upon herself to improve her protégée's prospects. She invited Ethel to come and stay with her on the Balmoral estate, and one blustery afternoon ushered her into the Queen's presence to perform some of her music.

While Ethel was reliably star-struck when she met her musical idols, royals were another matter. She was quite used to mixing among the upper echelons of society, and although she admitted that the Queen was a little 'awe-inspiring', she was becalmed by her smile, which she thought the 'sweetest, most entrancing' that she had 'ever seen on human face'. Undaunted, Ethel launched into a rendition of the Mass's Sanctus and Benedictus in her uniquely unselfconscious way, hollering out all the parts while accompanying herself at the piano and stomping her feet for additional percussion. Queen Victoria was so 'delighted with this novel experience' that she invited Ethel to Balmoral to give a repeat performance. Ethel managed to breach all kinds of court etiquette, but nonetheless she and Marco thrilled the stern Balmoral audience with a rendition of the Mass that was so loud and energetic that 'the presence of a real chorus and orchestra was scarcely missed!'

Eugénie's patronage proved more valuable than Ethel could have imagined, as did her own instincts to believe in her music, and not to lessen her personality for the sake of propriety. Alongside Eugénie, two of Victoria's daughters also undertook to attend any performance of the Mass. With such an outstanding vote of royal approval, the premiere was scheduled by the Royal Choral Society, at the prestigious Royal Albert Hall in January 1893.

o   o   o   o

'School', as Rebecca remembered it, 'was not a happy time.' She was incessantly talkative and quite a tomboy, which earned her the disapproval of many teachers. Her report from Miss Colbeck's primary school for girls bluntly stated that 'Rebecca would do well to cultivate a quieter and more ladylike manner'. She showed no signs of conforming to these expectations, however, and after a couple of years was expelled for scrapping with another girl in Harrow High Street, throwing Agnes into the unexpected position of home tutor. One of the long-standing impacts of these escapades was an acute consciousness of her class. She was sure that many of her troubles at Miss Colbeck's stemmed from the fact that the other students 'came from the "superior" and rather conventional families of Harrow' – families just like Ethel's. Rebecca, with her homemade clothes and clumpy boots, quite clearly did not belong to this group.

When Rebecca was ten, the Clarkes upgraded to a large house called Gayton Corner, complete with tennis court and no fewer than two indoor bathrooms, which was a considerable luxury in 1896. But the family were living a little beyond their means. Both the water and heat supplies were erratic, to put it generously. The house was furnished with a curious assortment of bargains that Joseph had foraged at sales, trinkets from his travels abroad, and opulent furniture inherited from his family in the States, including 'marble-topped tables, a set of sofa and chairs with beautifully carved oval backs, a wardrobe almost big enough to live in, lush red brocade curtains, and a lot of family portraits'. The acquisition of Gayton Corner clearly signalled that the family 'were going up in the world', and Rebecca was quite disappointed by the attendant 'inconvenient increase in propriety that would be demanded of us'. She was happiest when climbing trees with Eric and Hans, or tormenting the family's ten cats.

Having an income that *almost* allowed Joseph to indulge his pretensions of grandeur but that also kept him constantly looking for money-saving schemes left the Clarkes in a peculiar hinterland. They were clearly not among the monied well-to-do Harrow residents, but nor were they among those who worked 'in trade'. So while one of Rebecca's school friends was barred from Harrow's open-air swimming pool because her aunt owned a shop, the Clarkes were able to enjoy lazy summer days in the cool water, however much they might have been looked down on by some of its other occupants. Monetary concerns so obviously shaping other people's perceptions of her as a child instilled a fierce financial independence in Rebecca. Where Ethel viewed it as an achievement to have her income supplied by sponsors and inheritances, Rebecca was extremely proud when she eventually began earning her own money as a performer. And she was always economical, making many of her own clothes and repurposing and recycling her household items.

None of this did anything to quell her sense of being an 'outsider'.

When she started at South Hampstead High School after a few years of home-schooling, she looked as out of place as she felt. She was tall, 'gawky, shy and inclined to pimples'. And her family's politics marked her as different. When the Boer War between Britain and the Boer Republics in South Africa started in 1899, the other girls came in with 'general buttons' on their clothes – buttons with portraits of popular generals in the British army, worn to show support for the war. Joseph, however, was strongly against the war, and banned Rebecca from wearing the buttons even when she saved up her pocket money for them. His anti-war stance was so well known that when celebration broke out across Harrow after a British military success, the revellers threw bricks through the windows of the Clarkes' home. Rebecca's response to this general feeling of ostracisation was to adopt the role of class joker. She was developing a quick wit and used it to her advantage, her sarcastic comebacks to unsuspecting teachers garnering her favour among her classmates.

Even though becoming the class clown gave her some sense of belonging, she still liked to dream that she was someone and somewhere else, sometimes having the feeling 'of being jolted out of my identity, to return almost instantaneously with a sort of bump and a sense of surprise at finding myself the same person as before'. This longing to be elsewhere was exacerbated by Joseph's beatings, punishments and reprimands, which made Rebecca feel as though 'everything I did was always wrong, however much I tried.' But she refused to let Joseph's cruelty define her. She resolved to grow 'an extra skin' and see his disciplining as being 'all in the day's work'. While she was in many ways successful at brushing off Joseph's criticisms, it would have been impossible for them not to leave a mark in some way. Rebecca kept the rug that had once lain in the Gayton library all her life, but even when she was in her eighties, the mere sight of it was enough to transport her back to her teenage years, resurrecting the sense of 'desperation' that she had felt while being chastised for 'all the bad things I had done'.

Amid the regular anxieties of becoming a teenager and the particular difficulties of her home life, Rebecca was beginning to find solace in music. What had begun as torture was becoming an escape. True, she still loathed practising, but now she was able to at least get a decent tone out of the violin, she forgot some of the misery of practice when the family played pieces together, revelling in the rare moments of accord. She enjoyed popular, tuneful pieces, particularly late-Romantic works that she could play with plenty of 'ardour'. Music like this affected Rebecca physically. Occasionally she would be moved to tears while playing, and when she heard music that particularly stirred her, she was convinced that if anybody touched her at that moment they 'would get an electric shock'. She carried around scores in her pockets so that her favourite pieces could travel with her wherever she went, called upon at a moment's notice when she needed a reprieve. In short, she 'was fast becoming emotionally drenched' in music.

Music also gave Rebecca a way to find friends at school, giving her a feeling of belonging. She was banned from attending prayers at school, but so were all the other girls whose families did not follow the Church of England. One of the Jewish girls in her class, Margery Bentwich, also played the violin, and the two girls bonded over their shared enjoyment of music while sitting out of morning prayers. Margery came from a large, generous and formidably musically talented family, and would become one of Rebecca's lifelong friends. In their teenage years Rebecca and Margery went to concerts, passing judgement on all the stars who passed through London, finding that they shared a love of the more passionate and intense pieces. Rebecca dreamed that one day, she would be one of the performers to step out on to one of London's celebrated stages. Foremost among all her idols was violinist Eugène Ysaÿe, and she particularly enjoyed 'strutting around in one of Papa's suits' to try to mimic the way Ysaÿe 'walked onto the Queen's Hall platform'. Envisaging herself as a famous musician was the most cherished of all her fantasies, 'dressing-up to escape being who I was'.

A CHANGING WORLD

Ethel, at thirty-five, was beginning to get a taste of life as a famous musician. When the newspapers announced the details of the Mass's premiere, she gained a minor celebrity status overnight. A first performance with the Royal Choral Society was like gold dust even for well-established composers, let alone for relatively unknown names with only a couple of English appearances behind them. Naturally the critics were curious about 'E. M. Smyth', and interviews with Ethel began cropping up in the papers. Even the journalist from the *Women's Penny Paper* was taken aback by meeting her, declaring 'I hardly know whether I had made up any mental picture of a woman composer, but certainly I will own I was taken by surprise on seeing a tall, bright, lithe, active lady enter the room.'

Adding to the general sense of bewilderment that most people felt when they met Ethel was the fact that she had taken to wearing tweed skirt suits with a blouse and tie, sweeping her fair hair up under a boater hat. She wore this ensemble with very few variants until she died, but when she first donned her tweeds, this was a significant statement of political affiliation. By the 1890s, this style of dress was associated with the 'New Woman', a term created in 1894 by the generation of young women who were rejecting the mid-Victorian ideal of womanhood, escaping from being 'incapable of independent action, unfitted for liberty, a dependent and a parasite from the cradle to the grave'.

Nonetheless, Ethel's political rebellion remained on an individual level, for now. At first, she couldn't have been less interested in organised women's rights movements. Despite the fact that some of her close friends were signing up to the many British women's suffrage groups, Ethel stayed aloof of such proceedings. She couldn't see how such abstract political issues would benefit her individually, and besides, many of those involved with the women's movements of the late nineteenth century upheld the ideal of motherhood and middle-class models for women's behaviour. Ethel had little time for either, particularly working in such a male-dominated world as music. She distanced herself from these movements, but asserted herself by dressing in a masculine way, single-mindedly pursuing her own career, taking up sports and riding bicycles – which were considered both outrageous and indecorous for young ladies when they were first introduced. This was not what critics expected of a composing woman.

Positive press was crucial for securing repeat performances, but all composers were constantly at the mercy of events and alliances beyond their control that shaped how critics approached their work. In the case of her Mass, Ethel managed to annoy the critics before a single note had been played. A performance with such a distinguished choir was *so* unusual that the critics all had their favourite composers who they backed each season to get a concert. This year their front runner had been Hubert Parry and his oratorio *Job*, but he was left off the programme. This left Ethel and her Mass starting on the back foot, having to live up to raised expectations. Reviewers were chagrined that their favourite had been passed over in favour of a lesser-known composer, and a woman at that. Even though royal attendance had been a condition of the score's publication, the press now used the presence of royalty as a way to dismiss the Mass, suggesting that it was being performed only because of social pressure, not for any musical merit.

When the day finally came, the cavernous Royal Albert Hall in Kensington was packed out with Ethel's friends, family, royal supporters and H. B. She was wracked with nerves, particularly as the rehearsals had been a minor torment for the self-critical composer. When she first heard a work of hers, she 'seldom perceived anything but the distance between my idea and my attempt to realize it'. After she heard how her harmonies and instrumentation actually sounded, Ethel was overcome with the desire to revise her score. She sneaked in between rehearsal sessions armed with scissors, glue and manuscript paper, pasting her corrections into the performers' scores. This process of ongoing revision during rehearsals became a lifelong habit. Musicians who worked with Ethel learned to dread the sight of the scissors and paste pot, especially because she sometimes went beyond minor alterations and rescored entire movements, requiring performers to relearn their parts extremely quickly. Despite the hasty reworking, though, the performance came off superbly, with Ethel called to the stage for multiple curtain calls.

When she later looked back on this performance, Ethel concluded sadly that 'the Press went for the Mass almost unanimously – some with scorn, some with aversion'. This wasn't quite true; many newspapers declared that it was 'distinctly original', and both 'modern and singularly energetic'. But her forthright musical style was perceived as falling far short of a womanly ideal. 'Why will so many women of the present day', one complained, 'not recognise that they are women, and that they are most attractive when they are most womanly?' Ethel, they felt, 'necessarily and properly fails when she endeavours to become too masculine in her methods'. Then there was the assertion from George Bernard Shaw that the Mass was merely 'decorative' – which was only to be expected, because 'If you take an average mundane young lady, and ask her what service to religion she most enjoys rendering, she will probably, if she is a reasonably truthful person, instance the decoration of a church at Christmas.'

Ethel was utterly dismayed. The reviews cast a pall over the performance. Despite publication, royal patronage, a premiere at a respected venue *and* a positive reception from the audience in the Hall, the piece would not be performed again until 1924. This was a bitter formative experience. All her life, the Mass's disappearance remained one of Ethel's greatest disappointments, and she held the critics' outright gender prejudice entirely responsible.

Ethel had to put the criticisms out of mind, because she was already embarking on an even larger project. Hermann Levi believed that the Mass was 'evidence of a dramatic gift', and begged Ethel to start an opera. Ethel needed no further persuasion. The opera stage was a place where fortunes were made. Opera was a prestigious (and expensive) genre, and opera composers and singers were some of the best-known musical names of the nineteenth century. Sites of opulence and scandal, opera houses had historically been places exclusively for the upper classes, but that was slowly changing. Nineteenth-century composers like Verdi and Wagner insisted that opera should be a national art form, and throughout Ethel's lifetime opera became more accessible to the middle and working classes, especially after the invention of the gramophone. Ethel had confessed to her mother that one of her greatest dreams was to have 'an opera accepted at a first-class opera house by the time I was forty'. Ethel was turning thirty-six soon, so she had little time to lose.

For her libretto – the opera's text – Ethel settled on a comedy called *Fantasio*. Eugénie had originally suggested the play, thinking it might suit a light-hearted setting in the style of Gilbert and Sullivan, whose comic operettas about magic potions, pirates and the Royal Navy were enduringly popular in England. Ethel loved the play, but was not naturally inclined to frivolity. She set about writing music in an altogether more serious vein, and significantly altered the original story. Ethel's version is a tale full of disguises, mistaken identity and hopeful love, in which a Herzegovinian poet called Fantasio takes on multiple disguises to win the heart of Princess Danila and save her from a miserable marriage to the Count of Croatia.

Ethel constantly discussed her revisions with H. B., who was now a permanent fixture in her life and took on the informal role of literary adviser. Ethel and H. B.'s reunion had done nothing to repair the wreckage of her relationship with Lisl. When Lisl died suddenly and unexpectedly in 1892, it was without having reconciled with her old friend. In one of her least admirable moments, Ethel vented her anger at Julia. Just a few days after the death of her cherished sister, Julia received a furious letter from Ethel announcing that she intended 'to fashion my life as I choose, not giving you a thought', placing the blame for her estrangement from Lisl entirely at Julia's door. Ethel introduced H. B. to her friends and family and, having waited for this moment for years, when they were in the same country they co-existed discreetly as romantic partners.

Besides H. B. however, someone else had entered Ethel's world – a woman who Ethel felt changed 'the whole colour of my life'. Mary Elizabeth Ponsonby, or MEP, as she styled herself, was by any account an extraordinary woman. She moved in the most elite circles, as the wife of Queen Victoria's Private Secretary, having herself been a maid of honour to the Queen. She had an aristocratic demeanour and, above all, exceptional tactfulness and the ability to persuade others through wit and good manners – talents Ethel did not possess. But MEP was also surprisingly liberal for her social circle, fiercely opinionated and willing to campaign for causes she believed in. She believed passionately in women's advancement through education, and was involved in founding Girton College in Cambridge, the first college exclusively for women.

Like Ethel, MEP took a very dim view of people trying to dictate what she could or should do on account of her gender. She played billiards, was a keen shot with a rifle, set up a wood-workshop for herself in the garden shed and read voraciously. It was precisely this combination of varied personality traits, mixed with a wicked sense of humour and a wide-ranging interest in everything from politics to literature, that so attracted Ethel to her. 'She appeals to every side in me', she enthused – 'including the snob.' And being twenty-six years Ethel's senior, MEP fulfilled the maternal role that

Ethel craved, becoming something of a replacement for both Lisl and Ethel's mother.

It was hardly love at first sight. They first met when Ethel was invited for tea at MEP's home by a mutual acquaintance, and she had been quite bored by Ethel's 'hectoring manner'. At the time, MEP and her family lived in a redecorated apartment in the Tower of London, the old cell walls exposed to reveal 'inscriptions carved by the prisoners', which MEP had surrounded with books and her watercolours. As she listened to Ethel holding court about her latest projects and grudges, MEP felt unexpected solidarity for the room's previous inhabitants. She excused herself at the earliest opportunity, but after a short while found herself tempted back to the room by one of the most bewitching sounds she had ever heard. It was a haunting, melancholy melody that simultaneously expressed such longing, desire, fear and sadness that it was impossible to ignore. 'Come o'er the sea,' the singer beckoned – come to the waves, where there is 'No eye to watch, and no tongue to wound us / All earth forgot and all heaven around us.' And to MEP's shock, Ethel was the source of the music, accompanying herself at the piano. Stunned that this obnoxious woman was capable of such passion and refinement, MEP gave Ethel a second chance.

It was a shaky start, but by 1893 Ethel and MEP were entwined in each other's lives. Despite many 'Ethel-ians' – 'interruptions without either profit or pleasure' – MEP slowly came to appreciate Ethel's 'gentle tenderness'. MEP, it seems, was able to bring out a more considerate, caring side of Ethel. She attributed her change to being 'wanted [. . .] as much as you want', remarking that 'I often felt as if another manual had been added to the organ, one with richer, deeper stops, and to this day I think that is a good picture of what a new great emotion can do for you'. H. B. was delighted by this new development. In his characteristic way, he showed no hint of envy about Ethel's relationships with other women, even when she told him that 'my love for Lady P. & the nature of the alliance is on the same plane as ours'. Instead, he reassured Ethel that he was 'obscurely grateful' to MEP for bringing about Ethel's more affectionate attitude.

Serene and sweet-tempered the new Ethel might have been, but her relationship with MEP was anything but docile. Flaming rows were typical of their day-to-day interactions. Where Ethel tended to rage at a relatively consistent level, MEP would first fly into a temper, throwing out hurtful slurs and accusations, then immediately swap to a frosty stillness. This enraptured Ethel. She was convinced that 'in no human being I have ever met were hidden such inexhaustible stores of fire as in the heart of this apparently calm, deliberately reserved, rather sphinx-like being'.

Their relationship was not as sexual as Ethel would have liked. She complained that she was kept 'at arms length' without kisses and caresses. Nonetheless MEP became Ethel's confidante in sexual matters, particularly where H. B. was concerned. When Ethel had her first sexual experience with a man, consummating her relationship with H. B. in 1895, she turned to MEP. Ethel confessed that 'There *is* a mystery in this actual belonging to the best being you know – to the one too who knows you best – which has come upon me with all my thirty-seven years as a surprise, a new force in life.' Then when Julia died H. B. started making overtures of marriage towards Ethel, alarming her greatly. 'I must be free,' she explained to MEP. 'I love my own loves, my own life.' Eventually H. B. agreed to keep their arrangement as it was, greatly relieved to leave behind their 'matrimonial bickerings'.

With H. B. and MEP providing Ethel with constant support, *Fantasio* was 'written with immense pleasure and desire'. Echoes of each relationship made their way into the opera score: Ethel recycled passages from her earlier *Song of Love* cantata, written at the height of her difficulties with H. B. and Julia; and for Danila's solo aria at the heart of the opera, she used an arrangement of 'Come o'er the sea', the song that meant so much to her and MEP. Even in this most grand and public of genres, Ethel incorporated private, intimate meanings significant only for her and those she loved. By March 1894 the opera was complete, and she had to begin the exhausting rigmarole of trying to secure a performance and publisher.

If getting a Mass performed was difficult, getting an opera staged was even harder. Ethel didn't just have to convince the conductor, but also the director and opera house staff. Because of the sheer amount of money involved in staging any opera, houses tended to err on the side of caution where new works were concerned, so there were few recent precedents of women writing operas. The most significant exception was the composer Augusta Holmès in France, of whom Ethel was well aware. Nonetheless, Ethel never bothered correcting people who labelled her the 'first woman to write an opera', instead embracing any opportunity to portray herself as a lone pioneer.

Given that Ethel's reputation was better established in Germany than in England, and that Germany had a much larger number of opera houses, Ethel set off there to try to fix a venue. She embarked on a gruelling, four-year campaign through Karlsruhe, Dresden, Leipzig, Cologne, Wiesbaden and Munich, before finally managing to secure a premiere at Weimar. The date was set for January 1898, just three months before Ethel's fortieth birthday. With a few weeks to spare, Ethel had managed to achieve the goal she had only dared hope for as a teenage composer starting out her career. 'Darling,' she wrote to H. B., 'I am slowly and surely going mad with joy.'

o   o   o   o

Ethel's world was filled with royalty, opulence, stately homes and tradition. She was, as she put it, a 'snob', and revelled in the formality, conservatism and exclusivity of this small social club. But by 1900, there were two worlds rubbing alongside each other, one looking backwards and one reaching forwards to the new and modern, each vying for dominance throughout the twentieth century. As Ethel was wallowing in Victorian splendour, Rebecca's father was taking her to the Paris World Fair, the ultimate symbol of a turning point between the centuries. The 1900 World Fair was the most ambitious the world had ever seen, with 530 acres of land in the French capital dedicated to celebrating the idea of progress – the new, the exciting, the *modern*.

Fourteen-year-old Rebecca couldn't have been more excited. 'Never in my life had I imagined anything to compare to the fantastic buildings, the colours.' She wandered around the site in astonishment. An enormous fountain at the centre of the Water Castle flickered in a display of changing multicoloured lights, lit by the Palace of Electricity. The site was dotted with pavilions representing countries from all over the world. Rebecca could stand in the Finnish Pavilion and gaze up at the frescoes representing the fur-clad heroes from the country's national epic, the *Kalevala*, painted to symbolise Finland gaining political freedom from Russia – before passing under the dragons, flowers and phoenixes adorning the roof of the Japanese Pavilion, on her way to see some of Japan's most treasured art shipped to France specifically for the World Fair.

Rebecca was born into a period when Europe was re-establishing its fascination with China and Japan, shaping the way that Asian countries and people were viewed in the West. The first craze for chinoiserie that swept across Europe in the eighteenth century had died down in the early nineteenth, but the forced opening of ports in both Japan and China meant that East Asian items were again becoming part of the fashionable middle-class aesthetic. Travel was now easier than at any time in history, with previously remote countries made accessible by steam-powered boats and a network of railways that criss-crossed world maps. Goods, ideas and people travelled swiftly across these routes. British galleries and museums ran exhibitions about Chinese and Japanese art, and the shops of Rebecca's childhood were filled with a combination of imitation and imported Asian goods. Both Ethel and Rebecca's fathers had brought home items from abroad. But unlike Ethel, who viewed anything non-European as distinctly suspect, Rebecca was fascinated by the netsuke and Japanese sword hilts that she found dotted around her house, and wanted to know more about where they came from. She would sit in front of the Chinese prints and imagine herself miles from home, losing herself for hours in the muted colours. For Rebecca, Asia signified adventure and mystery.

Imperial ambition underpinned much of the motivation for the World Fairs, and there was a section specifically dedicated to pavilions from countries that were then colonised. Rebecca was captivated by the sound and sight of the gamelan – an Indonesian orchestra of hand-crafted gongs, drums and metallophones, set in exquisitely decorated wooden frames – and she would work the music she encountered at the Fair into many of her later compositions. She was not alone. Claude Debussy was also inspired by the gamelan, as was Benjamin Britten decades later. Rebecca's world was changing, and so, accordingly, was the sound of the music within it. As she wandered across the fairground, the ringing gamelan mingled with the blare of jazz bands, brass bands, choirs and folk singers from across the world. It was 'a dazzling experience'.

Over the coming years British concert halls would be filled with music by composers like Rebecca, who were trying to make sense of this bewildering world that inspired a combination of astonishment, excitement and no small amount of fear. Along with the unshakeable belief in the idea of progress came an anxiety about traditions being lost as the country changed at a dizzying rate.

Concern about Britain's position in global politics fuelled these worries. The British Empire had undergone unprecedented expansion, and by 1900 the British were engaged in the 'Scramble for Africa' with six other European countries, fighting each other to colonise the largest proportion of the continent. But at the same time, the Boer buttons that Rebecca's school mates proudly wore couldn't hide the fact that the war was revealing the limited extent of Britain's military power. Defeat followed defeat, and the increasing economic might of countries like America challenged narratives about British political dominance.

Where Rebecca embraced this new world with enthusiasm, Ethel's diary over the coming years became a litany of political worries, cataloguing the disappearance of the traditions she loved. Everywhere Ethel turned, it seemed, there were reminders that the beliefs and assumptions that had shaped her early years were slipping away.

This profound ambivalence about the new meant that in the early 1900s there was no consensus about what 'modern' and progressive music should sound like. While Beethoven and Schubert remained popular, over the next few years both composers and audiences would be completely divided by jazz, dance music, the sensual and ethereal harmonies of composers like Debussy, and the uncompromising, angular and dissonant music of Igor Stravinsky. Some embraced what became labelled 'modernist' music with fervour, but others dug in their heels, declaring that 'our English music is being ruined'.

Coming of age in this tumultuous world, Rebecca still had to negotiate the far more pressing and regular concerns of being a teenage girl. Desperate to fit in at school, she pored over fashion and beauty magazines in a largely unsuccessful quest to make herself prettier. Her attempts to rid herself of blackheads ended miserably after she scrubbed away 'a large patch of skin that took weeks to heal', and her efforts with modern hairstyles were curtailed by Joseph's insistence that she wear her hair in a pigtail. But at least she now had a sister with whom she could commiserate. Dora, named after Joseph's boat the *Dorian*, was nine years younger than Rebecca, and they adored each other. When Hans and Eric left England for Germany and America, Rebecca and Dora stayed together in London, sharing a flat while the older sister worked as a performer and the younger started out her career as a sculptor, studying at the Slade School of Fine Art.

Sex was also starting to appear on Rebecca's horizon, in a con-fused and abstract sort of way. Like most young girls of her gener-ation, Rebecca was woefully ignorant about any of the practicalities of sexual relationships. She was endlessly frustrated by certain ques-tions and words being illicit and taboo, giving sex 'an unknown mys-tery – half fascinating, half frightening'. And she couldn't ignore the fact that she was starting to find boys deeply attractive, and develop crushes on older girls at her school. Her attractions to women seem to have been motivated more by idolisation than sexual desire. She wanted so desperately to be beautiful and popular that she – and her friends – pedestalised the girls who appeared to have everything they didn't. Rebecca's small group would gather in the playground during breaks to complain about their teachers and work, and gossip about their latest crushes, trying to work out how to emulate the older girls in order to get more 'sex appeal'.

Practising in the music room at Gayton Corner, surrounded by the comforting, sweet smell of bow resin and old scores that lay strewn around the room, Rebecca would sometimes feel 'a moment-ary shiver' as she played. She didn't recognise the feeling at the time, but she would later describe it as 'something very much like a kind of rarefied sex'. For Rebecca, playing and listening to music was a bodily, multi-sensory experience that was both sensual and sexual. When she was older, she was able to explain that she felt as though 'the dividing line between music and sex is so tenuous as to be almost nonexistent'. As a teenager, the curious sensation that came over her when she encountered music she truly loved only made her even more absorbed by the violin practice that now dominated her days.

Shortly after she turned fifteen, Rebecca found herself expelled and being home-schooled yet again – this time through no fault of her own, but because Joseph refused to quarantine her after Dora caught the measles. Rather than battle with 'devastatingly dull' his-tory and geography, she turned her full attention to music. One of

Joseph's friends, Percy Miles, was a violin teacher at the Academy and frequently came to Gayton Corner to play chamber music with the family. He was so impressed by Rebecca's playing that he suggested she audition for the Academy, which became her goal for her sixteenth birthday.

Finally, 'the time arrived that I had been looking forward to – and dreading.' With Agnes at her side, a trembling Rebecca took the train from Harrow to Baker Street, clutching her violin case for comfort, finally arriving at the sprawling Academy building, then in Hanover Square. Making her way through the maze of passageways and practice rooms, she found a panel of suit-beclad men with uniform moustaches in her audition room. Rebecca was so nervous that she could remember nothing except the fact that the interviewers were eating strawberries and cream. But she made it through her pieces, calmed by Agnes accompanying her at the piano, smiling quiet encouragement through the whole process. It was enough to gain her a place. From January 1903, Rebecca's life would change completely.

o   o   o   o

Compared to Ethel's Mass, *Fantasio* received a relatively amiable reception. German critics seemed to be of the general opinion that it was difficult music, a bit overlong, but 'full of charm and melody, and replete with grace, delicacy, and refinement'. Nonetheless there was something that Ethel still wasn't happy with. It was the writer Maurice Baring who put his finger on it first. Ethel and Maurice (MEP's nephew) had first met at the Mass's premiere, and he had since become 'one of the two or three supreme friends I have possessed'. She trusted Maurice's artistic judgement in nearly all things, and he felt that *Fantasio*'s music was beautiful but it simply didn't suit the text. Agreeing completely, Ethel later gathered together the opera's parts, set fire to all of it and sprinkled the ashes on her rose garden, deciding that it would be better off as compost than as an example of her operatic abilities. Thankfully one version of the score survived incineration, but *Fantasio* met a similar fate to the Mass. It has not been performed since 1901.

Ethel marked up *Fantasio* as a valuable learning curve, and was already setting to work on her second opera, *Der Wald* (The Forest). No comedy this time. Following more modern literary trends, *Der Wald* would be a dark, symbolic drama set in a forest, and she took the unusual decision to write the libretto herself. Iolanthe the witch sets out to seduce a woodcutter, Heinrich, who is about to marry his sweetheart, Röschen. When Heinrich rejects Iolanthe she orders him to be murdered, and the devastated Röschen collapses beside him, dead of a broken heart. The opera starts and ends with a ritual conducted by elemental spirits, as though human tragedy is entirely inconsequential to the concerns of natural forces. Ethel wanted the opera to express the 'everlastingness of Nature' and 'the brevity of things human'.

She first came up with the idea while cycling around Italy with H. B., the trees lining the road and the breeze whipping her hair as they rushed along suggesting the cool glades of a forest. Once again H. B. took on the role of libretto-adviser-in-chief. They were now able to see each other whenever they wanted, because Ethel had moved out of Frimhurst into her own home, One Oak, after her father died in 1894. Ethel's new house was just a couple of miles away from Eugénie's, and the freedom of living on her own was 'a perpetual intoxication'. Even though One Oak was hideously impractical – it was far too large, had only a well as a water source, and the living rooms had previously been occupied by a donkey and a horse – she set about renovating it with help from H. B. Soon, Ethel could settle into the comfort and peace of composing in her own home, with only her dog, cat and housekeeper for company. H. B. was a regular guest, and in the quiet of Ethel's study they worked together on *Der Wald* in between chess sessions, sipping champagne chilled in the garden well and stroking the Old English Sheepdog that lay nibbling acquisitively on H. B.'s boots. This rascal was called Pan, after the god of nature, and his 'wistful human eyes' and absurdly shaggy fluff won Ethel over completely. Marco's successor was the first in a 'dynasty' of Sheepdog Pans (seven in total), who would be Ethel's lifelong companions.

Der Wald could not be more different to Fantasio. It's a one-act opera, so all the action is concentrated in a single burst of energy – Ethel wasn't risking a repeat of the reviews that had deemed her opera too long. But more importantly the libretto allowed Ethel to play to her strengths. The plot suited her style perfectly. Creating the nature spirits let her play with unusual, elusive harmonies that disorient the listener, enveloping them in the unsettling whispers of the ethereal and indifferent beings. And at the heart of the opera is a powerful woman, Iolanthe, who knows her own mind, and a passionate love story that gave Ethel the opportunity to unleash the full power of the modern orchestra. Uncharacteristically, Ethel modestly said of Der Wald only that she had 'a weakness' for this particular score. But it is one of the most compelling things she ever wrote.

Compelling or not, Der Wald would still have to undergo all the usual procedures to be staged. Ethel set out to Germany once again, calling on the most influential friends she had to support the opera: the German Chancellor Bernhard von Bülow and Kaiser Wilhelm II. Eugénie once again outdid herself as a patron by introducing Ethel to the Kaiser, who took quite a shine to her – unlike most of the souls who were ushered into his presence, Ethel was quite prepared to disagree with him. She first dined with him during the Boer War, which Germany emphatically opposed – cartoons regularly appeared in German newspapers that showed British soldiers bayonetting Boer babies. Ethel, however, with her brother Bob serving in the military, was in favour of the war. When the Kaiser criticised British actions in South Africa, Ethel roundly reprimanded him on the grounds that 'whether the war be right or wrong, it was splendid for character'. The Kaiser enjoyed Ethel's unrepentant self-belief (they shared a catchphrase, 'I know I'm right'), and how unladylike she seemed. Cigar-smoking Ethel was accepted as an exception among his male dinner-circle.

Ethel's connections helped her considerably in her quest to get *Der Wald* staged, and she managed to secure a performance at no less a venue than the Berlin Court Opera in 1902. But events out of Ethel's control played against her. As with the Mass, critics were chagrined about the opera house's programming. This time they complained about the small number of stagings of new German operas. And although the conductor might have been prepared to set aside his anger over the Boer War for the sake of the opera, the audience was not. The curtain lifted on a chorus of boos and hisses so vitriolic that Ethel dared not venture out on stage for her curtain calls. The reviews were a massacre. Emboldened by the unfavourable political climate, the German critics unleashed a wave of sexism upon *Der Wald*. Ethel was labelled a 'composing Amazon', one author admitting outright that 'The work of the English composeress did nothing to weaken the prejudice that one is generally accustomed to show for female compositional activity.'

More sensitive personalities than Ethel might have given up composing entirely in the face of such an onslaught. But nothing motivated Ethel more than a feeling of injustice. And MEP's influence was starting to have an impact on Ethel's views about women's rights. Ethel felt she 'must fight for *Der Wald*', because 'I want women to turn their minds to big and difficult jobs.' This was perhaps the first time that Ethel had seen herself not just as a lone pioneer, but as a possible role model for other women, her actions potentially changing circumstances for somebody other than herself. She left Germany in a rage, and set her sights on England instead.

Previously Ethel had dismissed England as a possibility because, to put it frankly, English opera was practically non-existent. Where Germany had multiple state-supported opera houses, England had a few touring companies, and Covent Garden Opera House was run by a syndicate who showed little enthusiasm for works by English composers. When operas were performed, they were Italian, German or French. And yet by 1902 there were the smallest indications that change was in the air. A couple of operas with English texts and music by English composers, Stanford and Sullivan (of Gilbert and Sullivan fame), had recently been produced by separate opera companies and received a fair amount of positive press. Critics, too, were starting to make noises about the lamentable state of opera in England, their views perhaps also shaped by the nationalism stoked by the Boer War. Covent Garden had previously been lukewarm about *Der Wald*, so Ethel was astonished to find that in the wake of the disastrous premiere they offered her a contract to produce the opera in July 1902, making her the first woman to have an opera staged there.

Ethel later looked back on the Covent Garden *Wald* as 'one of my few almost wholly delightful operatic experiences'. She got on famously with the stage director, Francis Neilson, who proved himself to be a most valuable collaborator. He thought the opera 'a strange and beautiful thing', but was quite astonished to find that Ethel 'knew so little about stage effects and how they were produced' that she had completely counterintuitive ideas about how her opera should be staged. She had relied heavily on H. B. as her dramatic mentor, which was perhaps a mistake – H. B.'s expertise was in long-winded philosophical treatises, and he had practically no experience of writing for the theatre. Francis overhauled the whole scenario, adding in dramatic details and lighting effects that made the staging look as modern as the music sounded. Ethel stayed by his side through the rehearsal period, learning from him, puffing away on her cigarettes and occasionally darting into the orchestra pit in her tweeds and tam-o'-shanter to paste corrections into the score.

With a stellar cast and some of the best collaborators Ethel ever worked with, the performance was an undeniable success. Sitting in her box, surrounded by family and friends, watching her own opera performed under the gilded arches of the opera house stage was one of the proudest moments of Ethel's life. She shoehorned herself into one of her sister Mary's lilac evening dresses especially for the occasion, looking so unlike her usual self that when she stepped out on stage to take her bows MEP shouted quite audibly from the audience 'I can't believe it. Ethel never looked like that.' The applause and cheers came in waves, the audience demanding repeated curtain calls for the composer. After the disappointment of the Berlin premiere, nothing could have been more welcome.

Ethel was hailed as the harbinger of a new English opera. The critics decreed it 'a really fine opera by a native composer'; an 'original opera of serious intention, of finely artistic construction, of first-rate inspiration, and most learned and sound musicianship'. A few grumbled about the libretto being in German rather than English – they felt that an English opera should have an English text that English audiences could understand – and of course there were some dismissive references to the composer being a woman. Overall, though, Ethel couldn't have hoped for a more positive response. *Der Wald* went down as 'a distinct and unique triumph' that could be counted among 'the most modern school of her art'. For all Ethel's conservative social circle, her music could still hold its own in the new world. Covent Garden scheduled *Der Wald* for a revival in 1903, and to add to Ethel's victory, the Metropolitan Opera House in New York offered her a contract. Again, Ethel was making history. The Met had never staged an opera by a woman before. She agreed to the production immediately, and set off in a state of elation to conquer America.

Full of anticipation, on the crossing over she wrote incessantly to H. B., filling hundreds of pages with her large, looping scrawl. And he patiently responded to every word, sending just as many pages in return despite his small, neat handwriting. As H. B. couldn't travel with her he demanded to know the exact position of her boat at every moment, so he could mentally accompany her across the Atlantic, from One Oak to Times Square. He always found their separations harder than Ethel did, and on this occasion he was beset by aches and pains that he, now fifty-three, put down to encroaching old age. Neither of them could have realised that H. B.'s headaches and weakness were symptoms of the cancer that would kill him within just five years.

By the time Ethel stepped off the ship, newspapers across the States had trumpeted the arrival of a famed woman composer and her opera. In America, even more than in England, Ethel was seen as the herald of a new age. And she embraced a more broad-minded, feminist attitude for her American audience. She gave interviews claiming passionately that she had 'a duty to all womankind in persevering in this field. Every woman that comes after me will find it easier because of my journey first over the rough road.'

Partly she was pandering to the crowd, but there was a part of Ethel so frustrated by her own difficulties in breaking down gender barriers that she was starting to see herself as a figurehead for other women. She still wanted her work to be evaluated on its merits, irrespective of her gender. But she was increasingly less inclined to hide the fact she was a woman, veiling her gender behind her initials. Why should she hide? Her treatment had been unjust. So Ethel took a new tack, deciding to try to force institutions to change instead of changing herself.

America, however, turned out to be a disappointment. Perhaps most importantly, Ethel didn't make friends as easily as she did in England. Loud, outspoken, tweedy Ethel was horribly out of place in the elegant soirées her sister Mary had learned to navigate so skilfully. Mary had a core of steel quite equal to Ethel's, but she bore it with style, convincing listeners with her easy wit, elegant hairstyles and layers of chiffon and furs. New Yorkers were used to Marys, and when presented with an Ethel they didn't quite know what to do with her. Then Ethel was not best pleased with the Met's production, and the reviews were lukewarm. It was a pity that 'the young woman could not burst her stays and be entirely natural and full in her expression', they sighed.

Ethel felt that her music was 'as out of place in America as one of the Muses would be at a football match', and didn't want to waste her time trying to lay foundations in a country where she felt uncomfortable. After another performance in Boston, Ethel returned to England without a second glance. Besides, she had other things to think about. She could feel something moving, stirring within her, faintly at first but growing with each passing week. It whispered to her when she woke and kept her awake at nights. Ethel couldn't have been happier. A new opera was taking shape.

DRAMAS, ROMANTIC AND OPERATIC

Concealed by the boom and rush and squall of the sea, a narrow crack in the Cornish cliffs becomes a tunnel that burrows deep into the hillside. Lit only by the dim flicker from oil torches, it plummets down, down under the sea, the brisk salt air becoming thick with the stench of weeds and rotting fish, the growl of the waves and shingle growing to an intense roar overhead. Then, suddenly, a sharp turn, and all is quiet. Just the sound of sea water dripping from the roof of an enormous cave into a completely still pool. The only living creatures are the blind fish circling in the water, robbed of their sight by the cave's darkness.

Legends linger around Piper's Hole – stories of lanterns being extinguished to deliberately lure ships onto the rocks, leading the crew to their deaths and the wreckers to the bounty of the ship's cargo. Tales about Cornish giants and ghosts that roam the coves at night pale in comparison to the horrors reported to have been committed by wreckers: survivors slaughtered in cold blood if they made their way to the shore, the corpses stripped of their valuables to add to the stash of goods smuggled across the country. The mystery and menace of Piper's Hole had struck Ethel so profoundly when she went on holiday to Cornwall in her twenties that she was still thinking about it two decades later as she turned forty-four, hunting for a topic for her new opera. She dreamed up a community of wreckers united by poverty, religion and ruthlessness; and at the heart of it, three lovers torn apart by greed and guilt. She sent off her sketches to H. B., and he was just as captivated by the idea as she was. Immediately he began crafting her notes into a libretto, giving shape to the very first outlines of *The Wreckers*.

No project had ever consumed Ethel or H. B. so completely as this opera. They worked at it ten, twelve hours a day, H. B. writing in Italy and Ethel composing at her desk at One Oak, Pan by her side and her housekeeper, Mrs Faulkner, occasionally wafting her way through thick clouds of cigar smoke to bring Ethel food. Letters flew between the two of them as they worked out the details of their plot. Slowly the characters began to take shape: Marc, compelled by compassion to betray the wreckers and warn ships away from the shore; Thurza, his lover, married to the town's preacher but similarly horrified by her people; and Avis, Thurza's rival, who loves Marc so desperately that she tries to save him even when she finds out he is warning the ships away. And Piper's Hole provided the scene for the climax, Thurza and Marc left chained to the rocks to die as traitors as the sea washes over them. Ethel and H. B. lost themselves so completely in the opera that Ethel became 'Beloved Thurza' in H. B.'s letters, and she herself admitted that she was starting to fall a little in love with the opera's hero. And no wonder – it's probably no coincidence that Ethel's second and third operas feature two women fighting over the same man. Perhaps at some level the love triangle of *The Wreckers* was based on Ethel's own experience with Julia and H. B. Everybody in *The Wreckers* fundamentally believes they are doing the right thing, and yet they tear one another apart anyway.

At least partly, the flames of Ethel's inspiration were being fanned by the appearance of a new love – Winnaretta Singer, Princesse de Polignac. Winnaretta was one of the best-connected women in Parisian society: she had her own money as heiress to the Singer sewing-machine fortune, and had married into status, to Prince Edmond de Polignac. In their own way, Winnaretta and Edmond loved each other, and they had a lavender marriage – a celibate marriage which gave them both social protection to pursue same-sex relationships – built on mutual respect and love of the arts. When Winnaretta met Ethel in 1903, she was recently widowed and had decided to devote her wealth and social standing to arts patronage.

She was herself an exceptional artist and organ player, and turned her home into a haven for France's avant-garde. In her wood-panelled salon Paris's most artistic rubbed shoulders with the most wealthy, nestled into one of the window seats or at a table with a cup of tea under the enormous vaulted ceiling that rose into blackness, all united by their love of music.

Ethel's increasing fame and the Covent Garden *Wald* had caught Winnaretta's attention, and after a brief meeting in England, she accepted Ethel and her music into this fellowship of art-worshippers. Winnaretta was not a conventionally beauti-ful woman – she had a long face and thick-set jaw that she flat-tered with judiciously chosen hats and haircuts – but Ethel was enthralled by her unique combination of intellect and artistic fer-vour, and not a little arrogance. 'I am certain of one thing as death – I love you more in five minutes than anyone else ever did in five years,' she assured Winnaretta. She gushed about her to H. B., who jokingly nicknamed her 'Vinigretta', never once jealous over the force of Ethel's affection. At least at first, Ethel's feelings were reciprocated, and this love became an inspiration for *The Wreckers*. Ethel later told her friends that the first act of the opera was com-posed 'in nomine W', meaning 'in the name of W'.

Relations were not always easy between the two women. Initially Winnaretta found Ethel entertaining and she adored her music, but her attention soon drifted to other younger, more beautiful and more aristocratic women. Ethel was beside herself. She opined that 'to be separate from her, as I love her, kills me'. She did everything she could to win Winnaretta over, except the one thing Winnaretta actually wanted – for Ethel to give her more space. Watching the object of her affections flirt with younger women plunged Ethel into jealous fits. She hated being just one of many. But Ethel refused to be deterred by her unruly muse. Act III, she lamented gloomily, was written 'in spite of W'.

With Winnaretta and H. B. to inspire her, Ethel composed with an unrivalled passion. 'I feel awfully full of power,' she wrote, 'deadly sure of what I am doing.' Even when she was revising (the most hated of all her compositional jobs), she was convinced that the music simply flowed through her. All she needed to do was simply notate the songs that already existed somewhere in her soul. As soon as she completed a section she would whip the pages off to H. B. as inspiration for the next part of the libretto. Having such an active collaboration between composer and librettist was unusual, but it worked for them – until progress ground to a halt because H. B. couldn't read music and was therefore unable to understand a note of Ethel's elaborate creation. So she set off for Rome so they could write the text for the third act together.

He seemed to her more frail than usual, wrapped up in his chair with rugs over his knees – but he was still her H. B., cigar in hand and enthusiasm for her music overflowing. Side by side they resumed their long working hours. Ethel immediately took H. B.'s new words to the piano to try out ideas, and hearing the woman he loved play spurred him on, giving him the fuel that he needed to drive the opera to its tragic climax. Spent from the effort of creating their work, Ethel and H. B. would sit on the balcony and watch the cypresses rise against the spring sunset that burned red and gold across the city. At sunrise they began again until, finally, the libretto for Act III was complete. Ethel returned to England to compose the rest of the music, informing H. B. about the birth of their operatic offspring by telegram: 'Safely delivered of fine female child, name Thirza Rampagia Smyth.'

When he heard *The Wreckers*, one of Ethel's critics thought that it 'conquers you with the sword'. Ethel's music was dramatic, powerful, modern – but the opera houses still wavered. The worst was Covent Garden, who simply informed her that despite the success of *Der Wald* they would not be taking *The Wreckers* because it was financial suicide to stage new works by little-known composers. Nonetheless, the esteemed conductor Arthur Nikisch agreed to give *Wreckers* its premiere in Leipzig, and after H. B. promised £1,000 (worth over £78,600 today) towards a Prague production, it was also accepted at the State Opera there. The English newspapers sprang into action, denouncing Covent Garden for turning down what promised to be the most exciting British opera of the new century. For once, the press were united in pledging allegiance to Ethel's cause. They felt that it was nothing short of a scandal that she should have to resort to a German premiere again. After the disappointment of America, the English press's unequivocal support was a great comfort to Ethel. She went into 1906 full of anticipation, hoping that this would be the year when her name would finally be indelibly marked on Europe's musical map.

o   o   o   o

Back in London, Rebecca was taking her first steps through the doors of the Royal Academy as a student. The whole building thrummed with music. Snippets of scales and melodies emanated from practice rooms, students hummed in the narrow corridors as they hauled their instruments from lesson to lesson, arms full of scores. Rebecca was in heaven. The commotion of the Academy took her away from her claustrophobic home, and she relished the independence. Being immersed in music gave her a renewed sense of purpose, and it brought her new friends. Many of her classmates were women, and the most precious friend she made at the Academy was a young pianist called Myra Hess. She was destined to become one of the most celebrated pianists of the twentieth century – but when Rebecca met her she was just a fourteen-year-old with a penchant for uncanny impressions of the rich and famous (her best was Queen Victoria), and a habit of hunching up her shoulders when she laughed that Rebecca found completely endearing. Rebecca warmed immediately to the constantly upbeat Myra, and together they giggled their way through rehearsals and French class. In quieter moments Rebecca sketched out her life at the Academy in a book she always kept with her, committing these treasured friends to paper as she listened to them perform.

Rebecca's sketch of pianist Myra Hess at
the Royal Academy of Music, c.1903.

Harmony was among the new lessons that Rebecca took. Being at the Academy brought her into direct contact with composition students she considered to be gods, their names familiar from concert programmes. She, too, was now a part of this elite club, and was determined to make the most of it. Her violin practice consumed her for hours a day, and she threw herself into harmony study. Although composition wasn't yet on her horizon, she would need to excel at harmony should she ever want to pursue composing seriously. Her hard work paid off. Her harmony improved, and she received her

Bronze and Silver Medals for violin in the first and second years.

Rebecca was delighted to find that her harmony tutor was Percy Miles, the family friend who had recommended she apply to the Academy. His moustache and meticulously groomed hair were a welcome familiarity, and being only eight years older than Rebecca, he was a slightly more relatable presence than some of the elderly tutors. She was grateful for his encouragement, and the reassuring chats they had after her lessons. Then chats turned into walks, and walks into lunches, until one day over a rhubarb and custard pudding he asked Rebecca to marry him. She was completely blindsided. Her 'first reaction was one of complete panic'. She had taken his interest in her to be purely professional, and had no romantic feelings whatsoever towards Mr Miles, as she still knew him. All she could do was push the pudding around her plate, stall for time, and try to remove herself from the situation as quickly as possible.

Rebecca playing guitar in her garden at Gayton Corner, *c.*1905.

Despite Rebecca's teenage fears that she would be forever gawky and unloveable, by seventeen she was an extremely attractive woman: talented and clever, with a quick sense of humour and a habit of speaking her mind. And with her thick dark hair and large eyes she was quite beautiful, always dressing her tall, slim figure in clothes she designed and made herself. She had already started to realise that being a woman came with particular risks, having experienced unwanted attention from family friends and a whole litany of harassments on London streets ranging from catcalls to indecent exposure. But Mr Miles's proposal presented a new problem. It was just the first of the hurdles created by male colleagues falling at her feet, creating an obstacle course in her professional life. Aside from the fact that Rebecca didn't love him, if she accepted his offer she would be expected to give up her career before it had even started. If she turned him down she risked him turning against her, producing the same result for her future.

It was an impossible situation. Having maintained her composure long enough to leave the cafe, when she reached home she locked herself in her room, threw herself onto the bed and 'cried my heart out the whole afternoon'. But she still had to face him at her next lesson. She absolutely dreaded it, finding it impossible 'to sit there at the piano playing my figured basses while all the time I could feel his eyes boring into me, pulling at me, pulling myself out of me'. She still gave him no answer, but at the end of the lesson he hovered by the door to claim an uninvited kiss before she fled the room.

Unable to work out what to do, Rebecca confided in her mother. But far from offering intervention on Rebecca's behalf, Agnes declared herself in Mr Miles's favour. She had already guessed from his previous family visits that he held a torch for Rebecca, and as she saw it, there were worse matches that could be made. Joseph, however, was unamused. The proposal precipitated an almighty row. If there was anything that could make Rebecca defend her teacher, it was Joseph taking such a firm stance against him, and she tried to convince her father that Mr Miles's intentions were honourable. But Joseph had a trump card. When Rebecca tried to reason with him that not *all* men were purely interested in sex because he had always been faithful to Agnes, Joseph triumphantly declared that he was living proof of the fact, because he had carried out affairs, and the 'family friend' he had invited to stay over the years had been his mistress.

This revelation was the final straw in an already fraught relationship. 'Suddenly a new and horrible light was thrown over everything.' It made Rebecca re-evaluate everything she thought she knew about her childhood, about her parents' marriage, and how to think about her relationships with men. She was furious at the distress that Joseph must have caused Agnes not only by taking one and possibly multiple lovers, but also by inviting them to the family home and parading his infidelity under his wife's nose. And Agnes, being naturally so caring, 'felt a responsibility towards these girls who were guests in her house: she feared, she said, that they might become pregnant'. Rebecca continued to see Mr Miles, more out of cussedness towards her father than any real affection for her tutor. Joseph, however, was just as stubborn as his daughter. As the harmony lessons and lunch dates continued, he decided to educate Rebecca with a medical study called *The Sexual Question*, telling her that if she really was going to get married, she should know what she was getting herself into.

What an introduction *The Sexual Question* must have been. Rebecca read it under the cover of darkness in the privacy of her bedsheets, and every page of this sexual encyclopedia she consumed added to a mounting feeling of horror. *The Sexual Question* didn't just lay out the mechanics of sex, but frankly discussed sexual fetishes, masturbation, female orgasm and menstruation. Coming from a position of almost no knowledge about sex at all, 'the result was an unreasonable fear – amounting almost to panic – of all men.' The book so shocked Rebecca that she stopped seeing Mr Miles altogether. Joseph had got his way in the short term, but in the long term his strategy may have backfired. Rebecca would eventually cultivate a liberal attitude towards sex and desire – because if the things described in the book were widespread, why on earth should she feel ashamed of them?

Rebecca may have managed to navigate her way out of Mr Miles's proposal, but the incident still took a toll on her career. Unwilling to keep his daughter enrolled in an institution that would allow such a situation to arise, in 1905 Joseph removed Rebecca from the Academy altogether after just two years of study. Gone were the harmony lessons, the orchestra, her friends and her teachers. Rebecca would just have to do the best she could on her own. The exciting future promised by the Academy seemed to be escaping her, leaving Rebecca to a life of fighting with Joseph until some suitable man carried her off to build a family of their own.

o o o o

For a year that was supposed to be the making of Ethel's fortunes, 1906 started exceptionally badly. Arthur Nikisch, who had shown such enthusiasm for Ethel's work and understood *The Wreckers* so well, left Leipzig Opera House having overspent his budget. Ethel couldn't believe her bad luck, wondering whether the curses of Cornish legend were destined to hang over the opera, or whether it was just the opera's association with Winnaretta. 'Everything connected with her, in my life, is doomed to be a cause of torture,' she moaned. Having thought she had already had her 'moment in the fairy-tale when the evil spell is broken and all difficulties melt away', she found herself once more travelling round German opera houses in a bid to save *The Wreckers*.

Everything else had to wait. She had planned a holiday to Greece with H. B., but it was now summarily put on hold until she had secured *The Wreckers*'s future. In handwriting so tense and small that it didn't even like look his own, H. B. quietly accepted Ethel's decision, agreeing it might all be for the best anyway. Ethel was so wrapped up in *The Wreckers* that she didn't seem to notice any change in H. B., and he, wanting to protect her, shielded her from the worst of his illness. The symptoms would pass, he told her. They could go to Greece another time. All that mattered was their opera.

After much panic, Ethel found that the situation was not quite as dire as she had feared. Leipzig was still committed to producing *The Wreckers*, just with a different conductor. Both houses were going into rehearsal to premiere at the end of the year; Leipzig in November, with Prague following in December. With the crisis averted, Ethel skipped the Leipzig rehearsals, assuming the performance would be a write-off without Nikisch's expert direction.

On the night of the premiere she slunk into the Leipzig stalls to watch what she thought would be the wreck of *The Wreckers*. It's unclear why Ethel was so convinced that Nikisch's understudy wouldn't be up to the job. He was a perfectly capable musical director, there had been plenty of rehearsal time, and the Leipzig orchestra and chorus were still among the best in the world. Accordingly, the Leipzig premiere of *The Wreckers* was an absolute triumph. As the final curtain fell the audience rose to their feet. Stunned and delighted, Ethel scrambled to the front of the hall, alarming the opera staff when she unexpectedly tripped out onto the stage. Winnaretta was in the audience, beaming with pride as she watched her friend take so many curtain calls that she lost count. Whether or not she wanted to be Ethel's lover, Winnaretta believed passionately in the opera she had helped to inspire, and wholeheartedly supported and advocated for Ethel's music.

Ethel left the opera house in a state of elation, and settled in to watch the rest of the performances in the run. There was only one issue. The conductor had made cuts to the third act, which she had expressly forbidden. It seemed, at first, to be a small problem. Delighted with the opera's success, the director assured her that the original material would be reinstated. But she woke up the next day to a hangover from her celebratory dinner – and to a particularly unwelcome telegram from the conductor, informing Ethel that he intended to keep his cuts. She was furious, and immediately fired off replies threatening to pull the work completely if a single note was removed. Thinking she was joking, or perhaps just irritated by her commands, the opera management did not respond. So the following morning Ethel made one of the worst decisions of her career. Flaming with righteous indignation, she went to the opera house and removed every last bit of the score that she could find. Players' parts, singers' scores and the conductor's manuscript all went. She packed them into her bag and caught the next train out of the city. But being Ethel, she didn't just leave it there. She wrote an open letter to the Leipzig press justifying her actions, naming, shaming and blaming the director.

Ethel couldn't have calculated a more efficient strategy of self-sabotage. Months of work and thousands of pounds had been thrown away on her pride. If any other opera houses had been considering staging *Wreckers*, this was more than enough to make them think twice. And if she had just waited to get her press notices, she would have realised that, for once, she had struck the right tone for the Leipzig press. What an opera needed to succeed was a whiff of scandal. In 1906 all of Europe was talking about *Salome* by Richard Strauss: it featured the titular soprano kissing the decapitated head of John the Baptist at the opera's close, all set to dissonant music that outraged the critics.

In this regard the Leipzig reviewers could have proved most useful for Ethel. They were appalled that a woman would set a story of such 'exceptionally nasty character', complaining unreservedly about the opera's lack of moral compass, and *especially* the insinuation that the church was complicit in the wreckers' theft and murder. Such comments were the outdated blusterings of a conservative press, but from Ethel's perspective they were free publicity. People were much more likely to queue up for an opera that provoked gossip and promised some outrage – and Ethel had pulled it from performance.

Things went from bad to worse. Ethel had assumed that she could afford to lose the Leipzig run because she was about to have a roaring success in Prague, but the conductor suffered a stroke. *The Wreckers* had to be handed over to another conductor at short notice, and the opera was performed with barely any rehearsal at all. Even Maurice Baring, who usually tried to find the positives in any situation, had to concede that the Prague production was a caterwauling mess that amounted to nothing short of a massacre of Ethel's work.

Utterly infuriated, Ethel travelled to Vienna to try to salvage what she could by securing a performance under the baton of Gustav Mahler, the city's most famous composer and opera conductor. But Ethel's reputation preceded her: Mahler hid. He did, however, send his deputy, Bruno Walter, to placate her. As it happened, this was an unprecedented stroke of luck. Mahler would die just a few years later – but Walter was an emerging leader, and he was blown away by Ethel's music. After he played through *The Wreckers* he declared her to be 'a composer of absolute originality and great significance, certain of a permanent place in musical history'. Ethel had won herself a long-standing friend. Walter would become one of her most fervent advocates, and conducted her work on many future occasions.

None of this, however, solved the immediate problem of *The Wreckers*. Ethel returned to England to regroup, recharge and begin composing again. The administrative exhaustion of securing opera performances had kept her away from her desk, but she was busy working on some new songs to French texts. Her relationship with Winnaretta had brought her into contact with the best that modern French music had to offer, and its flowing, diaphanous sounds intrigued her. So she wrote her Four Songs for voice and chamber orchestra, designed for the sultry atmosphere of Winnaretta's sumptuous salon. They featured a mezzo-soprano – Ethel's own voice type – accompanied by a small ensemble including the harp, the instrument beloved of the French musical impressionists for its subtle, suggestive timbre. Choosing an ensemble rather than piano accompaniment played perfectly to Ethel's strengths. With a very small number of instruments she managed to create the impression of a boudoir-size orchestra, combining seductive intimacy with power and solemnity. And besides the obvious connection with Winnaretta, the French texts had particular significance to Ethel and Francophile H. B. The poems are reflective meditations on love, regret and dying, which spoke particularly strongly to H. B. as he grew weaker and weaker, mulling over his life with his two great passions, Ethel and Julia. Ethel dedicated the songs to H. B., a gift from someone who 'must love happily' to one who could only love complicatedly.

Once again, Ethel postponed their Greek holiday to work on the songs. Next time, she promised him, next time. She had to oversee the songs' premiere first, and she didn't want to lose the momentum that she was gathering behind *The Wreckers*. English critics continued to be chagrined about the lack of innovative opera productions in England, and Ethel correctly sensed that they would be supportive of any attempts to have her opera performed in the UK. And her circle of influential supporters was by now formidable. Through MEP and Eugénie she had access to royalty, Maurice opened up contacts among the British aristocracy, Winnaretta drummed up enthusiasm among the artistic avant-garde, and to these could also be added the financial support of a reclusive and extremely wealthy American patron called Mary Dodge.

Like MEP, Mary was committed to the belief that women's position in society would be advanced through education and success in the workplace. Even though educational opportunities were opening up for women, there were still enormous barriers in their way to careers. From 1869 women could study at the College for Women at Hitchin, which later became Girton College, Cambridge, but they were not awarded degrees. When the university voted on women being awarded degrees in 1897, hundreds of male students poured onto the streets in protest, showering the cobbled roads with eggs and fireworks. The vote failed. Women would not be awarded Cambridge degrees until 1948. The University of London was the first in the UK to give women the same degrees as men in 1878, but even equipped with a London degree, in the early 1900s it was still illegal for women to enter the civil service or become lawyers.

Women like Mary Dodge were committed to challenging the prejudices behind these decisions, and supported exceptional individuals to hold them up as examples, demonstrating that women could do just as much as men given the opportunity. Mary provided Ethel with an annual salary, offered to finance future concerts, and put the beautifully wood-panelled music room in her London home at Ethel's disposal to use as a salon. She was too shy to be a hostess herself, so locked herself in the room next door to listen through the keyhole to the music she had paid for, studiously avoiding the agony of having to make small talk over post-concert tea and cakes. Ethel hoped that between them, they would be able to engineer an English *Wreckers* performance.

Slowly, things began to fall into place. Nikisch was coming to England in May and agreed to conduct the Prelude to Act II of *The Wreckers* at the Queen's Hall and, if £400 could be found, a concert performance of the first two acts with the London Symphony Orchestra. Mary Dodge and H. B. came to Ethel's rescue. Now mostly bedridden, wracked with bouts of pain that felt as though he had a nest of kittens nestled in his stomach trying to claw their way out, H. B. realised that the Greek holiday that he and Ethel had dreamed of for so long would never happen. He gathered together the £200 he had saved up for the trip and put it entirely at Ethel's disposal. If they could not have a final moment of escape together, he wanted to spend his last days watching the woman he loved succeed. Once again he reassured Ethel that he was not as ill as he seemed, and she believed him. Partly she was naive, partly self-absorbed, but mostly in denial, simply refusing to believe that H. B. might die. He was as necessary to her existence as breathing, and she could not bring herself to contemplate a world in which he was not by her side. So she accepted the money gratefully and put it towards the concert performance, with Mary making up the remainder.

The concert dates were set: the premiere of the Prelude on 2 May 1908, quickly followed by the concert performance on 30 May. Ethel turned the concerts into a campaign for a nationally subsidised opera house. Showing remarkable aptitude for personal publicity, she announced to the press that she was resorting to a concert performance because English opera houses were locked to English composers, quoting her rejection from Covent Garden as proof. It set the gossip pages alight. All of London was talking about *The Wreckers*, and at the first concert the hall was full to bursting with supporters, friends and critics. The press were unreserved in their praise. By the time 30 May came round, tickets would be impossible to come by.

H. B. was resolved to make it to the Queen's Hall no matter what. Having finally received a diagnosis of liver cancer and a bleak prognosis of only a few weeks, he set out from Rome against his doctor's orders. Ethel was delighted, believing that this demonstrated the truth of his reassurances that he was healthier than it seemed. But when he shuffled off the train at Victoria Station he was so obviously unwell that Ethel finally realised that she had clung 'to hope as the drowning clutch at the tiniest bits of floating wreckage'. His face was a ghostly yellow from jaundice, skin taut over his elegant cheekbones in a way that made him seem 'unearthly'. Supported by Ethel, he made his way to her box at the Queen's Hall, and they watched side by side as their creation came to life on the stage. He lived to see their collaboration become a triumph, hailed as 'one of the very few modern operas which must count among the great things of art'. Just a few days later, on 13 June, he passed away peacefully in his hotel room, Ethel holding his hand in hers.

H. B. was the one loss that Ethel never recovered from. She felt that he was with her, always, and his was the voice she heard in her head when she needed advice or consolation. In the weeks after his death she was completely inconsolable, unable to work or process his death enough to grieve properly. She stopped all work on an opera she had been sketching based on his play *Buondelmonte*. Ethel was a composer who usually found it easy to pour her heart onto the page, but it wasn't until 1930 that she accepted H. B.'s passing enough to be able to write another piece for him. She confided to her great-niece that her last work, a symphonic cantata set to one of H. B.'s books called *The Prison*, was 'my H. B. requiem', capturing something of his personality and what he meant to her. Maurice, always able to get to the heart of things, described H. B.'s *Prison* as being 'like a quiet tower hidden in the side street of a loud city [...] which those who visit find to be a place of peace, haunted by echoes'. He could have been describing H. B. himself.

DOROTHY

Her head bowed reverently in prayer, seven-year-old Dorothy Howell kneels with her family on the cool flagstone floor of St Francis's Catholic Church in Handsworth. Golden curls blossom out from under Dorothy's 'Sunday best' hat, framing her small face, the usually mischievous dimples and button nose now relaxed into a look of calm serenity. The church is so familiar to her – she was baptised here, and her family have worshipped here every week since. Occasionally she allows herself a glimpse up at the pretty patterned tiles on the ceiling which seem to flicker and shimmer on sunny days like this, given movement by the coloured light that dapples through the stained glass. But for the most part Dorothy keeps her eyes closed, listening intently to the music sung by the choir under the direction of her father, the church's organist and music director. It resonates round the high wooden arches, devout voices unified in worship. And there is nothing, Dorothy thinks, that sounds so beautiful.

The Howells' lives were shaped by their faith. In the early twentieth century, Catholics were seen as outsiders and were often subject to persecution in England, because they took authority from the Pope in Italy. Birmingham had a large Catholic population – 76,494 people in 1884, in a city of around 400,000. Nonetheless, children walking to their convent schools in Birmingham still learned to keep their heads down and stick together, as passing non-Catholic schoolchildren would jeer at them, shouting out derogatory nicknames. This hostility also created incredibly tight-knit Catholic communities. The congregants of a parish supported each other. People from all classes mixed together within the red-brick walls of the church, united by their beliefs. Inevitably this created an acute class consciousness, as school had for Rebecca, and relatively wealthy families like Dorothy's were expected to contribute what they could to the finances of their church. From a very young age, Dorothy was used to her family taking leading roles in their religious community, ranging from running the church's music to helping organise fundraisers.

Dorothy Gertrude Howell was born on 25 February 1898 in Handsworth, Birmingham, daughter to Charles Edward Howell and his wife Viola Rosetta Feeny. Theirs was a happy middle-class home which always rang with singing and laughter. The family had deep roots in Birmingham: both parents had been born there, too. Dorothy would later go to the school associated with the church where Charles Edward had been baptised, and attend convent schools just as her mother had.

Victorian Birmingham was a city of industry, seeming to belong to a different world from Ethel's quiet rural upbringing full of farm animals and apple orchards. When Queen Victoria visited Birmingham, she described it as a city of fire and machines, where 'the country continues black, engines flaming, coals in abundance, every where, smoking and burning coal heaps', the roads ringing with the roar of hammers and furnaces. This was Charles Edward's world, and by the time he married in 1892 he had a steady, respectable job as an iron manufacturer. By 1898, when Dorothy was born, he was a Secretary at the Midland Carriage and Wagon Company.

Dorothy's was a noisy and exuberant childhood, a little like Ethel's. She was fifth of six children – Charles Joseph (known as 'Carlo'), Mary Viola ('Sis'), Winifred ('Winkie'), Clifford, Dorothy and Alfred – and Dorothy, too, loved playing with her many siblings in the large back garden of the family's house at 3 Wye Cliff Road, just a ten-minute walk from St Francis's. An enormous see-saw stood near the back door, and Dorothy took great delight in her brothers' trick of all sitting on one end so she could be held aloft on the other. When they weren't in the garden, they were thundering

Dorothy with her brothers Clifford and Alfred in the garden at Handsworth.

Charles Edward and Viola Rosetta with their children Mary (Sis),
Dorothy, Clifford, Winnie and Carlo.

round the house with such enthusiasm that when Charles Edward travelled on a steamer in a room just above the pistons, its violent shaking only seemed 'as though Winkie & Dorothy were at play on the other side'.

The children played under the caring supervision of the family's nanny, Sarah Ward, affectionately nicknamed 'Pookie' by the children – and alongside Pookie the Howell family also employed a cook, housemaid and gardener to help Viola with the practicalities of running a large home with six children. Pookie 'wore black, always' and was never seen without her black hat, gloves and battered handbag, which gave the impression that she was 'extremely old, always'. She was profoundly deaf, so remained oblivious and accepting of the children's raucous playtimes. And she was 'completely devoted to the family'. They, in turn, were devoted to Pookie, so much so that she would continue to live with Dorothy until she died.

Charles Edward was frequently away on business, and when he returned he regaled his children with tales about his travels to Canada, the United States and Latin America, which, to them, sounded unbelievably exciting. He painted vivid pictures of Canada's 'noble mountains of the deepest, divinest blue, & over all a sky of delicate pearly grey', and told them how Niagara 'gripped me by the throat, literally, & I could not have spoken had I wanted to'. Listening to his stories instilled a deep longing for travel in Dorothy, just as Joseph's tales had done for Rebecca. Dorothy's house, too, was filled with items that Charles Edward had brought back with him, for he always remembered to buy small gifts for his children.

On his return from a 1904 trip, six-year-old Dorothy was most excited to hear that Charles Edward had met his first 'Gibson Girl' on the steamer. Dorothy had only ever seen their pictures in books: beautiful, elegant women with hourglass figures and their hair piled up in chignons, created as an American beauty ideal by the illustrator Charles Dana Gibson. The Gibson Girl was the conservative ideal of an emancipated modern woman – she was educated enough to have a job and be widely read, but would never campaign for women's suffrage, be loud or outspoken, or be seen in Ethel's scruffy attire. Dorothy had always believed that they were imaginary, but here was Charles Edward telling her that he had seen a woman who was 'exactly what I have seen dozens of times in the Gibson books', with 'large frank eyes, & a most fetching little dimple or something between her well-arched eyebrows, giving her an appealing expression'. With the exciting news that it was actually possible to look like the pictures, Dorothy paid extra attention to her features in the mirror, wondering whether her button nose and wispy hair would ever be able to look like a Gibson Girl's.

Even more than Charles Edward's travel stories, though, his children loved the music lessons he gave them. Like Joseph Clarke, the Howells had a dream of family music-making, but they made it far less of a chore for Dorothy than Joseph had for Rebecca. Charles Edward was a keen amateur musician who indulged his passion for music by directing the church choir and singing in amateur opera societies. Viola was an amateur soprano and violinist. Her family, hailing from Sligo in Ireland, adored music and the arts and had encouraged Viola's musical inclinations. Dorothy's grandfather, John Alfred Feeny, worked as the arts and music critic for his uncle's newspaper the *Birmingham Daily Post*, and his wife Rosetta Piercey was an accomplished amateur violinist.

It was Rosetta who had taught her daughter Viola to play violin, and she, in turn, passed this knowledge down to Dorothy. Many of Dorothy's childhood days were spent by the family's piano either trying her first notes on the violin as her parents carefully corrected her posture, or belting out favourite tunes with her siblings while Charles and Viola accompanied them at the keyboard. The Bechstein piano had been one of the Howells' wedding gifts, and when they died Dorothy inherited it, the smooth ivory keys able to bring back fond memories of making music with her beloved parents.

The Howells' musical enthusiasm was infectious so, unlike Rebecca, Dorothy needed no encouragement to practise. She progressed quickly on both violin and piano, and was soon able to contribute to the family's chamber groups. And she always wanted to know more. So Charles Edward began teaching her the fundamentals of music harmony. Before she had grasped basic arithmetic she had started to understand how her favourite pieces were put together – how chord progressions worked and which instrument combinations gave the sounds she liked the most. It was an invaluable foundation. Thanks to her parents, Dorothy would always associate music-making with happiness and security.

o   o   o   o

Ethel's world seemed pointless without H. B. in it. There was no reason to compose without him to write for, no incentive to fix performances knowing she could never look out from the stage and see his eyes smiling back at her. Her friends tried to help, but they all reminded her of him. Together they had gone to Maurice's plays, dined with the Ponsonbys and gossiped about Winnaretta. Every interaction with them was haunted by H. B.'s absence. It would take a new passion to pull Ethel through her grief – harpsichordist Violet Gordon Woodhouse. They had met early in 1908 at a soirée organised by Winnaretta, where Violet became one of the many people who were bowled over by Ethel's solo rendition of *The Wreckers*.

Violet and Ethel made a curious pair. Visually, Violet was everything Ethel was not. Tall, slim and elegant, she glided across stages bedecked in satins that shimmered under the lights, throwing out flashes and flecks of intense colour. Ethel stomped on covered in dog hair, with her own locks poking out like twigs beneath her hat. But, rather like Laurel and Hardy, they complemented each other. Violet was everything Ethel needed – she was kind, open-hearted, hopelessly impractical, and with an air of innocence that seemed completely at odds with her dark, sophisticated style of dress.

When H. B. died, Violet reached out to her new friend, inviting Ethel to come to stay at her Tudor mansion in Stratford-upon-Avon, where she lived in a *ménage à cinq* with her husband and three other men, while female loves floated in and out of their unusual living arrangement. Needing no further persuading, Ethel turned up at Armscote House and stayed for nearly a month. H. B. remained on her mind, but at least the change of scene was distracting. Violet gave Ethel the music room, hoping that it would entice her back to work, and when Ethel emerged from her mountain of glue pots and manuscript scraps the two would wander around the walled garden together, soaking up the rich summer scent of the kitchen herbs.

Ethel was slowly healing. Violet's enthusiasm was infectious. She spoke about Ethel's music with such generosity that Ethel couldn't help but feel a little optimistic. Violet seems to have intuited that what the composer needed was a project, and reassurance that her work still meant something. So she conspired to bring Ethel into contact with a young, ambitious conductor called Thomas Beecham, who was making a name for himself by specialising in relatively unknown works. Violet hoped that he might include *The Wreckers* in his London concerts. She might have been less enthusiastic had she realised that he had already heard the concert performance and thought it 'the most idiotic and miserable rubbish I have ever heard'. Remaining in happy ignorance, Violet invited Beecham to her home.

Ethel owed a great deal to Violet's gut instinct. By the end of the meeting, charmed by Violet's harpsichord playing and enraptured by Ethel's own rendition of *The Wreckers*, Beecham had completely changed his mind. He now saw Ethel as 'the one and only genuine fighting asset in Great Britain', potentially 'a tremendous ally', and *The Wreckers* as 'one of the three or four English operas of real musical merit and vitality'. He agreed to conduct the UK premiere in his 1909 opera season at His Majesty's Theatre.

This was the final encouragement that Ethel needed. Over a year after H. B.'s death, she picked up her pen again. This time Violet was her muse. The combination of gratitude, protectiveness and attraction that Ethel felt for Violet proved a heady mix, resulting in two extremely sexually charged works: *Sleepless Dreams* and *Hey Nonny No* for choir. The human voice was Ethel's favourite instrument: she loved the distinctive timbre of each voice and the intimacy created by the feeling that the singer was speaking directly to every single listener individually. For Violet, only voices would do.

To listeners who knew Violet was the inspiration for these pieces, Ethel made little secret of her feelings. The speaker in *Sleepless Dreams* tosses and turns at night, lonely and unable to sleep, tormented by erotic visions that appear whenever they close their eyes. As for *Hey Nonny No*, the words taken from a sixteenth-century manuscript, one alarmed but impressed reviewer likened it to being thrown into 'the midst of a Stygian orgy'. It was the first time that Ethel had shown interest in any literature from before her lifetime apart from Shakespeare, and this was certainly prompted by Violet. She and her harpsichord-playing were driving forces behind the revival of pre-seventeenth-century 'early' music. The movement took England by storm in the early 1900s, not least because it suited the nationalist agenda to uncover and reinvigorate music that tied England to a long and illustrious history. For Ethel, hearing this music through Violet's ears made it exciting, opening up avenues for innovation.

Hey Nonny's text is threatening, sinister – 'Men are fools that wish to die!', it says, asking 'Is 't not fine to dance and sing / When the bells of death do ring?' In Ethel's hands it became a bacchanalian frenzy, fear mixed with sardonic humour and wild abandon, all set to driving rhythms and dissonances that made the critics accuse Ethel of an 'almost brutal disregard for all the accepted laws of harmonic beauty'. And it is charged with sexual tension. The title is a nonsense phrase that was often used in the Elizabethan era to suggest a sexual subtext, alluding to acts that could not be explicitly spoken.

While she was composing, Ethel bought Violet a copy of Sappho's poems, dedicating it to 'Violet from Ethel – "Hey nonny no" epoch November 1909 – "I love delicacy, and for me love has the sun's splendour and beauty" (Motto written by Sappho on purpose for V. G. W.)'

After the UK premiere of *The Wreckers* and Beecham having billed a second staging at Covent Garden in 1910, Ethel's star was rising. The press recognised the *Wreckers* premiere as 'one of the most important musical events of the year'. She was given an entry in the latest edition of *Grove Dictionary of Music and Musicians* – then considered a definitive source for English musical life – that hailed her as being 'among the most eminent composers of her time'. Her works were widely performed, from the Four Songs to *The Wreckers* Overture, and even her spurned earlier works like the Violin Sonata were now finding a willing and appreciative audience. It seemed as though finally, at the age of fifty-two, her efforts were paying off.

To crown an already triumphant year, in June Durham University conferred an honorary doctorate on Ethel in recognition of her contributions to music. Of all the honours that she ever received, this remained the one that meant the most to her. Mixing as she did with royalty and the aristocracy, she was delighted to be given a title. And it was a mark of acceptance from the academic community that had otherwise cold-shouldered her because of her gender. The 'Dr' signalled respect, allowing Ethel to abandon the 'Miss' that she so hated because it invited easy dismissal. Beaming with pride and appreciation at the Convocation, Ethel processed under Durham's thick stone arches in her new doctoral robes of white brocade with a purple hood, the outfit marking a new phase in her musical life.

o   o   o   o

In Birmingham, Dorothy's own education was only just starting. Her first school was St Anne's Convent School in Deritend, on the other side of Birmingham to where her family lived. There were many much closer choices, but St Anne's School was attached to the church of Charles Edward's youth, and tradition meant a great deal to the Howells. Additionally, the school had been founded by John Henry Newman, one of Birmingham's most important Catholic figures. For the Howells, Dorothy's spiritual education was more important than anything else, so they felt it was vital that she attend a school whose founding religious principles they agreed with.

The Howells were not passive churchgoers. Many in Dorothy's family were members of Catholic societies and wrote about liturgical reform, actively participating in the liturgical debates that rumbled on throughout the nineteenth and twentieth centuries. Dorothy's brother Clifford would eventually become a priest, as would one of her nephews, Petroc. But the extent and manner of the family's involvement was divided by gender. For a young woman, the early twentieth-century Catholic church could be a difficult and confusing place. There were strong examples of women's leadership – the nuns at Dorothy's convent school being one such example – but these groups were always subordinate to men. And official women's groups were controversial. The clergy were at pains to ensure that women fell under their authority, while anti-Catholic groups tried (unsuccessfully) to enforce secular, Parliamentary inspection on convents, fearing that they were hotbeds of abuse.

Dorothy would never become one of the more obviously radical women within the Church, but she would lend her support to groups and causes that assisted women's participation – within the limits decreed by the Pope. And her first major encounter with women holding positions of responsibility in the Church came through her schooling. She studied usual subjects like literature, arithmetic and history, but the majority of her school life revolved around religious study. Dorothy wasn't exactly a star pupil. Even as a teenager her spelling was atrocious. She would much rather be at the piano. Nonetheless she always tried her best, and enjoyed her time at St Anne's. It served a parish with a congregation containing a high number of Irish immigrants, so the majority of Dorothy's classmates were the children of working-class families who had moved to England to escape the Famine of 1845–52.

Dorothy playing piano in her family home at Handsworth.

Dorothy was far less enthusiastic about her secondary school, a convent school in Belgium that she attended along with her elder sisters from the age of eleven. She was always extremely close to her family and despised boarding. And missing her family exacerbated all the other problems – the draughty corridors, food she didn't like, the Rupel river looking bleak and miserable, and everything just being too *quiet*. The population of Boom was minute compared to Birmingham, and even though convent life in both cities was shut off from the rest of the world, from the gardens in Boom Dorothy could hear nothing like the hubbub that had surrounded St Anne's.

It didn't take long for Dorothy to beg her parents to bring her back to England. Holidays were her salvation. She counted down the term days left until she went back to her cosy family house, not least because going home meant resuming her musical education. By now she had quite a taste for the classics: Schubert, Beethoven, Bach, Chopin, the very same composers who had captivated Ethel and Rebecca before her.

Added to these was the composer who would be Dorothy's enduring love: Sir Edward Elgar. Now best known for *Land of Hope and Glory*, he was England's leading musical figure by Dorothy's eleventh birthday in 1909. Elgar was a man of many nuances, but at the height of the British Empire it was his most bombastic and pompous music that caught the British imagination. He was knighted in 1904, the same year that a three-day festival of his music was held at Covent Garden – the kind of recognition that Ethel only dreamed of. (With perhaps a hint of jealousy, Ethel declared Elgar 'the greatest <u>bore</u> I ever met in my life'.)

Importantly for Dorothy, Elgar was Catholic. His magnum opus was an enormous Catholic choral work called *The Dream of Gerontius*, set to a text by Newman, the man who had founded Dorothy's first school. And Elgar was a prominent figure in Birmingham. He was the University of Birmingham's first music professor, composed major choral works for the Birmingham Festival, and *Gerontius* had been premiered in the city, in the same Town Hall that Dorothy would later perform in herself. He was a figure who Dorothy could aspire to emulate – successful enough to encourage ambition, and familiar enough to feel like a role model, as though her dreams might be achievable. And as Dorothy grew, it became obvious that her dream was music. She was never in any doubt. She lived and breathed it. Dorothy knew she wanted to be a musician. The only question was what kind of musician she would be.

o   o   o   o

Having tasted the promise of the Royal Academy, twenty-two-year-old Rebecca was certain she wanted to become a professional performer. But so long as she was in Joseph's house, there was no question of her taking a job. Her father informed her that her purpose was to 'make some good man happy', and he objected in the strongest terms to her having an income. Stuck at home, there was little for Rebecca to do but fill her days with practice, practice, practice.

In the evenings she escaped to St James's Hall in London, as Ethel had so many years before her when faced with paternal resistance, to hear the world-famous musicians that she idolised. Visiting thirty years apart, the two women would have heard much of the same music. Beethoven, Bach and Brahms were continuously on concert programmes in both their lifetimes. But Brahms had been new in Ethel's teenage years – now, the new music that Rebecca heard was more harmonically daring, breaking from traditions that Brahms represented. She came home from the concerts with her head full of music. Snippets of chords and melodies rang in her ears, helping to drown out Joseph's inevitable tide of shouting.

Miserable knowing that Joseph's parade of 'guests' were his lovers, Rebecca buried herself in composition. It became 'a refuge, an outlet, and finally a passion'. Her first pieces were songs, very Brahms-like in style, with an attempt to incorporate some of the modern directions that she had heard at St James's Hall. Rebecca had an ear for dissonance that Ethel never had and that Dorothy never would. The crunchy chords peppered throughout Rebecca's earliest pieces would become the searing, intense, uncomfortable discords that make her later works so powerful.

Joseph's response to Rebecca's compositions was characteristically contradictory. On the one hand, he sneered at her music, telling her that her problem was having 'the temperament of a genius but no genius'. On the other, he sent some of her songs to Sir Charles Villiers Stanford, Professor of Composition at the Royal College of Music, and one of the most eminent composers of the day. Compared to the Academy the College was a relatively new institution – only thirty years old – and was considered much more upper-class. The imposing red-brick building was nestled in the heart of Kensington, directly opposite the Royal Albert Hall. The Academy turned out brilliant performers, while the College trained England's most promising composers including Ralph Vaughan Williams. If Joseph wanted to support Rebecca's compositional aspirations, he could have done nothing better than try to secure her tuition with Stanford. Perhaps he secretly hoped that Stanford would dismiss Rebecca's efforts. Whatever Joseph's intentions, the professor judged that Rebecca had 'a possibility of poetical feeling'. Within a few weeks she was enrolled at the College as a composer, one of the few women whom Stanford ever taught.

Sporting pince-nez, a thick moustache and an aggressive side-parting, Stanford was one of the College's most revered tutors. His pupils thought he had 'a sort of splendour, as if the hero of a fairy-tale' had 'strolled unconcernedly into a world of ordinary mortals'. Besides being a founding figure of the College, he was also a Professor of Music at the University of Cambridge and, by the time Rebecca met him, the composer of eight operas.

Like Ethel he had premiered many of his operas abroad and had difficulty publishing them, and as a result also campaigned on behalf of English opera. Indeed, Ethel and Stanford should have been natural allies. They might have achieved a great deal if they had worked together. With his multiple professorships and conservative style Stanford was the very embodiment of what Ethel called the 'Machine': the English musical establishment that she felt locked out of. His musical contacts combined with Ethel's access to the aristocracy might have changed both their prospects, but they never joined forces, perhaps precisely because they were so different.

Instead it was Rebecca who would benefit from Stanford's contact book and influence. Despite his reputation for being taciturn and dismissive, when he believed in a student he supported them wholeheartedly. Rebecca was one of the few Stanford took under his wing. She stood up for herself in lessons, and he admired her courage, determination and sense of humour. Once they knew each other well she had the good grace to laugh at herself when he gently but sarcastically poked at her more pretentious statements – and vice versa. Stanford was 'always so nice to me that I could not fail to see the soft heart he so carefully hid underneath his crusty shell', and he became something of a father figure to her during her time at the College.

Rebecca flourished under Stanford's tutelage. He had a conservative teaching style, rooted in the classics, which was precisely what Rebecca needed. She naturally had an ear for modern harmony. What she lacked was the foundation to pour these sounds into. Stanford encouraged her to write sonatas and suites, and she completed a violin sonata in 1908 that he thought of very highly. Rebecca was deeply perplexed when she handed him the second movement and, having read it through for a moment, he promptly disappeared with her score. She later found out that he was so impressed that he had taken it next door to show another tutor. 'I was told I ought to be very flattered; and I was. It was the only time it ever happened to me.'

Stanford might have deplored modern music in general, but he recognised talent when he saw it and allowed his students to develop their individual styles. Rebecca began to find her voice. Her first attempts at songs closely followed pre-existing models in the late-Romantic, German style. After a while, however, she turned from German to Chinese texts that had been recently translated into English. Given her fascination with Asia it's unsurprising that

Rebecca found these short poems so inspiring. Compared to the German poems she was used to working with, these seemed more suggestive, fleeting. The songs that resulted, 'The Color of Life', 'Return of Spring' and 'Tears', were the most accomplished of all Rebecca's early pieces. They have an originality that points towards her later work. Even though 'Tears' is only a minute and a half long, it is particularly evocative, Rebecca setting the images of moonlight and the weeping singer to a piano accompaniment that is so sparse it seems to simply hang in mid-air. Time stops for a moment, only restarting when the final note has faded into silence.

Rebecca was rewarded for her progress with composition prizes from the College, earning herself scholarships that covered her fees. No matter what else was happening, composition was Rebecca's solace. Starting was always difficult – a blank manuscript is a terrifying thing – but when ideas did come 'everything would fall into place with a suddenness almost like switching on an electric light.' It was the most intoxicating feeling Rebecca knew. As soon as the light came on 'I had no illusions whatever about the value of my work – I was flooded with a wonderful feeling of potential power – a miracle that made anything seem possible.'

When she wasn't in composition lessons, Rebecca was playing in the College orchestra where, from her seat in the strings, she caught occasional glimpses of a tall, blond man called James Friskin playing the timpani. He was best known as Stanford's star composition pupil, 'the apple of Sir Charles's eye', who had already had some 'enviable successes' with his chamber works – not that those who met him would ever guess, as he was unfailingly modest about his achievements. Extremely shy, he hovered unobtrusively in the background of the orchestra where Rebecca watched him 'tuning his drums or anxiously counting his bar rests', little realising that this earnest young man was her future husband.

Nudging Rebecca towards orchestral composition, Stanford suggested that she swap her main instrument from violin to viola.

Violins usually took the melodies, while violas were harmony instruments, the core of orchestral composition. Stanford advised her that taking up the viola would place her 'right in the middle of the sound' so she could 'tell how it's all done'.

Changing instrument turned out to be an astute career move. Solo violists were extremely rare in the early twentieth century, and women violists even more so. Although Rebecca never chose to write for orchestra, playing the viola put her in high demand as an instrumentalist. It opened up opportunities to play with some of the most sought-after performers of her day. Her training days in the orchestra provided Rebecca with some of her most treasured moments at the College, spending summer nights under the concert hall's 'great domed roof' saturated with evening light that changed 'from blue to intense blue to violet and finally to black'.

Finally, after her miserable school days, Rebecca had found the place where she no longer felt like 'a fish out of water'. Here, she was appreciated for who she was. She didn't have to play the fool to find friends. At the College she was popular without having to try. Her classmates loved her for her generosity, and respected her for her talent. Some of them would be her lifelong friends – even if these friendships had their more peculiar aspects.

She shared an interest in the Renaissance composer Palestrina with a pianist called Beryl Reeves, so they started up a Palestrina Society together, inviting Vaughan Williams to conduct their choir. Although Beryl was intellectually stimulating, she was also 'moody and unpredictable, alternately ingratiating and crotchety', and she and Rebecca frequently ended up in fiery rows. Beryl got into the habit of buying Rebecca reconciliatory rubber ducks by way of apology. She would eventually marry Rebecca's brother Eric and become her sister-in-law, with the result that Rebecca became 'the owner of quite a fleet of ducks in various shapes and sizes'.

Ducks aside, Beryl remained one of Rebecca's closer friends at the College. She was joined by a singer called Muriel Soames, who was 'as goodnatured and easy to get on with as Beryl was the reverse', and together the trio supported and challenged each other through their studies. Beryl and Muriel tried out Rebecca's songs, and in return she provided a willing audience for their practice recitals, offering feedback on Beryl's passagework and Muriel's 'insuperable intonation problems'.

Rebecca's College days were 'a happy time, an ecstatic time', but they were always clouded by the fact that come nightfall she had to return to Gayton Corner, and to Joseph's abuse. As soon as they could, Eric and Hans moved far away from the claustrophobic family home – Eric to America and Hans to take up a chemistry fellowship in Berlin – leaving Agnes, Rebecca and Dora to weather Joseph's wrath together.

Watching twenty-three-year-old Rebecca flourish seemed to provoke Joseph to unprecedented levels of unpleasantness, exacerbated by his fear of encroaching middle age. He swung between ignoring her completely and making an inventory of her faults. She was ungrateful, lazy and dressed provocatively. When Rebecca tried to leave he followed her around the house, and his volley of complaints kept her awake at all hours.

Teenage Dora tried to help her older sister. With the boys out of the house the two sisters grew closer, bonding over a shared love of fashion. Dora had an impeccable eye for colours and textures that would eventually make her a well-respected sculptor, and she helped Rebecca pick out clothes and make her concert dresses, a service for which Rebecca was especially grateful. But even with Agnes and Dora by her side, Rebecca found it increasingly difficult to separate her work and home lives; Joseph's words echoed around her as she made her way up the sweeping College staircase.

He managed to turn her proudest moments into nightmares. At the end of her second year, Rebecca's *Danse Bizarre* for two violins won an exhibition to cover two terms of her third-year fees. She went home exultant, sure that her father would be appreciative.

Instead, Joseph flew into a rage, telling her that if they really valued her they should pay for the full year. He framed the award as an insult, and sent a vituperative letter to the College refusing to pay for Rebecca's final term.

Rebecca appealed to the head of the College, Sir Hubert Parry, who was understandably incredulous. Parry was, by 1910, a famous elderly gentleman with a few wisps of grey hair that seemed incongruous in contrast to his dense, boot-brush moustache that gave him the air of a military officer. Rebecca had to sit before him in his imposing office and try to explain her father's absurd actions, all the time feeling heartbroken and embarrassed that Joseph should have put her in such a humiliating position.

Thankfully for Rebecca, Parry was known for his kind-heartedness. He was not prepared to lose one of the College's better students to the whims of an unreasonable and controlling father. Parry offered to pay for the remaining term himself, and when she would not hear of that, he proposed that her fees be covered by the College's hardship fund. Overwhelmed with gratitude, Rebecca consented and enrolled for her final year. It was only many years later that she discovered the College had no such fund. Parry paid her fees.

Being outmanoeuvred did nothing to calm Joseph's temper. On one occasion he banished Rebecca for a week, hoping to demonstrate that she was unable to manage on her own. But, like his stunt with *The Sexual Question*, this particular punishment backfired spectacularly. Her week of exile was 'quite an adventure and I felt rather exhilarated', enjoying the freedom of seeing her friends when and where she wanted. It only made her more determined to succeed at her career, and save up enough money to buy her way out of Gayton Corner.

As soon as she returned the fights resumed, making it impossible to focus on her work. Stanford did what he could to help. He didn't know exactly what was going on, but it was obvious that Rebecca was distracted and miserable. When she turned up for lessons without new work he didn't reprimand her, just set technical exercises that required less creative input than composing original music from scratch. Not really knowing how to comfort her, he took her aside after a lesson and gave her the most personal advice he probably offered to any student: 'Don't kick against the pricks.' Rebecca was so touched that it 'gave me a nice warm feeling towards him'.

Sick of Joseph's persecution, Rebecca snapped. Letters from his lover piled up on their doormat while he was away on business trips, and at first she discreetly shut them away into a drawer as he wanted. But each click of the letterbox made her angrier. Finally, during one of these trips she decided to heap the letters performatively on his desk on top of his ashtrays. She was not prepared to put up with his behaviour any longer. When Joseph returned to be confronted by his post, he knew that Rebecca intended every envelope as a testament to his shortcomings as a husband and father. Once again she was banished from the house, but this time it was for good. Joseph wanted her gone. She would be given no money. By the evening, Rebecca was homeless.

FREEDOM

Rebecca was not one to shy away from a challenge. Perhaps Joseph thought she would crumble, and beg to be allowed back home. She did nothing of the sort. As she watched the stations she knew so well rumble past the train window, she mulled over her options. Apart from £12 in her Post Office savings account, all she had in the world she carried with her – a viola and one battered suitcase full of clothes. Her first priority was accommodation. Once she had somewhere to sleep, she could think about the next problem: money.

By the time she stepped off the train into the bustling Baker Street station, Rebecca had a plan. She might not have much money, but she did have friends. Her first stop was Kensington to visit Audrey Ffolkes, her deskmate in the College orchestra. On nights when Audrey's flatmate was out she had offered Rebecca a room after evening concerts. Maybe, just maybe, tonight was one of those nights. It might not be a permanent solution, but it would allow her to work out her next steps.

Rebecca was exhausted by the time she reached Audrey's flat. Much to her dismay the flatmate was very much at home. But Audrey wouldn't turn a friend out on to the street. She was less surprised than she might have been to hear Rebecca's story, having suspected for weeks that something was amiss as she watched her friend grow increasingly distracted during rehearsals. A few years older and wiser than Rebecca, Audrey proved to be a guardian angel when Rebecca needed one most. The next morning, having set Rebecca up in a cosy chair with some warming tea and her flatmate for company, Audrey set out to find a room on her behalf. She managed to secure one almost directly opposite her, above the green-grocer's shop. It wasn't much, but for five shillings a week it offered the stability Rebecca needed – and for an extra sixpence she could have the luxury of warm water delivered to her room every morning.

As if that wasn't enough, Audrey also put Rebecca on the path to finding a job. Tea finished, she was packed off on a bus to the Royal College, to ask Parry for a paid job in the College orchestra. Good viola players, as Audrey explained, were hard to come by, and the College sometimes hired independent musicians to boost the section. Once again, Rebecca found herself in Parry's office because of her father. And again, Parry came to her rescue. He agreed to employ her at a rate of ten shillings a week, with an additional guinea for concerts. It was just enough for her to afford her little room. Rebecca's life as a musician had begun.

This day was, as she later described it, 'a watershed'. In the morning she had been homeless with no means of paying her way. By the evening she was a self-employed musician living on her own. Rebecca had joined the small but growing population of young, unmarried women who were entering employment in the early 1900s, determined to work for personal freedom. Rebecca went back to her new quarters on Kensington's Abingdon Road in a state of euphoria, to share her first dinner as an independent woman with Audrey.

Over the next few months Rebecca set about building the networks she would need to survive. Connections were everything for a musician, especially for young women, and she took any and every job available. Her friends rallied around her, and as soon as news got around that Rebecca had struck out on her own, her old schoolfriend Margery Bentwich turned up on her doorstep with a bunch of lilies and an offer for her to come and stay with Margery's enormous family of thirteen in St John's Wood.

Although extremely grateful for her friend's kindness, Rebecca was resolute in her decision to keep her new-found independence. She stayed in her small Kensington room, but began performing regularly in a trio with Margery and her sister, cellist Thelma

Bentwich. All three women were around the same age, and in the process of setting up their careers. Sharing this experience created bonds of friendship between them that would last their whole lives.

They helped each other as much as they could, and for a while their weekly rehearsals were an anchor in Rebecca's week. These resulted in regular concerts at 67 Finchley Road near Regent's Park, the home of Ernest Howard, a wealthy arts patron. He came into Rebecca's life as one of Margery's violin students, but would become one of her most constant supporters and, all-importantly, a way in to London's artistic circles. The attendees of his drawing room concerts were always a lively and well-connected crowd, including 'Huxleys, Galsworthys, and artists of all sorts'.

Before long Rebecca had built herself enough of a reputation as a performer that she could increase her concert fee from five shillings to seven shillings and sixpence – a move that she considered both audacious and well deserved. And she upgraded from her greengrocer's room to move in with Audrey in her basement flat. The somewhat generous address, No. 12 Abingdon Mansions, made Rebecca feel as though she was living the life of the landed gentry. So what if there were rats, and the flat was burgled, and she and Audrey would sit of an evening listening to the sounds of people's footsteps on the pavement above them. Rebecca was overcome with pride when she had saved up enough to buy her first pieces of furniture with her own money, and nothing brought her more satisfaction than performing in a concert before wandering home with Audrey, chatting away as they munched on takeaway fish and chips.

Living with Audrey was as formative for Rebecca's politics as it was for her career. Audrey was, for her time, extremely liberal. She employed a home help called Maud in full knowledge that Maud had an illegitimate son, who would occasionally appear at Abingdon Mansions to see his mother. Rebecca was 'greatly impressed by Audrey's broad-mindedness', and grew to care for the ever-cheerful Maud as much as Audrey.

But of all the women who Rebecca encountered in these early years, the one who would be the strongest influence and her life-long friend was the cellist May Mukle. The two met not long after Rebecca left home. May was the cellist in an all-woman group called the Nora Clench Quartet, who invited Rebecca to audition for the position of their new violist. Rebecca was uncharacteristically anxious when she turned up to the audition. After all, the Quartet was both famous and highly regarded by the press. Only after fifty years of friendship would May divulge that they had contacted her on Stanford's recommendation, and that he had written to them asking the group to give Rebecca 'a helping hand'.

By 1910, all-women ensembles were still rare but not unheard of; the first all-woman quartet in England had been founded in 1886. Women were still barred from professional orchestras, so chamber groups like the string quartet became a way for the best performers to build careers. They needed nobody to hire them to set up their own ensemble, and they could rent halls for performances or play in private salons. By grouping together, women musicians could bypass the patriarchal norms that ruled musical institutions – most audiences were just as willing to hear women perform as men, if they were good. The Clench Quartet's leader, Nora, had performed for royalty, and May had an established international reputation as a soloist. Rebecca was used to walking past the Quartet's publicity posters in the Underground, which to her 'meant fame, so I was full of awe and so nervous that I played my very worst'.

Rebecca finished her piece expecting to leave and never see the group again, until she heard May pipe up from across the room, saying, 'Don't she play nice?' May 'knew quite well that I had done nothing of the sort. Of course I adored her from that moment.' May's vote of confidence secured Rebecca's place in the group, and for the next few months she travelled between Kensington, St John's Wood and Nora's house, where the four women would rehearse. Sadly Rebecca's career with the Quartet was short-lived. Soon after she joined the group Nora became pregnant, and decided to retire to devote more time to her husband and family – an extremely common path for married women. Nonetheless, Rebecca's months with the Quartet were among the most important weeks of her professional life, because they brought her May.

May had that rare combination of extraordinary talent and copious generosity. She and Rebecca came from similar middle-class backgrounds – May's father was an organ-builder and also an immigrant. Unlike Ethel, whose social privilege allowed her to grow into music later, May had been performing in public since she was nine years old, astonishing audiences on both sides of the Atlantic with her prodigious abilities. Critics were captivated by her forthright, carefree personality that contrasted with a reserved onstage presence exuding 'self-possession'. Having worked her way to independence by performing throughout her teenage years, May was constantly helping other younger women trying to follow the same path as her. Sometimes this took the form of friendship, or setting up contacts to help navigate the difficulties of professional life – and occasionally she lent her own rare and extremely expensive cello to her students for their performances.

May's concern for the wellbeing and careers of other women led her to join the campaign for women's suffrage, which had been gaining significant momentum. Votes for women was now headline news thanks to the Pankhursts and the militant WSPU. Alongside education and the abolition of a sexual double standard, women's suffrage was one of the most sought-after goals of those who wanted gender equality. In 1908, May had joined more than five hundred thousand women at an enormous rally organised by the WSPU to raise awareness of the campaign and demonstrate support for the cause. May had led the musicians' section wearing the WSPU's colours, marching through Hyde Park alongside thirty thousand other campaigners, proudly holding up the musicians' banner.

It was probably under May's influence, therefore, that Rebecca came to be playing for an event organised by the Women Writers' Suffrage League in January 1911. As one of the all-woman band (including May's sister Louise on percussion), Rebecca took her seat on the stage of London's Little Theatre, and watched the small auditorium filling up with the leading figures of the suffrage campaign, including Emmeline and Christabel Pankhurst. As the lights dimmed and the chatter subsided, the band took up their instruments to begin the evening's music – composed and conducted by none other than Dr Ethel Smyth, resplendent in her new academic robes.

o o o o

Given how closely Ethel followed current affairs, it took her a surprisingly long time to join the campaign for women's suffrage. Partly, she was loath to engage in anything that would draw her away from her music. But she also didn't see how the vote would benefit her directly. She had been deeply suspicious that the Votes for Women campaign was merely 'a fad of visionaries', and had no time at all for the peaceful campaigns co-ordinated by the National Union of Women's Suffrage Societies (NUWSS). Ethel was a woman of action, and it wasn't until the WSPU began adopting militant tactics that she started paying attention to women's suffrage. Even then, she stayed aloof, inclined to view the suffragettes with 'indifference tinged with distaste'.

The recognition brought by the Durham appointment, however, seems to have mellowed Ethel's stance. All her old fears about being seen as a 'woman composer' were still present, not least because the WSPU emphasised women's alterity to men, claiming femininity as its own form of strength and foregrounding the importance of bonds between women. Being associated with this may well have been, from Ethel's perspective, potentially damaging to her musical credibility.

But Ethel was increasingly inclined to agree with the WSPU. She had tried to play by men's rules and had met with gender prejudice that might have ended her career, had it not been for the women who supported her. And at fifty-four, Ethel was now well known enough that she felt she could, perhaps, afford to take some time to support other women herself.

In the wake of her becoming a Doctor, Ethel's postbag was filled with letters asking about her stance on women's rights, including from one of her old friends, Lady Constance Lytton. Constance was a committed suffragette, jailed for militancy and force-fed multiple times, and she reminded Ethel that her status in England was now so significant that she was a figurehead with responsibilities, whether she liked it or not. Ethel saw the reasoning in Constance's argument. She wrote to Emmeline Pankhurst in September 1910 declaring that from this point forward nobody could 'be a more profoundly convinced suffragist than I'. After many years of rejection, she finally accepted one of Constance's invitations to a WSPU event.

It was here that Ethel met Emmeline. This extraordinary woman had built an international reputation on her charismatic leadership, compelling public speaking and single-minded devotion to women's suffrage. Those who knew Emmeline were struck by her singularly exceptional force of will, which could be all-consuming. One of her colleagues remembered that 'To work alongside of her day by day was to run the risk of losing yourself.' She was strategic and ruthless, sparing nobody's feelings – even her own family's – to make sure that the course of action she felt best for the campaign was followed. But she combined this with a grace and charm that her opponents found completely disarming. As, too, did Ethel.

From their first meeting Ethel was captivated by Emmeline's 'bright eyes that on occasion could emit lambent flame'. But it was Emmeline's voice that she truly fell in love with, believing it sounded 'like a stringed instrument in the hand of a great artist'.

Emmeline was the final push Ethel needed to join the suffrage campaign. Never one to do a thing by halves, she decided to abandon musical work for two years to devote herself entirely to women's suffrage – and to Emmeline.

Emmeline's initial response to Ethel was decidedly lukewarm. She took a dim view of women with high societal standing who hadn't pledged themselves to the campaign. But despite this frosty start, Ethel would become one of Emmeline's closest companions in these pre-war years. She stormed into Emmeline's life during a period when she was at her most vulnerable. Within the space of a year Emmeline had been left devastated by losing her son from diphtheria and her sister from a brain haemorrhage attributed to her being force-fed in prison. Ethel's brusqueness perhaps provided her with a distraction she desperately needed.

Importantly, Ethel was a WSPU outsider, standing apart from the intrigues and drama of the personal relationships within the tight-knit organisation. From the very beginning Emmeline had faced criticism of her leadership. She was seen by some as being too autocratic, and too willing to follow her daughter Christabel's strategy of courting deliberate arrest, regardless of the cost. Ethel, however, was prepared to follow her without question, giving support when Emmeline faced resistance from her closest friends and family members. And from Ethel's perspective, Emmeline was precisely the kind of woman she most admired, whose vision and drive gave her purpose. She viewed Emmeline as 'an even more astounding figure than Joan of Arc', and in this early period there was an element of hero-worship about her attitude. By the start of 1911, the two women were an inseparable unit.

Despite her supposedly having sworn off music, Ethel's first act as a suffragette was to compose the song that would become the suffragette anthem – *The March of the Women*. Theatricality was at the heart of the WSPU's publicity strategy. Their outdoor marches through Hyde Park and enormous fundraising rallies in venues like the Royal Albert Hall were carefully co-ordinated spectacles, and music was a crucial part of the performance.

Until Ethel, however, they had been making do by setting new words to the *Marseillaise*, and sometimes singing *Rule Britannia*. Ethel's *March* gave the WSPU its own voice. It premiered on 21 January 1911 to considerable fanfare and pageantry, Ethel offering her music to the packed hall. And even here, at the door to her new life, H. B. was still with her. He had once jokingly suggested that she should write a March for the suffragettes, and now, three years later, Ethel thought of him as she conducted the piece that he had unwittingly prophesied.

Ethel at a suffrage rally, *c.*1910.

It must have been quite a night for Ethel, to stand with the woman she loved at her side, leading a chorus of women wearing the WSPU colours in singing her anthem of women's emancipation, hearing the sound of the entire audience joining in the repeat. She had always desperately wanted her music to be popular. The WSPU gave her that. Her *March* was adopted by suffrage groups in both the UK and America, sung in halls, parks, homes and on the steps of the United States Capitol. The WSPU's newspaper, *Votes for Women*, ran multiple articles that praised the *March* for containing 'all the spirit of the Women's Movement, the tenderness, the hope, the faith, and the cheerful and triumphant thrill of victory'.

After the premiere it was immediately performed across London – including at the Little Theatre with Rebecca and May in the band – culminating in a rally at the Royal Albert Hall in March, at which Emmeline presented Ethel with an engraved conductor's baton encircled with a gold band, in recognition of her services to the movement. Ethel remembered the whole event being simply 'wonderful'. For the next two years, she and her music were inextricably tied to the suffrage campaign, further boosting her fame in England.

In the days after this Albert Hall concert, Emmeline was busy rallying support for a census boycott on 2 April. If women weren't going to be treated as citizens, Emmeline argued, they should not act like them. She urged women to either spoil their census forms, or avoid the count altogether by leaving the house for the night. Once again, Ethel and her music rallied to the cause. On 1 April Ethel conducted the London Symphony Orchestra in a concert of her own works at the Queen's Hall, premiering her new set of choral songs, *Songs of Sunrise*, her first works explicitly associated with suffrage.

A triumphant victory coming after a prolonged struggle was a familiar narrative often read into music – Beethoven's *Eroica* Symphony, for example – and usually, the heroic figure was a lone man, battling against fate. In *Songs of Sunrise*, Ethel rewrote the musical hero narrative. She made women her heroines, struggling not against fate but against political oppression. The first song, 'Laggard Dawn', lays out a beautiful vision of hope, the text telling of women all over the world watching the sun rise, a sun so radiant that it sets the 'east aglow'. It's an uncharacteristically mellow piece, and beyond the obvious metaphor for women's emancipation, Ethel hid more personal meanings in it. The song is based on a melody written by Prince Edmond de Polignac, Winnaretta's late husband. Ethel still cared deeply for Winnaretta, and took great delight in being able to introduce her to her new passion, Emmeline. 'Laggard Dawn' is a private confession of love between three women, written into a public declaration of solidarity with women across the world fighting for political representation.

From the sincere to the sarcastic, the second song in the set, '1910', provides the 'battle' part of the narrative. Ethel wove together political slogans, snippets from nursery rhymes and fragments from anti-suffrage speeches. By making these her source material for a suffrage song, Ethel subverted the violence committed against suffragettes in the only way she knew how – by creating a musical farce out of objections to women's suffrage. Brutality was a sadly familiar part of the suffrage campaign. On 18 November 1910 a peaceful march on Parliament turned into a day of exceptional police violence and mass arrests, with women subjected to sexual assaults and severe injury from hostile authorities and the gathered anti-suffrage crowds. It was nicknamed 'Black Friday', and stayed in suffragettes' memories as one of the most terrifying and bleak episodes of the campaign.

Emerging from the battleground, Ethel finished off the set with the ebullient 'March of the Women', bringing her triumphal trilogy to a close. Critics were unenthused by the songs' political message, and tried to separate Ethel the composer from Ethel the suffragette. The general verdict was that 'the concert would have gained in dignity had these effusions been omitted', the critics expressing particular saltiness about '1910'. Her pieces that challenged accepted norms of musical 'masculinity' were dismissed as unbecoming political trifles. But reviewers had nothing but praise for the other choral and orchestral pieces in the concert – even if they still found it shocking that 'the product of a female brain' could command such a 'virile power of climax'.

By now Ethel was used to such condescension. On this occasion, it didn't matter to her: critics liked her concert music, and suffragettes liked her political music. The day after the concert she scrawled 'No vote no census' across her census paper, and set out to spend the night with Emmeline, joining other protesters in a rally at Trafalgar Square before they processed to the Aldwych Skating Rink for hours of entertainments from singing to speeches. Before the rink closed and the weary protestors headed home, Ethel and Emmeline sneaked away to Emmeline's hotel room to watch the sun rise over the Thames. Standing together in their dressing gowns, the two women watched the first rays of light push through the mist curling in lace spirals over the river. Flushed from the excitement of the census protest and exhausted from days of campaigning, they stayed with their 'foreheads pressed against the window pane [. . .] standing on the spot in a madly spinning world where nothing stirs, where there is eternal stillness'. Census night would remain etched into Ethel's memory for the rest of her life.

Over the next few years, when Emmeline needed to get away from London or to recover from a spell in prison, Ethel's newly built home on Hook Heath in Woking became her refuge. In an extraordinary act of generosity, the ever-elusive Mary Dodge had offered to completely finance Ethel building her own cottage, allowing her to leave the ramshackle, time-consuming edifice that was One Oak. The plot of land Ethel chose overlooked Woking Golf Course – her two stipulations for her residence were that it must be close to both London and a golf course – and she designed the simple and unpretentious property herself, all in a pared-back modern style with plenty of light and a garden for Pan. Ethel adored the town (she described herself as the 'Duchess of Woking'), and threw herself into local life with gusto, becoming a member of the Golf Club and, later, Woking Musical Society. She called her little cottage 'Coign', and it would be her home for the rest of her life.

Wanting to give any support to the suffrage campaign that she could, Mary also hired a chauffeur, Aileen Preston, and bought Emmeline a new car so she could travel to Ethel's in comfort and style. Ethel and Emmeline would sit together for hours in the drawing room, Pan snoring in a corner while the composer improvised quietly at her piano. Aileen was never invited to these intimate soirées, but occasionally found herself a spot on a bench by the open window so she, too, could listen, 'with the nightingales literally within a few yards from me in the woods'. When Emmeline was fully rested, Ethel would haul her over the road onto the golf course with Pan in tow, lugging a bag of stones so they could practise for their window-smashing campaigns.

By 1911, after repeated rejections and defeats, relations between suffragettes and politicians were rapidly deteriorating. In November the Prime Minister Herbert Asquith reintroduced a Manhood Suffrage Bill, which was a clear and provocative move against women's suffrage. For years, Parliament had hovered between two voting reforms: first, a Conciliation Bill which would extend the vote to some women; second, a Manhood Suffrage Bill which would remove the restriction of land ownership on men's right to vote. Because voting reform bills were passed so rarely, introducing the Manhood Suffrage Bill was an underhand way to avoid giving women the vote, because it appeased the Labour Party (who were most likely to support women's suffrage) by enfranchising working-class men. Anti-suffrage politicians like Asquith gambled on the assumption that enfranchising more men would push women's rights and demands further down the electorate's list of concerns.

The WSPU responded accordingly. On 21 November, a band of innocuously dressed women headed out shopping. They browsed the same stores they always did – Dunn's Hat Shop, Lyons Tea Shop, the businesses that Rebecca and her friends spent much of their time in – but today, as they exited the buildings, they drew out hammers and stones from their mufflers and coat pockets and began smashing the windows of shops, hotels, newspaper offices and government buildings. Two hundred and twenty-three women were arrested. On 1 March 1912 they repeated the exercise, this time on a much larger scale in the fashionable West End. Emmeline was arrested for breaking two of the windows in 10 Downing Street, and on 4 March Ethel was arrested for throwing stones at the residence of a Liberal politician. Christabel fled to Paris to avoid incarceration.

Thanks to Ethel's connections, Christabel was able to co-ordinate the WSPU campaign from Paris while living in luxury and enjoying the support of an elite, monied social network, helped by the ever-generous Winnaretta. Back in England, the situation for Ethel and Emmeline was less glamorous. Both were sentenced to time in Holloway prison, Ethel to two months with hard labour. In the event, however, there was to be no hard labour, and she did not serve her full sentence. She tackled her short time in Holloway with her usual gung-ho optimism, and when Beecham came to visit her he was astonished to find battalions of Ethel's fellow suffrage inmates parading around the yard, bellowing *The March of the Women* while the composer conducted from her window with her toothbrush. If the intention of sending Ethel to Holloway was for her to reflect and repent, Beecham observed, 'she neither reflected nor repented'.

Emmeline's time in Holloway was far less jovial. As a repeat offender and with a special status as leader of the WSPU, she was initially confined in a separate block from the majority of suffrage prisoners, in a small, damp, dark cell. The conditions were so poor that she developed bronchitis, and it was only after several days in a different cell with cockroaches as her only company that she was finally moved next to Ethel.

Once they were reunited, Ethel did her best to keep her friend's spirits up. She sewed a pair of knickerbockers with the slogan 'A Mus. Doc.'s notion of small clothes' and hung them outside. When the more prudish Emmeline objected to these, Ethel joined other prisoners in making slogans and banners in WSPU colours to hang up until they were discovered and removed, and partook of the sports competitions held in the yard. When Ethel was finally released, the deputy medical officer declared her 'mentally unstable', 'highly histerical [*sic*]' and 'neurotic'.

o   o   o   o

Little aware of these unfolding events that would decide her future political rights, Dorothy was making her first tentative steps towards becoming a composer. She turned thirteen in 1911, and her love of piano and violin was slowly transforming into a growing curiosity about the fabric of the music that she played. She was learning how to conjure the harmonies and melodies that she loved so much out of thin air. As with all her work, Dorothy took her first compositions incredibly seriously. Using what little theory she had learned from Charles Edward, she sat at the keyboard for hours to sketch her musical thoughts into existence. Stuck in the unfamiliar convent that she disliked so much, composing helped her feel connected to her family far away in Birmingham. Each note brought her closer to home.

Charles Edward and Viola were inordinately proud of their talented daughter. Many other parents of their class might have dismissed Dorothy's attempts at composing as unbecoming for a young woman, but she had the good fortune to have middle-class parents who not only supported her but were forward-looking in their attitude towards women's careers. They recognised the societal shift that had happened over their lifetimes. Where Ethel's father had fought tooth and claw to prevent his daughter from pursuing her musical ambitions, when Dorothy came to Charles Edward with a set of six short pieces, he published them himself as her Opus 1.

The pieces in Dorothy's op. 1 are capricious, whimsical and just a little bit silly, with titles like 'Puddle Duck' or 'Double, Double, Toil and Trouble'. But they show an advanced grasp of harmony and capacity for melodic writing, and are representative of her fabulous sense of humour, demonstrating why she would become such a popular composer of music for children. As Joseph had for Rebecca, Charles Edward sent off Dorothy's pieces to one of Britain's most eminent composers – Granville Bantock. They were sufficiently promising that he agreed to take Dorothy on. Securing Bantock as a tutor was an extremely astute move. By 1911 he was an incredibly important figure in Midlands music-making, holding both of Birmingham's top music-teaching jobs. If anybody had the connections to put Dorothy on the road to a compositional career, it was Bantock.

He also introduced Dorothy to a whole new musical world. Bantock was well versed in the classics like Beethoven and Schubert, who formed the focus of the Howell family's music-making, but he was also steeped in the most modern music of the day. He was fascinated by the Finnish composer Jean Sibelius, who appeared at the 1912 Birmingham Festival at Bantock's invitation to conduct the UK premiere of his Fourth Symphony – a work which sounded to British ears so radically sparse and uncompromising that the critics felt 'obliged to state frankly that we do not at present understand it sufficiently'. Bantock's lessons expanded Dorothy's ideas of how new music could and should sound. Added into this mix was his interest in Classical literature and his overt Orientalism – when Dorothy came to him he had just completed songs to texts by Sappho, and an enormous choral work based on the *Rubáiyát of Omar Khayyám*. Orientalism would become an integral aspect of much of Dorothy's work as well.

Winters melted into springs around Dorothy as she sat at her piano, brow furrowed, working at the exercises that Bantock set her. Her family was moving up in the world – in 1912, Charles Edward was promoted to company director at Noah Hingley Iron and Steel Works in Netherton, famous for having made the anchor for the *Titanic*. The Howells moved from their semi-detached home in

Handsworth to the much larger Wollescote House in Stourbridge. Finally, after many years of miserable letters home, Dorothy's parents relented and allowed her to move school. She returned from Belgium to take up a place at the Notre Dame Convent School in Clapham, a grand, neo-Gothic building, its turrets and tennis courts a far cry from Dorothy's small primary school in Deritend. And still Dorothy composed, finding her way around new harmonies and musical ideas, deciding what she did and didn't want to incorporate into her own music.

By the end of 1913, after two years of tuition, Bantock was quite certain that Dorothy was an unusually gifted student. She had progressed from dancing mice and splashing ducks to impromptus for solo piano, trying her hand at larger forms. Dorothy was well on her way to developing the characteristic tone that would define her mature works. Bantock recommended that she apply for a place at the Royal Academy of Music. Charles Edward and Viola probably took some persuading. Going to the Academy meant that she would leave her Convent education unfinished, to attend a co-educational institution with much older men at an age when her naivety might make her vulnerable. This was a daunting prospect for most parents in 1913, let alone ones with such a religious background.

Nonetheless, they agreed to her sitting the audition. In January 1914, fifteen-year-old Dorothy walked into the Academy's new, far more imposing property on the Marylebone Road, up the shallow stone steps into the towering cream and terracotta building. She impressed the audition panel, and was granted a place. The compromise on her living arrangements was that while at the Academy, she would be chaperoned by her cousin-in-law Dick Sampson, and she would live at St Dominic's Convent in Harrow to continue some of her convent education in her spare time. The Convent was just a short walk from Rebecca's family home, so for the next four years Dorothy followed quite literally in Rebecca's footsteps, taking the same familiar train from Harrow to Baker Street with instrument, manuscripts and scores in tow. As it had for Rebecca six years before, the Royal Academy would change Dorothy's life.

o   o   o   o

In a political climate where women's rights were headline news, and a cultural climate in which women musicians were becoming commonplace, a few enterprising women grouped together to create the Society of Women Musicians (SWM). Frustrated with the expectation that women were either unwelcome or an oddity in the social spaces created with male musicians in mind, SWM was set up to give women 'a centre for the exchange of ideas', where they could network freely and, importantly, build connections between composers and performers. Ethel frequently lamented that one of the main obstacles to a composer's success was finding good performers to play their music. And this was especially true when they were faced, as Rebecca noted, with an additional 'prejudice against women's compositions'.

The SWM held their inaugural meeting in July 1911 at 92 Victoria Street, home to the Women's Institute, lying in the shadow of Westminster Cathedral just a short walk from where the mass arrests of Black Friday had been made. Rebecca was one of the many musicians who gathered to hear the founders lay out their vision for the SWM's future. Carving out her space in London's professional musical world, Rebecca was still working out how to navigate the barriers put in the way of women's success. She was no public firebrand like Ethel, and would later explain to an interviewer that music 'has nothing to do with the sex of the artist. I would sooner be regarded as a sixteenth-rate composer than be judged as if there were one kind of musical art for men and another for women.' But she couldn't change the fact that others chose to see her as a woman first and a musician second – and that women composers were still 'about as much of a freak as the bearded lady of the circus'.

Rebecca's presence at the first SWM meeting suggests that she was prepared to investigate whether the Society could help her negotiate these difficulties. The fact that it was never intended as a woman-only organisation probably appealed to her – the founders were, after all, trying to move towards an ideal in which men and women worked equally alongside one another, so men were welcome as associates, if not as full members. But as the years progressed Rebecca distanced herself from any strategy that explicitly differentiated between men and women. Her support for the SWM proved short-lived, and although she maintained contact with several of the founding members, she didn't get involved with the organisation in any substantial way.

Instead, she tried to put herself in contexts that showcased her exceptional musicianship and demonstrated that she was equal to her colleagues of any gender. And she asserted as much authority over people's perceptions of her as she could. Rebecca was aware that as a performer and particularly as a woman, her body was on display as soon as she stepped onto the stage. So she put her love of fashion to good professional use, using her dresses to curate her public image. When she had her photo taken in a small studio on Hyde Park Corner, she opted for a far more modern, feminine image than Ethel's tweeds and ties, reflecting the musician she was becoming. Dressed in a loose-fitting patterned dress with a delicately embellished, low neckline and her hair swept up in a fashionable low coiffure, this was a woman who wanted to be seen as up-to-date, artistic, youthful – and not a little beautiful.

Now Rebecca was settled into her new life, the desire to compose was coming back to her. She worked mainly on songs, and the very best from these years, like 'Infant Joy' and 'The Cloths of Heaven', have all her most distinctive hallmarks. They have an incredible theatricality – Rebecca builds fragile musical structures on haunting, ethereal harmonies, and then traps yearning, soaring, rhapsodic melodies in these frames that seem far too delicate to contain them.

And yet, somehow, despite the flashes of fire that threaten to burst into roaring flames, the most exquisite songs end quietly, ambivalently. They stop but don't end, the final notes always containing a final twist or surprise. Rebecca finishes her songs like a novelist concluding with a final sentence that contains the single most important question of the whole book, making you reappraise everything you've just read.

Rebecca still had to build her reputation as a composer, but as a performer she was embedded into London's musical life. In 1913 she was selected as one of only six women to play in the string section of the Queen's Hall Orchestra – the first women in England to be employed in a professional orchestra. Although women were widely accepted as soloists and all-women orchestras had been popular for decades, women's orchestras were seen as amateur affairs and their concerts usually had a philanthropic purpose.

The conductor Sir Henry Wood accepting women into his orchestra was, therefore, headline news, especially as it was one of the most respected musical institutions in the UK. In 1895 they gave the first Promenade Concerts at the Queen's Hall: a summer series set up to bring high-quality, affordable music to London in a concert format that blended the new and the popular. The concerts were so successful that they are still running annually as the BBC Proms.

Henry wanted to hire the best, and time and again he gave jobs to women when others would not. Rebecca hoped to get on with her job without comment, but audiences and journalists had different ideas. During their first concert, the new women of the orchestra 'slunk into their places', trying to draw as little attention to themselves as possible – but they still got a cheer from a man in the Hall's gallery, which made Rebecca feel 'as if I could have dropped into the floor, because I knew how the orchestra were annoyed at having women'. God knows what she would have made of Ethel's comment that having women in the orchestra gave the sound a 'blend of sensuous charm and rhythmic energy'.

The NUWSS's weekly newspaper also brought the public's attention to the newly appointed ladies. As far as the suffrage campaign was concerned, having women in one of London's premier orchestras was a significant coup, and they ran an extensive article on their achievement, complete with a large photograph of all six women. The tone was jubilant, over-optimistically announcing that 'Sir Henry's innovation will do much to vanquish prejudice and win a fair field for women throughout the musical world.'

Rebecca may not have set out to be a feminist pioneer, but she was becoming one anyway. And although she didn't want to draw attention to her new role, she still wasn't afraid to stand out a little bit. The women's dress code was all black with a white collar, but Rebecca's wide, white lace collar swept down to her waist – a look 'that was considered a little bit daring'.

Alongside her Queen's Hall job, Rebecca was still gigging as a soloist and chamber player, often with May at her side. Increasingly they were performing with a young violinist called Marjorie Hayward, who had first played alongside them under Ethel's baton at the Suffrage 'At Home'. Another rising star, Marjorie was a regular soloist at the Proms, and would become one of Rebecca's closest friends. She, May and Rebecca all shared a passion for new music, and the trio came together to play the latest offerings from Britain's most celebrated composers, including Vaughan Williams, who was already working on *The Lark Ascending*.

It was at one such concert that Rebecca found herself working alongside a teenage pianist called Evangeline Livens, who was delighting critics with a performance of her own works which 'showed remarkable skill' and conveyed 'a perfectly definite idea of her own'. Born eleven years after Rebecca, Evangeline was just beginning to make her mark with delicate, fleeting piano miniatures – and she was writing them in the lessons she shared at the Royal Academy with her classmate Dorothy Howell.

WOMEN IN ORCHESTRAS.

October 18th was a red letter day for women ambitious of making their way as instrumentalists. The lady harpist is a familiar figure, but on Saturday women were seen for the first time in this century among the violins and violas of one of our principal orchestras; six ladies being engaged to play in the series of Symphony Concerts which Sir Henry Wood is conducting at Queen's Hall. Several women are members of the Colonne and Lamoureux orchestras in Paris, but hitherto there has been a strong prejudice against admitting female performers to membership of our leading English orchestras, though some have done good work in the provinces. The Moody-Manners Orchestra, for instance, has for some time included ladies.

It seems illogical and absurd to treat women as if they were unfit for the orchestra, while welcoming them as soloists and performers of chamber music—in which capacity a number of lady violinists have come to the fore; and no doubt Sir Henry's innovation will do much to vanquish prejudice and win a fair field for women throughout the musical world. His experiment is no hastily conceived idea. For some time past he has intended to give women an opportunity of showing what they can do, and in increasing the number of his Queen's Hall Orchestra this season to 110, for the Symphony Concerts, he persuaded the directors to consent to his recruiting some of the extra string players from among the ranks of lady performers. Some years ago, Ysaye made the suggestion to him, but Sir Henry, though sympathetic, did not consider that the time was then ripe. Lady Wood and Lady Speyer—a well-known solo violinist — have, however, been pressing the women's claims, and their influence has secured not only an open-door for women but the same rate of pay as for men.

This Sir Henry readily conceded; for he was most favourably impressed with the technique of the ladies who came before him as competitors, and also with the accuracy of their reading and the truth of their rendering. He was, moreover, anxious not to prejudice his innovation by introducing unfair competition.

The experiment has the cordial support of many leading professors of the violin, and there is a growing feeling that it is only fair to give a chance to the numerous women students who are being trained in our colleges and schools. Many of these have achieved a really high standard; but after all, it is only a select few who can hope to make a name as soloists. Occasional engagements in our smaller concert halls merely provide a little pocket money, while teaching is arduous work, and requires qualities which many a brilliant player may lack. The large majority of players, both male and female, can only hope to earn a living by performing in an orchestra.

The six ladies selected from among some fifty or sixty candidates are all students of the Royal College of Music, and have had excellent opportunities of perfecting their art in the College Orchestra, under Sir Charles Stanford. Miss Jessie Grimson and Miss Elsie Dudding are first violins, Miss Dora Garland and Miss Jessie Stewart, second violins; Miss Sybil Maturin and Miss Rebecca Clarke, violas. They have all had considerable experience on the concert platform, both in chamber and orchestral music, but they are delighted at the opportunity of performing in one of our leading London orchestras.

Miss Elsie Dudding leads the first violins in the Orchestra of the Royal College of Music. Miss Jessie Grimson is leader of the well-known Grimson Quartet, in which her husband, Mr. Edward Mason, also an old student of the College, plays the 'cello.

Queen's Hall. Miss Sybil Maturin, whose name is well-known as a concert player, is a pupil of Mr. Inwards and of Señor Arbos. She took an Exhibition at the College and is an A.R.C.M. For several years Miss Maturin has been leader of the violas in the Strolling Players' Amateur Orchestra and the Oxford House Orchestra (both mixed orchestras for men and women), and she is also engaged as principal viola for the final rehearsal and concert by various provincial societies. She has played in quartets at London concert halls, with well-known artists, and on one occasion played in Berlin with Hausmann, the late 'cellist of the Joachim quartet. Miss Jessie Stewart is a composer as well as a performer, being a pupil of Sir Charles Stanford for composition.

At first there seems to have been a little heart-burning among male members of the musical profession at the threatened inroad—prompted, perhaps, by the fear that the women would undersell them and bring down the rate of remuneration for orchestra work. But it was soon made clear that women members of the Queen's Hall Orchestra were to be paid at the recognised rate; and no opposition was offered to their admission. Indeed, they all speak highly of the courtesy and consideration which has been shown to them, not only by Sir Henry and the officials, but by the gentlemen of the orchestra, whose kindness in making them welcome they keenly appreciate. Miss Maturin adds that altogether their first experience has been a most enjoyable one.

Sir Henry Wood's experiment is naturally regarded as the thin end of the wedge, and there is considerable speculation as to where it will lead. It seems not unlikely that in the near future women may become permanent members of the Queen's Hall Orchestra, as vacancies occur among the strings, and may find an entrance into other leading orchestras; but whether they will ever qualify as first-rate performers of wind instruments seems more doubtful.

So far there has not been much scope for women in this capacity, and not very many girls take up this branch of the musical profession. The writer was told that at one time a woman played the flute in the Orchestra of the Royal College, and another played the oboe; but that at the present time there are no ladies among the performers of wind instruments in that orchestra.

Miss Elsie Wild, one of our most successful lady flautists, considers that it is very bad for the health of a delicate girl to play a wind instrument, but that for anyone with good lungs and a good constitution, it is a splendid thing. Performing on a wind instrument, she says, is generally considered more fatiguing than playing the strings; but not more difficult. The oboe and bassoon are the most tiring, and there are very few women who take them up; consequently these are greatly in demand in the various ladies' bands which have recently been started. Horns and trombones are very difficult instruments, at which not many ladies are capable of becoming expert. The flute is their principal wind instrument for solos, and is also used a good deal for obligato work with the voice.

The large majority of professional lady wind players join ladies' bands, which are not as a rule really first-class or very well paid, while some find employment as soloists, mainly on the Music Halls. In London men only are employed in all the leading orchestras and at the theatres, and Miss Wild does not consider that there is much likelihood of alteration in this direction at present. Several attempts have been made to start a large ladies' orchestra, and some of these have been really good, but the expenses of such undertakings are heavy, and they have always resulted in financial failure. The difficulties in the way of the

WOMEN MEMBERS OF QUEEN'S HALL ORCHESTRA.

(London News Agency.)

Rebecca (front centre) with the ladies of the Queen's Hall Orchestra pictured in *The Common Cause*, 24 October 1913.

o o o o

Dorothy's enthusiasm for life at the Academy knew no bounds. She wrote long, gushing letters home, excited to share every moment of her new existence. The concerts she went to were 'heavenly', the orchestras 'the most perfect I could possibly dream' and her new friends 'a marvel'. When she wasn't composing she was shopping, or sitting in the sunshine listening to the birds in the convent garden. In short, she declared, 'things are most inspiring'.

She met Evangeline in her first composition lesson, taught by the Scottish composer John Blackwood McEwen. He was an unusual man – a composer of copious works who did little to promote them, and both an ardent socialist and a tutor at one of the UK's most prestigious institutions. Dorothy clearly warmed to his mix of contradictory personality traits, and he to both her music and her generous, upbeat attitude. He became one of her most sincere advocates and eventually a close personal friend.

When McEwen had a particularly talented student he was a demanding teacher. In Dorothy's first lesson he told her to write three 'characteristic pieces' for violin, for an upcoming competition. Thrown in at the deep end, Dorothy implored her parents to come up with suggestions for titles or topics to start her off, because 'I can't think of anything to do'. Ultimately she completed her pieces within a couple of months, christened by her composition class as the 'Air Sprite', 'Water Sprite' and 'Earth Sprite' (but not placed in the competition, much to Dorothy's disappointment).

Dorothy's classmates chose well. The titles convey something quite distinct about her compositional style. There's a playful, sparkling, sprightly quality to her early piano works. Perhaps McEwen encouraged this style of composition, because several of the students in Dorothy's class wrote with a similar harmonic boldness and lightness of touch. Evangeline's pieces with evocative titles like 'Gossamer' are comparably breezy and impossible to play without an excellent technique, as they require the pianist to flutter across the keyboard at lightning speed. So, too, do the piano works of Leo

Livens, Evangeline's brother – described by Dorothy as 'a sleeky-haired youth with rather an opinion of himself' – who was one of the few men in the class. Clubbed together in McEwen's teaching room, light streaming in through the enormous windows onto the grand piano, they would all workshop their compositions together, offering feedback, guidance and encouragement. Within these four walls, at least, it was not just accepted but normal for a woman to compose. In these moments Dorothy and her friends felt full of promise, the future of British music at their fingertips.

Outside of those four walls, however, Dorothy was testing the constraints of being a woman in pre-war London. McEwen encouraged her to attend concerts to learn how to write for orchestra. He often gave her spare tickets, but concert attendance had different conditions for women and men. On one occasion she turned up to a chamber concert only to find that women had to wear academic dress – a white dress with a scarlet sash which, a disgruntled Dorothy noted, cost eight shillings and sixpence – and that they were required to sit in a particular section of the auditorium. That time she managed to sneak past the ticket attendant. On other days, however, she simply had to miss out. She needed a chaperone for evening concerts, and when Dick was busy that meant she couldn't go. This prevented her from benefitting from all the opportunities that were available to her male colleagues of a similar age and class.

These frustrations aside, Dorothy managed to attend a wealth of concerts in her first year, and took full advantage of living in the capital with its extraordinary array of music-making. She got to see Wagner's operas for the first time, which she enjoyed 'immensely' even if Dick was 'bored all through', and expanded her performance horizons by listening to interpretations of her staple repertoire of Schumann, Chopin and Rachmaninoff. One of the performances she enjoyed the most was Elgar's *Dream of Gerontius*, writing home that she adored his 'heavenly' music.

On the other end of the spectrum lay modernist music, which

Dorothy was quite certain that she hated. Between classes in March 1914, she wandered down the road to Steinway Hall to catch the first London recital given by the Russian-American pianist Leo Ornstein, playing a selection of his own works and pieces by Schoenberg. Dorothy was not impressed. 'I have never heard such a noise in my life,' she snorted. 'It was so awful that I began to laugh, & the fearful antics of the pianist only added to my mirth.' Dick and her piano teacher, Percy Waller, 'nearly collapsed on the floor'. She found the whole affair so amusing that she sent her sisters a parodic sketch poking fun at the latest artistic styles entitled 'Masterpiece by Rubrant-rembens-vangelico' depicting 'futuristic impressions' of her life.

Dorothy's complete dismissal of this kind of music was a significant departure from Rebecca or Ethel's attitudes. When Rebecca later heard Ornstein perform in America, she found that she 'rather liked his queer compositions'. Ethel, for her part, had developed her own style and was not interested in adapting to the latest developments in musical language. But she at least appreciated what Schoenberg was trying to do in his early works, declaring that his detractors should 'brush up on one's intelligence and take trouble', because he was 'worth the effort'.

It's difficult to imagine how shocking this music must have sounded in 1914. The music that Dorothy grew up with was tonal, meaning that it was written in a particular key – even though there were moments of dissonance, it sounded as though the piece resolved, beginning and returning to a 'home' key. But Schoenberg and Ornstein were using a different system altogether to structure their music. This music was moving towards atonality. Rejecting the idea that any one key should be more important than another, atonal music had no central key. It had few of the memorable, singable melodies that Dorothy was used to. This was the direction that modern music was heading, but to Dorothy it just sounded as though someone had unleashed an angry cat on a keyboard.

Most British critics agreed with Dorothy, recommending that only 'sufferers from complete deafness should attend the next recital'. This kind of incomprehension and derision was a common reaction to works that have since become giants of the twentieth-century repertoire. But in a world that was obsessed with the new, these were also the composers many saw as progressive, innovative, driving music forward. Stravinsky's ballet *The Rite of Spring* had premiered a year previously, and the combination of his shockingly dissonant pulsating music and Vaslav Nijinsky's angular, violent choreography had caused considerable controversy. Stravinsky and Schoenberg, who were abandoning keys and conventional harmony altogether, were fast becoming the names that were synonymous with modern music, and the gold standard against which new compositions were measured. This would become a serious problem for Dorothy. She was simply not prepared to follow their paths.

o   o   o   o

Soaking up new compositions and lunching with Schoenberg himself on a trip to Vienna, Ethel clearly didn't quite make good her promise to give up music entirely for suffrage. She and Emmeline had an understanding that work, whether creative or political, was central to their existence. She didn't try to stop Emmeline from seeking arrest, and Emmeline didn't begrudge her a few months off campaigning to watch Bruno Walter perform some of her works in a concert that also included the Austrian premiere of Gustav Mahler's orchestral song cycle *Das Lied von der Erde*. This billing was, as *The Suffragette* reported, 'a notable tribute to Dr. Smyth'. Mahler had passed away in 1911, so a posthumous premiere was guaranteed to have a full audience and extensive press coverage – and the audience adored Ethel and her music.

Even while soaking up Viennese adulation, Ethel did not rest on her suffrage laurels. She used her trip as an opportunity to radicalise

Austrian musical circles, giving speeches at venues like the Vienna 'New Woman Club' and leaving suffrage newspapers where she could. She conducted a one-woman literary campaign, shedding copies of *The Suffragette* from her tweeds in banks and the waiting rooms of unsuspecting dentists. Perhaps she even managed to smuggle one in to the Opera House, one of Vienna's most potent symbols of patriarchy, when she saw *Der Rosenkavalier* by Richard Strauss. Showing her usual level of reverence for esteemed gentlemen, she declared that his music had a 'whiff of boredom' about it. At least Schoenberg's music was 'wrung in a sort of contraction of passion from the soul'.

For Ethel, it was Emmeline who provided the 'contraction of passion from the soul' that she needed to compose. Inspired by her suffrage experiences, she revisited a string quartet that she had started as a student but since abandoned. The Quartet opens with a cello solo, a yearning call straight from the heart. But in the final movement Ethel suddenly unleashes a torrent of fierce yet contained aggression that threatens to spiral out of control at any moment. She combines two musical forms that seem to battle each other throughout the entire movement before coming to an abrupt halt in a final, blazing spectacle. Ethel considered this one of her most ingenious pieces. 'Mountains of male quartetts cd. be buried under mine and look like a pinch of dust,' she boasted to Emmeline. And the final movement, 'If it is anything, it is. . . "Suffragette!"' Even in this most abstract form of art, stripped of all narrative, she wrote her being into every single note.

Her pieces with texts had an even more obvious and explicit link to suffrage. In between brick-brandishing and court appearances, she also composed three songs: the first was set to 'The Clown' by Maurice Baring, the second dedicated to Emmeline and the third to Christabel. 'The Clown' was part of Ethel's crusade to convert the anti-suffrage Maurice to her cause, inviting him to empathise with her perspective through a sympathetic setting of his poem which describes a clown dancing in chains, longing for a freedom that they know will never come. Meanwhile Christabel's song, 'On the Road', was a call to arms. Set to a poem by working-class feminist Ethel Carnie Holdsworth, the song asserts that it is better to choose 'death on the field with an honour bright shield / Than the soft bed that coward souls find', Ethel setting her fighting words to a marching rhythm. It's telling that Ethel chose to write a song to Christabel, not the less combative Sylvia. The Pankhurst family politics were increasingly complex during these years, with Sylvia falling out of Emmeline's favour. Ethel took Christabel's side in the family debacle, agreeing with Emmeline that her daughter's tactics gave the WSPU the best chance of success.

Emmeline's song, 'Possession', is of an entirely different ilk. A song about letting go, it's one of the most personal, tender pieces that Ethel ever composed. The singer realises that she stifles her friend by trying to hold on to them, so she commands them to 'Sing thy song, roam the world glad and free'. She knows that 'By the holding I lose, by the giving I gain / And the gods cannot take thee from me.' When Ethel composed 'Possession', she was beside herself with worry over Emmeline's health. Emmeline was already struggling with illness from her bouts in prison, and her periods of convalescence at Coign were never quite enough to restore her fully before she returned to jail.

In April 1913, Emmeline had joined the ranks of suffragettes going on hunger strike to ensure release. Her state deteriorated to such an extent that after nine days of living on only water, believing that she would die, she wrote two farewell postcards to Ethel. In them, she reassured her that she would die content in the knowledge that she had done all she could for the cause. Emmeline thanked her dearest friend for her music, letting her know that 'during sleepless nights I sang the "March" and "Laggard Dawn" in such a queer cracked voice' to bring herself comfort in what she believed were her final hours. Ethel never disclosed the rest of the postcards' contents. They were 'too sacred to quote'.

Emmeline collapsing onto Ethel outside Coign, during her re-arrest.

But it was not Emmeline's time to die. She was released just a few days before the notorious Prisoners (Temporary Discharge for Ill-Health) Act, nicknamed the 'Cat and Mouse Act', passed through Parliament on 25 April. The Act allowed hunger-striking suffragettes to be temporarily released to recover their health, before they were recommitted to finish their sentence. Emmeline was rushed to a nursing home, and Ethel immediately came to her side. She was horrified. Emmeline was 'heartrending to look on, her skin yellow, and so tightly drawn over her face that you wondered the bone structure did not come through'. But just as disturbing was 'the strange, pervasive, sweetish odour' caused by her starving body consuming itself.

Emmeline was transferred to Coign to recover, but once there she could not leave without ending up in jail. Police officers were stationed at Ethel's garden gate, where Pan continually harassed them for tidbits. Come rain or shine they stayed in post. Emmeline banned Ethel's umbrella-offerings to the shivering men sheltering under the gorse bushes. 'Don't make things pleasant for them!' she would call from her bed, adding that it was Ethel's duty 'to bring home to the minions of the law the odiousness of their job'. After a month of house arrest, Emmeline broke the stalemate on 26 May by attempting to attend a WSPU meeting. Supported by Ethel and her nurse, she made it as far as her waiting car before she was seized. Fainting onto Ethel's sturdy frame, she was borne away by taxi to Holloway to begin her second hunger strike. There was nothing Ethel could do but watch.

This deadly dance was now Emmeline's existence. Ethel knew that she could not dissuade her from continuing her campaign, but it was too much to bear to watch the woman she loved waste away in agony. And music was calling to her once again. 1913 marked the end of her sworn two years, and she was longing to throw herself into a big musical project. She couldn't concentrate when all her efforts were focused on worrying about Emmeline. So Ethel decided to leave the country. In November she set off for Egypt, where it would take weeks for suffrage news to reach her, telling Emmeline that she hoped she would learn 'patience and gain power over myself. In your honor, my darling, if not for my own sake, it must & shall be done.'

Ethel composing at her hotel in Egypt.

To Ethel's face, a somewhat surprised Emmeline gave the plan 'her blessing'. What she really thought about her closest friend moving to the other side of the world when she was constantly courting death remains a mystery. But Ethel's decision highlighted the chasm between the two women's outlook on the world. For Emmeline, suffrage campaigning was her life. She was prepared to die for the cause, and 'it obsessed her like a passion'. Ethel lent her energies to suffrage on a temporary basis. She took it seriously, but it was music that structured her existence.

As she sailed across the world Ethel kept Emmeline apprised of all her exploits, providing a distraction that Emmeline desperately needed. And there were a lot of letters, because not only was Ethel concerned about her friend, she also initially hated Egypt and wanted to vent. The pyramids were 'loathsome', the sun a hateful 'glare', and her main wish for the Egyptian Museum was that suffragettes would 'burn down the whole filthy place'. And when she wasn't complaining, Ethel was completely absorbed in her new opera project, *The Boatswain's Mate*, keeping Emmeline updated on the opera's genesis. After the customary period of procrastination and battling with existential dread that preceded all major work, Ethel was now composing furiously. She was comfortably installed in a pavilion at her hotel in Helwan, on the banks of the Nile, where she could write either at her piano or in a cosy wicker chair with enormous palms and papyrus plants sheltering her from the sun.

Boatswain was to be a suffrage comedy, an adaptation of a story by the British writer W. W. Jacobs. Ethel's heroine was a pub landlady called Mrs Waters, and the plot revolves around her repeated rejections of a retired boatswain (deck officer) who is infatuated with her. The opera took shape amid the flurried exchange of letters between her and Emmeline, who provided the inspiration for Mrs Waters, and in few of Ethel's works is her life so literally transcribed on to the page. She included in-jokes intended specifically for Emmeline or Christabel, hoping that they would be amused by her 'making the boatswain a typical instance of male fatuousness'. And for her audience more broadly, sympathetic to suffrage or not, she included musical jokes that poked fun at canonic figures. The policeman, a figure representative of patriarchal authority, is introduced with a reference to Beethoven's Fifth Symphony and soon sent packing by Mrs Waters.

Being so far apart allowed Ethel to imagine Emmeline as 'a great lighthouse, visible through all the thousand miles of fog between us', her beam of light guiding Ethel to the notes and words she needed to finish her opera. With Emmeline as her muse, 'come to bring fresh love & flame into my life', she took *Boatswain* from conception to completion in only five months. On 16 May 1914 she made the final tweaks to the Overture, made up from her suffrage songs, and began laying plans to have it performed. She sped from Helwan to Germany, intent on securing a premiere at Frankfurt Opera House.

Given *Boatswain*'s subject matter and English libretto, combined with the fact that the English papers had been hassling Ethel for a comic opera for years, it's surprising that she was so intent on Germany for the premiere. But she was so used to the pattern of needing foreign acceptance before British opera companies would look at her work that she still chose to prioritise Germany for this most English of operas. And after weeks of intense negotiation, Ethel managed to secure not just one opera production, but two. Frankfurt Opera House accepted *Boatswain* for a premiere in 1915, and Munich Court Theatre agreed to stage *The Wreckers* in February 1915.

Ethel was overcome with joy. These were two of the world's most esteemed opera houses. To have one opera performed at either was extraordinary for any composer. To have two different operas running in the same season was unheard of. 'I have touched the goal I have been aiming at for 8 years,' she wrote to Emmeline. 'I know everyone worth having believes in me, & so all is well.'

Ethel and Emmeline decided to meet in France to celebrate, and to allow Emmeline to recover from her latest round in Holloway. They agreed on Saint-Brieuc in Brittany, with its stunningly beautiful coastal views for Emmeline and exceptional golf courses for Ethel. In the heat of the summer sun they could bathe in the turquoise waters of the bay, roam the windswept cliffs and retire to their rooms in the evenings to enjoy a banquet of freshly picked mussels. Ethel waited impatiently for Emmeline to arrive. At last, at the end of July 1914, 'the ghost of what had been Mrs. Pankhurst tottered on to the quay', accompanied by Christabel. Within a few days Emmeline was strong enough to try swimming, and even began teaching Ethel how to float. Ethel was completely oblivious as to the fragility of this bliss, and how precious these moments would become over the coming years as their world plunged into chaos.

WAR (I)

Like the majority of British citizens, Ethel couldn't have been more shocked by the declaration of war. The news was made all the more unreal as it came while she and Emmeline were basking in the golden sunshine of Saint-Brieuc. The sea still sparkled in the hazy summer heat, and tourists embarked on the golf course every morning. But even in this Arcadia, the signs of war were there. The hotel's German waiters were discreetly dismissed, and the tenor of dinnertime conversation became more anxious, guarded, as foreign guests hurriedly checked out.

Ethel was shaken to her foundations, and immediately went back to England. Truly her father's daughter, once war was declared she supported it without question. The only thing that mattered to her now was that England should win. Work paled into insignificance. Ethel wanted to feel practical, useful, and threw herself into supporting the war effort, firing off patriotic letters to newspapers, donating to war funds and loudly denouncing pacifists. Emmeline, meanwhile, saw the war as a good opportunity for women to prove themselves worthy of citizenship and she called a halt to all militancy, throwing the WSPU's resources behind the war effort.

The England Ethel returned to was already changed by war. She had to push through crowds of men waiting to enlist as she made her way across London. The queues outside public buildings that had been hastily repurposed as administrative offices were so long that it was impossible for Ethel to see from one side of the road to the other over the sea of flat caps, boaters and bowler hats as thirty thousand men a day hurried to volunteer for the army. War might have been unexpected, but it was received enthusiastically across the country. On the night of the declaration, Trafalgar Square and the streets outside Buckingham Palace rang with the songs and cheers and laughter of thousands, gathering to celebrate a war they believed would be won by Christmas.

In musical circles, the war gave focus to the undercurrents of anti-German sentiment that had simmered in England for decades. Under the banner of patriotism, German citizens were evicted from orchestras, and German music wiped from programmes. Even the Proms were not immune to the increasingly hysterical attacks on Teutonic culture. Henry Wood had to bow to public pressure for his planned second night, replacing the all-Wagner programme with a potpourri of music from Allied countries. Nonetheless he refused to boycott German music altogether: Brahms, Bach, Mozart and Beethoven appeared in the 1914 season as much as any other year. Even Wagner returned from Monday 24 August – albeit in a watered-down form, interspersed with Allied music and bookended by the British and French national anthems.

World War I quickly became a culture war. It was portrayed in the newspapers as a clash of Allied civilisation versus the German *Kultur* that became synonymous in the English press with barbarism and cruelty. The *Daily Mail* denounced German atrocities in Belgium with the aside 'Such are the methods of this people which claims the privileges of culture and civilization.' This put British musical institutions in a tricky position. German names had dominated programmes for decades. What should be done with the German performers who were so popular on British stages?

The musical establishment was divided. In September 1914 Ernest Newman, chief music critic for both the *Manchester Guardian* and *Sunday Times*, spoke out for music's cosmopolitanism, making an emotional appeal for the war to foster 'a new sense of the emotional solidarity of mankind', sweeping away 'old racial hatreds and distrusts'. Others were less magnanimous. A composer recovering from injuries sustained at the Somme complained bitterly after he 'went into a London concert hall and heard a public vociferously applauding a German soloist'.

Some tried to disassociate their favourite composers from modern Germany altogether. Everyone before Wagner represented a more exalted Germany that spoke to 'a world-wide brotherhood of man', but contemporary composers could be avoided without guilt, because their music was true to wartime Germany – 'unpleasant heaped-up cacophony, betraying an orgy of brutish forcefulness'. As the war dragged on, the tone of discussion around German music grew ever more bleak. By 1916 even Newman had changed his tune, abandoning his previous open-hearted stance towards what he now called 'our bestial foe'.

World War I provided both vindication and ammunition for the campaign to promote English music. Having finally managed to negotiate her dream of having both *Wreckers* and *Boatswain's Mate* staged in the same year, Ethel was bitterly disappointed by the war putting a stop to all English opera productions in Germany. But British concert halls and opera houses offered some hope, as conductors sought to replace German repertoire with the British music their audiences demanded. This was not an opportunity Ethel would let slip.

Ethel began travelling around the country to conduct her music in person, taking to the podium in her doctoral robes. The tour resulted in overwhelmingly positive press coverage. Her pro-war stance helped, as did the fact that her suffragette activity had already made her a famous figure. At the start of the war she had few English bookings lined up, but after a couple of performances of *The Wreckers* Overture in January 1915, enthusiasm for her music quickly snowballed. Over the coming months Ethel's pieces graced platforms in multiple cities to rave reviews. Her String Quartet was 'one of the best pieces of chamber music' written by an English composer. Her musical style lived up to that British ideal, 'simple and unpretentious in character'. Ethel's new-found fans blustered that 'English music has much to answer for for the neglect of this lady composer'. She was still a 'lady composer' – her frustrated pleas for critics to 'give up labelling me "the leading woman composer"' were falling on deaf ears – but she was now at least *our own* lady composer'. Ethel would just have to take what victories she was offered.

Her biggest victory came in January 1916, when she managed to secure the premiere of *The Boatswain's Mate* with the Beecham Opera Company at the Shaftesbury Theatre. There were vanishingly few opportunities for British opera during the war. The Royal Opera House was requisitioned for government use as a furniture store, and touring companies were hard pressed to stage works, particularly as so many musicians signed up for active service. Beecham's company was one of the few lights in a bleak operatic landscape, and he took full advantage of the hunger for English music. He staged three British operas in quick succession: Liza Lehmann's forty-five-minute *Everyman* on Boxing Day 1915, followed in January 1916 by *The Critic* composed by Rebecca's old tutor, Stanford, and finally Ethel's *Boatswain's Mate* later in the month.

Boatswain was hailed as 'a landmark in the development of British art'. Ethel's opera was the right work for the time – its slapstick humour was precisely what audiences were looking for, to 'amuse them and help them to forget'. Critics were trying to clamber out from under German influence, and struggled to define how a national English music should sound. They heard in *Boatswain* what they wanted to hear. The reviews showed how slippery the idea of an 'English' sound was: the main criticisms *Boatswain* received were for sounding like 'Wagnerian stuffing and Strauss sauce', but one reviewer complained that the music evoked 'palms and minarets'! Thankfully for Ethel, however, the majority heard *Boatswain* as the future of English music. It was 'clever and modern, without ever becoming pretentious', used folk music here and there, and had an English libretto with characters that were 'intensely human'. By any standards, *Boatswain* was an unmitigated success.

Ethel herself conducted the premiere, but she was only on a passing visit. Surrounded by the chaos of war, she found that she 'could no more work than fly'. Just as she had felt the need to set aside composition for suffrage, once again she felt herself called to a greater purpose. In 1915 she joined her sister Nina at the Italian front to train as a radiographer, and was eventually posted to an enormous war hospital in Vichy.

Here, what had once been hotels now provided refuge for the wounded and dying. Ethel wove through ballrooms where the rain beat against the high windows, the murky skies casting a grey light over the thousands of bandaged bodies lying in narrow wooden beds under the chandeliers. When trainloads full of soldiers arrived from the front, Ethel was called upon to locate shards of shell shrapnel embedded in their wounds before sending the patients off for surgery in one of the many operating theatres, perhaps to a large room in which the thick curtains were the only evidence of its former role as a bedroom, or a wood-panelled billiard room where oil paintings still hung on the walls.

Composition would have to wait. Watching a doctor 'plunge into a live though anaesthetised body the knife that shall prove you either an expert or a bungler, is not a music-inspiring job'. Ever pragmatic, Ethel tried to get on with her new role with as little fuss as possible. She didn't give herself time to reflect on the miseries that surrounded her daily. In her periods of leave, she volunteered at a vegetable garden.

Yet it was during these sun-drenched afternoons, the rich scent of peat surrounding her, that Ethel was most troubled. The world should have been quiet, but she heard a persistent booming, like a rumble of thunder or a distant air raid. At the hospital, these noises were just part of the sounds of war, mingled with the screams of the dying and the blasts of faraway bombs. But here, Ethel had to admit that the booming came from her own head. Her greatest fear was going deaf. Deafness would distance her from music and from talking with her friends, the two things that made her life worth living. She had watched her mother struggle with hearing loss in her final years, withdrawing from the world rather than face the distress of not being able to join in conversations. So it was not the hospital that haunted Ethel. It was the quiet garden in the Bois de Boulogne that became her torture chamber, forcing her to confront her own vulnerability.

o   o   o   o

The war brought about no such existential re-evaluations for Dorothy, happily continuing her studies at the Royal Academy. At least, not at first. She absorbed the new circumstances of war into her daily routine, performing in fundraising concerts and wandering across to Regent's Park between classes to watch recruits drilling. And when a group of Belgian refugees sought shelter at St Dominic's, Dorothy took it upon herself to look after and entertain them. Besides providing musical distractions, which included impromptu concerts of national anthems and rag-time pieces in the convent parlour, Dorothy would whip out a slapstick routine, playing the fool until the children collapsed in hysterics. By the end of the war she was such close friends with these families that she stayed in contact with them long after they returned to Belgium to rebuild their lives.

Initially, many responded to the war with enthusiasm and certainty that it would be over in no time. But by January 1915 there was unease in the air. Christmas had been and gone, and there were no indications that hostilities would be ending any time soon. The trenches of the Western Front had been dug, over four hundred miles long, and the first British civilian casualties came in mid-December when the German navy attacked Hartlepool, Scarborough and Whitby. And then, in May 1915, the first bombing raids on London began. The writer D. H. Lawrence described watching the Zeppelins swooping silently over the city as being like watching 'war in heaven'. 'I cannot get over it', he wrote.

Dorothy, however, took it in her stride. 'Pleasant all these Zepps flitting about, what?' she wrote to her parents. 'Well, if I'm going to be blowed up I'll be blowed up; if I'm going to survive I'll survive! – so there's no use worrying about it.' But as usual when she adopted a blasé humour, it was to cover an underlying fear. The consequences of war were becoming increasingly apparent to her. On her way to the Academy she regularly walked past trucks bearing wounded soldiers from the Front. Harrow had seemed miles from central London when she made her first impatient trip from the convent to the Academy, but now as she watched the searchlights sweep through the skies searching for Zeppelins and felt the rumbles from their deadly cargo shaking the convent walls, she realised how very close she was to danger. Dorothy no doubt wanted to reassure her parents, who would have been fraught with concern. Their daughter was still only sixteen after all.

The one thing that Dorothy found it impossible to joke about was her family and friends leaving to fight. Her beloved brother Carlo was among the 478,893 men who volunteered in the first six weeks of the war. He visited Dorothy at the Academy when he was on leave (causing 'no end of a flutter among the girls'), and he and his sister wrote to each other as often as they could. For Carlo's sake she kept her letters light, chatting about music, but when she didn't get a reply she would send an anxious note to her parents, asking if they had heard from him. The Howells were one of the many families across the world who lived with the daily fear that they would wake up to the news that a son, husband, brother, cousin had been killed. After Carlo, Dorothy's chaperone Dick Sampson also signed up, and her classmates slowly began disappearing to fight. They would be commemorated with a white marble memorial that still hangs in the Academy's entrance foyer.

There was little Dorothy could do except throw herself into her work, which was going from strength to strength. She had settled herself into a routine at the Convent: breakfast by 8.30 a.m., piano practice until 11 and afternoons spent composing at the parlour piano for as long as inspiration struck her, sometimes until bed at 8 or 9 p.m. By 1915 she had quite a list of compositions to her name, mostly songs and solo piano pieces. She was extremely smug when one of her songs earned her the Academy's Hine Gift for composition, a prize of £12 for the best English ballad written by students under seventeen. She was clearly excelling in the smaller forms, so both McEwen and Percy Waller (who Dorothy nicknamed 'the Hard-to-please, the Scanty-praise-giver') encouraged her to write longer pieces for bigger ensembles. By June 1915 she was diving into a string quartet with gusto, producing a first movement in her 'patent rag-time style' in just a month.

Performance was equally promising. When she finally screwed up enough courage to perform at one of the Academy's fortnightly concerts, her piece was no less than Rachmaninoff's imposing Second Piano Concerto with the Royal Academy Orchestra. She was blisteringly nervous, and sat shaking uncontrollably while she waited her turn. Soaking her freezing hands in hot water added little to the situation except mild pain, so by the time she made it on to the platform it was with icy fingers, knocking knees and a worryingly pale complexion. Stage nerves were just something she would have to get used to as a professional pianist. Having settled into the familiar chords of the first movement and made it through the glorious slow movement without a hitch, she finally found herself enjoying the thrill of pouring out her heart with the full power of the orchestra behind her as she launched into the finale, hurtling to the extravagant, climactic close at an impossibly fast speed. As first concerto performances go, Dorothy's was impressive. The famous pianist Harriet Cohen was in the audience, and found Dorothy afterwards to tell her it was 'ripping, topping, gorgeous, magnificent'.

Dorothy wearing her Royal Academy Prizes.

Dorothy's piano playing eventually brought her to the attention of Tobias Matthay, the Academy's most esteemed piano teacher, and a figure who would become increasingly important in her life. Matthay's fame was not misplaced: his students became some of the most celebrated pianists of the early twentieth century, including Rebecca's friend Myra Hess. His receding hairline and small glasses made him look a little like a thin Father Christmas, and his grandfatherly demeanour earned him the nickname 'Uncle Tobs' among his students. 'Tobs' took Dorothy under his wing, and she began to have lessons with him as well as Waller – as high a vote of confidence in her potential as any she had yet received.

Dorothy was extremely modest in public, but she wasn't oblivious to her obvious successes and the fact that she often stood out as excellent among her older peers. She'd never say so to anyone other than her parents, but as she racked up praise and prizes she began to feel a little indignant when denied a first place she felt she deserved. When she missed out on the Liszt Performance Scholarship she put it down to sexism on the jury's part. Maybe there was some truth to this, but when a young woman called Eva was given a prize instead of her in 1916, gender bias was clearly not the issue. When Dorothy found out the result she 'simply screamed with laughter', adding that 'my examiners sadly risked what reputation they had by not mentioning me. [. . .] All of which sounds very cocky, but is strictly true.'

Dorothy found rejection hard to take. Her tendency towards parody was sometimes a self-defence mechanism, covering feelings of insecurity. And she never wanted to feel as though she had let her parents down, so it probably helped her to assuage any feelings of guilt by blaming a lack of success on the jury rather than herself. But she also knew that she was good, and it bothered her when this wasn't recognised. This wasn't a problem when she was doing well – she blotted out this particular disappointment by winning two other competitions for piano performance in 1916 – but this combination of character traits would make it difficult for her to handle future setbacks when they came.

o   o   o   o

Rebecca was revelling in her life of freedom when the war hit. She had found a daily rhythm that would last for the whole of her career, mixing rehearsals and concerts with composition, parties and shopping trips with Dora and May. And her professional network was growing. Apart from May, Rebecca's rock and right hand, two women who were becoming more important in Rebecca's life were the violinists Adila Fachiri and Jelly d'Arányi. These Hungarian sisters had caused an absolute sensation when they moved to the UK a few years previously, performing together in all of London's most prestigious venues.

Part of their appeal was how very different they were. Jelly was a law unto herself. She was a born star, exuding an endlessly alluring air of mystery and danger. Maurice Ravel, Béla Bartók and Ethel were among the many composers who fell under her spell – Ethel would later write a concerto for her. There was a popular rumour that when Jelly played she was possessed by the devil, and she did nothing to quash these rumours. She swept on to the stage in sumptuously decorated gowns, draped in jewels that flashed and glittered as she swayed, completely lost in her music, glaring out at the audience with a searing gaze beneath thick dark eyebrows knotted in concentration.

Adila, by contrast, was outgoing and full of fun, a smile always flickering over her round face framed by dark curly hair, her playing full of warmth and sincerity. Rebecca loved her earnest personality, and when they weren't performing together she was frequently found at Adila's house enjoying teas and parties.

Rebecca thrived on her many relationships with the ambitious, extraordinary women who graced concert stages in the 1900s.

This put her in an excellent position professionally. As with Ethel, Rebecca's friendships were the very fabric of her world. Nonetheless, their social circles were very different. Rebecca befriended young, middle-class professionals, not the landed gentry, and when she wasn't playing or composing, she loved nothing better than to window-shop in Regent Street, arm in arm with a friend while they shared the latest gossip. An incurable love of fashion combined with the realities of surviving on a musician's salary instilled in Rebecca a lifelong habit of bargain hunting. She was just as likely to dive into one of London's less salubrious markets as she was to buy hats and coats from department stores.

As the war rumbled on, shopping in London became a far less attractive activity. By 1915 the first wave of panic-buying had passed, but food supplies were still variable, money was tight and wartime fashions were focused on thrift and recycling old clothes rather than buying new ones. And while Londoners tried to keep their spirits up, sadness and anger loomed ever-present over the city. The once-busy recruitment offices were now almost deserted, sporting the latest posters in the government's last-ditch efforts to increase enlistment numbers before they introduced conscription.

Particularly troubling to Rebecca were the photographs covering the front pages of her daily newspapers in May, showing German businesses with their windows smashed in, looted by locals and neighbours in revenge both for the sinking of the *Lusitania* that killed over a thousand, and the unleashing of poison gas on the Front. The first gas attack had murdered six thousand Allied soldiers in just ten minutes. Rebecca worried about Agnes, with her clear German accent, and hoped that she would not be caught in the wrong place at the wrong time.

Rebecca gave regular fundraising concerts, but her 1915 diary was far from being as packed as she liked it. So on 1 July 1916, she and Dora set off for America to stay with Eric and Hans, who now both lived in America. They travelled aboard the *Philadelphia* from

Liverpool, but the New York they arrived in was not quite as they had expected. The city was in the grip of a polio epidemic. Cinemas were closed, entire streets quarantined, and everyone who could afford it was packing their children on to trains bound for rural areas to escape 'the Dreaded Infantile Paralysis'. Dora and Rebecca didn't linger, travelling on to Eric's home in Detroit for a summer of concert-giving, hiking, sightseeing and shopping. And when they weren't outdoors Rebecca was usually found sprawled over a sofa, skirts hitched up around her waist, nose buried in the latest edition of *Vogue* to find inspiration for her concert dresses.

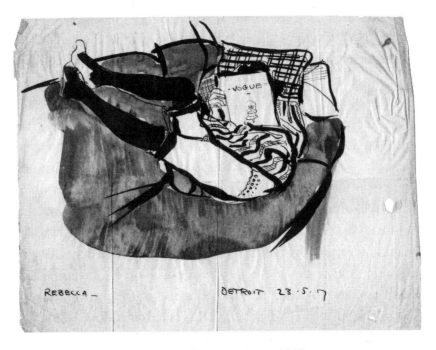

REBECCA — DETROIT 23·5·17

Rebecca as Dora saw her in 1917.

Happily, Rebecca's trip coincided with May's latest American tour, so the two performed together when they could. Rebecca offered up a dazzling array of repertoire in her wartime programmes, always blending her staples of Mozart, Beethoven and Brahms with a selection of modern pieces. As well as composers like Ravel, she played works by names that are very little known now but were formative for her compositional development. Ernest Bloch, for example, fascinated Rebecca with his hard-edged modern sound, so different from the French school or the gentle lyricism of Vaughan Williams. Rebecca soaked up all these influences, well on her way to developing a unique compositional style that seamlessly mixed the classic and the contemporary.

American life was clearly conducive to composing, because between 1916 and 1918 Rebecca produced no fewer than four concert works. Her working method was capricious: she composed when ideas struck her, but didn't sit labouring at the piano if inspiration wasn't there. When lightning struck she worked quickly, pieces sometimes going from conception to completion in a matter of days.

The most substantial of her war works is a concert piece for viola and piano named *Morpheus*, after the Greek shapeshifter, son of the god of sleep. It's a gorgeously theatrical piece, full of virtuoso passages for the violist and sweeping glissandos running up and down the piano. Perhaps the title was simply meant to evoke a rhapsodic dream-world. Or maybe it was a reference to Ovid's *Metamorphoses*: Morpheus appears to Alcyone in a dream as her husband Ceyx, telling her that he has drowned, after which Alcyone is so stricken with grief that the gods take pity on her and transform both her and her husband into kingfishers. Possibly Clarke's soaring, diving, whimsical passages simulated the birds' flight over the water. Whatever the intention behind *Morpheus*, Rebecca mixed Greek fables with sonorities clearly inspired by the gamelan that she had found so fascinating at the World Fair, creating a sound world that still sounded modern in 1917.

When she wasn't composing Rebecca was networking, and it was on this American trip that she met a woman who was to play a pivotal role in her career: Elizabeth Sprague Coolidge. Elizabeth was a formidable character, with a forthright professionalism and lack of tolerance for nonsense that immediately endeared her to Rebecca. She was fascinated by music history, and had trained as a pianist and given lectures on early music and the avant-garde as a young woman. Musicology was an unusual career for women to pursue, and her budding career as an academic musician petered out after her marriage. Then in 1916, at the age of fifty-two, she unexpectedly found herself heiress to a fortune of several million dollars after both her parents and her husband died within a year of each other.

Elizabeth devoted her wealth to promoting chamber music, which had always been her overriding passion. Chamber music was increasingly popular in the United States, but it was missing large-scale institutional promotion. Concert halls were designed for symphony concerts, and the musicians who raked in enormous fortunes through concert-hall tours were instrumentalist soloists and opera singers. Ever practical and business-minded, Elizabeth spotted a niche where her money could make a difference to her country's musical life, and she set about raising the status of chamber music in America.

Rebecca and Elizabeth met in 1917 through a mutual acquaintance: another heiress, called Gertrude 'Ariantje' Watson. Like Elizabeth, Ariantje was to become one of Rebecca's closer friends and colleagues. She was also a formidably talented pianist, and performed with Rebecca and May whenever they stayed with her.

Elizabeth's introduction to Rebecca came at the perfect time. She was about to announce her plans for an annual chamber music festival, to be held on her estate on South Mountain in Berkshire. Not only was she building a concert hall designed specifically for chamber music, but she was also patronising a new string quartet and, most significantly as far as Rebecca was concerned, establishing a composition competition to run concurrently with the festival. The prize was $1,000, equivalent to around $20,000 today. This was a serious intervention on behalf of chamber music in the United States. News of the festival and competition hit all the big newspapers.

Rebecca wasn't ready to enter in 1917, but it would, eventually, be this competition that launched her as a composer to be reckoned with.

o   o   o   o

Perhaps it was, in some ways, a relief that Ethel couldn't properly hear the agonised screams of the wounded soldiers who were flooding into her hospital. Despite the best efforts of the specialists she consulted about her hearing, none were able to stop the attacks of ringing and booming. Voices and everyday sounds were muffled, as though Ethel was listening to the world through a thick pane of glass separating her from reality, and from her music. During bad attacks she could not pick out individual instruments in an orchestra, and she lost the details in very high and low pitches. When she was honest with herself she knew that her hearing probably wouldn't ever fully recover, but that didn't stop her hoping for a miracle.

Ethel desperately needed a friend to lean on. Her war work required boundless energy, but she was finding that her physical reserves were slightly less than they used to be. After all, she had turned fifty-eight in 1916. She tried to confide in Emmeline, but Emmeline was lost without militant campaigning to organise and far too wrapped up in her own affairs to realise Ethel's needs. She had tried to raise funds for a Home for War-Babies – an idea that Ethel vehemently disagreed with – and was bitterly disappointed when she couldn't find enough donors to set up the orphanage.

Instead, Emmeline settled for adopting four young girls, intending to raise them as feminists. Ethel was unimpressed and told her so, which frustrated her no end. As Ethel put it, 'She did not like her ideas being adversely judged; what autocrat does?' So instead it was Maurice Baring who provided Ethel's spiritual comfort during the final years of the war. 'Life is a strain now, isn't it?' he wrote. 'One seems to live in a permanent eclipse and a *seasonless* world.'

Ethel and Emmeline kept up their correspondence, but the fire that had welded them together since 1910 was beginning to dim. They could put aside their differences in personality when they were united by a common enemy and burning with righteous outrage. But at a distance from one another and facing quite a different kind of war, the cracks in their relationship widened. Christabel was one particularly powerful force widening the gap. She had found God with such a fervour that she moved to the States after the war to become an evangelist for Second Adventism. Ethel had little patience with religious fundamentalism at the best of times. When it came from somebody as single-minded as Christabel, she found it completely intolerable. Emmeline, however, would bear no reproofs against her beloved daughter, and always took Christabel's side should disagreements arise. And arise they did.

And then, quietly, women were given the vote in January 1918. Not all women – only those who were married or over thirty – leaving out many of the young women who had toiled for Britain in factories and in the fields. But it was enough for Emmeline to feel satisfied that the cause was won. Like Ethel and Emmeline's relationship, British feminism began to lose its direction after the vote was granted. Having been relentlessly focused on a single issue for so long, internally diverse feminist groups had to decide what their new priority should be. Some wanted to campaign for equal pay, others for reproductive rights, sexual morality, women's education – but there was little agreement.

British feminists lost momentum at precisely the moment when they needed to be at their most fierce. Because while the war had been a wonderful opportunity to demonstrate women's ability to contribute to civil life, it had also thrown an exaggerated emphasis on gender. A person's gender determined who went to the Front and died, and who stayed at home and lived. Wartime society was fraught with gendered tension. Propaganda posters for the Women's Land Army showed images of strong, healthy women enjoying lives of independence and freedom – and however misleading these images were, they were both galling and threatening to men who returned from the Front physically and mentally shattered, feeling emasculated by their experience of war. Post-war culture explored a litany of anxieties about masculinity, from the skeletal figures that haunt Otto Dix's canvases to D. H. Lawrence's *Lady Chatterley's Lover*, and discordant, fraught operas that mercilessly killed off seductive women who sent men mad. Additionally, the plummeting birth rate meant that Britain became fixated on motherhood, marriage and family, encouraging women away from the workplace and back in to the home. Far from being a period of clear progress, the war threatened to bring major setbacks for women's rights.

For once these problems were far from Ethel's mind. In March 1918 Germany initiated the Spring Offensive, a last effort to push back the Allied line before America entered the war. They succeeded in moving the Front several miles west, forcing Allied troops into retreat, and to those in Paris it looked as though the Offensive might well be a success. Ethel secured her passage out of France by train and by boat. Flashes and flares lit up the night sky as her train crept through the French countryside past prisoner-of-war camps. Her Channel crossing was no less perilous. Travelling in a convoy of destroyers, Ethel wrapped herself into a dirty life jacket, praying she would not need to use it.

When Ethel finally landed safe on British soil, she spent the following months at Coign, planting potatoes and recovering her strength in an attempt to protect her ailing ears. But her service in France had completely exhausted her. She caught Spanish influenza during the second wave of the pandemic that hit in the winter of 1918. It started just as a shiver, then became an agony so intense that she was only able to scream down the phone to her doctor that she would shoot herself if he couldn't stop the pain, before she passed out on the floor. Come Armistice Day she was fighting for her life, completely delirious with pleuropneumonia. Emmeline still cared enough that when she heard Ethel was close to death she rushed to her bedside, bringing a doctor with her. Emmeline stayed with her until finally, miraculously, the sixty-year-old Ethel began to recover. Even after they completely severed ties in 1921, Ethel never forgot this last kindness, maintaining that she owed her life to Emmeline and her doctor.

o   o   o   o

Across the Atlantic, far from the immediate impacts of war, with four new works under her belt Rebecca was ready to announce herself to New York City as both composer and performer. She and May booked a joint recital date in February 1918, in the city's most prestigious chamber music venue: Aeolian Hall. This was a relatively new building, erected in 1912 by a company that made pianos. The concert hall lay on the third floor of an eighteen-storey building that was advertised as 'the first really complete musical center the world has seen'. There was a showroom for Aeolian pianos, a music store selling the latest scores, and floors of studios that musicians could book. The concert hall was the building's *pièce de résistance*, the first in New York designed with chamber music in mind. Solo musicians could perform here without the sound being swamped as it was in the halls designed for orchestras. If you wanted a venue to signal your ambition, Aeolian Hall was it.

It was a smart move to make her debut a double bill with May. May already had an established reputation in America as an astonishing cellist, and the double bill put the lesser-known Rebecca on an equal footing with her. The concert's promotional poster featured photographs of both of them, and their names stood in bold at the top of the bill.

They picked two of Rebecca's new pieces to perform: the *Lullaby & Grotesque*, and *Morpheus*, which would be getting its world premiere. But Rebecca wasn't listed as *Morpheus*'s composer. For the first and only time in her life she adopted a male pseudonym,

Anthony Trent. It wasn't uncommon for women to adopt gender-neutral initials (as Ethel had done) or male pseudonyms to introduce new works, to avoid gender prejudice. Perhaps Rebecca wanted to test the critics, but the explanation she later gave was that it broke up the number of 'Rebecca Clarkes' on the concert poster, stopping the concert from looking like a Rebecca Clarke vanity showcase.

If it was a test, the critics passed. Trent and Clarke got equal consideration. When *Vogue* ran their season round-up in April, directing readers to new musical trends filling the void left by the eradication of German music, they featured Rebecca three times over as someone to watch: as performer, composer and as Anthony Trent. Alongside the opera divas and trendsetters they included a photograph of Rebecca taken by one of America's leading celebrity photographers; she looked as fashionable as ever in a patterned dress and thick necklace of beads, with her hair swept up loosely. Given how devotedly she followed *Vogue*, this feature was probably just as exciting for her as the positive notices in the New York papers.

By the end of 1918 Spanish flu was sweeping across the States, leading to concert cancellations across the continent. One of the few places still able to run a concert series was Hawaii, so in October May and Rebecca set off for the islands, booked as high-profile guest artists. The Honolulu press were delighted. The newspapers sang their praises for several weeks in the run-up to their October arrival. As in New York, May was the main event, 'one of the most fascinating 'cellists of the day', while Rebecca was famous by association.

May was so supportive of Rebecca that her relative fame never seemed to cause insecurity on Rebecca's part. Artistically they viewed each other as equals, and their friendship shone through on the stage. Audiences adored them. Their first concert was the 'finest evening of instrumental music the city has ever heard'. The *Honolulu Advertiser*'s critic seemed to have instantly fallen in love with May, rhapsodising about her 'great, dark eyes that bespeak a knowledge of the deep things of life', her face 'a picture as beautiful to the eye as her artistry is to the ear'.

For their second concert, Rebecca was placed front and centre as the soloist. By 1918, it was still unusual to see a solo violist. The critics were fascinated by this woman who was able to transform what they thought of as a dull orchestral filler into a vibrant, virtuoso instrument. Rebecca was deemed a true 'pioneer', whose playing managed to mix 'sonority with sweetness and total dignity with fire and verve'. The hall sold out, and the cheering, whistling audience showered Rebecca with applause and enormous orange-gold lilies that covered the stage like a blanket of flames.

The concert series continued through the winter, generating such publicity that Rebecca started giving pre-concert analytical lectures to introduce the pieces they were playing. Lectures illustrated with live music were a nineteenth-century phenomenon, developed as a kind of adult education programme. Then as now, classical music, particularly contemporary classical, was widely thought to be difficult to understand. Educators, however, believed that being able to enjoy classical music was good for the brain and the soul, so used lectures as a way to help audiences understand what they were hearing, in the belief that it would aid appreciation of classical music. Rebecca followed in this vein, pointing audiences towards moments they might want to particularly listen out for, and showing why, from a performer's perspective, she loved this music so much.

When she wasn't performing or writing her lectures, Rebecca was off exploring Hawaii with May and the other musicians booked for the series. In the evenings they set out for drives along the oceanfront, revelling in the cool night breeze that swept across the open-topped car. Ribbons of silver and purple moonlight spooled out over the surface of the waves. As the small group rumbled through the avenues of green palm trees they played games to see who could spot a shark first. In March Rebecca trekked up the shallow slopes of Kīlauea. Persisting through the distinctive, putrid odour of rotten eggs and spent matches, when she reached the summit and looked down into the volcano she was mesmerised by the 'glare of fire miles away'. She travelled back to her hotel on 'beautiful roads – tree-ferns, wild arum lilies, wild roses, strange birds – like a fairy-story'.

It wasn't just the natural world that Rebecca marvelled at. Hawaii introduced Rebecca to a whole wealth of new sights, smells, tastes and sounds. She ate Hawaiian food at lunches given for the per-formers, saw geishas at Japanese dinners, bought May suits made out of rich blue Chinese silks, heard a Chinese orchestra play in the New Year, and went to plays and concerts. With this inspiration around her, Rebecca's Hawaii compositions marked a new phase in her compositional development. In a single day she penned a song set to W. B. Yeats's poem 'Down by the Salley Gardens'. This is a com-position that signals a supreme self-confidence on the composer's part. Rebecca strips everything back. It's just a folk-like melody with a simple accompaniment that makes the piano sound a little like a plucked instrument, perhaps evoking the Chinese orchestra she had heard the night before. Apart from four chords, the most the pianist ever plays is two notes at the same time. It captures the text's melancholy perfectly. There isn't really a firm key. The music hangs in mid-air until the last chord – and even when the piece seems to settle Rebecca adds a final note that leaves the song unresolved, a dissonance that sounds like a single, escaping tear.

'Salley Gardens' was a brief break from another, larger project. Rebecca and Elizabeth Coolidge had remained in regular contact since they met, Rebecca giving guidance and suggestions about per-formers and repertoire for the festival. She had plucked up the cour-age to suggest May as a soloist for 1919, writing to Elizabeth that 'a great cause is served in putting the work of women executants on an equal footing with that of men, – that is, only when it really *is* equal'. This was one of the rare occasions when Rebecca outspokenly adopted a feminist line. As far as Rebecca was concerned, May was 'one of the very finest artists on *any* instrument, quite irrespective of sex', and putting forward her name for the festival was an opportunity to repay her for her kindness in promoting Rebecca as a soloist on her tour.

Most importantly for Rebecca's composition, Elizabeth decided that the $1,000 prize for her 1919 Festival Competition would be for a viola work. Surrounded by the beauty of Hawaii and now with plenty of experience writing concert pieces for the viola, Rebecca began trying out ideas. By April 1919 the form of the first movement was starting to come together, and she confided to her diary that she was 'beginning to get quite excited' about the piece. Composition was interrupted by an unexpected, hasty exit from Hawaii before all boats out got cancelled because of the pandemic. She passed the Olympic Mountains on her way to Detroit to stay with Eric and Beryl, where she immediately resumed work.

Routine was vital for successful composition, and over the next few months Rebecca found hers: composition in the morning, walking in the afternoon, sewing or reading in the evening. When May left for England Rebecca made the difficult decision to stay behind in America so she could work, even if she would miss her friend terribly. She was caught in the passion of composing, only pausing when she caught the flu, and when there was a heatwave. She sewed as the temperature soared, making 'a négligée of orchid crepe-de-chine & lace', which she wore 'at supper to the great disapproval of the others'.

By 3 July she had finished her masterpiece, just twelve days before the competition deadline. In three substantial movements, the Sonata was far more formidable than anything Rebecca had written before. She was a born performer, and there have been few pieces written for the viola before or since that so brilliantly showcase what a beautiful instrument it can be, exploiting its uniquely rich tones. The opening fanfare and virtuoso flourish for the soloist grabs you from the moment it begins and does not let you go as the viola sweeps, soars and floats across the three movements, never stopping.

It's one of those rare pieces that makes you feel as though you're the protagonist lost in a fantastic world, a place of magic where danger lurks behind a carnivalesque facade of excitement and gaiety – but it's all the more thrilling for that undercurrent of peril. You can almost hear the fearful excitement of staring into Kīlauea, the awe of gazing at America's mountains, and the sheer pleasure of those moonlit evenings gazing out over the ocean. There are still the French influences, particularly in the texture, mixed with a classical approach to structure, and harmonies coming from the gamelan and the Chinese music she heard in Hawaii that give the music an Orientalist feel. In combination they are pure Rebecca, and the Sonata would become her best-known and most-played work.

Rebecca put in a final prodigious effort to get the piece written out for performance, Beryl chipping in to help by copying out the viola part. On 11 July she submitted the manuscript, even though she could 'hardly believe I really have got it done'. There was nothing left to do but wait. She set off for Ariantje's farm in Pittsfield to enjoy the summer while the competition's judges decided her fate.

o   o   o   o

Back in London, Dorothy was far from Rebecca's 'fairy-tale'. Her days were filled with the buzz and bangs of air raids and the screech of the Tube as she shuttled between convent and conservatoire. The war shaped her days, but she was nonetheless able to lead a relatively quiet life at St Dominic's. She attended services at the convent, composed in the day, went early to bed and amused herself with benefit concerts on her days off. On one occasion the convent staged an outdoor operetta as a fundraiser for the local parish schools, transforming the gardens for *A Visit to Fairyland*, which Dorothy accompanied at the piano.

When Carlo sent her some of his diary to read, she was horrified by the 'awful things he's seen and endured!', musing that 'One can't help realise it all from this safe distance'. Temporarily posted to Lemnos, Carlo was constantly in and out of the camp hospital with enteritis, not helped by the flies and dust and heat, nor the sight of his friends lying wounded in beds beside him. When he was well enough he was sent straight to the trenches, fighting against the Turkish army, surrounded by 'shrapnel, high explosive, star shells, bombs, rifles, machine-guns'. The deaths of his soldiers were so commonplace that Carlo couldn't let himself grieve each fully.

Far away in the relative security of Harrow, Dorothy felt practically helpless. What she *could* do to support the war was give regular fundraising performances – and concerts meant gowns. She was especially delighted with an extravagant frock of grey georgette over pink silk trimmed with white lace that she bought for her first fundraiser with royalty attending – which set her family back by an eye-watering £5, equivalent to around £300 today. Even in wartime, when faced with a beautiful dress Dorothy seemed to lose all sense of her parents' finances, and couldn't quite help herself from splashing out on accessories and haircuts. On this occasion she apologised for spending so much, saying her money had 'simply melted away' – but after all, she needed to look the part. She began signing off her letters 'P.B.R.', 'Performed Before Royalty', revelling in the excitement of the whole affair.

Then on 25 January 1917 the Howells got the letter that every family dreaded. Carlo had been killed in action in Mesopotamia, buried in an unmarked grave near Al-Kut. Charles Edward recorded the news in his diary in a hand wracked by grief: a shaky, near-illegible scrawl in a book that's otherwise filled with neat, meticulous handwriting. For Dorothy, the loss was incalculable. Carlo had been her anchor, the sibling who she looked up to, trusted the most, and whose presence always made her feel safe. She immediately returned to Birmingham to mourn, attending a Mass for him that was held at their local church in February. Dorothy's family was forced to relive their grief over and over as letters continued arriving from Carlo up until March, as though his spirit refused to accept that he had died. His kit finally arrived from Mesopotamia in July and the Howells unpacked his small collection of belongings together, heartbroken but grateful to have some finality.

Carlo's death changed Dorothy's world completely. Immediately after he died she began working on pieces of a much greater scope and emotional maturity than she had attempted before. She was growing up anyway: by 1917 she was nineteen, and had been studying at the Academy for three years. But there was a new urgency to her work from January onwards. Perhaps Carlo dying gave her a renewed energy, making her realise that a life could be snuffed out at any moment – or maybe she wanted to live up to what Carlo believed she could be. Her music had always brought them together, Carlo quietly encouraging her work. Composing was a way for Dorothy to remember her brother.

The largest works Dorothy had written until this point were a piano sonata and a small string quartet, but in 1917 she began sketching an opera. It was based on Shakespeare's tragicomedy *The Winter's Tale*, but Dorothy renamed her version *Perdita*, adapting the play to focus on the story of the abandoned princess Perdita. If she ever finished the opera, it has not survived. The only trace is a single scene – a duet between Perdita and her lover Prince Florizel, followed by a Shepherds' Dance.

Clearly, Dorothy was as influenced by French modernism as Rebecca. Debussy's harmonic style lingers over the whole piece. And yet it's still distinctively Dorothy. There are sprightly leaps and turns of phrase that show what an imaginative composer she was becoming. She wrote up this first operatic attempt in a beautiful wine-red presentation book. Presumably she planned to send it to conductors to see if there was any interest. But if she did try, she was unsuccessful. She gave the premiere of a piano version of the Shepherds' Dance herself, to very little fanfare, at one of her fundraising concerts in Stourbridge. Beyond this, though, there's no record of *Perdita* ever having been performed. It got forgotten, left off her full list of works, eventually buried in an old cardboard apple box under a heap of other scores.

Dorothy was inexperienced at writing theatrical music and, understandably, her first attempt at a full-scale opera wasn't as sophisticated or idiomatic as the piano works she was writing at the same time. But *Perdita* provided a stepping-stone to her next piece, which she began sketching in 1918. She chose as her topic a Keats poem called *Lamia*, which had been a favourite of Carlo's. It tells the story of a serpent transformed into a woman, Lamia, who is fated to return to her original form should her true identity be revealed. Lamia falls in love with Lycius, and she convinces him to hide their love from the world. But when, finally, she consents to marry him, she is recognised at their wedding feast, and immediately vanishes into thin air.

Dorothy was a true romantic at heart, even if her convent life precluded the possibility of boyfriends. Any love life she had as a teenager was purely fantasy, which is perhaps one of the reasons why Keats's overwrought poem about an all-consuming but doomed love appealed to her. And *Lamia*'s story provided her with all the elements for a big set-piece. She had been working hard at orchestration and attending as many concerts as she could to get a feel for how an orchestra worked. So she decided to make *Lamia* a symphonic poem: an orchestral piece, usually of one movement, which expressed a poetic idea or programme.

Symphonic poems had been wildly popular in the pre-war years, but few modern composers troubled themselves with the genre. It was considered too indulgent for modernist sensibilities. Dorothy, however, had no such qualms. Her mornings at the convent's parlour piano now took on an unusual earnestness, as she spent months trying out themes for her new piece. Unlike Rebecca she was a great believer in continuous work. Dorothy laboured at *Lamia* every day. She only broke her routine when inspiration left her entirely, taking the morning off to go and play tennis in the sunshine.

Lamia occupied Dorothy for months, through the most significant events of her early twenties. The first was her graduation, and with it the question of what to do and where to live after leaving the Academy. Dorothy's parents were desperate for her to return to them in Birmingham. They missed her terribly, and after Carlo – and then Dick Sampson's death on the Somme in 1918 – they wanted to keep the family as close as possible. But Dorothy's odds of making a career as a composer were much higher if she lived in London, with easy access to performers, agents and publishers.

Dorothy's tutors intervened on her behalf. 'You must not run to seed in the wilds of Worcestershire,' Tobias Matthay wrote to her, promising to find her students at his piano school to supplement her income. McEwen took a more direct approach. He wrote to Charles Edward, imploring him to let Dorothy stay in London. 'Apart from the question of sex there is no doubt that she is possessed of quite an unusual talent,' he explained. 'That it should be found in a girl is I think a very extraordinary & suggestive thing. I venture to think that 20 or 30 years ago such an occasion was both physically & mentally impossible.' Despite Ethel's public battles over the last thirty years, in 1919 it was still the case that nobody, not even composition tutors, *expected* a woman to be a composer. There had been just as many women as men at the Academy for years, and thanks to the war the statistics became even more skewed in favour of them; in Dorothy's graduation year there were only 46 men to 379 women. Nonetheless, it still required a suspension of disbelief for tutors to promote the music of a talented woman student.

Ultimately both Charles Edward and Viola wanted what was best for Dorothy. They finally relented and helped to set her up with accommodation in London, where she continued to compose and perform. The other big event of 1919 was her public London debut as a concert pianist. On 11 March she took to the stage in Aeolian Hall, the London partner to the building that had housed Rebecca's New

York debut. London's Aeolian had a much more English flavour: where the New York Aeolian was newly built with flashy show-rooms, the London building erected on New Bond Street in 1876 had once been an art gallery, and still sported the elaborate facades from its previous existence. But they were both halls for chamber music. The London hall seated hundreds, but it had a distinctly intimate feel. There were no boxes or tiered seats. Everybody sat on the same level, facing the same direction, focusing all attention on the soloist under the high archway that framed the stage.

Just as Rebecca had, Dorothy chose to announce herself simultan-eously as a composer and pianist. She put her *Humoresque* and Five Studies on her debut programme alongside some Robert Schumann and a McEwen sonata. The lively *Humoresque* has an air of playful mystery to it – like the musical answer to Agatha Christie – with occasional, unexpected flashes of joy that burst through at the top of the piano. It would become one of her most popular pieces. The critics decreed that she was 'a very encouraging and candid talent', and her compositions 'showed a real inventive power and a rare gift of imagination'.

Dorothy was overjoyed with her success, but nothing would distract her from *Lamia*, which was nearing completion. She only needed to put the finishing touches on the orchestration – and to secure an orchestra for the premiere. Her nationality already put her in a good position. Even once peace was declared, the tide of musical patriotism unleashed by war showed no signs of subsiding. Both conductors and audiences were keen to give new British works a hearing. Dorothy decided to aim as high as she could: the Proms. It was, to put it mildly, a long shot. She had no real compositional reputation to speak of, and *Lamia* was her first substantial orchestral work. But she submitted the score for consideration anyway, secretly hoping against hope that it would catch Henry Wood's attention.

The unthinkable happened. On 11 June 1919, she got a letter call-ing her for an audition at the Queen's Hall. Henry saw promise in the vivid, imaginative tone poem, and when Dorothy turned up for her audition he was completely charmed by her cheerful sincerity. They warmed to each other immediately, which made it all the more enjoyable for him to deliver the good news. Dorothy couldn't believe it. But there it was, written in black and white. The date was set. *Lamia* would be put to the public at the Queen's Hall on 10 September 1919.

BREAKTHROUGH

As she took her seat in the Queen's Hall, Dorothy surreptitiously surveyed the audience around her, thrilled that they were all reading her name when they glanced at their programmes, unaware that they were right next to the composer of the evening's world premiere. It's unlikely that the other audience members noticed Dorothy at all, as she sat with her proud parents.

Even had they known who she was, the audience were far too pre-occupied with the oppressive heat in the auditorium to pay her any attention. London had been baking in a heatwave, and by the evening of 10 September temperatures were still topping 30 degrees. Ladies in silks and chiffons fanned themselves furiously as they sweltered in their plush upholstered seats, their jewels glistening under the blood-red lampshades. Faced with less sartorial freedom, the gentle-men wilted in their bow ties and dinner jackets, those in the furnace of the upper balcony glaring with envy at those on the ground floor. These were hardly auspicious circumstances for the premiere of a new work. Patience for new music was limited at the best of times. The fate of Dorothy's work was in the hands of Henry Wood and his orchestra, and there was nothing left for her to do now except pray.

The murmur of chatter dimmed politely as the Queen's Hall orchestra came on stage, before swelling to a roar of applause as Henry stepped out on to the rostrum. He was still London's favour-ite conductor, resplendent with his thick moustache, white bow tie and long black tails as he soaked up the audience's welcome. Finally the clapping subsided and he turned to raise his baton. The evening had begun.

Dorothy had a long time to wait. *Lamia* was sixth on the pro-gramme, and before it lay nearly an hour of music by established

Proms favourites and some of the best-known names in the repertoire: Schubert, Lalo, Puccini, Saint-Saëns and Robert Schumann. These were tough acts to follow. But finally, silence fell. Dorothy's moment had come.

Lamia begins with a seductive, undulating chromatic line woven between two flutes – an invitation to enter into a mythical world of magic, secrets and deadly desire. As the flutes continue their dance the rest of the orchestra wakes: the strings softly introduce a melody that in turn becomes the backdrop for repeated horn calls, shining through the orchestra like rays of the rising sun piercing a bank of mist.

Dorothy paints the whole poem in sound so vividly you can almost see the drama unfolding in front of you. Lamia and Lycius fall in love to the sound of a yearning, aching melody – first in the oboe, then the violins, before the cellos arrive to sweep the music to a glorious climax, the instruments intertwining and the whole orchestra moving as one. The dance at their wedding feast changes the mood completely. This is playful, fantastic music peppered with the sounds of tambourines and harp; there's only the faintest hint of danger lurking in the bass as the dance sweeps along. But Lamia's joy cannot last. Her snake theme starts to creep back into the flutes, and the once-distant danger comes ever closer as the piece pulses towards its tragic finale. When Lycius finally dies, the symphonic poem – like the mythological woman who inspired it – melts into the silence from which it came, closing with three quiet, funereal chords.

The silence lasted just a little longer than it normally would – usually a sign that listeners either hated a piece or were completely confused by it. But then this English audience, hardly famous for effusive displays of enthusiasm, erupted into euphoric applause. Temporarily forgetting the discomfort of the heat-hazed hall, they whistled and clapped, calling the composer to the stage.

Dorothy couldn't quite believe it at first. It was only when she stepped out to take her bow that she began to realise that *Lamia* had been a phenomenal success. She was called back to the stage two, three, four times, the audience thundering their astonished admiration for this slim, pretty young woman wearing a simple, loose-fitting dress gathered with a sash at the waist, her light brown hair cut in a bob. She beamed as she took in the most rapturous response that a new work had received in years.

After the concert Dorothy was surrounded by well-wishers and journalists curious to find out anything they could about this new-comer. It was well into the morning hours before the Howells finally reached Stourbridge and Dorothy could collapse, exhausted, into bed. She woke the next day to a flurry of press requests and notes of congratulations – and her first reviews.

A flicker of nerves returned as she picked up the newspapers, but the critics were as excited as the audience had been. Their general focus, however, was more on Dorothy herself than on *Lamia*. Just as critics had been shocked by Ethel decades ago, they now noted in astonishment that Dorothy was 'one of the sunniest, most natural, and unassuming girls', and therefore 'the very antithesis of what the general public imagine a musical genius to be'. Reviewers were so incredulous that McEwen had to confirm that *Lamia* was indeed all Dorothy's own work.

The more critical writers agreed that although *Lamia* was popular and showed that Dorothy had promise, the symphonic poem in itself was nothing extraordinary. Her writing was 'a little facile', her ideas 'immature and imitative'. They felt she was too influenced by others – she needed to 'shake herself free' to become 'her true musical self'. Critics wanted something modernist, groundbreaking, daring – a work fit for the Roaring Twenties. *Lamia* launching her in such an extraordinary way was a double-edged sword. Reviewers gave Dorothy immediate fame, but they set a phenomenally high bar for her future work which would be hard to reach once the novelty of her age and gender had worn off.

PERSONAL : PEOPLE OF THE MOMENT.

PHOTOGRAPHS BY ALFIERI, FARRINGDON, ILLUSTRATIONS BUREAU, AND LAFAYETTE.

LEADER OF THE "OCCUPIERS" OF FIUME : GABRIELE D'ANNUNZIO—
AS AIRMAN.

A semi-official Italian Note of September 13 stated that news had come that some detachments of grenadiers and bands of Arditi (storm troops), with machine-guns and armoured cars, had arrived at Fiume. The Government, it was said, would take the most energetic steps to check the movement at once and discover those responsible for "an act which is as rash as it is harmful." Gabriele d'Annunzio, Italy's famous poet—and airman—was named as the leader. Certain of the Italian papers defend the exploit.

COMPOSER OF "LAMIA," GIVEN TWICE IN A WEEK AT THE PROMS. :
MISS DOROTHY HOWELL.

D'Annunzio, it will be recalled, played a gallant part during the war.——Miss Dorothy Howell, a young British composer, had the unusual honour of having her symphonic poem, "Lamia," given twice in a week at the Queen's Hall, at Promenade Concerts. A critic writes of her : "A further acquaintance confirmed the view that the young composer has still far to go before she finds an individual note, but that she has the power which will carry right to the foremost rank if only she is not spoilt by success."

MOTHER OF FIELD-MARSHAL ALLENBY : MRS. HYNMAN ALLENBY.

Mrs. Hynman Allenby, mother of Field-Marshal Allenby, who gained the highest rank of the British Army and a Viscounty for his splendid victories against the Turks, was, it need hardly be said, one of the most eager to greet him on his return.——Dr. William

PRESIDENT OF THE BRITISH ASSOCIATION FOR 1920-21 : DR. WILLIAM HERDMAN.

Herdman has been chosen President of the British Association for the year 1920-21, when the meeting will be at Cardiff. He is Professor of Natural History at Liverpool University, and was General Secretary of the British Association from 1903 until the present year.

Dorothy (top right) photographed at home as one of the
Illustrated London News's 'People of the Moment'
after the success of *Lamia*.

For now, though, she revelled in her new-found celebrity. She gave interviews to journalists who delighted over the fact that she played tennis, approved of her having 'an enthusiastic belief' in 'forwarding the cause of British music', and nicknamed her the 'English Strauss'. The critics wanted an English stick with which to beat the Germans, and Dorothy fitted the bill perfectly. A repeat performance of *Lamia* was hastily scheduled for 13 September to allow listeners a second chance to hear the piece that had taken London by storm. This was, as Henry Wood later wrote, 'exceptional for a British composer's work – for a woman, a triumph'.

The press furore allowed Dorothy to leap over the first barrier that had presented Ethel with such problems since the 1870s – publication. Attracted by *Lamia*'s popularity, Novello offered her £100 for the copyright to *Lamia*, which amounts to about £3,000 today. For a relatively unknown composer this was an enormous sum, a clear show of faith in Dorothy's skills. By comparison, Novello gave Elgar no money for the first work of his that they published, just 100 free copies of the score.

Henry was delighted that the piece had 'made such an excellent impression', and put an unusual proposal to Dorothy: he would conduct *Lamia* in the provinces if she gave him exclusive performance rights for a whole year. It should have been a difficult decision. If a work was to achieve lasting success, high-quality repeat performances were crucial – and Henry would provide these. But other conductors were also falling over themselves to conduct the piece that was the talk of 'all musical London' – Dorothy even had performance requests coming in from Italy. Nonetheless, she immediately agreed to Henry's terms.

Unlike Ethel or even Rebecca, Dorothy was never one for self-promotion or taking risks. She was unlikely to make the necessary business decisions that a more shrewd, hard-headed person might have made. She missed – or felt too shy to take – several big opportunities following *Lamia*'s success. Having the rare qualities of modesty and generosity did, however, make her well liked by colleagues, and she inspired fierce loyalty. And although she was selective about her commissions, if she accepted them she worked quickly and efficiently. In September, Henry proposed a commission to write two orchestral songs for the celebrated contralto Phyllis Lett, for a recital in December 1919. Dorothy leapt at the chance. A few weeks later she delivered two songs, 'A Sunset' and 'A South-Wester', well in time for the world premiere with Henry conducting.

As if two orchestral world premieres in a single year weren't enough, Dorothy added a third – *Two Dances for Orchestra*, which received their first performance in Birmingham under the baton of Appleby Matthews, Artistic Director of the newly forming City of Birmingham Orchestra. Appleby was Dorothy's complete opposite: sharp-tongued (Ethel described him as being 'as big a beast as I ever met'), opportunistically charming and aggressively ambitious. He spotted the appeal of this local composer, and billed Dorothy's fun and flavourful work in a Sunday concert full of classic favourites aimed at a popular audience. It didn't make the same splash as *Lamia*, but the *Two Dances* were nonetheless picked up for performance at no less a venue than Buckingham Palace in November. The conductor, Raymond Rose, reported that the Palace performance was 'greatly appreciated by the distinguished audience'. Rose liked the *Dances* so much that he took them on tour the following year, playing them across the UK with his symphony orchestra of ex-servicemen.

At the start of 1919, Dorothy was an upcoming pianist. By the end of the year she was a famous woman with three world premieres to her name, hailed as one of the UK's most promising composers. She was in her element, and as the dust settled around *Lamia* she was already working on her next major piece – an epic of forbidden love, heartbreak and murder.

o   o   o   o

After the gargantuan effort of writing her Viola Sonata, Rebecca was free to spend a perfect summer on Ariantje's farm in Pittsfield. She spent her days practising, taking long walks, hosting teas and heading out for drives. And in the evening after the flurry of socialising, she, May and Ariantje would rest under the vine-covered porch, eating dinner while they watched the sun throwing out its final rays of red and gold over the fields. Sometimes Rebecca would sit and sew as long as the light lasted. Other nights May would take up her cello, Ariantje accompanying her on the piano, Rebecca listening. She had no other word for it but 'heavenly'.

On one of these golden August evenings, there was a knock at the door as they sat eating supper. When Elizabeth Coolidge and one of the prize judges walked in, Rebecca's heart leapt. She had been waiting for this news for nearly a month. The competition had been fierce, they explained. More than seventy anonymous manuscripts had been submitted. The standard was so high that in the end the jury had been split between two works. Elizabeth was given the casting vote. She chose the piece that turned out to be by Ernest Bloch, a composer whom Rebecca admired greatly. And the runner-up was Rebecca Clarke.

Rebecca was ecstatic. 'A red-letter day for me,' she wrote in her diary. 'Very excited indeed.' She and Elizabeth shared plans and ideas for the forthcoming festival, scheduling the Sonata for the first day, 25 September, alongside the US premiere of Elgar's new String Quartet. Rebecca couldn't have asked for more. Everything about this month was blissful. She threw herself into rehearsing the performers, and on 27 August she celebrated her thirty-third birthday with Ariantje. That year her friend gave her two gifts: a beautiful Chinese amber pendant, and an invitation for Rebecca's mother to attend the Sonata's premiere. Ariantje 'really is incredible', Rebecca wrote. 'I'm so happy.'

After weeks of rehearsal, the day of the premiere finally arrived. The September heatwave that hung over *Lamia*'s premiere was also felt across the Atlantic, draping a golden haze over the Berkshire mountains. Here, tucked away in the forests, was Elizabeth's temple. It's a simple, timber-frame building, designed to be a place of worship for America's chamber music disciples. The seats are wooden pews, salvaged from a church. Sat in their pews, listeners can look out of one of the enormous French doors that open on to a lawn that falls away into green woodlands peppered with silver birches, their autumn leaves blazing yellow, orange and copper-red against the vivid blue sky. There couldn't have been a more perfect setting for the romance and drama of Rebecca's Sonata. Nonetheless she was wracked with nerves. Ever-exacting, she felt that the violist 'did not play very well', but the performance was good enough that she was called to the stage to take her bow and 'overwhelmed with congratulations'.

Reviewers were uniformly impressed – certainly more than they were with Elgar's Quartet. It sounded dull and antediluvian when placed next to Rebecca's firecracker of a work, fizzing with modern harmonies and innovative timbres, with a second movement that was 'the elfish, tricksy sort of thing the moderns like to do'. The *New York Times* judged that Rebecca 'had unquestionably something of her own to say, she is moved by a strong feeling for beauty, and much of her work is charming and really engrossing'. A rumour flew round that the judges had originally believed that the Sonata was written by a French composer – probably Ravel.

This was all phenomenal publicity. Rebecca had the business savvy that Dorothy did not, and set about capitalising on her new-found fame. She wanted to give the New York premiere of her Sonata herself, so booked herself a recital date at, of course, Aeolian Hall. On the weeks running up to the concert she practised furiously, even though as usual she was living life at a break-neck speed, juggling these rehearsals with concerts, dress-fittings, parties (not even a fever would keep her from her New Year's party) and yet more rehearsals.

Rebecca in a publicity image, *c.*1919.

Having spent years as a freelancer Rebecca knew precisely how the musical publicity machine worked. She sent out strategic invitations to get the right people in the audience, ensuring that the Aeolian concert had the highest impact possible. The day of the recital rolled round: 26 January 1920. As always before a big concert, May was there to wait on her friend hand and foot. Her cheerful presence helped calm Rebecca's nerves. Both knew how miserable the day before a concert could be, and they took turns before each other's important recitals to bring soothing cups of tea and help fix each other's outfits. Rebecca had put together a truly ambitious programme to announce herself to New York as both composer and performer, placing some virtuoso showstoppers alongside her own Sonata. She played beautifully, whipping up enormous applause and streams of congratulations at the after-party.

Having come down from her post-concert adrenaline rush, Rebecca woke up the next day feeling glum. But being presented with her 'splendid notices' soon cheered her up. New York's response to the Sonata was, frankly, embarrassingly positive, hailing it a work of 'genius'. And now, she had another country to conquer: England.

o   o   o   o

August 1919 found Ethel in pursuit of quite different goals to Rebecca and Dorothy. They were starting their careers, but Ethel was in her autumn years. War had made her meditative, and while she had been tending the wounded she had begun jotting down reflections on her childhood, working towards an autobiography. As luck would have it, she had found that a helpfully immobilised patient provided a captive audience for her first drafts. Sitting and reading at him became part of Ethel's nursing routine. The final two-volume memoir that resulted, *Impressions that Remained*, is as extraordinary as Ethel herself. It covers her fights with her father, her studies and travails in Leipzig and her first attempts to have her music published and performed up until 1890, all woven together with humorous anecdotes and irreverent personality portraits that are so realistic she makes you feel as though you, too, knew and loved her friends and family.

When *Impressions* was published in October 1919, it was hailed as 'one of the most remarkable books of memoirs that has appeared in recent times', no less than the most important musical book ever printed in England. Readers delighted in the 'perfect sincerity' of Ethel's writing, admired the way she portrayed 'the psychology of feminine friendship', and fell in love with her blend of egotism, self-deprecation and willingness to analyse her own actions as well as those of others. Even if women writers were still associated with particular genres such as memoirs (which certainly helped Ethel in this instance), it was far more accepted that women should be authors than composers. The only time that gendered language sneaked into the reviews was when the authors were considering her music. 'Those of us who have wondered at the masculine vigour of Miss Smyth's music', one wrote, 'will wonder no longer after reading these memoirs.'

Writing *Impressions* proved to be Ethel's best career decision yet. She became a literary sensation. The book was sold in America and translated for sale abroad in multiple editions. She was in the society pages, gossip columns and women's magazines. *Impressions* was *the* book you had to read in winter 1919. When the *Daily Mirror* drew up a list for an ideal women's government, it was Ethel who they imagined would 'organise our concerts and direct musical scholarship'. *Impressions* boosted her not inconsiderable fame, making the 1920s some of her most successful years. People wanted to know the music behind the memoir, and performance requests came rolling in.

Most delightful of all was that Ethel had a new-found passion to share her successes with. As the war was ending, she had picked up a book called *Irish Reminiscences* by the Irish author and artist Edith Somerville. Encroaching deafness and being surrounded by death had filled Ethel with a desperate longing for H. B. And here, unexpectedly, she found herself reading a book that described precisely the profound feeling of loneliness and emptiness she felt without him. *Irish Reminiscences* was Edith's attempt to come to terms with losing Violet Martin, her second cousin, co-author and (possibly romantic) companion, who had died from a brain tumour in 1915. Together they had written fourteen books, Violet writing under the pseudonym 'Martin Ross', and in their lifetimes they were inseparable. Violet Martin had been to Edith what H. B. had been to Ethel – a soulmate without whom life was unimaginable.

Ethel wrote what was essentially a fan letter to Edith. 'I don't know when anything has moved me more deeply,' she stated simply. 'I wish I could thank you adequately.' Edith was touched by the sincerity of the composer's letter, and a cautious correspondence followed. After a year of exchanging a few letters they finally met at a railway station in September 1919, when Ethel was visiting Ireland. The connection was immediate. Edith was a gentle and fiercely intelligent woman with a marvellous ability to see the humour in any situation. The same age as Ethel, she was small, slim, with kind eyes and a perfectly straight nose that gave her a striking profile. And they had plenty in common. Both loved riding, writing and animals (Edith's companion of choice was a fox terrier). Ethel marked the date in her diary: 'I have had the unhoped-for, undreamed-of fortune to strike..in my Autumn..a new & perfect friend.'

Ethel had intended a short trip to Ireland, but having met Edith she did not return to Woking until mid-October. She stayed with Edith at her family home, Drishane House, in County Cork, where their relationship blossomed. Days were spent walking, riding and writing, while evenings were occupied by Edith playing the piano, Ethel roaring corrections from her comfortable armchair by the fire as she completed the *Times* crossword. Ethel was in love. But loving Edith also meant loving Violet Martin, or Martin, as she was known for short. Disconsolate with grief, Edith had turned to spiritualism after Martin's death. Spiritualism had been popular in the UK for several decades, but had gained new momentum in the wake of World War I and the Spanish flu. Bereaved family and friends often consulted mediums, desperately hoping to gain some comfort by contacting their loved ones after death. London's Society of Psychical Research gave spiritualism a veneer of credibility by leading academic research into the paranormal, and boasted such distinguished members as Sir Arthur Conan Doyle and Arthur Balfour, the former British Prime Minister. So Edith was not wildly unusual in believing that she was in constant contact with her cousin's spirit. From beyond the grave Martin remained Edith's writing partner, confidante and companion.

If Ethel was to stand any chance with Edith, she had to get Martin's approval first. So when she decided to declare her love for Edith, just three days after coming home from Drishane House, she had to write to both of them. She had no idea whether her feelings for Edith were reciprocated. Nonetheless, she laid her feelings out on paper, placing her heart at the mercy of both woman and ghost. She posted her letter, and waited anxiously on their reply. She needn't have worried. Edith cared for her, and Martin gave her blessing. Ethel was overjoyed. 'That such a happiness is given to me who so little expected any more happiness makes me wonder if it's a dream,' she gushed. 'And, best of all that yr. cousin is glad I am in your life.'

It was an unconventional love affair, to say the least. But everything about Ethel was unconventional, and her relationship with Edith would be one of the most fulfilling she ever had. Theirs was a love built on laughter. Edith was an inveterate prankster, and was constantly coming up with new ways to amuse Ethel. Whenever she was feeling morose Edith was there to cheer her up, and Ethel, in turn, doted on Edith. After Martin's death Edith had found it difficult to believe in her writing, and her natural tendency towards self-doubt had intensified. Ethel encouraged and supported her, gave her feedback on her book drafts, and negotiated with galleries on Edith's behalf to arrange exhibitions of her paintings. They drew each other out of themselves. And at sixty-one, they were each old enough not to bother standing on ceremony. Edith was often immobilised from a combination of sciatica and lumbago, and their ailing health was a common topic of conversation. Ethel shared her dietary tips, and Edith consulted the ghosts of dead doctors on Ethel's behalf to try to help when her hearing was particularly bad.

Above all else, Edith's love for Martin allowed Ethel to relive her passion for H. B. Both women knew how it felt to live alone after losing the love of your life. As time went on Martin started to pass on messages from H. B., which filled Ethel with joy. The *ménage à trois* expanded to become a *ménage à quatre* – Edith and Ethel in this world, and Martin and H. B. in the afterlife. The only thing missing, for Ethel, was physicality. Edith wanted their love on a purely spiritual plane. Ethel disagreed. 'If I thought that I would have become a nun long ago,' she lamented.

By December 1919 Edith and Ethel were revelling in their new-found love. They wrote continuously to one another from across the Irish Channel, sometimes running to several letters a day that detailed every aspect of their lives and feelings for one another. Edith sent Ethel a matchbox that had once belonged to Martin as a token of their affection. Having this physical reminder of their joint presence made Ethel 'so happy that I can't talk about it', and she took the matchbox with her everywhere, even – especially – to bed.

They were desperate to see one another again. Eventually Ethel suggested a trip to Sicily. Not only was it a gloriously romantic location, but the Mediterranean sun and sea air would do a world of good for their various ailments. At first Edith tried to bring family members, which would have ruined Ethel's romantic getaway, but Ethel finally got her way. The two of them set off for Taormina, alone, in February 1920.

o   o   o   o

Beneath a willow tree lies a pagoda, the home of a powerful mandarin who lives with his beautiful daughter, Koong-se. The mandarin plans for Koong-se to marry for wealth and power, but her heart belongs to the mandarin's bookkeeper, Chang. The lovers meet a tragic end. Chang is murdered by the mandarin's soldiers and Koong-se, desperate with grief, sets fire to her home and dies in the blaze. Seeing the lovers' plight, the gods take pity on them and transform them into doves, allowing them to live together, free, for all eternity.

The story of Koong-se has many of the same fantastical elements as *Lamia*. Both revolve around a doomed love, and a transformation wrought by the gods. Again, it appealed to Dorothy's sense of fairy-tale romance, and she set about adapting it as a ballet. She believed the tale to be an ancient Chinese legend, little realising that it was an eighteenth-century British invention devised to sell a porcelain design called the Willow Pattern (which Dorothy's family had on their best china for special occasions).

With the twentieth-century resurgence of interest in chinoiserie, by the 1920s both the Willow Pattern and the accompanying legend were as well known as *Cinderella* and *Snow White* are today. The story gave Dorothy all the ingredients she needed to participate in this craze for the imagined East. As she had for *Lamia*, she settled in to compose, locking herself away at the piano every morning. When inspiration flowed Dorothy could still be found writing at dinner time, immersed in the world of Koong-se. The piece would take two years to complete, absorbing her night and day.

Combining ballet and chinoiserie was extremely savvy. Ethel might have seen a future for English opera, but to Dorothy's gener-ation with their penchants for bobbed hair, calf-skimming dresses and make-up, ballet was the modern genre. Opera was decidedly fusty. Where fashion magazines had once followed opera stars, the pages of *Vogue* were now graced by glamorous ballerinas. Parisian fashionistas avidly followed the Ballets Russes, the most famous and influential ballet company of the twentieth century. Anybody who considered herself a modern woman knew the Parisian dresses and perfumes based on their productions. And from 1918, the Ballets Russes's image in London was all about chinoiserie. They were hoping to capitalise on the runaway success of London's most popular musical ever, an orientalist comedy called *Chu Chin Chow*. Dorothy couldn't have missed the posters that bedecked the Underground, advertising their 1918 season with one of Picasso's costume designs for a Chinese conjuror. She was starting to think like an entrepreneur, bringing together two of London's hottest trends.

When she wasn't composing, Dorothy was busy zipping around the country, satisfying the demand for appearances from London's new musical darling. She gave piano recitals across the length and breadth of England, distinguishing herself in a crowded field. It was composing, though, that was Dorothy's life. In between her ballet writing, she penned a short piece for violin and piano called *Rosalind*, which she herself premiered at the Aeolian Hall in October 1920. Performer-composers like Dorothy and Rebecca had a huge advantage over composers like Ethel, because they didn't need to wait on other people to get their chamber music played. *Rosalind* is a short, melodious salon piece, and was immediately published. Its tuneful gaiety made it one of Dorothy's most popular pieces in her own lifetime – even if it wasn't the modern rule-breaker that the critics wanted.

After *Lamia*'s success Dorothy also had plenty of other players wanting to programme her work. Throughout 1920 her music was on schedules across the UK, including two lecture recital series. Lecture recitals about classical music took on a new importance in the early twentieth century, because jazz and dance music had spread through London like wildfire. When the Original Dixieland Jazz Band toured the capital they sold out clubs with people wanting to experience the thrilling new sounds coming from America. But the conservative classes were keen to ward off what they felt to be the corrupting, deviant influence of jazz and dance. Lecture recitals became a crucial weapon in the fight for cultural education, and by the 1920s they had become a pastime of choice for the socially and culturally aspirant.

Dorothy herself adored jazz, but there are very few audible jazz influences in her works. And while she sometimes used unusual harmonies and complex instrumentation, her music was not atonal like the pieces that she had found so risible in 1914. She represented a modern path for music that could be both popular and melodious, making her the conservative contemporary composer of choice. For a lecture recital touring northern cities, one pianist put Dorothy alongside similar English composers, presenting them as the natural successors to Bach, Beethoven and Chopin. She was represented by three works in his lecture recital, including a clever little piece called *Spindrift*. It has a dignified restraint and poise, but still manages to keep a feeling of fun and liveliness. Nothing is overblown or overstated.

Dorothy's name was also becoming associated with children's musical education. Her old piano teacher, Tobias Matthay, was on a mission to revolutionise music teaching in England, arguing that in a post-war world England needed more intellectual independence from the continent. What English children needed was not German music, but good English pieces by good English composers – of which Dorothy was one. He included her *Pieces for the Bairns* in his lecture recital, using it as an example of his ideal as it managed to combine a simplicity of expression with writing that stretched learners' technique. For Dorothy, this call for an educational renaissance couldn't have been more welcome. She adored writing children's music, but traditionally this kind of composition was seen as trivial 'women's work', beneath the 'great' composers. Ethel would *never* have allowed her music to be associated with children. But if Matthay's position represented a sea change in the musical establishment, it might pave the way for Dorothy's music for children being seen as an asset, rather than a detriment to her profile as a composer.

For now, though, writing children's music was not going to make Dorothy's name. Having worked tirelessly for nearly two years, by mid-1921 she put the finishing touches on her ballet score, now with the anglicised title *Koong Shee*. But having chosen such a promising topic, Dorothy then made a colossal mistake with the premiere. Had *Koong Shee* been staged at a theatre that specialised in big, spectacular productions, it might have been a roaring success. But Dorothy had few contacts in the theatrical world. And the UK's dismal artistic infrastructure meant that outside the big theatres, the options for staging ballet were extremely limited.

Dorothy faced the same problem with her ballet that Ethel had faced with her operas many times over. The Royal Ballet wasn't established until 1931, and English National Ballet not until 1950. So Dorothy went straight to Henry Wood with her new score. He loved it, and scheduled an unstaged concert performance for that year's Proms. This would have been perfect had *Koong Shee* been another symphonic poem, but Dorothy had written a spectacular ballet for a young audience who enjoyed musical theatre, not a self-sufficient concert work appropriate for the Proms.

Nonetheless, *Koong Shee*'s premiere was set for October. The newspapers were delighted that Dorothy's music would be gracing the Queen's Hall stage. Once again, Dorothy and Ethel were the only two women to have orchestral works programmed – Dorothy with *Koong Shee* and *Lamia*, and Ethel with extracts from both *The Boatswain's Mate* and *The Wreckers*. Dorothy knew Ethel, of course, by reputation, so she was both astonished and delighted to receive a letter out of the blue from the famous composer, asking permission to attend the *Koong Shee* rehearsals. 'If a thing has originality, a real personal idea behind it,' Ethel explained, 'I often feel rather lost at a first hearing' – not letting on that this was because of her encroaching deafness. She had been full of admiration for *Lamia*, assuring Dorothy that her 'command of means, absolutely astonishing, is so obvious as not to escape even a slow listener like myself!'

Dorothy was already buoyed with the natural excitement of a premiere, and the encouragement of another woman considered a 'serious' composer meant a great deal to her. There *were* a number of other women composers scheduled in the Proms season, but because their contributions were popular songs with titles like 'There Are Fairies at the Bottom of Our Garden', they were ignored by the press. Unlike Dorothy's projects, these songs did not break the mould of what women were thought capable of achieving in music.

Unfortunately, once again Dorothy's style was held against her. *Koong Shee* has the same imaginative orchestration and feel for melody as *Lamia* – if Tchaikovsky had written a ballet on the Willow Pattern legend, it might have sounded similar. But in 1921, Dorothy wasn't being measured against Tchaikovsky. She was being judged against modern ballet composers: Stravinsky and his *Rite of Spring*, with its thundering, pulsating rhythms that had outraged Paris in 1913; Ravel's seductive, ethereal *Daphnis et Chloé*, premiered in 1912. And in both these cases, the choreography and staging had been as crucial as the music for the ballet's reception. Without an innovative staging, Dorothy's work couldn't compete. The reviews for *Koong Shee* were muted at best, sexist at worst: one dismissed it as having not a single 'note of originality', adding that Dorothy's talent was 'merely an imitative feminine gift'. This was a major setback. What should have been a triumph became a disaster. *Koong Shee* was never published, and to this day it has yet to receive a full staging.

o   o   o   o

While Dorothy was dealing with disappointment, Rebecca was still euphoric after the excitement of the Berkshire Festival. She sent a heartfelt note to Elizabeth Sprague Coolidge, telling her that the Sonata premiere 'was the most wonderful day I have ever had [. . .]. You have given me the greatest impetus to further work that anything possibly could.' And work she did. When she returned to

England in April 1920 her concert schedule resumed at a furious pace. Her mornings were spent composing, and the afternoons and evenings performing or rehearsing.

As she had done in New York, Rebecca booked herself a recital at London's Aeolian Hall at the end of May to premiere her Sonata. British critics were a little more reticent than the Americans about new music in general, but the Sonata nonetheless came off as a 'distinctly clever work'. Rebecca was at the forefront of modern composition in England, and reviewers were divided accordingly. The same critic who lambasted Dorothy's *Koong Shee* for having 'no novel outlook' was delighted by Rebecca's Sonata, but another scorned Rebecca's 'use and abuse of mannerisms'.

Three of Rebecca's songs were published during these years, and again the reviews were similarly mixed. Some called them 'distinguished work' that was both 'fragile and beautiful' – but the critic Ernest Newman, never one to mince words, decreed that her songs were an 'expert refurbishing of old clichés in a modern style or attempts at originality that were frustrated in almost every line', belonging to a large group of English works 'that ought never to have been made either visible or audible'. Rebecca had to learn to brush off unconstructive criticism.

In one respect, though, Rebecca was quite lucky: compared with Ethel and Dorothy, her gender was rarely mentioned explicitly in reviews. Perhaps it was because she wrote chamber works instead of orchestral music, the latter tending to attract more sensationalist journalism. Or possibly her anonymous leap to fame through a prestigious competition earned her a certain amount of critical respect. Whatever the reason, this was precisely how Rebecca wanted it. On one of the rare occasions that she gave a performance for the Society of Women Musicians and a speech was given about her, she wished the ground would swallow her up. 'Couldn't help wishing I wasn't either a woman or a musician,' she moaned bitterly.

Rebecca played with a staggering number of different groups and individuals during these years, learning a vast amount of repertoire at lightning speed. It was exhausting work, but so, so rewarding. She adored the social, personal, physical process of music-making. The dynamic in each group was unique, each individual giving a distinctive nuance to the music that they created together. For her next fixed ensemble, she joined violinists André Mangeot and Kenneth Skeaping, and of course the quirkily brilliant May provided the quartet's foundations on the cello. With a Byronic profile – sporting thick dark hair and an impossibly straight nose – André was the quartet's showman. He was passionate about contemporary composition, and threw himself with gusto into finding new works for them to play. Kenneth, the second violin, provided a gentle humour to balance André's intensity. Like Rebecca, he was personable and well liked, possessing a boundless energy. Rebecca was the emotional core of this group and May brought a touch of the unexpected; together the alchemy of their personalities seemed to work. They gave their first performance in June 1920 – 'everybody enthusiastic about our future'. Rebecca spent much of July in rehearsals with these three, sometimes for six hours straight, working tirelessly to maintain their impressive concert schedule.

As Rebecca's career flourished her family life grew less complicated. Her father had slipped further into the background to a point of near non-existence. He no longer had the power over her that he once did, and when she spotted his face in the audience at London concerts she wouldn't bother going to say hello. And although she was still technically exiled from the Harrow family home, she and Dora stayed with Agnes for months at a time when Joseph was away travelling. Occasionally May would spend the night, joining them for dinner and an evening of sewing, reading and playing music, before heading home the next morning with an enormous bunch of tulips from the garden. When Joseph returned, Rebecca and Dora would make a scrambled, speedy exit, bundling their suitcases into taxis to central London. Rebecca was travelling so much for work that she bounced between addresses, staying in Harrow or with London friends, never resting in one place for long. She didn't mind this 'jolly' nomadic existence, but balancing so much at the same time was still 'a great strain'.

Joseph had died in September 1920, his death bringing with it emotional and financial liberation. Rebecca's feelings towards him were complicated: she couldn't help but care for him a little, and she was sad to see the pain that his loss caused Agnes. And since she had been living in London, away from his immediate control, she had come to view her father with 'something almost like pity', realising how fully he had succeeded in alienating all his children. Nonetheless in many ways she had hated him, and his death, at least, made it much easier for her to see her mother. There would be no more sneaking to Gayton Corner. Agnes was free to live where she liked and she chose to move in with her two daughters, the three of them making a cosy home together in St John's Wood. It was the perfect spot – close to galleries for Dora and concert halls for Rebecca, and large enough that in the evening they could all relax in comfort, Rebecca sewing as Agnes (or 'Bartchy' as her children nicknamed her) read to them from her favourite books. And Regent's Park was close enough that Rebecca could go on long morning walks to compose, trying out all the ideas that had come to her on the piano when she returned.

Joseph's death had also left Rebecca with a basic income of $930 a year (around $13,000 today), which freed her from a great deal of her financial constraints. She could now afford to turn down some of the concerts that she really only agreed to for money, and concentrate instead on composition.

Amid all of this, Rebecca was mulling over ideas for her next big work. By October 1920 she was thinking ahead to the 1921 Coolidge Competition, and began sketching out ideas for her Piano Trio. Where the Sonata had flowed effortlessly, the Trio was a more laborious undertaking. 'Dismayed about my work, it doesn't seem to come these days, dash it all.' But this didn't last long. After a year of composition sessions punctuated by shopping trips and hat painting, she finally submitted the Trio in July 1921, 'really quite pleased with it'.

If the critics had considered the Sonata modern, they were in for a shock with the Trio. It was Rebecca's most experimental work yet – darker, more violent and far, far more dissonant than the Sonata had been. She may still have been influenced by Ravel and Debussy, but they never wrote anything as terrifying as this. It opens with a war cry, chords hammered out in the piano while the strings hold notes that clash forcefully against each other. The first movement has military horn calls dotted throughout it during moments of transition, played quietly on the piano as though signalling from far away, seeming to determine the music's direction.

The return to England in 1920 from the idyllic shores of Hawaii might have been quite a shock, coming back to find some friends and colleagues irreparably altered by the experience of war, others killed on active service. Perhaps the Trio was part of Rebecca's coming to terms with this changed world, consciously or unconsciously. She doesn't present any conclusions or answers – this is a contemplative, ambiguous work. The military horns come thundering back in the final movement, but they don't bring the Trio to a close. Instead they are met with a tense, reflective passage interrupted by an abrupt flourish that propels the work onwards. It feels almost as though the piece ends before its questions and problems are resolved, leaving a lingering air of unease after the final notes fade away.

Once again, Rebecca's piece came second in the Competition. The winning composer was in many ways more conventional than her, which perhaps swung the vote in his direction. But Rebecca was still pleased, and set about arranging a premiere to unleash the Trio on London audiences in the coming year.

o   o   o   o

Ethel and Edith spent three blissful spring months in Sicily in 1920. The trip wasn't without its hiccups, but rail strikes, lost luggage and chaotic hotels brought them closer together. At night they sat together and watched the stars, tracing the outline of the city's spires against the velvet sky. Mount Etna loomed, dominating the skyline. Ethel, burning with desire for Edith, saw the volcano's bubbling energy and unpredictable eruptions as a sexual metaphor for her feelings towards her travelling companion. Edith, trying to contain Ethel's ardour, preferred to imagine Etna's streams of molten lava as a metaphor for artistic creativity. By day the two of them would sit in gardens of abundant colour; Edith painted while Ethel sat by her side, smoking, clad in her tweeds and obligatory tricornered hat, impervious to the spring heat.

Ethel was so deliriously happy that it had to be too good to last. Travelling back home through Rome in May, she came down with influenza. Edith nursed her day and night, coaxing her back to health. Ethel's body recovered, but her hearing did not. By the time she got back to Coign the booming had returned, accompanied by an alarming noise like a sail flapping in the wind. And this time the noises thundered in both ears. Ethel was disconsolate, and immediately made plans to travel to Paris to see an ear specialist. Edith was her anchor throughout this period of heartrending anxiety, providing gentle solace and support. 'Thank you', Ethel wrote to her, for what 'you say I have in you. It remakes my life. Merely that.' She thought about Edith all day, whispered her name in bed before she went to sleep, and kept Martin's matchbox by her side at all times. Ethel lost herself fully in loving Edith.

Ethel promptly took matters in to her own hands after a few exasperating sessions with a specialist. She was convinced that creating more space in her sinuses would help, so she took herself off to a Parisian doctor to excavate bone from her nose, which left it 'raining blood'. She was desperate, prepared to try anything that might offer a sliver of hope. She simply couldn't imagine being shut off from her music or unable to keep up a conversation. This was the closest Ethel ever came to contemplating suicide, writing to Edith that 'when I think that you would be lonelier without me I say decidedly "yes ... I do want to live." For I believe I love you more than myself.'

Perhaps without Edith's prompts to keep composing, Ethel might have given it up entirely. Her 'music spirit' felt diminished. She believed that if she could just 'accept that my gift is gone – at least not gone but that I am hindered from using it – I can work out a happy & sane remnant of life'. But Edith knew that Ethel would fade without her work. Work 'is the core of ourselves', Ethel had once written to her. So she kept up her gentle encouragements.

In the meantime, Ethel turned to literature. After her years of campaigning, she had become catnip for newspaper editors looking for inflammatory opinions about the state of British opera. She turned out a five-part series putting forward an impassioned plea for state subsidy. Ethel's articles were reprinted in British presses as far afield as India and China, and they certainly had the intended effect of sparking debate. Her insistence that the situation in Germany was far superior to that in England was especially inflammatory, as it played on post-war insecurities about English identity and pride. Were English composers capable of competing with Italy or Germany? Was England a country that wanted to support art forms that were seen as foreign, and had a dubious class status? What kind of culture should the state be subsidising? In essence: what did the English want their culture to be?

Ethel was seen as English opera's greatest hope. Thanks to publicity from *Impressions*, English opera enthusiasts suddenly seemed to remember that they had in their midst a composer of four operas. Sections of both *The Wreckers* and *The Boatswain's Mate* were performed across the country and she conducted her own music at both the 1920 and 1921 Proms: Henry Wood knew that her celebrity drew a crowd. And Ethel did naturally what others might have done as publicity stunts. In the weeks running up to her Proms appearance she was photographed in her back garden, tweeds, tie, hat and all – conducting while tied to a tree, 'to discipline my muscles'. Her reputation as a loveable eccentric grew.

It wasn't just Ethel's operas that were getting more attention. Several of her works were dusted off for performance in 1920, including her String Quartet. A gala concert was held in her honour in November, featuring movements from the Quartet alongside her songs. The ladies attending took the opportunity to show off their luxurious gowns, the room filled with 'huge combs and fishtail trains', furs covering black evening dresses. Ethel donned the outfit of which she was proudest: her doctoral gown and cap. The cruel irony was that this uptake in interest came just a little too late. Listening to her own work being performed was one of Ethel's greatest joys, but she could hear little of her music's miniature revival.

Ethel may have finally been receiving the acclaim she deserved, but musical women's lives more broadly were not getting any easier. There had been some post-war gains: in 1919 the Sex Disqualification (Removal) Act was passed, allowing women to enter the civil service and legal professions. There were hints of a more open attitude towards sex and birth control in the wake of Marie Stopes's 1918 book *Married Love*, which tried to 'increase the joys of marriage' by teaching couples to have enjoyable sex.

But all of these were qualified triumphs. Women could only vote if they were over thirty and fulfilled various other criteria. The Sex Disqualification (Removal) Act was a watered-down substitution for a much more liberal Women's Emancipation Bill, which would have extended more significant rights to women. Sex could be discussed more openly, but only if it was in the context of marriage. Even Stopes framed marital pleasure as a service to country and government that ensured a stable family unit by reducing divorce numbers. And although women had taken on men's jobs while they fought at the Front, the assumption was that when the soldiers returned, women would go back to home and hearth.

Rather than put an end to debates about what women could be and do, World War I had simply shifted the goalposts. And in musical circles, women's increased visibility during the war led to pockets of protest. In October 1920, Hamilton Harty, the new conductor of the Hallé Orchestra in Manchester, dismissed every single one of the Orchestra's women players. Ethel took up arms on behalf of the ladies of the Hallé. She gave a furious speech condemning the decision as 'a cruel, wicked, and unfair thing'. Unfair it certainly was, but there were no legal grounds on which to challenge Harty's decision. A major loophole of the Sex Disqualification (Removal) Act was that it didn't extend to avenues of employment other than the legal and civil services. Orchestral women's careers were still dependent on the good will of the conductor. As usual Ethel's bluntness ignited the correspondence pages, and for several months the local presses were awash with opinions about women's relative merits and shortcomings as orchestral players. Despite Ethel's best efforts, the debate would rumble on for many years. Except for Henry Wood, conductors of national orchestras employed very few women, if any.

After Ethel's despondency over her ears, all this gunslinging perked her up considerably. She was arguing her way back to health, Edith supporting her the whole way. Their letters hadn't lost the gushing, almost giddy passion of their early love, their ardour heightened by living so far apart. But this was now combined with the easy familiarity of a long-term relationship. They knew each other inside out, affectionately coining Edith's bouts of insecurity as 'typical Edith', and Ethel's impassioned tirades at the slightest provocations as typical Ethel.

They saw each other when they could, but travel was difficult because Ireland was in the midst of its War of Independence, which started in 1919 after Sinn Féin's breakaway government declared political autonomy. Not only were rail strikes widespread, but the bridge outside Edith's home in Cork was blown up by Sinn Féin operatives. Edith made light of this, but war was tearing Ireland apart. The IRA sometimes intercepted her correspondence (prompting an occasional aside to the IRA in letters, lamenting that unbidden readers would probably 'die of boredom'), and when Edith wanted to update Ethel on the realities of the war she entrusted the letter to a friend to carry it in person. Edith and Ethel disagreed vehemently about Home Rule. Edith was passionately pro-independence, but Ethel, egged on by her military brother Bob, was belligerent about supporting English rule. She seemed incapable of understanding the complexities of Irish politics or the subsequent difficulties of Edith's daily life during the war. Edith avoided this impasse by slapping a ban on all political discussion.

Between exploded roads and orchestral arguments, Ethel and Edith were the busiest they had ever been. Ethel had been writing throughout 1920 and her new book *Streaks of Life*, a collection of essays, was published in March 1921. Some essays were biographical sketches of her friends, others dealt with the opera problem and women in orchestras. As with *Impressions*, *Streaks* got rave reviews (even if some readers were disappointed that it wasn't an autobiographical account of her suffragette days). And now, music was calling to Ethel again. She had been mulling over an idea for a new opera for months: a comedy based on a short story by Maurice Baring. She had so far felt unable to commit anything to paper, but by December 1921 she could finally tell Edith that she had begun composing again. Edith was overjoyed. 'The "crust" is broken and that you are again "stepping down to the deep wells of light"' – bringing forth Ethel's fifth opera, *Fête Galante*.

THE ROARING TWENTIES

The disappointment of *Koong Shee*'s bad reviews hit Dorothy hard. Until now she had received relatively constant public affirmation and praise, and without it she doubted herself and her music. 'Don't bother your head about any of it,' McEwen tried to reassure her – 'steer your own course & think only of your own development.' But Dorothy found it almost impossible to banish critical words from her mind. They invaded her thoughts whenever she tried to compose. She needed a mentor to spur her on – and so she turned to Ethel, who had been so encouraging before the premiere. Ethel let Dorothy know she had been advocating for *Koong Shee*, reminding her that the only way to get performances was 'to <u>pester</u>' conductors. In response Dorothy poured out her heart to Ethel, admitting her fear that, only a few years out of the Academy, she was about to be buried as a relic. Struggling with a lack of performances and feeling outdated was a feeling Ethel knew well. 'Don't think for a second that *Koong Shee* & you are antiquities,' she responded. 'If one goes on, undismayed by these firework-fabricators, trying to express one's thought as one feels it in one's own language it is <u>quite sure</u> to be wanted by those who feel as one does oneself.'

Ethel tried to be as practical as possible, and strongly encouraged Dorothy to diversify her portfolio and take up conducting. 'You must cling to each rung of the ladder,' she explained. Henry Wood also put in a plea, offering Dorothy a conducting slot at the 1925 Proms if she took classes at the Royal Academy. But she would not be swayed. She didn't like to be on display, or to strike out in an area in which she felt inexpert. The fact that one of the very reasons that Henry wanted her to conduct was the complete lack of women in the Academy's conducting class probably only contributed to her resolve. She wanted all attention to be on her music rather than on her, and even when papers ran features she would advise them to 'talk for most of the column, and then bring me in casually at the end', signing off with a brief 'Excuse haste; I have to get on with my trumpets and trombones.'

Rather than 'pestering', as Ethel put it, Dorothy went on giving performances where she could, hoping that her music would make its own way in the world. She gave London concerts at sought-after venues, but her heart really lay in provincial performance. One of her favourite places to play was Birmingham Town Hall, a building that felt homely to Dorothy despite its colonnades, ornate ceilings and cavernous auditorium. Another was Netherton Public Hall, just a few miles west, where she delighted audiences with Chopin and some favourites from her own compositions, often giving her services for free to help raise money for good causes.

The local press rewarded Dorothy for her loyalty, covering her performances extensively and lavishing her with praise. But as Dorothy had once pointed out herself, pianists were easy to come by. It was almost impossible to make a living from performance without an international reputation. Again, her reluctance to spend time away from her family put limits on her career. Nonetheless, now she was a famous composer, local support provided her with confidence when she felt disillusioned with composition.

Dorothy's music for children, at least, was nationally embraced. By the 1920s the UK had a vast, institutionalised network of music-making aimed at children that is still in place today, from Associated Board exams to music festivals which ran competitions for students. With their sprightly tunes and unconventional harmonies, Dorothy's piano pieces and small choral works made perfect test pieces for the festivals. By the middle of the 1920s children up and down the country were making their first tentative steps onto the concert stage, dressed in their Sunday best, playing her music.

With her usual generosity, Dorothy sometimes adjudicated these classes and motivated her young interpreters, gently reminding them that 'Imagination was the most important thing', and 'what mattered was the meaning behind the music'. Teaching was one of her great gifts – certainly one that Ethel never possessed. Dorothy had a wonderful way of making children feel encouraged, even when her feedback and teaching methods were both strict and uncompromising.

It took Dorothy a full year to put *Koong Shee* behind her, but by 1922 the memory of the reviews was distant enough that she could turn her attention to a large work again. She returned to where she felt safest – a fantasy piece for her own instrument, which she had begun sketching just before *Lamia*. She had the main theme, a horn call beckoning like a summons from the distant past. The shades and colours of sound begin to change as the strings respond, shimmering in gentle ripples underneath the horns. Harmonies shift as the orchestra moves into a dance, gathering momentum for the piano's opening flourish which immediately turns the dance into a drama, the lone pianist navigating their way through a treacherous musical landscape. From this opening idea the rest of the piece slowly began to flow, Dorothy working consistently at her piano until the final notes had fallen into place. In its final form, the fantasy work was her single-movement Piano Concerto, an epic playing out in twenty minutes of unbroken music.

Almost the day when Dorothy finished the Concerto, she received a commission for a Phantasy for Violin and Pianoforte – only £10, but nonetheless from a well-known and prestigious awarding body. 'Have of course accepted this honour!' she noted. In the wake of this commission she sent off the Concerto score to Henry Wood, and he accepted it for a Proms performance without hesitation. Her stomach churning with nerves, Dorothy returned to the familiar Queen's Hall for the world premiere on 23 August 1923 – but this time rather than being able to hide away in the audience, she was stepping out as the soloist in her own work. The audience embraced Dorothy's Concerto unreservedly, recalling her to the stage five times.

A month later she was on the Proms platform again to take her bows at a repeat performance of *Lamia* – and this time one of the enthusiastic applauders was Ethel, who turned up to support her. The two women had corresponded sporadically for the last two years, but this was the first time that they met. In her characteristic way Ethel invaded the Artists' Room after the performance to embrace Dorothy and shower her with compliments about the work. During a period when Dorothy's faith in her own abilities was so precarious, Ethel's buoyant and unmitigated enthusiasm was a tonic she desperately needed.

It had taken Ethel forty years to ignore reviewers – Dorothy was not yet at that stage, still anxiously poring over the papers. But the press judged the Concerto to be 'full of life and spirit', with some 'unusually ingenious' moments. Dorothy cut these positive words out of the papers to read whenever she needed reassurance.

o   o   o   o

Although Ethel had begun composing again, it was 'without a shred of inspiration & with almost physical distaste'. The booming in her ears killed 'all impulse to write'. Nonetheless, she was determined not to let her music slip away without a fight. Ignoring the pain from her arthritis, using all her energy to drown out the noises and imagine the music she knew she still had in her, Ethel composed. She set down the first notes of *Fête Galante* just a few days before Christmas 1921, tucked up at her great oak desk with Pan II by her side. He, too, was growing old now, his muzzle greying, and he was quite content to lollop by the fire rather than face the frost-covered firs dominating the view from Ethel's window.

Fête Galante was unlike anything Ethel had ever written before. It has some similarities to *Fantasio*, being another story of mistaken identities and courtly games of love. But it has a far more sinister undertone than her earlier opera. It's set in a romantic moonlit garden with *commedia dell'arte* characters, but danger runs through this idyllic setting. The plot hinges around Pierrot seeing the Queen with a lover, and the opera ends with Pierrot, sentenced to death because of his refusal to name the Queen's lover and thus dishonour her, killing himself to avoid being murdered. He stabs himself as a dance swirls around him. Even so, he cannot escape the ending he most fears – the final curtain falls in front of his body hanging from a beam centre-stage. More disturbing still is the gentle chorus that succeeds his demise – the same that opens the opera. The world, it seems, is indifferent to Pierrot's fate. After his death everything continues almost as before.

Maurice's play has a coolness and detachment that's markedly different from the romance of *Wreckers* or the silliness of *Boatswain*, and Ethel changed her musical style accordingly. Gone are her sweeping melodies and vast orchestrations, replaced with refined, courtly dances straight from the eighteenth century, written for a small ensemble. Partly, this was a practical move. Ethel was sick of being told her operas were 'too big' or 'too expensive' to stage. This time she was going to write an opera small enough that amateur and touring companies could stage it, so it couldn't possibly be refused with that excuse.

But Ethel was also moving with the times. In 1920 the trend-setting Ballets Russes had devised the pioneering ballet *Pulcinella*, which combined sets by Picasso with stock Italian *commedia dell'arte* characters and a neoclassical score by Stravinsky. There were some modern trends that Ethel flatly refused to embrace, but her imagination was fired by neoclassicism and its promise of aristocratic flirtation and forbidden pleasures. She filled her score with sprightly, elegant music, and it was the first of her operas to incorporate several extended dances, to the extent that she subtitled it 'A Dance-Dream in One Act'.

Composition was interrupted by an extremely welcome letter arriving on 21 December, informing Ethel that she was to become a Dame Commander of the British Empire. Once again her name was emblazoned across the newspapers. She was now 'not only the greatest British composer, but the greatest woman composer of the world'. She was applauded for her perseverance despite being 'a musical prophet without honour in her country'. The furore surrounding her DBE was so widespread that Ethel even had to politely decline a request from a young woman who wanted her to adopt her three-year-old child, whom she was certain was 'a musical genius'. But for one normally so concerned with status and honours, Ethel was curiously ambivalent about the damehood. It was all, she felt, a little too late. When the time came to meet the King she thought it all underwhelming, most concerned that the pin shouldn't damage her precious doctoral robes.

But Ethel used the publicity from the DBE to whip up support. She fired off a letter to the *Daily Mail* pointing out that although she was one of the most famous women in Britain, her music was still repeatedly rejected by decision committees for the UK's big annual music festivals. Now in her sixties, with an established reputation and her hearing deteriorating, she was too tired of discrimination to keep up appearances. 'For 30 years I have vainly hoped that some work of mine might be accepted for performance at one of the great provincial musical festivals,' she wrote. 'It has not happened yet.'

The *Daily Mail* embarked on a minor campaign to get Dame Ethel's pieces performed. It worked. Flooded with letters from angry readers, conductors grudgingly included Ethel's music on their programmes, starting with a big orchestral concert at the Royal Albert Hall. And finally, Ethel got a foot in the door at the Leeds Musical Festival. Wearing a dazzling gold brocade gown with a fur-trimmed black coat, Ethel took to the podium to conduct the well-received *Hey Nonny No*, sending the chorus into fits of laughter when she gave them their first line at the rehearsal with a wry smile: 'Men are fools.'

She put the finishing touches on *Fête Galante* in May 1922. The macabre, sensual brutality of *Hey Nonny* had been on Ethel's mind, and she wove references to it through Pierrot's final moments. Where she had revelled in completing *Wreckers* and *Boatswain*, *Fête Galante* was finished to very little fanfare. 'Now it's done,' she put simply in her diary. Edith reassured Ethel that 'it is going to be a perfectly lovely thing & a triumph, & I am <u>longing</u> to hear it is a Fête accompli (<u>French joke, quite impromptu</u>)'. At least the damehood meant that securing a premiere was no longer a battle. This time, it was Ethel who snubbed Covent Garden, choosing instead to give the first performance to the Birmingham Repertory Theatre in June 1923 in a double bill with *Boatswain*, with a London performance following a week later. Sadly, the opera was not quite a *fête accompli*, with a few reviewers expressing reservations that Ethel's music was 'frequently on the point of over-weighing the fantasy'.

By this point, however, Ethel had given up on reading her press notices. Let the critics say what they would – she would carry on regardless. *Fête Galante* unleashed a torrent of creativity, and just a few weeks later Ethel was moving gleefully on to a new opera. 'I've written a divine Libretto called <u>Entente Cordiale</u> & am composing it – greatest fun!', she enthused. *Entente* went back to the familiar comic territory of *Boatswain*, which was still her most popular opera by a wide margin. It's a farce focused on British soldiers in France during World War I, full of blunders and puns and slapstick humour, designed to provide the light comic relief that Ethel and her postwar audiences so desperately craved. She continued in the neoclassical vein, this time harnessing airy classical forms for comedy rather than tragedy, peppering her score with Gilbert and Sullivan-esque flourishes, and the military calls that she remembered from her childhood. *Entente* would be dedicated 'To my own branch – the Army', a rollicking salute to her family's past that would stave off the misery of her booming ears during the cold winter days.

o o o o

From the cupola over the Wigmore Hall stage, the Soul of Music gazed down on Myra, May and Marjorie as they stepped out to share Rebecca's Trio with London audiences. Flanked by female embodiments of Love and Psyche, Music, naked, holds aloft a blazing gold orb of eternal fire representing Harmony, shining enlightenment on to all who come into its sphere. But the path to Music is not without barriers. He is ensnared by thick vines of brambles that keep humanity from Harmony in its purest, most abstract form. The metaphor must have felt particularly apt to those sat in the velvet seats trying to make sense of Rebecca's barbed, aggressive piece, watching the lights cast unpredictable sparks from the performers' gowns and instruments as they threw themselves into her music. They paired it with Ravel's Trio, which seemed tame by comparison. Clarke's Trio was 'really brilliant', the papers raved afterwards, showing her to be 'a frank disciple of modernity'. Publication would follow later. It was the kind of reception that Dorothy dreamed of. At the after-party at Myra's house, Rebecca dined on praise and cocktails, overwhelmed by congratulations.

She didn't stop to revel for long, however, and was soon back at her piano, composing. The Trio seems to have unlocked something in Rebecca. Over the coming decade, she wrote some of her most dark and impassioned pieces. In November 1921 she began work on 'The Seal Man', a song of fatal desire, told from the perspective of a woman who goes to her death following her lover into the sea.

This was neither the calm sea that Dorothy liked to envisage, nor the mysterious ocean of Ethel's 1913 orchestral songs *Three Moods of the Sea*, nor even the violent but predictable waters of *The Wreckers*. Rebecca's sea is ominous and forbidding, pulsing and smouldering with sexual energy. She uses the very lowest registers of the piano to represent it – a kind of ghostly groaning at the bottom of the instrument. The singer has to struggle to be heard over the tempest of the piano part as she describes how the sea becomes 'a flame before them', and their love 'a great love like the love of the Old Ones'. The physicality of the piece is extraordinary. Pianist and singer have to be a single unit, pianist listening intensely to the nuances of the singer's breath and singer watching the pianist's every expression to make sure they keep together. Lose each other even for a second and the song will fall apart. Finally, Rebecca rips away the piano at the revelation that the man 'wasn't a man at all', the sudden silence driving home the shock of this macabre twist in the tale. Nowhere is it more apparent that Rebecca felt music and sex were two sides of the same coin.

As soon as 'The Seal Man' was edited, Rebecca could turn her attention to an even larger project. Following her success in the Berkshire Festivals, Elizabeth Coolidge had presented her with a $1,000 ($14,000 today) commission for a cello rhapsody, the only piece Elizabeth ever commissioned from a woman. Rebecca began work in March 1922, composing in a friend's flat for peace and quiet while they were away in Vienna. The Rhapsody took a while to come to her, but by November she was 'getting quite pleased' with the progress she had made. The first movement inhabits a similar sound world to 'The Seal Man', sinister and disconcerting. Glimpses of the melodiousness she had cultivated in the Viola Sonata sometimes shimmer through the texture, but they're quickly submerged again into the gloom.

Composition, though, would have to wait, because in December Rebecca set off for a concert tour with May and Ariantje that would take them to Sri Lanka, India, Singapore, Malaysia, Myanmar, China and Japan. An Asian tour like this was unusual. Even in a world where foreign travel was considered obligatory for the upper classes, British travellers more regularly went to Europe, Africa or America than Asia. Only the best and most intrepid performers would have bothered undertaking such a long journey.

Aboard the ship that would take her from Paris to Sri Lanka,

Rebecca filled her days with bridge, dancing, teas, cocktails and evening walks along the deck 'to cool off & look at the stars & moon & phosphorescence'. Having taken dance classes with Dora in London especially in preparation, Rebecca 'danced the New Year in', foxtrotting the night away in the smoke-filled, cocktail-fuelled ship's ballroom until midnight, when one of her friends 'burst through a paper screen', showering the dancers with confetti to a round of wild applause welcoming 1923.

Rebecca had dreamed of travelling to Asia since she was a little girl in her small room in Harrow. Now, she saw elephants in Sri Lanka and monkeys in Jaipur, and was enchanted by the peacocks and parrots populating the Amber Palace that she rode to on the back of an elephant. She struggled to fully record her experience in the small space of her engagement diary, jotting down only the briefest of impressions – 'Brilliant green rice-fields, palms, cocoa, coffee, tamarind trees', hibiscus and 'brilliant sarongs against the red earth, & the green trees' in Sri Lanka, 'Glorious scenes & singing-birds everywhere, chiefly bulbuls' in Penang.

Best of all was visiting the Taj Mahal by moonlight, which Rebecca thought the 'Most beautiful thing in the world & most touching'. And everywhere in the cities of India and China, she inhaled the warm scents of jasmine and hibiscus with pleasure. She had been saving the payment from her Viola Sonata publication for a special occasion, and in Jaipur she finally found 'a small but lovely pearl necklace! Very thrilled.' And she gave concerts almost nightly, with responses ranging from 'general indifference' to 'a splendid success'.

As she had in Hawaii and at the World Fair, Rebecca soaked up the sounds of the new world around her. She was intrigued by the music that she heard in Hindu temples, but as always she was more drawn to everyday sounds. She was given an impromptu drumming lesson in Kolkata, and sailing from Malaysia to Myanmar she was surrounded by Burmese citizens playing 'native instruments, & it mingles with the voices [of] sailors chanting', and the sounds of 'cooking apparatus & children'. Ashore in Yangon, it was the 'balls that tinkle in the wind' hanging from pagodas that left the deepest impression.

Flooded with new possibilities for harmonies, rhythms, timbres and resonances, Rebecca was desperate to compose, but with their packed travel itinerary there was simply no time to set down a single note. It wasn't until May 1923, when they arrived in Beijing for twenty days, that she was in the same place for long enough to order a piano to her room. 'I have missed my work so awfully all this time,' she confessed, spending every available morning moment at the keyboard working on the Rhapsody. The creeping cello line that opens the second movement has all the menace of the crocodiles she saw in Jaipur, while the fragile accompanying piano part sounds almost like a memory of those Burmese chimes. But writing was interrupted, again, by the tour schedule, and when the piano was removed from her room Rebecca 'felt as though I had lost a friend'.

The trio finally came to the end of its six-month tour in Tokyo, sailing to Honolulu with the blessings of a 'most enthusiastic' audience. In Hawaii the friends and listeners who remembered them from their 1918 trip showered them with flowers at concerts they gave by special request. Exhausted and triumphant, Rebecca finally settled at a friend's ranch on Molokai in July, where she alternated watching the cowboys ('fine-looking chaps') with intense work on the Rhapsody.

She was now composing every day with her imagination fired by the tour. Within a month the first draft was ready to share with May, who would give the premiere with Myra. With a twenty-five-minute running time, it was Rebecca's longest work to date, and by far her most forbidding – both in tone and in difficulty. Rebecca was delighted with it. 'Am so glad I have taken my time over it, as I am sure it is much better than if I had hurried.' She wrote eagerly to Elizabeth to tell her the commission was complete; 'some of my best work'. The coming weeks would be spent buried in rehearsal with May and Myra, preparing the Rhapsody for its unveiling in the Berkshire hills, where she would be the only woman to have a work performed at the Festival.

o   o   o   o

On a cold, dry night in November 1922, the words 'This is 2LO, Marconi House, London calling' made their way into British homes for the first time. Nearly twenty thousand families gathered curiously around their new radio sets to hear the BBC's first broadcast news bulletin. Some were gathered around the fire and dressed in gowns and dinner jackets. Others only just got in on time, out of breath, still in travelling clothes, having cut short afternoon visits especially just to tune in. Whether they knew it or not, these pioneering listeners were witnessing a historic moment that would change British entertainment for good. From its minimal origins with just four employees, the BBC would grow to become the national British broadcaster, accumulating more than five million listeners in its first decade. They would provide news in war, comedy during peace-time, and dramas that gripped the entire nation. And throughout all of it, of course, there would be music.

Broadcasting changed all musicians' lives, whether they were opera divas or dance-hall singers. The radio was a mixed blessing: it offered musicians larger audiences than they had ever dreamed of, but the BBC monopoly meant that its patronage was vital. Without radio slots, musicians would struggle to make a name for themselves at all. So when Dorothy was invited to give a broadcast concert in February 1923, she didn't hesitate. Sheltering from one of the wettest Februaries on record, listeners tuned in to hear her performance from the Wesleyan Chapel in Biggleswade, interspersed with the news, songs and cello music.

Over the coming years Dorothy would appear on multiple programmes, particularly on *The Children's Hour* at 5 p.m. The show combined stories and music and proved extremely popular, providing tired parents with the welcome relief of a regular hour of ready-made entertainment. Dorothy's light-hearted piano pieces made excellent material for it, from the 'Paper Boat' in *Pieces for the Bairns* to the 'Half a Pound of Butter' in *A-Shopping We Will Go*.

The BBC's first General Manager John Reith saw its mission as being to 'inform, educate, and entertain'. Informing and educating were foremost, directing the BBC's sometimes high-minded attitude towards programming in its early years. From the start the BBC tried to project an air of authority, even insisting that anonymous newsreaders wear dinner jackets while broadcasting. Its ongoing attempts to balance entertainment and betterment often made their programming choices feel frustratingly opaque to those outside the organisation. 'It is all a world of mystery to me,' a perplexed Ethel confided to Dorothy.

In the 1920s the barometer swung in the direction of 'education', so once adult listeners had sent their children off to bed, they also got to hear Dorothy as both pianist and composer in her more 'serious' guise. As they enjoyed an after-dinner brandy or cup of tea, households across Britain tuned in to Dorothy performing her own *Spindrift*, *Humoresque* or *Toccata* for piano, and occasionally caught her chamber works like *Rosalind*. Because of her tuneful style, she fitted the remit of 'light' music that was both contemporary and popular with listeners, and this made her a useful choice for early evening programmes. A more significant platform came in March 1925, when an entire concert dedicated to Dorothy's music was broadcast, mixing songs with piano and chamber music to give a varied showcase of her work. Being accorded this kind of recognition at just twenty-seven years old was a formidable achievement for any composer.

This was followed by two broadcasts dedicated entirely to women composers, which put Ethel, Rebecca and Dorothy all on the same radio programme for the first time. They were, by now, widely recognised as the three most significant women composers working in Britain – when a guide to contemporary British composers was published in 1925, they were the only three women featured.

Naturally, then, when the BBC wanted to exhibit women's musical efforts, the corporation turned to their music. Rebecca's song 'Shy One' was programmed next to Dorothy playing her own Piano Concerto, Ethel leading the Wireless Symphony Orchestra in the 'Cliffs of Cornwall' and Overture from *The Wreckers*, and works by three lesser-known composers: Muriel Herbert, Ivy Clayton and Amy Woodforde-Finden. Thanks to a conductor called Dan Godfrey – the only conductor apart from Henry Wood whom Ethel credited with truly supporting women's work – this 1925 broadcast was built on two years later with a women's orchestral concert at Bournemouth Festival, which put both Dorothy and Ethel alongside big orchestral pieces by rising stars Susan Spain-Dunk, Vivien Lambelet, Dora Bright and Edith Swepstone. The number of women composers in Britain was steadily increasing, and even though there were still fewer of them than their male counterparts, by the 1920s it was easy to programme an orchestral concert featuring only music by British women and have plenty of choice for pieces.

Reflecting in her diary, Ethel noted that 'The finest thing [. . .] I have heard for ages was Dorothy Howell's Piano Concerto, beautifully played by herself. Newspapers of course utterly patronising & infuriating about it.' Sadly, Ethel was right. Lamenting that the concert left them unable to make 'profound generalizations about feminine music' beyond 'a tendency towards topography', one criticised the Concerto for being 'neither very original nor very deep'. It was merely 'a sincere piece of competent work tinged with imagination'. It probably didn't help that reviewers heard the concerto as part of an all-woman programme. In the 1920s these were something of a necessary evil – they were intended as a gesture to raise awareness of women's music – but at the same time by separating music written by women from men's, they reinforced the idea that it was in some way 'different' or 'other', encouraging essentialisation.

Dorothy pictured in the 1920s.

All the same, with three years of successful broadcasts behind her, Dorothy was granted a spot in the BBC's 1926 Spring Concert series at the Chenil Gallery in Chelsea, which introduced 'new or unfamiliar works of merit'. In a programme that also featured Vaughan Williams, Dorothy's contribution was the world premiere of her *Nocturne for String Orchestra*. Short and reserved, the mysterious, muted *Nocturne* moved away from the ebullient Concerto into a calmer, more introspective world. It was a piece perfectly suited to late-night radio. Her hair now cut into a short shingle bob, Dorothy donned her most fashionable dress to fit in with the chic clique who frequented the various art galleries along the King's Road. She sat among the paintings annotating her programme as she always did, commenting on the players and noting down small alterations she wanted to make to her work. The critics wasted few words, labelling the *Nocturne* 'colourful and workmanlike' and 'musicianly and chaste', whatever that meant.

These casual platitudes set Dorothy's compositional self-belief back again. She retreated into teaching at the Royal Academy, where she had been appointed as Professor of Composition in 1924. Dorothy stood out among the older and entirely male composition staff, looking almost young enough to be a student. She made friends instead among the instrumental tutors. She bonded especially with a violinist called Elsie Owen; they enjoyed the same kind of clothes, music and magazines, sported matching bobs, and took up cinema and shopping trips in Marylebone after teaching. It would be some time before Dorothy regained the confidence to put a major new work before the public.

o   o   o   o

After the excitement of the *Fête Galante* premiere, in 1924 Birmingham hosted another major milestone in Ethel's career: the revival of her Mass, untouched since its premiere in 1893. Ethel was now so famous that her earlier works were being increasingly sought out, especially for first performances outside the capital. So on 7 February hordes of curious listeners crowded into the Town Hall to finally hear something by the famous woman whose books they had enjoyed and whose name was so familiar from the papers.

Ethel had waited for this moment for thirty-one years, and was determined it would be a success. All work on *Entente Cordiale* was put on hold to allow her to oversee (or, from the conductor's perspective, interfere with) the rehearsals, constantly adjusting the tempo. The conductor in question was an upcoming talent called Adrian Boult, who would become an increasingly important figure in all British composers' lives over the coming decades, especially after he was appointed the BBC's Director of Music. Disagreements with Ethel's conducting advice aside, Boult felt that her Mass's 'power and beauty impress me more and more every time I touch it'. The revival of the Mass was his first step towards becoming quite an advocate for Ethel's music.

1893 had not been the right time for Ethel's Mass. Then, the musical world was too conservative, and she was too unknown to have the critics accept a work that large and unconventional. But English society – and Ethel's place in it – had changed beyond recognition by 1924. This time, the Mass was welcomed without reservation. Reviewers were stunned by the 'novelty of the outlook, the intense earnestness' of the piece, praising it as 'extraordinarily beautiful in its gradually growing intensity'.

This did prompt, at least, a little sheepish self-reflection from critics. Put in the *Daily Mail*'s characteristically blunt style, the Mass's revival exposed 'British musical leaders of that time as stupid and unjust. Was, then, England so rich in original music in the 1890's that they could afford to cold-shoulder such a manifest talent?' Conductors, at least, seemed prepared to make up for lost time, and multiple performances of the Mass were scheduled in venues from the Royal Albert Hall to Gloucester Cathedral, where Ethel became the first woman ever to have a work performed.

The 'glorious resuscitation', as Ethel called it, was one of the greatest comforts of her later years. Encroaching arthritis prohibited golf and tennis, and without these distractions she spent long periods of time reflecting on her past. She was increasingly fearful about her legacy and filled her diary with catalogues of past resentments, fixating on the might-have-beens prevented by bad luck, systemic prejudice or, as she believed, personal vendettas. At other times she singled out ebullient press statements that gave her some hope that she might go down in history as a 'great' composer. Her deepest fear was having no control or influence over the fate of her music. She could not bear the thought of being forgotten.

Death was becoming an everyday part of Ethel's life. In the space of a few years she lost both her sister Violet, and Emmeline Pankhurst. Although Ethel and Emmeline had drifted apart, when she died Ethel penned pages of reminiscences and furious outbursts in her diary, convinced that 'this death might have been prevented'. 'I think she is the greatest woman that has ever lived,' Ethel wrote sadly. Violet's passing was much more visceral – Ethel saw her just days before she died from agonising cirrhosis. 'There never was a greater tragedy,' Ethel lamented. And then came the death of Pan II, put to sleep while Ethel was away at a concert. Ethel couldn't forgive herself for being absent at the last. 'Often in the first days I wished I could die. The thought of it all happening when I was away [. . .] was intolerable.' Worst of all was returning to an empty house, without the reassuring welcome of bounding, panting hair that had greeted her in the hallway every day for the last eleven years. 'Nothing can, in the nature of things, go so near to one living as I do as the death of your dog,' Ethel admitted. 'I can hardly bear life without him.'

Unable to be without her dog, after a fortnight Ethel brought home a new puppy, Pan III, expecting that he would 'probably be the last of my series – see me out!' And she tried to fill her life with people who made her feel younger. In 1925 she set off for Greece with her great-niece Elizabeth Williamson. Ethel had been one of the guiding forces in Elizabeth's life, supporting her desire to study. Elizabeth explained to Ethel that 'When I first grew up you made me see what sort of life I really wanted', taking courage from her great-aunt's single-minded dedication to her career. Elizabeth followed in Ethel's footsteps, studying at university and going on to become an astronomer at University College London. She brought energy to Ethel's life, disagreeing robustly with her about the merits of *Paradise Lost* and enthusing wildly about her great-aunt's music. Ethel so valued their Greek holiday that she penned a travel book about it a year later, finished off while she was visiting Edith at Drishane.

Ethel with Pan III, 1927.

Feeling her mortality keenly gave Ethel a renewed sense of urgency. *Entente Cordiale* was finished in record time. Ethel conducted the premiere, broadcast from the Royal College of Music only a month after she finished orchestrating the full score. She had correctly gauged the national mood, and her libretto was deemed 'a capital idea for a farce' which produced 'the homeliest little piece' – not that Ethel read her reviews.

To have broadcast anything comprehensible was nothing short of a miracle. The performance took place during a terrific summer thunderstorm, and early radio broadcasting was so haphazard that halfway through Ethel noticed 'that a stream of water was issuing from beneath my little chair'. Ethel kept conducting as a caretaker tried to control the levels from rising past the players' toes, bailing water out with a bucket. All in all, Ethel thought it was 'Great fun', and joined the players in applauding themselves 'frantically' to give the impression that the broadcast was taking place with a live audience.

Depending on the state of her hearing Ethel fluctuated between despondency and stoicism. Just before Christmas 1925 she feared that 'I shall never compose again' because 'My ears make life too intolerable & make me dread any sort of enterprise needing ears to application.' But by New Year's Eve she was composing a set of variations, 'just to see if I can master the ear-disturbances'. Where she had previously composed at her desk, only using the piano for reference, now she worked out her music at the keyboard first to drown out the booming.

She was rewarded almost immediately with the hints and flickers of tunes that she could craft into a new work – the Concerto for Violin, Horn and Orchestra. It opens with such an energetic, joyful motif that this could almost be the Ethel of her Serenade days, standing before her audience for the very first time, full of excitement. The first movement is infused with a true wistfulness, but the beating heart of the work is its second movement, which

Ethel publicly titled 'Elegy'. Privately, she also gave it a subtitle from Goethe's *Faust*: 'Thou shalt forgo, shalt do without.' She poured into it the anguish of loss, of intense loneliness, of having the only things that gave her life meaning stripped from her – but facing them all with resignation and grace.

Illness delayed the third movement, but when she returned to it after a few months Ethel was able to produce one of the most frolicking, buoyant pieces she ever composed. It's certainly the most entertaining of the three movements, and reviewers enjoyed its 'quips and outbursts of high spirits'. But on the whole, the Concerto flummoxed the critics. It was just too personal. Multiple listens are needed to really get past the surface.

While Ethel composed, honours and acclaim continued to rain down upon her. Following in Durham's footsteps, in 1926 the University of Oxford awarded Ethel an honorary doctorate. She was 'delighted', but nonetheless 'everything comes too late'. Her ears were worsening again, and she began to despair, admitting that 'this perpetual noise is mastering me'.

But her seventieth birthday fell in 1928, and her friends and supporters were determined to help her make it a jubilee to remember. She conducted her own works in Bristol, Edinburgh and Cheltenham, the newspapers noting that no matter how popular the other male conductors were, 'their reception was not so great as that accorded to Dame Ethel Smyth'. Another of her books was published to great critical acclaim, this time a collection of essays on the theme of gender prejudice, and after she had received a third honorary doctorate, from St Andrews University, Ethel was able to sit beside Queen Mary in a box at the Royal Albert Hall to watch a performance of her Mass.

The experience was bittersweet. All Ethel's life she had longed for this recognition, and now when it came she struggled to make out any of her own notes at all. Her family and friends raised nearly £600 for her to go to Berlin to become the first woman to conduct the Berlin Philharmonic, leading a concert dedicated entirely to her music. Dressed in her doctoral gown, Ethel conducted her Concerto, *Sleepless Dreams* and *Hey Nonny No*. When she turned to face the audience she saw they had left their seats to crowd round the stage, applauding her and calling her to the platform over and over again to take a bow. Ethel tried not to let her emotion show, but this year meant more to her than nearly anything else in her career. It was the first time that she truly felt the acceptance she had fought for her entire life.

o   o   o   o

Even before the Rhapsody premiere came to its close, Rebecca could feel that something was different. The audience were shuffling in their unforgiving wooden pews, glancing out of the window to bask in the final rays of sunshine, rustling their programmes. The applause, when it came, was muted. 'Some of her sincerest admirers may think that she is not following a promising path,' wrote the *New York Times*, declaring the Rhapsody 'very gloomy'. Rebecca had been so sure – was still sure – that this was one of her finest works, and yet it was her first piece that the audience did not immediately 'get'.

The premiere left her 'very depressed'. Unlike Dorothy, however, she faced her critics with resolve, concluding that 'it is very good for me to have a failure'. Besides, Elizabeth loved the Rhapsody and was still happy to be the piece's dedicatee. 'The chief thing I feel is gratitude to you for your interest in me,' Rebecca told her. Nonetheless, she withheld her piece from publication. It remained in manuscript until 2020.

Rebecca decided to go and stay with Myra for a while in New York to recharge. They took long afternoon walks together, overlooking seas of auburn trees with autumn mists swirling around them, mulling over Rebecca's future and drawing up shortlists of potential performers for 'The Seal Man'. In the evenings Myra practised Beethoven and Bach for her concerts, Rebecca listening through with the scores to offer feedback. She resolved to make the Rhapsody disappointment an incentive to try something new. Travelling around the States to visit family and friends before returning to England, she set to writing some folk song arrangements, 'Trying to write absolutely simply for a bit of practice.' Rebecca's instincts were right – with their jovial combination of voice and violin, her folk songs would be some of her most enduringly popular pieces.

Then came a short violin piece, *Midsummer Moon*, which sits far away from the terrifying sound of the Rhapsody. The violin glides over the piano part like summer moonlight on a clear night, rippling on the surface of the sea in Hawaii or creating shadows in the Taj Mahal's curves and crevices as it advances across the sky. *Midsummer Moon* was immediately published by Oxford University Press alongside Rebecca's most explicitly orientalist piece, an earlier violin work from 1921 called *Chinese Puzzle*. It was the only time she attempted to mimic the sound of Chinese music, perhaps copying the musicians she heard in Hawaii, and she based it on a tune that a Chinese family friend had hummed to her.

Dora designed prints for the cover, and both pieces were premiered by Adila. Having criticised Rebecca for writing a Rhapsody that was long and difficult, the critics welcomed her more manageable, digestible, 'feminine' forms. Armed with her new set of compositions, Rebecca and her friends headed back to the Wigmore to give a concert showcasing her work, with the Sonata and Trio as the centrepieces. As usual, some of the newspapers blithely judged that her larger works were 'reflective of preceding masculine creations', but the smaller pieces displayed 'real feminine personality'. Prejudice aside, though, even they had to admit that her 'bold modern style [...] placed her among the musicians "who count"'. A week later the BBC broadcast an evening concert dedicated entirely to Rebecca, further cementing her reputation. And Ethel, listening as well as she could in the Wigmore, was distinctly impressed. After the concert she invited Rebecca to Christmas lunch with her at Coign, laying out a spread with copious cups of tea.

Walking past Ethel's rose bushes into her cosy, quiet home, Rebecca was struck by just how different their two existences were. Rebecca spent her free evenings sipping cocktails with celebrity authors like Arnold Bennett and Rebecca West, while Ethel, in her tricornered hat and baggy cardigan, was more likely to be found reminiscing nostalgically with her aristocratic friends, who felt themselves displaced by Rebecca's world. Ethel was a 'Funny, cracked old thing', Rebecca thought, 'but very nice'. Ethel asked her to play through 'The Seal Man' and a couple of other songs. Admittedly, with her shaky piano capabilities Rebecca produced an 'awful performance', but nonetheless Ethel 'seemed interested'. More than just interested – she told her great-niece that she considered Rebecca 'very very gifted and I loved the songs'.

As lunch slipped in to tea-time Ethel brought the conversation round to H. B., feeling that she could trust Rebecca enough to show her some of their letters and admit that they had an affair, which she had kept ambiguous in her autobiographies. She felt that Rebecca was 'a perfect darling – and a lady', who would not betray her confidence. Although their paths would cross in future – Rebecca played Ethel's works, and their music was programmed together often enough that they sometimes bumped into each other in green rooms and studio corridors – this was the last time that they sought each other out especially. Rebecca later regretted that she had not 'followed up and known her better', but at the time they were too different to sustain a real friendship. Rebecca was a strategist who appreciated tact and discretion, but Ethel said whatever came into her head.

Even had they been natural companions, Rebecca was so busy that it would have been difficult to maintain anything but the lightest of friendships. She was more in demand as a performer than ever before. As a chamber music specialist, she was one of the musicians who particularly benefitted from the advent of radio, because small ensembles were much easier to broadcast clearly than a full symphony orchestra or an opera. The 1920s were *the* decade for chamber performance. Rebecca was in front of a microphone almost weekly, and when she wasn't broadcasting she was booked for informal 'tea-time' chamber concerts. Allowing the audience to take tea as well as smoke while they heard new music, the tea-time concert took chamber music out of the fusty formality of the concert hall and brought it back to its origins as an intimate, social form of music-making.

Rebecca was almost permanently on the radio, not just because she was a good musician but because she was also a shrewd businesswoman. She recognised gaps in the musical market, and signed herself up for ensembles that were unique in some way. From 1925 she began performing with a flautist, violinist and pianist under the name of the Aeolian Players. The unusual combination of instruments meant they could offer repertoire that provided a contrast to the endless supply of singers and solo pianists – a definite attraction for nightly music broadcasting. And then in February 1927 she, May, Marjorie and a pianist called Kathleen Long gave their first appearance at the Aeolian Hall as a piano quartet named the English Ensemble. There were ample numbers of professional string quartets, but the addition of the piano again opened up the possibility of performing lesser-heard pieces. Their first concert was a riotous success. They were labelled 'a new organisation of excellent promise', and within a year they were also gracing the airwaves. Setting up the English Ensemble would turn out to be one of Rebecca's most formative career decisions. It brought her yet more fame as a performer, and touring with her friends gave her some of her happiest moments – but their success inevitably took her away from composition.

DOREEN

In the middle of a field filled with tents, pets and brightly coloured bunting, seven-year-old Doreen Carwithen stands beaming with a slightly lopsided smile, her dark curly hair frizzy in the wind. She trots along beside her mother, Dulcie, as they peruse the offerings at the Monks Risborough Horticultural Society annual show. It's the flowers clutched to Doreen's chest that are the source of her grin – she has just won her first ever award (second prize for bunch of wild flowers, under 14s), following in a proud family tradition of returning with armfuls of rosettes and the occasional jar of jam, for which they have worked much of the year round.

This year Dulcie will retire with seven prizes, ranging from first place for handmade woman's overall to second prize for bottle of preserved gooseberries (with a graceful acknowledgement to Mrs Dorey, with whom Dulcie has a friendly rivalry). As a special treat Doreen is allowed a slice of cake from the Women's Institute stall as they wait for her father, Reginald, to finish up his duties as the Society's Honorary Secretary. There is a lot of business to attend to – missing rabbits, gramophone difficulties – and Doreen has long finished her Victoria sponge by the time the family can head down the hill to their house and begin to think about dinner.

Aptly named 'Underhill', the Carwithen home is a large Victorian building, with a creaking wooden staircase that always betrays Doreen when she sneaks out of bed for a glass of milk at night, and a beautiful garden that Reginald devotedly cares for every weekend. The house sits at a crossroads: on the right-hand side, from the large bay windows Doreen can see the 'Whiteleaf Cross' chalk hill carving, enormous, white and mysterious opposite the house, overshadowing the entire hamlet. Her grandmother,

Mary, tells her that it is a sign from God (Doreen is not sure if she believes this). Beyond the hill, further up Peters Lane, lies the wood where Doreen loves to play in the holidays, the burnished beauty of silver bark mingling with the smell of sap and rich mulch of leaves, a perfect haven to pretend that she is a fairy or even a witch. But occasionally Doreen's family will turn left out of Underhill on to the main road. This leads into the unknown – sometimes to Oxford, or Thame, or somewhere new entirely, beyond the known comfort of Monks Risborough. These rare journeys are a source of enormous excitement for Doreen.

Most often, though, trips down the main road lead to Haddenham, and her grandparents' house. Mary and Freeman Clarke have lived in the village all their lives. Freeman has worked since he was nine years old – as a baker's boy and an apprentice wheelwright before setting up his own bakery at the age of twenty-one. In the same year he married Mary Ann Harris, daughter of a sheep-dipper. She, too, knew no other life than that of hard work. At seven she was a lace-maker, and a talented one at that; she then moved into service before marrying Freeman. Together they built up a business with little more than 'a basket and a sack of flour'. From bread they expanded to sweets and pastries, eventually providing catering for the whole village. Whether it was a funeral or the village fete the Clarkes were there, reliable, with finger sandwiches and scrumptious tarts oozing with jam made from the berries in their garden. After a decade they had saved enough to build a new premises that would double as a home for them and their three children – Cyril, the eldest, born in 1890, Ivy (born 1891) and Dulcie (born 1895).

The Clarkes began construction on the High Street. Local stories have it that Freeman made it the highest building in the village (apart from the church) to signify their status as one of the most respected and established families in the parish. They called it 'Clementine'. The top two floors were the family rooms, and the bakery and shop lay on the ground floor. Flour deliveries came in through the enormous wooden doors leading off the road into the courtyard turning circle for the carts, the sacks either stored in the barn or hurried into the tiled kitchen with its cavernous ovens so the day's baking could begin. This was the house where Doreen was born in 1922. She arrived into the bustle of a working household, Dulcie hearing the horses in the yard below and the constant ringing of the shop bell throughout her hours of labour with Mary at her side.

The Clarkes' bakery in Haddenham where Doreen was born.

Having worked their way into the lower middle class, Freeman and Mary wanted to give their children the best start in life that they could. They encouraged Cyril to work hard at school and he was later rewarded with a scholarship to a grammar school in Thame. As soon as they were old enough, both Ivy and Dulcie were given music lessons. Dulcie in particular showed a remarkable aptitude for the piano. Knowing little about music themselves, the Clarkes sought advice from her piano teacher, who suggested that she apply to the prestigious Matthay School in London, run by Dorothy's old teacher. Managing to obtain a place, Dulcie practised daily for hours, hoping to be among the lucky few whom she saw leave the school to become stars on London's concert stages.

But fame is fickle, and Dulcie was never quite in the right place at the right time. She became one of the hundreds of girls whose ambitions to be a concert pianist were never realised, and who went into teaching instead. Soon after World War I ended, she settled at a school in Clacton where she met Reginald Carwithen. He was a kind, earnest man, working as an accountant for the North British & Mercantile Company. He was somewhat musical himself, singing in his company's operatic society and conducting his local church choir. Dulcie knew Reginald was a good match. So after a short courtship they married at St Mary's Church in Haddenham, a small service with a few family and friends, Dulcie wearing an ivory satin dress and bearing a bouquet of roses and white heather, her brides-maids in cream crêpe de Chine with pink carnations. They had their reception in Freeman and Mary's garden, the cake's delicate decorations matching the orange blossoms on Dulcie's dress.

After marriage, Dulcie advertised herself as a music teacher, working in the Monks Risborough schools and accepting private students at Underhill. Doreen and, later, her sister Barbara, born in 1926, had a childhood steeped in music. Their daily soundtrack was the sound of scratching violins, squeaking recorders and enthusiastically wielded cymbals, as Dulcie's piano, violin, recorder, percussion and singing pupils threw themselves into their lessons with gusto. And in the evenings when the hubbub subsided, Doreen and Barbara became an audience of two upstairs in bed, as they listened to Dulcie play the Chopin, Beethoven and Mozart that she had dreamed of one day performing at the Wigmore, or the Queen's Hall. Sometimes Reginald would join her to sing, and the children fell asleep to the gentle lilt of Schubert and Brahms lieder.

o   o   o   o

By 1928 Rebecca was such a familiar radio name that when she gave live concerts she was advertised as being 'of wireless fame'. Her days were an endless reel of rehearsals, concerts and parties. When Ravel (then one of the biggest celebrities of modern music) visited the UK in 1928, Rebecca was selected to play in his London concerts. At the after-party at May's house she produced a set of tarot cards from her bag and set up in a dimly lit corner to indulge her latest hobby of reading people's fortunes. Ravel sidled over, 'strangely quiet, reserved, rather secretive', fascinated by the tall, elegantly dressed violist offering to uncover people's innermost feelings and fates – but then found himself rather perturbed by the accuracy of some of Rebecca's readings.

Rebecca couldn't decide whether she believed in her own powers of divination or not. Sometimes, secretly, she took out her cards and asked them for guidance on her own future. Because when the parties ended and she had time to mull over her thoughts, Rebecca was quite troubled by the men in her life. Being single in her forties and both beautiful and talented, she received a formidable amount of romantic attention. But marriage, unless it was to exactly the right person, would almost certainly mean giving up the career that meant everything to her. She had waited so long to get independence from her father that it would be hard to give up that freedom again. It would be an extraordinary man who would either agree to her continuing working, or entice her from the concert stage.

So Rebecca turned down the various proposals that came her way. Which would have been the end of the matter, had these and other propositions not usually come from her colleagues. It was a constant tightrope – every unwanted advance risked souring a working relationship. Thankfully, most came from people who were only intermittently involved in her working life, and took no for an answer. Fellow composer and violist Cecil Forsyth often cast a useful critical eye over Rebecca's work, but he was no great loss when she 'had to turn him out as he was beginning to get too affectionate'. To his credit, Cecil accepted Rebecca's decision and they remained on cordial terms – even if he did carry a torch for her for many years, like Mr Miles before him. Rebecca's old tutor never moved on from her. When he died from pneumonia in 1922, he left her his Stradivarius violin in his will.

Occasionally, though, Rebecca's would-be suitors were more persistent, or more complicated to distance herself from. The most troublesome was Gordon Bryan: an affable, business-like individual with a large chin and short dark hair, and the pianist for the Aeolian Players. Even without romantic dramas, the dynamics within the Aeolian had the potential to become a little volatile. Gordon was an extremely talented concert manager (it was he who booked Rebecca as a player for Ravel), but not the world's most gifted pianist. He would only have needed to be a slightly different personality to have become jealous about never being the star attraction. On this front, luckily, he was amiable enough. But he was not someone Rebecca wanted to marry.

Rebecca was as firm as possible, but it was difficult when they saw each other almost every day for rehearsals. She had to resort to increasingly desperate measures to avoid being left alone with him. After one business lunch he followed her shopping and she had to seek refuge in the nearest women's club until he lost patience and went home. Rebecca suspected that he wanted 'people to go on talking about us', in the hope that circulating gossip that they were 'already supposed to be engaged' might convince her to give in to his advances.

With amorous men causing a maelstrom of frustrations, it's perhaps unsurprising that when Rebecca did finally enter a relationship, it was with a man who was unavailable. In 1924, the married singer John Goss came into her life unobtrusively via a note expressing his admiration for 'The Seal Man'. She arranged a meeting, as she usually did for performers who conveyed interest in her work, and he performed his rendition of her song over tea. He did it 'simply beautifully', Rebecca noted, his deep voice bringing a new, almost predatory dimension to this song about fated love that had so far been sung mostly by women.

They had plenty to talk about – John came from a working-class background and had worked in a whole host of jobs from golf caddie to errand boy, and had also won a scholarship to Ruskin College in Oxford, an institution set up by two Americans to provide talented individuals with free higher education. Over the years he had developed strongly held socialist and pacifist views that he was only too happy to discuss with Rebecca. She thought him 'very jolly & most friendly', and they agreed to meet again soon.

It was hardly love at first sight. The combination of John being married and Rebecca's existing dilemmas meant that romance didn't initially cross her mind. But they continued to meet, sometimes at concerts, sometimes at parties. Their blossoming relationship was shrouded in secrecy and mystery. Rebecca, usually so forthcoming in her diary, left little about her impressions of him at all. And John was, publicly, a family man. He was hardly likely to divulge details about his affairs in the memoir that he co-wrote with his wife, Mabel.

Traces of John linger in the reviews of his singing. They paint a portrait of a quiet, engaging man with a 'pleasant light baritone voice' who sang 'earnestly and beautifully'. Was it his voice that

Rebecca became most attracted to, as she listened to him give such understanding performances of her songs that she almost thought he had reached into her musical soul? Or perhaps it was his ability to 'laugh at anything, and defy the solemn with his ridicule', making her giggle when they were ensconced in some corner together at a late-night party? Or maybe it was 'his gentle, modest manner and quiet way of speaking', belying the strength of his political convictions? Quite probably she appreciated his tall, slender figure that seemed so simultaneously animated and composed when he stepped out on to the stage.

By 1927 they were lovers. They snatched moments when they could after rehearsals, and, very occasionally, they found a day of glorious sunshine to go motoring around Enfield, where John had grown up. Being the 'other woman' was not how Rebecca had imagined her first serious relationship. But John would not, at least, ask her to abandon her own life – so she decided that, for now, she would take whatever happiness she could find.

o o o o

Alone in her little room in Chelsea, Dorothy closed her eyes and cast herself off for Gibraltar. A few years earlier she had gone there on holiday with her mother, and if she focused hard enough, despite the cloying London smog she could still almost smell the algae, taste the sea salt surrounding the little fishing boat that carried her to the peninsula from the SS *Maloja*. When they reached the shore Dorothy was surrounded by the sound of Spanish, Maltese, Maghrebi Arabic, as street vendors called out their wares. Donkey brays layered over panpipes announcing small bleating goat herds. 'This street is narrow and crooked,' Dorothy remembered, 'crowded with little shops on either side displaying wonderful embroidered shawls, carved ivory figures.'

From the bustling Royal Academy, Dorothy revisited Gibraltar's winding, noisy streets in any quiet moments, jotting down phrases and rhythms on napkins and scrap paper. Goat-herders' panpipes became flute melodies, the strings evoked the lapping waves against the harbour, and to the horns she entrusted the feeling of majesty that overwhelmed her when she stood in the square, gazing up at the Rock that loomed over the tiled roofs. Snatching composition time in the evenings and on her days off from teaching, through 1928 Dorothy slowly sculpted an overture that she titled *The Rock*. As supportive as ever, Henry Wood agreed to perform the work immediately – and selected it as one of the premieres for the Last Night of the Proms, the most anticipated and well-attended concert of the whole season.

Dorothy was almost sick with nerves when she took her seat in the hall. She knew it would be conducted to perfection, and she trusted the orchestra unconditionally, but even the raucous Last Night atmosphere with the audience bursting into a spontaneous round of 'For He's a Jolly Good Fellow' could not distract her attention from the inevitable reckoning with the newspaper reviews. The critics' pens hovered over Dorothy the whole night, poised to strike her down with a single, well-placed barbed comment.

When she picked up her copy of the morning papers the next day, Dorothy could hardly believe her eyes. *The Rock* was 'a forceful and picturesque composition that gave great pleasure', and 'an advance in point of workmanship on any recent composition of Miss Howell's.' Dorothy hoped that with this kind of review, publication of *The Rock* would surely follow. Buoyed by her success, she continued to fill every non-teaching moment with composing. In 1930 she premiered her *Andante and Allegro* for violin and piano, accompanying Elsie on the violin part. Dorothy and Elsie were now firm friends. Earlier in the year they had travelled to Florence with Elsie's husband, Arthur. Perhaps they had unknowingly wandered past H. B.'s old home as they strolled around the passageways, trying to find the best viewpoint to watch the sun set over the city.

On this wave of good news, Ethel also dropped back into Dorothy's life. Might Dorothy have any suitable compositions for brass band, for Ethel to conduct at the unveiling of Emmeline Pankhurst's statue in the Victoria Tower Gardens? Ethel was very keen that women other than herself should be represented. Dorothy was hesitant at first – after all, she had not been old enough to participate actively in the suffrage campaign. But Ethel reassured her that 'Mrs Pankhurst was too big a woman to have put the bringing forward of women's work second to <u>anything</u>'.

So, on 6 March 1930 Dorothy stood in the cold listening to Ethel lead the Police Band in one of her Minuets, rearranged for brass band. The irony of the moment was not lost on those attending. Those who had stood shoulder to shoulder with Emmeline, suffered in prison with her, experienced 'a strange thrill' as the fabrics were pulled away from the statue, revealing her shining in the March sun, one hand lowered as though caught in the middle of a sentence.

After these encouragements, however, neither the publication nor the anticipated performances of *The Rock* ever materialised. Shortly after the premiere, the conductor Dan Godfrey, Dorothy's most committed advocate after Henry Wood, scheduled a rendition in Bournemouth. Henry programmed it in Liverpool, and there was a performance by the Royal Academy Orchestra in 1934. But after that, performances simply dried up. Ethel would surely have encouraged Dorothy to 'pester' conductors. Works foundered without sustained bombardment on the composer's part. And without performances, *The Rock* met the same fate as *Koong Shee* and the Piano Concerto. They are still unpublished, which has prevented the performances that would allow Dorothy's works to enter the canon.

Dorothy was already frustrated and demotivated, and when her father died in March 1932 she took it especially hard. She returned to Our Lady and All Saints Church at Stourbridge for his Requiem Mass, and as she stood where they had all worshipped as a family before the war, tears blotted out the pink and grey granite columns when she looked to the end of her family pew and did not see Charles Edward and Carlo smiling back at her. Dorothy suspended her teaching to help Viola sort and box away all Charles Edward's belongings (the Howells, as a rule, never threw anything away). To get away from the silence of the depleted family home, mother and daughter set off on a fortnight-long sail to Egypt to visit Dorothy's brother Alfred, who had been posted to Ismailia with the RAF. When Dorothy had sailed to Gibraltar in 1924 she had been listed in the ship's log as a composer – now, in 1932, she was registered simply as 'spinster'.

However, Dorothy always found inspiration in changes of scene and routine. They gave her different perspectives, a renewed focus. In Ismailia, she spent every moment she could at prayer, attending Mass in the Church of the Holy Family. In the heat of the Egyptian sun, her path seemed to reveal itself with astonishing clarity. What she had always cared about – almost exclusively – was God, music and her family. And they did not have to be separate entities, running on parallel tracks. For the first time, she turned her attention to writing religious music. Composing for the extremely limited resources of the Holy Family Church (a handful of singers and a small organ), Dorothy produced three Masses in a few months. She had very strong opinions about music in the liturgy, believing that music should be clear, unadorned and at the service of the words. All her Masses follow this principle. Unlike Ethel's Mass, Dorothy's settings are short, uncomplicated and easily singable by amateurs.

Upon returning to London, Dorothy largely divided her time between the Church and teaching. She composed the theatre music for multiple religious plays, most of which were produced by the Grail, a Catholic women's society. Established in 1921, the Grail was conceived to get out of the 'ultra-masculine' rut some felt the Catholic Church had fallen into. The society called upon lay women to act as spiritual leaders, integrating life and worship to 'counteract in the world all masculine hardness', their mission being to deliver the world from spiritual crisis. One of the Grail's key strategies for youth involvement was enormous, colourful stagings of plays with a Catholic message. In 1936 Dorothy's music for *The Hound of Heaven* was heard by an audience of thousands at the Royal Albert Hall. The stalls were filled with young Catholic women, gathered together to share in the play's story of deliverance.

In terms of audience numbers, the 1930s were some of Dorothy's most successful years. Her pieces for students were set for the Associated Board grade exams, meaning that thousands of students across the world played her pieces. Theatre music was usually much more widely heard than music written exclusively for the concert hall – and productions like the Grail's would always outstrip the audience numbers for classical music, especially for un-broadcast pieces like *Koong Shee*. But because the emphasis in theatre was on visuals rather than sound, very few people even consciously registered that they were hearing music at all. Theatre composers were rarely credited or acknowledged, and this anonymity was exacerbated in the case of the Grail, with its emphasis on individual sublimation to a higher calling. So Dorothy stepped into the background, her work indispensable but unattributed.

Dorothy found pleasure, comradeship and fulfilment working with the Grail, but in her heart she still longed to write concert music. She turned to Ethel in desperation. Novello had rejected her Piano Concerto for publication, and the 1920s requests for BBC performances had simply stopped coming. The BBC was now far more interested in the new 'ultra-modernist' music that Dorothy reviled, and even Rebecca found difficult to accommodate. What was she to do? Again, she turned to Ethel. 'Oh! don't I know the misery of it all!' the older composer commiserated. 'I am (you must remember) of a very dead & gone generation.' She felt as ostracised by London's musical community as Dorothy did. 'I have nothing to suggest.' Without a hint of bitterness Dorothy reassured Ethel that she had, in fact, been of help, 'if not with advice with sympathetic understanding', and they parted with Dorothy giving 'for what they are worth, my sympathy, my admiration, & my gratitude'. They would be the last words she ever wrote to Ethel.

Dorothy's only motivation for living in London had been to further her career as a composer, but with performances and broadcasts in short supply there seemed nothing worth staying for. She could compose perfectly well elsewhere, so she moved to the leafy calm of Letchworth in Hertfordshire to live with her mother and Pookie, the woman who had nursed her as a child. Intensely secretive about her private life, Dorothy never appeared to show any inclination towards romantic relationships. Even though she was still only thirty-four, there wasn't a flurry of suitors around her as there was around Rebecca. And she certainly didn't go in for the demonstrative displays of ardour that Ethel favoured. She liked children, but seemed uninterested in having her own. Dorothy was certain she would be happiest living a quiet life in Letchworth, commuting to London to teach.

o   o   o   o

On 20 February 1930, an abrupt bell-ring interrupted the cool calm of Virginia Woolf's home at 52 Tavistock Square. Moments later, announced by 'a brisk tramp' that echoed up the stairs, Ethel burst forth into the room where Virginia lay on her sofa, recovering from flu. Flushed with excitement to meet one of her literary heroines, Ethel bounded up to Virginia, roared 'Let me look at you,' and simply stood watching her for a while.

Gazing back, Virginia saw 'a bluff, military old woman (older than I expected)', who was 'a little glazed flyaway & abrupt; in a three cornered hat & tailor made suit'. Her unconventional opening gambit complete, Ethel drew out a notebook and pencil, settled herself into a chair by the bookcases and began questioning Virginia about her life. Four hours and many cups of tea later, Ethel and Virginia were still animatedly discussing music, writing, biography, art, their friends: Virginia back on her sofa, Ethel resting her sore legs on the basket belonging to Pinker, Virginia's cocker spaniel.

The two women certainly had much in common, and were well aware of each other's work. Virginia was one of the most famous women in London, having already penned works including *To the Lighthouse*, *Jacob's Room*, 'Monday or Tuesday' (Ethel's favourites) and *Orlando* (of which she was less fond). She and Ethel had in fact first crossed paths – not that Ethel had realised – a few years before, in the hallway of the Wigmore Hall, where Virginia had seen Ethel bustling past with 'a general look of angry energy' in a way that 'reminded me of a ptarmigan – those speckled birds with fetlocks'. Ever a shrewd observer, Virginia saw Ethel as ludicrous and eminently vulnerable to caricature: she 'has a vein, like a large worm, in her temple which swells. Her cheeks redden. Her faded eyes flash.' But she also felt everything about Ethel that was admirable. 'So sincere & abrupt is she', Virginia noted, that they had laid 'the basis of an undying friendship [. . .] in 15 minutes: – how sensible; how rapid'.

Ethel, for her part, was completely smitten. The BBC had provided her with the perfect opportunity to reach out to the writer, by inviting Ethel to be the only woman on their essay programme *Points of View*. She chose to talk about feminism (which stood out in the series – other contributions included H. G. Wells on physics), so asked Virginia if they might discuss her feminist polemic *A Room of One's Own*. The writer responded with enthusiasm. 'If you only knew how often I have wanted to write to you – and only didn't for fear of boring you – to thank you for your books and articles.' Now they had met, Ethel could admit that 'I did love you before I saw you, wholly & solely because of "A room of one's own"'. For Virginia's sake she tried to explain exactly what she meant by love. It wasn't sexual per se; even in Ethel's sexual relationships, 'the real part has always been (as H. B. used to remark) the prestige the person had for me – the thing that compelled admiration & a desire for human near-ness'. After all, 'with me & I think many women the root of love is in the imaginative part of one – its violence, its tenderness, its hunger'.

Virginia and Ethel, *c.*1930.

It was destined to be a tempestuous relationship. For every topic that united Ethel and Virginia, they had at least three about which they disagreed. Ethel was boisterous and wore her heart on her sleeve. Vita Sackville-West – Virginia's lover, Ethel's friend and fellow eccentric – shrewdly observed that Ethel 'might concisely have entitled her successive books Me One, Me Two, Me Three, and so on'. Virginia was reserved, and hated personal publicity of any kind.

She despised arguments, Ethel thrived on them. Ethel wrote dozens and dozens of letters, sometimes several a day, to the point where Virginia often became overwhelmed and retreated for a lie-down. And they fought, repeatedly and bitterly. Ethel would get jealous of Vita; Virginia despised Ethel dragging her to uproarious parties.

Virginia also had a sarcastic, socially conscious side that could prompt her to be cruel about Ethel behind her back. In her diary Virginia praised Ethel as 'a very genuine, breeze blown mind; a free, entirely energised character'. She was, overall, 'a game old bird'. But to her friends, Virginia painted quite a different picture. She viewed Ethel's circle with deep disdain, and was wary of the social implications of befriending this hectic, hectoring old lady who tramped about 'in her spotted fur, like an unclipped & rather overgrown woodland wild beast, species indeterminate'.

So while Virginia responded kindly to Ethel in person, and reasoned in her diary that 'it would be mere poltroonery for me to hold off for fear of ridicule', she wrote to her nephew Quentin Bell that being loved by the seventy-one-year-old Ethel was 'at once hideous and horrid and melancholy-sad'. To her sister, Vanessa Bell, she despaired that 'Ethel Smyth is mad'. She cautioned Vita not to let Ethel know their movements, 'or she'll come too', and then 'every instant will be ravaged by the rapacity of Ethel Smyth'.

And yet, somehow, the two kept up an eleven-year friendship that was only ended by Virginia's suicide in 1941, after prolonged battles with mental health problems. True, Ethel could be an over-enthusiastic guest and occasionally took up more of Virginia's time and energy than she was able or willing to give. But she also had the grace to realise when she had overstepped, and would retreat until Virginia was ready to speak to her again. She, in turn, forgave Virginia's sometimes venomous outbursts born of vanity, insecurity, frustration and sheer exhaustion. 'I think you are worth anything – any sacrifice,' Ethel told her. 'Where you lodge is in a deep part of my consciousness that no one has ever been in before – it needed you – your genius, your lovableness to make the place you live in.' And so they always made up from their fights. Virginia would return to Ethel, 'my old uncastrated wild cat', for there were days when she needed 'one of Ethels most violent, disruptive, abruptive, fuliginious, catastrophic, panoramic, I cant think of any other adjectives – effusions'. Ethel always responded with alacrity.

Spurred on by her new friendship, Ethel was composing again, this time with H. B. in mind. After his death Ethel had felt stripped of all words, all music. But now, with twenty years' distance, she could begin to piece together her eulogy, a final farewell. She still missed H. B. desperately, and wanted so much to be able to talk to him about his work, her music, old age. Now seventy-two, she did not want to die without having shared with the world all that H. B. meant to her. She immersed herself in his book *The Prison*, a philosophical poem about death and sin. The Prisoner realises he is dying, and communes with his soul in an attempt to make sense of his existence – asking questions that now occupied Ethel at almost every waking moment. When she feared her music dying with her, she turned to *The Prison* and read the lines 'Tell them that no man lives in vain [. . .] We are full of immortality.' She felt as though H. B. was speaking to her through his text.

As she read these words music flowed into Ethel's mind. She composed the whole of *The Prison* in agony due to a persistent injury from a fall when conducting. Ethel could only write for half an hour before the discomfort became too much. She played piano 'as a fly crawls over a window pane – & often as I did so wept from pain'. Her lengthier letters to Virginia deteriorated into an almost illegible scrawl as she struggled to write. And yet 'inspiration never flagged'. In the past, composing had sometimes felt like a battle and a puzzle combined as she fought to find where the themes slotted into the right places. *The Prison* was different. It was as though there could be no other way of setting the text. The ideas marched logically to their allotted spots of their own accord. On 11 August 1930 she wrote

'The End' on *The Prison*. 'I have never been happier in my life than this year – working furiously at what I believe to be a good opus.' A couple of weeks later Ethel wondered to herself whether *The Prison* 'is as good as I think', worrying that 'the intoxication of the text has deprived me of judgment'.

The Prison wasn't just a good opus, it was an extraordinary one. It is reserved and careful, nothing like the ebullience of *The March of the Women* or *The Wreckers*. There are moments of passion and fear, even anger, but Ethel combines them with such exquisite musical caresses that the piece has a pervading atmosphere of peace and acceptance. Virginia came to a private rehearsal at Portland Place, accompanied by some of Ethel's friends and her sister Mary ('a swathed satin sausage'). As Ethel conducted, 'She sang now & then; & once, taking the bass, made a cat squalling sound – but everything she does with such forthrightness directness that there is nothing ridiculous. She loses self-consciousness completely.' Ethel acted, Virginia thought, as though 'this is about the most important event now taking place in London. And perhaps it is.' Virginia outsourced her opinions on Ethel's music, asking her musically informed friends for their judgements, but she would go to the first London performance nonetheless. And Ethel, knowing that her hearing was very nearly gone completely, hoped that *The Prison* would allow her to leave music in a final blaze of glory.

o   o   o   o

Quite uncharacteristically, Rebecca hovered on the fringes of the party. Cocktails flowed, the room filled with musical celebrities and the noise dropped to a murmur as they gathered to listen to a singer. But Rebecca did not hear him. She was far too distracted by John, who had come with Mabel – and was studiously ignoring Rebecca. The realities of having an affair with a married man had long been clear. Every blissful moment was tinged with guilt. The secrecy made their clandestine trysts exciting, but the lack of stability and feelings of betrayal created no end of difficulties. Discussions became arguments, meetings obligations. John would often cancel at short notice, or neglect to call when he had promised. Wracked with worry, Rebecca soothed herself to sleep in the evenings by working through her compositions in her head, the familiar notes comforting her like old friends.

One hot, uncomfortable night in July when she had been waiting for what seemed like a lifetime for any word from John, Rebecca finally confided in Dora. She didn't know where else to turn. Her hectic concert schedule left her with so little free time that she felt more isolated from her friends than she had ever been. Long shopping trips with May had been curtailed by rehearsals and recordings, and John's unpredictable availability only made the situation worse. Dora, at least, had been in the same situation with a married man, so had plenty of sympathetic advice. They spent the whole evening talking, mulling over Rebecca's options. The answer was obvious. Rebecca admitted to herself that 'the John affair must come to an end, but feel very unhappy about it all'. Steeling herself for the inevitable, she left a letter for John telling him it was over.

Soon, Rebecca was dancing at parties with Dora again, and took a trip to Brighton with May to take her mind off things. But a cloud was cast over Christmas Day 1928 by John's name popping up in a newspaper advert, putting him in America at the same time that Rebecca had been planning to travel. May provided a shoulder to cry on, sending her home 'with instructions to take a hot bath & go early to bed & forget it'. She really did try, but she couldn't control the way her heart leapt whenever John's name was mentioned, or when she heard his voice across the room. Despite Rebecca's best intentions, the affair would rumble on and off for years, well into the 1930s. She stopped keeping a diary in 1933, shrouding the end of the relationship in silence. They probably only parted of necessity, when John and his wife moved to Tokyo.

THE ENGLISH ENSEMBLE

" Their ensemble is an ensemble of understanding, not merely of time and notes ".
Times

KATHLEEN LONG, *Piano*
" an artist of whom this country should be proud."
Manchester Guardian

MARJORIE HAYWARD, *Violin*
" her playing is distinguished by its liquid tone, its intense feeling—and individuality." *Morning Post*

REBECCA CLARKE, *Viola*
" we have seldom heard more beautiful tone and phrasing from a viola player." *Times*

MAY MUKLE, *'Cello*
" in the very front rank of living violoncellists."
Times

Publicity flyer for the English Ensemble. From left to right: May, Rebecca, Marjorie and Kathleen.

Between concerts and her private life, Rebecca composed only a small number of works. In 1929 she wrote just three songs: a 'Cradle Song'; a humorous, quirky piece called 'The Aspidistra'; and 'Tiger, Tiger', a vivid, chilling song set to William Blake's poem full of 'deadly terrors' and 'fearful symmetry'. It follows a similar path to 'The Seal Man', theatrical in a way that suited John's voice particularly well – Rebecca certainly had him in mind. What's so disconcerting is its complete lack of vulnerability, of humanity. The pianist and singer move as one – a single, relentless, rumbling, soaring unit advancing without mercy.

It took Rebecca two years to finish 'Tiger, Tiger', revised in between home and hotel rooms as the English Ensemble toured both Holland and the UK throughout 1931, with newspapers praising them for their 'fire and devotion'. After the Wall Street Crash in 1929 the British economy slumped, with unemployment doubling through 1930, causing a crisis of faith in the Labour government that resulted in a landslide Conservative victory in the 1931 election, and the introduction of emergency spending cuts and tax hikes to save the plummeting pound. And yet for the upper middle classes, concerts continued as usual – within three months the English Ensemble toured eighteen cities, from Dundee in Scotland to Denbigh in Wales, taking in both Dublin and Belfast, playing in Exeter, Liverpool, Lincoln, Cambridge – and between those Rebecca also had concerts where she was booked as a soloist. The pace was exhausting. In 1932 the Ensemble was back in Holland again, still raking in rave reviews. Come 1935, Rebecca would be grateful for this frantic pace of life. The Ensemble provided some welcome solace when Agnes passed away, leaving Rebecca feeling more alone than ever. At least when her performance diary was filled she barely even had a moment for a cigarette, let alone time to dwell on the loss of her mother.

But having such a successful performance career also meant less space for composition. Thankfully, Rebecca's old works wore well. Her 1919 Viola Sonata was still 'powerful and pungent, but wears its modernities with good grace', the Trio showing 'a creative talent that is at once strange and fascinating'. The gritty, macabre, dissonant element of Rebecca's style meant that, unlike Dorothy, she could still find a place in a musical landscape obsessed with 'modernity'. But this was changing rapidly. Just as important as where Rebecca's music was played was where it was not. The International Society for Contemporary Music Festival was one of the biggest and most important events for composers. But at the 1931 Festival held in Oxford and London there were no women represented at all. Similarly, between 1928 and 1939 the BBC ran a series called Concerts of Contemporary Music, and in those eleven years entire concerts were dedicated to the music of Schoenberg, Stravinsky and newer names like Bartók, Paul Hindemith, Darius Milhaud and Sergei Prokofiev, who would come to dominate twentieth-century music. They programmed music by only *one* woman: Elizabeth Maconchy, an emerging modernist.

Modern music wasn't just being defined as atonal – it was being defined as male. Sixty years after Ethel first stepped foot in Leipzig and began to realise the systemic prejudices against women, musical institutions and organisations were as closed as they ever had been. The people who made up the 'Machine' might have changed, but their rules were still the same. Despite Ethel, Rebecca and Dorothy's very best efforts, a woman composer was still considered a novelty.

It wasn't because women weren't composing. In the 1930s a new, young group of modernist women composers was coming up through the Royal College – Elizabeth Maconchy, Elisabeth Lutyens and Grace Williams – whose music was even more challenging than Rebecca's. Like Ethel before them, these three defied expectations, writing substantial works including operas, film scores and large orchestral pieces. They were, unquestionably, among the more famous composers in Britain during the 1930s and 1940s. But women were still in the double bind that Ethel had faced with her Mass. If they wrote pretty, tuneful music, it was dismissed as 'feminine', trivial and unprogressive. If they moved away from expectations of what women should write, embracing 'modern' idioms, they were attacked. When Maconchy, Lutyens and Williams gave a concert of their own music in 1935 the press complained that 'No lipstick, silk stocking or saucily tilted hat adorns the music [. . .] All is grim, intense, and cerebral [. . .] these three ladies were too formidably clever, or tried to be.' It was impossible to win. Relatively speaking, the 1920s had been a halcyon era, with no consensus about what 'modern' music was or should be. By 1939, modern was male.

o   o   o   o

Whenever she left Underhill, six-year-old Doreen would ask to be lifted up so she could run her fingers over the embossed brass plate that hung by the door: 'Dulcie D. Carwithen LRAM, ATCL', her mother's teaching notice. Even though Dulcie saw her teaching career as the 'second-best' option to performance, Freeman and Mary were immensely proud of their talented daughter. Doreen, too, looked up to her mother. She couldn't miss the fondness in Dulcie's voice when she spoke about music. The Royal Academy took on an almost hallowed aura for Doreen, as Leipzig Conservatoire had for Ethel. One day, she hoped, she would make her family proud, and it would be her name that hung by her mother's.

Dulcie knew how to give her children the best possible chance at a musical career, and began teaching both Doreen and Barbara instruments when they were very small. Doreen started out on the piano and violin at the age of just five, passing her first ABRSM piano exam when she was eight. Unlike Rebecca, she never saw practising as a chore. She loved working out pieces on the family's upright piano in the hall, and her most treasured sixth birthday present was a miniature violin that allowed her small fingers to reach the notes more easily. Family music-making was as much of a joy for Doreen as it was for her parents. She felt terribly grown-up when Dulcie accompanied her at the piano, and she practised as hard as she could to get to the stage where she, too, could accompany Reginald singing.

The Carwithens made sure that music was prioritised in their daughter's school life as well. Doreen's first school was Whiteleaf High School, which followed the ideas of the Victorian educationalist Charlotte Mason. She believed in holistic, nurturing teaching that helped children to develop as individuals by giving them a broad education including music and art. Every morning Doreen trotted next door to Whiteleaf, which stood directly beside Underhill in an almost identical Victorian house with homely classrooms. Music lessons, though, took place in a large wooden building, with enough space for the whole school to practise for their end-of-year play. In kindergarten Doreen trod the boards in her pyjamas to sing a 'slumber song' in *Ali Baba*, later upgrading to play a fairy in *Snow White*. For both plays Dulcie was at the piano, accompanying the children as they whirled around the stage.

Dulcie (right) with her daughters Doreen (left) and Barbara (centre), at the beach on holiday in Exeter.

After this, Doreen had a spell at Woodlands School, where Dulcie taught singing and percussion. Then, when she turned eleven, her parents sent her to the Chiltern School. This was a much grander, exclusive private girls' school housed in the Old Rectory at Monks Risborough. It still wasn't far from Underhill – just a short walk up the hill and past the churchyard's enormous trees. Music and art were included on the curriculum, as well as sports from cricket to riding, and there were only forty students. A middle-class girl hoping for a musical career couldn't have hoped for better.

When Doreen came back from school the house would still be full of the sounds of music lessons. Afterwards, she and Barbara would commandeer the two pianos – the upright in the hall and, from 1937, a baby grand in the music room – to play duets together. Or Doreen would listen to the evening's concert on the wireless, reading along with the scores she had. Some nights she heard Beethoven's music, some nights Ethel's, and she also got her introduction to musical modernism. The music of Doreen's childhood was very different to the music that Ethel, Rebecca and Dorothy grew up with. Of course, she heard all the classics that had shaped their early years. She knew the passion of Beethoven's piano sonatas, and the welcoming lyricism of Schubert's songs. But thanks to her mother and to the radio, Doreen had early access to a much wider range of music. Alongside all the repertoire staples, musicians growing up in the 1920s also heard the shocking sounds of the new, pushing the very boundaries of what 'music' was thought to be, denounced by perplexed critics as 'either excruciatingly hideous or irritatingly meaningless'. Doreen would never go as far as this – her music was always melodious – but she was bound to be a quite different composer to her three predecessors. She would fill her pieces with spicy harmonic and rhythmic surprises, the aural equivalent of finding a chunk of chilli at the middle of a Werther's Original.

By the time Doreen was fifteen she had added the cello to her roster of instruments (she nicknamed hers 'Perky'), and the two sisters tried out pieces from Dulcie's collection of scores. Initially Doreen taught herself cello, but when it became clear that she had a natural gift for it Dulcie sent her for lessons with a local cellist called (Kathleen) Peers Coetmore. Peers was not as famous as May, but by the time Doreen came to her for lessons in 1938 she had made a respectable name for herself. She and Doreen got along tremendously, and she became as much a friend to Doreen as a teacher. Peers knew how difficult it was for women to make their way into professional music – she herself was part of a group of women cellists who tried to support each other's careers – so was more than happy to be a role model, offering her pupil encouragement and advice over cups of tea.

Doreen dressed for her confirmation,
aged sixteen.

From playing in school concerts, Doreen progressed to local music festivals. Fiercely competitive, she regularly took home first prizes for solo piano from the Buckingham Music Festival. Even when she was competing in the same classes as Barbara, she wanted to win. She sailed through her ABRSM exams. And then, finally, came a moment of breakthrough, bringing her a step closer to her cherished ambition of the Royal Academy, where Dorothy was still teaching. The examiner for her Grade 8 piano was an Academy teacher, Frederick Moore, and he was so impressed with her performance that he offered to give Doreen private lessons, with the goal of her transferring to study with him at the Academy. Doreen could hardly believe it. She agreed immediately, overjoyed that the dream which had once seemed so far away was becoming a reality.

o   o   o   o

The Prison was not destined to be a triumph. After the premiere in Edinburgh and the first London performance shortly afterwards, the press annihilated it. One reviewer decreed it had 'little evidence of real musical talent', another quipped that 'Both Ethel Smyth and Henry Brewster have made brave attempts at mediocrity'. It would never have been performed 'had its composer been a man and not a woman, whom our critics still feel it is unchivalrous to criticize adversely' – although the press seemed to have had no qualms about cutting this outspoken advocate for women's rights down to size. By writing an hour-long symphonic cantata on metaphysics Ethel had overstepped the boundaries set around her, as she had with the Mass forty years before.

Reneging on her commitment to ignore her press notices, Ethel was understandably devastated. 'The story of the Prison has (really) broken my musical heart,' she wept. Despite Virginia's half-hearted attempts to stop her, Ethel hit back and lashed out. She accused the BBC of murdering her magnum opus, despite the fact that they had broadcast the performance from the Queen's Hall. Infuriated, Adrian Boult (then the BBC's Director of Music) told Ethel that he quite disagreed with her high estimation of the piece.

Ethel treasured her letters from admiring listeners, but they were few. 'Serious' classical music persistently ranked lowest among radio listeners' preferences (lower even than 'tennis commentaries'). In the 1930s radio broadcasting was dominated by dance music, musical comedy and serial dramas that provided good gossip – not Ethel and H. B.'s philosophical tracts. The kind of music Ethel wrote was slipping from public interest faster than she had realised.

Shattered by *The Prison*'s reception and unable to fight encroaching deafness, Ethel decided she could not compose again. She had the piano removed from her study. Her manuscripts were packed away. She would devote her final years to promoting her existing work – and writing, when she could muster the energy. At least she had Virginia to encourage her. 'I wonder how it feels', Virginia mused, 'to be so candid; and convinced that the public will be enthralled. I couldnt do it; but then you can.' Elements of Ethel may have even made their way into Virginia's autobiographical essay 'A Sketch of the Past'. Openly addressing the sexual abuse she had experienced as a child, the essay was far more personally revealing than any of Virginia's fiction. Ultimately she decided not to publish it. But the subject of autobiography – and how much one should reveal of oneself to the public – was a constant topic of conversation between the two women. Over the 1930s Ethel published no fewer than five books – some essays, some autobiographical and some biographical. But whatever the alleged focus, Ethel was the real subject.

In 1933 Ethel turned seventy-five, which she would not allow to go unmarked. As they had in 1928, her friends and supporters rallied around. After much fundraising and hassling behind the scenes, the BBC agreed to broadcast a rendition of *The Prison*, give a concert of her chamber music and conclude the celebrations with the Mass at the Queen's Hall, conducted by Ethel's old friend-cum-nemesis, Thomas Beecham. Virginia remarked cattily that for a couple of months, Ethel was 'deafening us every evening on the wireless with her caterwauling'. Nonetheless, she turned up to the Queen's Hall for the Mass in March 1934, even making an appearance at Ethel's after-party – which took place at a Lyons tea shop, much to Virginia's horror. Lyons was distinctly lower middle-class, and Virginia considered the venue a 'sordid crumby room', filled with Ethel's 'garish' crowd 'amid clerks & shop girls eating cream buns'; she cringed when Ethel rolled up her skirts to fetch a purse from among her undergarments. But Ethel's old flame Violet Gordon Woodhouse was also among the 'garish' mob. 'Who but Ethel could collect such a distinguished company at Lyons 6d tea,' she enthused, chuckling at a guest's verdict that 'This is the maddest tea-party since the Mad Hatters.'

Ethel's 1934 jubilee would be the last celebration of her music in her lifetime. Sporadic concerts followed, with highlights being a revival of *The Wreckers* at Sadler's Wells and a ballet version of *Fête Galante* with sets designed by artist Vanessa Bell, Virginia's sister. But even on Ethel's eightieth birthday there was no outpouring of admiration on the scale of 1934. The rest of the decade presented her with disappointment after disappointment. She disappeared from Proms programmes after Henry Wood took offence at one of her published comments. Her income collapsed when the financial crisis left her shares almost worthless. In 1935 she was presented with a £1,600 bill in unpaid tax. She was delivered from having to sell Coign thanks to the generosity of her friends – especially Maurice, who paid £900 of the bill – but she couldn't afford to devote time to composition that might or might not pay off. She had to accept almost every writing commission she was offered. With her arms in agony from arthritis, Ethel nonetheless sat scribbling at her desk, firing off opinions to any newspaper that wanted them.

But the worst tragedy of the 1930s was the death of Pan VI. When out walking with Pan trotting along beside her, a car approached behind them. Ethel, now too deaf to hear it, didn't call Pan out of the way in time. 'It was my own fault,' she sobbed in her diary:

I rushed to him 'Pan Pan' he staggered up whimpered, fell again..&
I saw he was dead tho' I tried to think he was stunned. [...] He was
the most beautiful of all my Pans, and getting more so every day.
He was just 19 months old, absolutely adorable – learning to be the
companion I wanted.

Ethel was inconsolable. Her friends immediately stepped in and
clubbed together to buy her a new puppy – Pan VII arrived in
December 1937.

Ethel could not mourn Pan for long, though, because there were
other, larger worries on the horizon. As politically engaged as ever,
she watched Hitler's rise to power in Germany with increasing horror. Unlike in the years before World War I, anyone with a modi-
cum of political interest in the 1930s saw the encroaching possibility
of an international crisis. 'These spectacular displays make me sick
and ashamed,' Ethel raged to her great-niece Elizabeth, troubled by
the annexation of Austria, and Hitler's and Mussolini's ostentatious
overtures to one another. Having always considered herself almost
an honorary German citizen, Ethel felt the rise of the Nazis personally, despairing that the country and people she loved so dearly
could capitulate to such a regime.

Right up until the outbreak of war, Ethel vainly held out hope that
a peace would be brokered, perhaps through mass sanctions being
imposed on Germany. When the Munich Agreement was concluded on 30 September 1938, ceding the Sudetenland to Germany,
Ethel wrote joyously in her diary that Neville Chamberlain was 'the
biggest man England has yet produced!!!!' Nonetheless she admitted
that it probably didn't mean 'anything but a postponement. As long
as that madman is alive there can be no stable place in Europe &
we must all go on arming.' She did her part by preparing her dining
room as a refuge from gas attacks, keeping all her necessary equipment nearby in a 'war box' in her dressing room.

Just a few days later, Ethel realised that the Munich Agreement would not be the end, which left her feeling 'so powerless with misery that I can hardly write these words & cannot (so far) work up the effort necessary for beginning the new set of memoirs'. She was so distraught that she even briefly considered joining the Labour Party in protest against the Conservative Prime Minister. She tried distracting herself by going to see Disney's *Snow White and the Seven Dwarfs* with friends, but she 'loathed' it: 'Everything rushed along so quickly that I couldn't see what it was before it was gone,' and she couldn't hear the soundtrack at all. Consolation came from throwing herself into another autobiography, *What Happened Next*, which would keep her company through the first years of the war. By 26 August 1938 conflict seemed 'inevitable', and Ethel went round the house 'darkening my windows'.

When Germany finally invaded Poland, the 1939 Proms season was in full swing at the Queen's Hall. Midway into the concert on 1 September, with the final, glowing chords of Beethoven's *Pastoral* Symphony still hanging in the air, Henry Wood stepped onto the stage to announce that the festival was to close with immediate effect. Baton in hand and moustache drooping, he cut a rather miserable figure, his usually larger-than-life personality deflated by his festival being cancelled.

A couple of days later, when war was formally declared, all theatres, cinemas and concert halls were shut down. The ban didn't last long – entertainment was thought to be so important for public morale that they reopened again a fortnight later with additional safety precautions. But it was clear for most musicians that life could not carry on as usual. In London, May had been running an underground social club, 'Mostly Musicians', for musicians and artists in central London, which she now transformed into an air-raid-shelter-cum-basement-concert-venue; Myra signed up as an Air Raid Warden; in rural Letchworth Dorothy volunteered for the Women's Land Army. She had been too young to serve in World War I, but this time she wanted to know she had done everything she could to help the war effort.

This was Doreen's first war, so for her there was a frisson of excitement at having to pin fabrics to windows and rush to the shelter when the sirens sounded. But for everybody who had already lived through one world war, September 1939 felt like a familiar nightmare. Rebecca was, again, out of Britain, visiting family in America. This time she was unable to return. The British Consul denied her a visa to travel, telling her that as a musician she was an 'unproductive mouth' and would not be allowed back into the country during wartime. Rebecca was distraught, desperately worried about her friends back in London, but there was nothing she could do. She could only watch from a distance, scouring the newspapers for news as the bombs began to fall on Ethel, Dorothy and Doreen.

WAR (II)

As the sun rose over Letchworth on 7 September 1940, Dorothy pulled on her threadbare cord trousers and army pullover, and set off for another day at the wheat harvest with her fellow Land Girls. They would spend their time bumping through fields on the threshing machine, scooping the precious grain into bags and hauling these heavy sacks onto trailers to be driven up to the barn, oblivious until the evening that the Blitz had begun.

In Monks Risborough, Doreen cycled her usual route to play tennis with friends, the village as quiet as ever. All she could hear as she cycled was birdsong, the rustle of autumn leaves and the familiar click of her bicycle wheels as she sped along the path, her curly hair flying out behind her in the wind. And in Woking, Ethel strode out for her daily walk with Pan VII. To her, the world sounded the same as it ever did – but had a bomb been whistling towards her that very second she wouldn't have heard it anyway. Although she'd never admit it except in her diary, she lived in constant fear of being unable to hear the warnings of a raid that might kill her.

When bombs began falling on London in the late afternoon, Rebecca was turning her thoughts towards lunch. Living with her brothers in New York, she was making the most of the life of leisure she had been forced into. Getting up late on most mornings, she would gather her long hair back into a bun and put on her favourite bathrobe before making her way to the piano to compose, losing herself for hours. Like Dorothy, Doreen and Ethel, Rebecca wouldn't realise the Blitz had begun until the news broke over the wireless.

At first, the Blitz didn't mark a significant change in their lives. These were not, after all, the first bombs to be dropped on Britain.

And Rebecca's world had already been turned upside down in 1939, when she was denied permission to return to the UK. But the impact that the Blitz would have on Britain's musical life affected all of them. London's concert scene had only just been surviving at a significantly reduced capacity. The daily raids would make it impossible for concerts to continue as usual. Musicians were going to have to improvise.

As far as the Proms programmers were concerned the show would go on, bombs or no bombs. Henry Wood was infuriated that the Proms had been interrupted by the changes to public broadcasting. He laid plans for the 1940 festival to go ahead, whether or not the BBC was still prepared to fund and broadcast the concerts. As venues go, the Queen's Hall was not a sensible bet during wartime. It seated more than 2,500, had no air raid shelter, and its sumptuously decorated interior with padded Venetian red seats and matching lampshades was worryingly flammable. It was also close to the BBC in the middle of Fitzrovia, a prime bombing target. But Henry was not going to be dissuaded. The Queen's Hall was the symbolic heart of London's music-making and had been home to the Proms from its very first concert in 1895. And the acoustics had no equivalent in London. Even in the upper balcony, right at the back, audiences could hear every word whispered by the singers on stage. For Henry, there was no other venue that would do.

Partly, at least, he was so belligerent because he assumed the dangers would be similar to those faced during World War I. He had weathered those with little difficulty. During one 1915 Prom a bomb fell close enough to the Queen's Hall to bring ceiling plaster showering down onto the audience and orchestra. A couple of orchestra members fled, but Henry simply kept conducting. He and the orchestra played an impromptu waltz after the programme finished to occupy the trapped audience as they waited for the all-clear. Finally, after several hours of dancing and improvised entertainment, everyone left unscathed at one in the morning.

With this as his experience of wartime peril, Henry saw no reason why the 1940 Proms shouldn't proceed as planned. So in January he secured permission for the Queen's Hall to be used as a concert venue, and the Proms season began at 8 p.m. sharp on 10 August. Safety concessions mainly involved putting up warning signs saying either 'Air Raid Alert' or 'All Clear', or preparing entertainment – ranging from musical quizzes to communal singing – for those audience members who decided to stay in the hall during the raids.

The war hadn't diminished the scope of Henry's ambition as far as programming was concerned, either. He compiled a season that brought together some of the most exciting voices of contemporary music from around the world, and he clearly had little intention of letting politics and patriotism shape his programmes. In one concert, for instance, a lilting setting of a Blake poem by Granville Bantock, Dorothy's old composition teacher, was placed alongside Soviet composer Alexander Mosolov's terrifying Futurist orchestral piece *Iron Foundry* – a churning, violent evocation of the modern factory, the orchestra used like one giant industrial machine. French composers Ravel and Paul Dukas were included alongside Brits Vaughan Williams and William Walton – and of course Ethel, whose overtures to both *The Boatswain's Mate* and *The Wreckers* were scheduled for performance. Prom 3, meanwhile, had a Nordic theme, and although Norway had been recently occupied by Nazi forces, Henry programmed Norwegians Edvard Grieg and Johan Halvorsen alongside the music of Germans Robert Schumann and Felix Mendelssohn.

While the BBC was blacklisting German music still in copyright, the 1940 Proms season defiantly included living German composers. And not just any composers. Henry programmed several pieces by Richard Strauss, who, despite his mistrust of the Nazi regime, had been prominent in the Third Reich as President of the official Reich Chamber of Music from 1933 to 1935. Henry's message was that music should transcend politics. His commitment was to the highest musical quality, no matter the composer's nationality or personal views. Nonetheless, the world premieres in the season were reserved for British composers. Women were better represented than usual (bringing them up to a grand total of 4 per cent of the composers programmed). Both Elisabeth Lutyens and Elizabeth Maconchy had world premieres billed – as did Dorothy, with a newly commissioned orchestral piece, *Three Divertissements*.

Henry quite possibly hoped that the accessible and tuneful *Divertissements* would appease concertgoers after the shock of Lutyens's and Maconchy's far more aggressive styles. He loved a good scandal as much as the next conductor, but even he was quite concerned about what the audience would make of Lutyens's experimental, atonal work which was, he remarked snidely, 'Thank God, only 5 minutes of excessive boredom.' Apparently the British musical establishment still wasn't quite ready for atonal music, even though the audience received this piece without uproar.

Fast-paced, sumptuously melodic and richly orchestrated, the three movements of *Divertissements* show Dorothy at her most imaginative and light-hearted. In its joviality the work was, perhaps, a perfect wartime piece, a crowd-pleasing distraction from the increasing difficulty of life outside the concert hall. Its premiere, in a programme also featuring Dorothy's beloved Bach, was set for 18 September.

The 1940 Proms got off to a roaring start, with the newspapers reporting full houses on most nights – 'not a little remarkable' given the 'transport difficulties during the black-out hours'. Contrasting with pre-war finery, listeners now came to concerts in sensible, practical clothing, expecting that they might have to spend a good deal of time in the Hall should the air raid sirens sound. Soldiers on leave came in their uniforms, as did those who had just clocked off from their duties as wardens and ambulance drivers. In general, critics framed the large audiences as a symbol of Londoners' stalwartness and common sense. Bemoaning the closing of the 1939 season as an unnecessary official measure, *The Times* wrote that 'principalities and powers have once more failed to kill the Promenades'. Dorothy's *Lamia* got a repeat performance, as did Ethel's *Boatswain* overture – both pieces had become veritable Proms regulars.

But history was to repeat itself. On the day the Blitz began, Henry insisted on continuing with a Prom that both began and ended during an air raid, with an audience of over 1,200. London authorities took matters into their own hands and closed down the festival just days before the *Divertissements* were to be performed. This was a considerable blow for Dorothy. It was supposed to have been her first big premiere in several years, keeping her name on London's musical map – and it wouldn't be easy to reschedule, with orchestras being gutted by conscription and concert venues at risk of destruction from bombing raids. The Proms was the most established orchestral concert programme in London. If Henry couldn't perform it there was very little chance of getting another orchestra to take a chance on a new work.

When the authorities gave permission for a pared-back Proms to go ahead in 1941, Dorothy tried to get the premiere rescheduled, but Henry had to disappoint her. The dramatically shortened season would include no premieres at all – and the *Divertissements* would wait a decade to be performed. Henry was right to be cautious. On 10 May 1941 the Queen's Hall was destroyed by an incendiary bomb. Nothing survived but the frame of the amphitheatre. Once-beautiful seats now rained rubble down onto the floor below, and as firefighters and journalists stepped into the ruins of the building they walked among the remains of composers' busts that had been smashed into pieces. Newspaper photographs showed the names 'Wagner', 'Handel' and 'Haydn' lying amid the charred and crumbling walls. The classical music world went into mourning. Not only had London's premier concert venue been destroyed, but the resident orchestra, the London Philharmonic, lost all the instruments and scores that had been kept in the Hall.

Yet in the face of so devastating a loss, audiences snapped into action. Hundreds of people donated to the fund to help the orchestra. Some even gave their instruments to the Philharmonic's musicians, 'from lovely old Italian violins by famous makers down to mandolins, guitars, a table-zither, a xylophone, and a Sousaphone'. Mourning became defiance, and plans were laid to rebuild the Hall as 'a symbol' that 'Germany no longer stands in the forefront of the musical nations'. Those plans for a new building were never realised, but the destruction of the Queen's Hall continued to fan the flames of hostility towards German music.

o o o o

Far away from London, Ethel sat at her desk in the quiet of Coign's cosy study, writing to Virginia. By 1940 they had become accustomed to each other's habits, quirks, flaws and strengths, and their friendship had moved beyond the tempestuous quarrels of the early 1930s. The war occupied a prominent place in their correspondence, and although Virginia put on a rather braver face to Ethel than she did in her diary, her fear of the regular air raids came through all too clearly. Bombs fell all round her London house in Mecklenburgh Square – and on 10 September 1940 the houses opposite hers took a direct hit. Everyone who lived there 'had sheltered in the basement. All killed I suppose.' In her letters to Ethel she described her and her husband Leonard's attempts to retrieve their belongings and move the Hogarth Press to Sussex. They drove to Holborn, which was 'like a nightmare. All heaps of glass, water running, a great gap at top of Chancery Lane; my typists office demolished.' A few days later she wrote again, saying that a bomb had blown out 'all windows, all ceilings, and smashed all my china'.

Not that Lewes or Woking were all that much safer. Virginia watched German planes being shot down over Lewes, bombs falling in the river near her home creating 'an island sea, of such indescribable beauty [...] that I cant take my eyes off it', and incendiaries fell around Ethel's house, leaving her 'secretly terrified'. Despite her age and frailty, she took it upon herself to take charge, calming down her hysterical housekeeper. Having Ethel calm the situation must have been quite alarming in itself. By this point her hearing was so poor that conversations were largely carried out with pen and paper, and her naturally loud voice had crescendoed to a mighty bellow. She tried the best she could with an ear trumpet, but seeing as she usually forgot to plug it into the box and simply wandered around with the wires trailing after her, conversation with Ethel was a 'screaming howling party', as Virginia put it.

When they weren't discussing the war, the pair exchanged notes about their autobiographical writings. *What Happened Next*, the final volume of Ethel's memoirs – packed with stories about her travels, her friendship with H. B. and her travails as both musician and suffragette – was published in the summer of 1940. Virginia was effusive. 'Virginia comes off very badly compared with Ethel, cant think how Ethel ever liked me, such a new moon slip of a life, compared with her full orange harvest glow. How when shes picked every plum off the tree, can she have fingered my crude little unripe apple?' (Virginia no doubt inserted the sexual imagery deliberately, to amuse Ethel.)

Given Ethel's ability to be so open about her life and experiences, Virginia saw her as a potential pioneer for women's writing. 'Why shouldnt you be not only the first woman to write an opera,' she asked, 'but equally the first to tell the truths about herself? Isnt the great artist the only person to tell the truths about herself?' She encouraged her to write openly about her sex life and masturbation. But Ethel reacted with consternation. There was still a little of her Victorian upbringing in her, and being open about her sexuality was one barrier she was simply not prepared to cross. Besides, although lesbianism was not strictly illegal, it was still considered taboo, and men were still being prosecuted for homosexuality. To admit romantic and sexual relationships with other women in such a public forum could have extremely negative social consequences for Ethel – and given that she mainly used her writing to promote awareness of her music, she was unwilling to give anyone a reason not to perform her work. Virginia replied that 'so much of life is sexual – or so they say – it rather limits autobiography if this is blacked out'.

Sex aside, Ethel was heartened enough by Virginia's feedback that she did begin writing another autobiography. She wrote to Virginia that she could continue writing, 'but it darkens my days trying to'. 'I do feel that *pro tem* my brain force, such as it is, has deteriorated.' She was struck with attacks of pneumonia, bronchitis, rheumatism, high blood pressure and, late in 1940, she was diagnosed with diabetes. After she was told the diagnosis, Virginia responded:

Leonard showed me a tiny snapshot of you in some paper: and my heart – ah hah! – the organ you dont believe in – gave one of those pleasurable leaps when the blood fills it and a release from non-liking becomes a positive rapture. There she sat, with her little bow tie and her great forehead, my uncastrated cat, challenging the world, yet divinely compassionate of its (so to speak my) infirmities. Thats why I want facts about diabetes.

How could Ethel know that this would be one of the last letters she would ever receive from Virginia? She had no idea that her friend's depression had resurfaced to the point that, on 28 March 1941, Virginia loaded her pockets with stones and drowned herself in the River Ouse. She had written to Ethel just a few months before that she felt 'convinced we shall all survive' the war, adding 'But thats because I want to.' Their final exchange of letters was a poignant end to such a tumultuous friendship. On 1 February 1941 Virginia sat down in the early morning hours to write, saying she had penned 'ever so many beautiful letters – cigarette letters – you know the kind, when one's devotion to Ethel rises like a silver smoke, too fine for words. [. . .] I would like to ask, quite simply, do you still love me?' Without hesitation, Ethel responded. 'You have given, and give me the greatest joy of my latter end. As it said in that wonderful American poem: "I am content," said the soldier. Yes, by God, I *am*. Bless you, my dear.'

They had last seen each other for tea in June 1940 – a separation so long Virginia considered it 'damnable'. Arrangements had been made for Virginia to come and stay at Coign in April, but it was never to be. The shock of Virginia's death left Ethel – for perhaps the first and only time in her life – speechless. When Vanessa Bell wrote to ask her if she would write a tribute, she couldn't bring herself to do it. 'Later perhaps – but my god not now. You see it was not only that I loved her; it was that my life [was] literally based on her.' How could she sum up the woman who for over a decade had surprised her, elated her, driven her completely to distraction? 'She was the centre of the one horse life I have led since music left me in the lurch,' she wrote to Henry Wood. There was little more that could be said.

o   o   o   o

Living in remote Monks Risborough with her parents, eighteen-year-old Doreen still found her daily life shaped by German bombs. Most dates in her 1940 diary record an air raid of some kind, but to her they represented more of an inconvenience than an existential threat. Amid taping up her grandmother's windows and blacking out her family home, life went on as usual. Unconcernedly declaring the raids 'very boring <u>and</u> tiring', Doreen continued to play tennis as machine-gun fire clattered overhead, take her music lessons through ongoing air raids and hunt for dresses in high-street shops with windows blown out by shard mines.

A few days a week, she would walk to her old school, Chilterns, where she taught throughout 1940 and 1941 for her compulsory service. She never particularly enjoyed teaching, but it would later prove a useful fallback when she found herself between commissions. She was starting to compose a little – just a couple of songs. These earliest works are lost, perhaps thrown away later in life because at this stage Doreen saw herself first and foremost as a performer. She might well have felt that her early efforts weren't yet representative of her ability as a composer. When she wasn't teaching she was performing in chamber groups with her family, or practising piano and cello: learning Chopin nocturnes, and Beethoven and Rachmaninoff's cello sonatas. She relished the opportunity to go to concerts, and travelled to see both Henry Wood and Imogen Holst conduct.

Doreen had a formidable work ethic, and a strong desire to please and impress her tutors. The big event of 1941, for which she had been preparing since January, was her Licentiate of the Royal Academy of Music exam in September: a prestigious and difficult teaching qualification involving performance, harmony and aural tests. Should she succeed she would get the letters LRAM after her name, bringing her one step closer to her brass plate at Underhill. She 'practised furiously' and submitted endless practice papers to her teachers. Doreen wanted to excel.

The day finally arrived, and on 8 September Doreen took the 10.56 train down to London for her performance exam. Her piano teacher Frederick Moore dropped by to wish her luck, sneaking her into the exam room so she could try the piano before she played. For pianists, not knowing what unfamiliar piano you'll be faced with is one of the most nerve-wracking parts of concert life. As Doreen put it, 'those few minutes helped me a lot.'

She thought her exam board were a 'very nice crowd' and the pieces 'went off well', but she still had her written papers, aural exam and an agonising wait. The next day she took the train to London again, this time with her sister Barbara. The aural exams were first, and due to her perfect pitch and years of practice, after just one minute, the examiner 'said "Thank God for a good ear" & pushed me out of the door!' The same afternoon she sat the written paper, thinking it 'quite good', and returned to Monks Risborough. On 17 September a letter arrived proclaiming Doreen an LRAM, with 78 per cent in her harmony exam and 91 per cent in her aural. Ecstatic, she 'rang up all the family', 'wrote to everyone else' and then cycled to her teachers to tell them 'the good news'.

Later that month, as Rebecca and Dorothy had decades before, Doreen began her studies at the Royal Academy of Music; her sister Barbara would follow her a little while after. Several days a week Doreen made the forty-mile train journey from Monks Risborough to London, setting off early, tramping to the train station with her cello on her back, also lugging along her handbag, music bag and gas mask. In contrast to her sheltered existence in Monks Risborough, where her diary entries recorded the minutiae of her days (events of note included teas with the family, music lessons and even washing her hair) the Academy was frantically busy.

Doreen stepped from Monks Risborough's narrow country lanes into the bustling chaos of Marylebone Road. On her way from the train station she passed Regent's Park, with its enormous tree-lined avenues leading to vast lawns dotted with walkers admiring the rose gardens and throwing food for the herons. As she approached the Academy itself the institution became as audible as it was visible: the rehearsal noises of hundreds of students all playing scales, split notes cutting through the cacophony of buses, shoppers and cafe-goers.

Now nearly every day was packed full of concerts, lessons, exams and social engagements with her new friends. Even though being in London meant the constant threat of bombs, air raid warnings became a footnote amid the whirlwind of rehearsals and recitals. She continued her piano lessons with Frederick, studied cello with the famed teacher Alison Dalrymple (who later taught Jacqueline du Pré) and attended harmony and musicianship classes. It was in one of these aural skills classes that she met fellow pianist and cat-lover Violet Graham, nicknamed 'V', who would become her closest friend. The teacher asked Violet to demonstrate the exercises, saying 'Just listen to this girl – with practice you students could do the same!' Doreen 'was quite dazzled by her effortless skill' – quite a compliment.

The pair went for coffee after the class, chatting about Violet's love of jazz – it transpired that she was an excellent singer as well as an exceptional pianist. They shared a mutual love of table tennis, so put a date in the diary for a game the next week. These weekly pre-aural-class games became a fixture in their joint calendar. Soon, the two women were inseparable. On Tuesday afternoons, they would watch Henry Wood rehearsing the First Student Orchestra in the Duke's Hall. Doreen doubted 'if we ever missed one of these occasions'.

Doreen and Violet excelled within their year group. Both received performance scholarships and they were regularly awarded the Academy's coveted end-of-year prizes. In one year 'we sat together and I asked her which prizes she was to receive and she said, "I really don't know. What are you getting?" Now, there are two prizes which are only announced on the day [. . .] I had one and V the other.' They were even chosen to represent the Academy when the Queen attended the prize-giving, for which they had to rehearse 'walking gracefully' and curtseying. When the day finally came, Doreen was relieved that she managed to retreat 'down the stairs in a long white dress with a red sash' without falling.

Between rehearsals, Violet and Doreen played piano duets together when they could. 'We discovered that we could more often get a room when the Air Raid warning had sounded as most professors etc. had retreated to the comparative safety of the basement and a cup of coffee!' So when the sirens sounded the two young women would throw caution to the wind and race upstairs, taking the threat of bombs as an opportunity to try out whatever scores they could lay their hands on.

For Rebecca, the Blitz was less perilous. News from London made its way to her through the newspapers and on the radio. When the bombing began, the American reporter Ed Murrow was living in Hallam Street in London's Fitzrovia – just a few streets away from the Royal Academy of Music – and sent regular broadcasts back to the States describing the devastation that the raids were wreaking on the capital. In a transmission on the evening of 21 September 1940, Murrow stood on a London rooftop and painted the scene for his listeners in America. He could see the 'faint-red angry snap of anti-aircraft bursts against a steel blue sky', and buildings that had been destroyed by bombs. 'You'll hear two explosions', Murrow says, ' —— there they are', as two muffled thumps interrupt him. Then the bombs are 'moving still just a little closer [. . .] the searchlights are stretching out now'. The thumps become thundering booms, the explosions moving closer still to his rooftop.

Rebecca could only listen in despair from across the Atlantic, where she sat basking in the sun that streamed into her brother's peaceful apartment. When the Queen's Hall was destroyed, the place where she had performed in her first professional orchestral job, she read about it in the newspapers. The *New York Times* described the 'clouds of white smoke pouring still from the ruin', with 'water dripping everywhere'. One can only imagine the sense of loss that Rebecca would have felt reading these lines from such a distance, and powerless to help.

The forced separation from Britain and daily reports of its destruction continually turned her thoughts towards home. She pondered how it was that 'we can project our memories like a searchlight to touch now this, now the Regent's Park, now someone we knew. But the people one loves most one cannot see – they elude one. Their faces have been worn away in one's memory by the friction of constant thought.' And she had many faces to remember. Frank Bridge, a friend and colleague, died unexpectedly from heart failure in January 1941. Unable to travel back for the funeral, Rebecca instead played in his memorial concert in Washington. Then there were those who were very much alive but whose presence was sorely missed in the States. Foremost among them were Dora and May, who had kept up her role as impresario at her Mostly Musicians Club with her usual gregariousness, directing operations while she clattered about in a battered tin helmet that she kept at the ready – just in case.

Far away from all this, Rebecca did what she could – she composed. Historical British music had been a sporadic source of inspiration for her, and in 1941 she turned to the music of the Tudor period. Against the backdrop of the Blitz broadcasts, she set to work on the *Passacaglia on an Old English Tune* for viola and piano. The old English tune in question was by Thomas Tallis, the same Tudor choral composer who had inspired Vaughan Williams. Rebecca used Tallis's theme as the basis for her passacaglia – a set of variations on a repeated bass. It starts simply, a melancholy viola melody in a minor key, that shifts briefly to the major – a glimmer of hope – before closing in the minor.

It's an unexceptional theme, but what she does with it is phenomenal. In the third variation the viola part bursts suddenly into a furious, virtuosic set of chords. From this point on the theme is broken down, fragmented, as Rebecca transforms Tallis's idea into something wholly new. Finally, the theme returns complete for a heart-stopping, triumphant conclusion. It's tempting to hear the *Passacaglia* as an ode to a Britain that Rebecca knew was changing – not a nostalgic lament, but more an expression of hope that change can bring renewal and transformation.

She dedicated the piece to her niece Magdalen, to whom she gave lessons while she was staying with her brother Eric and his wife, Beryl, in their Manhattan apartment. Compositionally speaking at least, this arrangement was relatively productive. Rebecca slept in late, composing at their piano as and when she wanted. During this period she produced *Daybreak*, a setting of John Donne's erotic poem 'Stay, O sweet and do not rise!' for voice and string quartet, followed by *Dumka* for violin, viola and piano, and the *Prelude, Allegro, and Pastorale* for viola and clarinet.

In some ways, *Dumka* and the *Prelude* couldn't be further apart. Written so close together, they demonstrate what a formidable compositional range Rebecca had. *Dumka* is a sumptuous rhapsody which has recently found popularity. Much of it is steeped in the Romantic sound world of Dvořák and Brahms – but this is contrasted with moments in a far more modern style, close to Rebecca's contemporaries Bartók and Sibelius. The crunchy harmonies and driving rhythms lend it a crisp freshness. It ends in a curiously understated way, with the string instruments meandering through fragments of melody, while the piano quietly rocks in its lowest registers, like a tolling funeral bell.

If *Dumka* has something of the modern about it, then the *Prelude, Allegro, and Pastorale* is nothing *but* modernity. No lush melodies or rich harmonies here. Each movement is just a few minutes long, like a musical epigram. Written for the unusual combination of clarinet and viola, the piece is texturally sparse and uncompromising, the timbres dissimilar enough that you can hear each melodic line clearly. The instruments always maintain their individuality, two equal partners working together rather than ever truly joining forces. Everything is restrained, thoughtful and enigmatic – it is, in the composer's words, a 'very unpretentious' piece.

Unsurprisingly, the *Prelude* was well received when it premiered at the 1942 Festival of the International Society for Contemporary Music, declared among 'the most important work' on the programme. As far as the critics were concerned, Rebecca was still a part of the international avant-garde. But her new works did not bring in much money. With little sign of the war ending, and unable to transfer her money from the UK to the US, Rebecca had to find some way to make ends meet. She certainly wasn't going to be receiving huge royalties for UK performances of her work. With a couple of exceptions, these had dried up entirely. So she turned to performing in the US, in 1940 securing an important showcase at the Composers' Forum-Laboratory, an organisation dedicated to promoting new music in New York. Other smaller concerts followed, and other musicians occasionally gave performances of her works, 'The Seal Man' continuing to prove popular among singers.

But these performances alone couldn't provide her with enough money to survive. So in 1942 she took up a temporary position as a children's nurse for a family in Connecticut. There, with four children to look after and educate – a toddler and three young boys – and an endless list of chores, she found it impossible to compose because 'my mind will not run that way, it is sucked up by all the other things I have to do'. She furtively taught the children to play a little piano and found time to practise before lunch and to play chamber music with other musicians in the evenings. But her fingers were 'puckered from all the washing', and it is 'hard to play well'. In place of composition, however, Rebecca wrote. She started jotting down bits of conversations, observations and memories, some of which would later find their way into her memoir or short stories. These notes became a welcome creative outlet, breaking the monotony of bathing the children and watching them argue in the sandpit.

o   o   o   o

Back in the UK, Dorothy was enjoying her temporary career change at the age of forty-two. She kept working for the Women's Land Army throughout the war. While she relished riding the threshing machine around the farm, the majority of her time was spent doing back-breaking work – everything from digging ditches to birthing cows, sowing seeds and pulling up vegetables. But it was also a time of happiness and liberation away from the dangers of

London. Dorothy adored the freedom and physicality of working at a Hertfordshire farm close to her home, returning exhausted each evening to a hot meal cooked by Pookie.

The Land Army kept Dorothy away from bombs and gunfire, but it could not save her from personal tragedy. In January 1941 Elsie Owen, with whom she had travelled in Italy, performed on so many occasions and taught at the Royal Academy, was found dead in her home in Hampstead. At just forty-nine years old, she was murdered by her husband, Arthur. Up until the war their marriage had been a happy one, but the constant air raids and threat of death brought on a depressive psychosis in Arthur, and in late 1940 he went to a nursing home following a breakdown. Only three days after he left the nursing home he killed Elsie with household implements, telling police that 'rather than ask her to face a bleak future I decided she should die and not be asked to face it'. He was found guilty but insane and was admitted to Broadmoor Criminal Lunatic Asylum, where he committed suicide two years later. A prize was established in Elsie's memory at the Royal Academy – of which Doreen would be one of the first recipients. Dorothy never really came to terms with the suddenness and violence of Elsie's murder, and the loss of such a close friend.

Then Viola's health took a turn for the worse. She had been unwell for some time, and Dorothy had turned down a job in the BBC's music department partly because of her extensive commitments as her mother's carer. Between working as a Land Girl and looking after Viola, a BBC job would have left her no time to work on the Symphony and Violin Sonata that she was sketching, the Sonata perhaps in memory of Elsie. Dorothy was well aware that her mother was ailing, but when the moment came in 1942 her death was nonetheless devastating. Composition was put to one side; the Symphony would never be finished.

By day Dorothy was now a farmer, but by night she kept up her career as a pianist. With performance opportunities for her orchestral compositions rapidly disappearing, she focused her attention on giving piano recitals across the country to boost morale. She broadcast for the BBC throughout the war, which brought her into contact with fellow composer Elizabeth Poston, who was working as the director of music for the European Service. The two women struck up a friendly correspondence. Elizabeth thought it 'splendid' that Dorothy was in the Land Army, working close to Elizabeth's own hometown, and was especially impressed that she kept performing as well. She admired her compositions, and requested that her programme should 'include your most delightful "Humoresque"'. She was extremely specific about timings – although this might not just have been standard broadcasting fare. It was rumoured that Elizabeth was working for the intelligence services, and would send coded messages to the Resistance via the music that she broadcast on the European Service. So as Dorothy played in the dead of night in a secret studio protected by barbed wire fences, it's quite possible that she was unknowingly participating in a moment of wartime espionage.

From 1942 Dorothy began giving concerts via the recently established Council for the Encouragement of Music and the Arts (CEMA, which would eventually become the Arts Council). The protection of British artistic life was felt to be especially pressing during wartime, with the government devoting precious funds to support Britain's cultural infrastructure – £50,000 for CEMA's first year. With a mandate to 'provide opportunities for hearing good music' for 'people who, on account of wartime conditions, are cut off from these things', and to 'encourage music-making and play-acting among the people themselves', CEMA funded concerts in factories, churches, shops and town halls, and gave money to Women's Institutes across the country to help them stage plays and set up local choirs, democratising access to music.

Dorothy's work for CEMA took her up and down the UK, from Southend-on-Sea in Essex to Trowbridge in Wiltshire, playing in hospitals, town halls and community and adult education centres. Resources were stretched – she had to share hotel rooms with her fellow performers and the pianos were generally not 'all they should be'. Despite these less than ideal circumstances, Dorothy's performances were received with joy and thanks, providing spiritual solace in a time of anguish and fear. And they were important for her, too. She loved her work as a Land Girl, but it wasn't where her heart lay. These concerts kept her own spirits up, her beloved Chopin and Bach offering a refuge from the realities of wartime life.

o   o   o   o

Dodging through London's bomb-ravaged streets in 1944, Doreen and Violet would sometimes glance at each other in fear as they heard a disembodied buzzing sound approaching like the gentle hum of summer bees, then becoming a mechanical drone as it came closer. These were V-2 and V-1 flying bombs, which had begun terrorising London in 1944, and which were nicknamed 'doodlebugs' for their distinctive noise. Powered by a jet engine which would cut out over the city, the bombs would either fall straight to the ground or continue on their trajectory for an unknown length of time. It was almost impossible to know where they would land.

By this time Violet was working as an ambulance driver, and she nicknamed the doodlebugs 'Gambler's Choice', because you had to choose whether to

throw yourself down covering your ears for the expected bang – (feeling a complete idiot when it disappeared over the rooftops and you heard a faint bang from streets away) or did you hope for the best!!! The worst ones simply crept up on you in silence – having been drifting for quite long distances.

Violet was called out to attend the scenes of countless doodlebug attacks, but after pulling bodies from rubble and fighting to save the wounded, she would return to her other life, joining Doreen at the Academy for coffee and piano and table tennis. Doreen also started sharing her own compositions with her friend so she could play them through and give her feedback. Violet went on to become an important interpreter of Doreen's early work, and when she performed during the war it was often dressed in her ambulance driver's uniform, 'her heavy shoes clumping onto the platform'.

Although Doreen had come to the Academy as a performer, composition became increasingly important to her as she progressed. She ended up in the harmony class of the thirty-six-year-old William Alwyn, at the time a well-known composer and flautist. He had dark, slicked-back hair, with blue eyes behind distinctive circular glasses with thick black frames. Doreen had her first lesson with him in October 1941. At first, they made little personal impression on one another. 'He is very nice – rather shy,' she wrote in her diary. Doreen's songs, however, clearly made their mark. The first song she took him was called 'Daffodils', and he told her that she had 'a gift for melody – wants me to write some more songs'. From the very start, William encouraged Doreen, and upgraded her harmony lessons to composition. As her lessons continued, so did his praise of her work. On 24 October she was delighted that he liked her new song, 'The Moon', and had decreed she had 'a "flair" for this sort of composition'.

As the months passed, Doreen grew in confidence as a composer. She was clearly influenced by Vaughan Williams, but also by upcoming figures like Britten and Walton, whose rhythmic punchiness she particularly admired. Sadly she only kept the music that she wrote after a few years of study. But if her 1943 *Humoresque* and *Nocturne* for cello are anything to go by, Doreen established her own unique voice early on, full of rhythmic energy and harmonic invention. No wonder William was so impressed. As her music developed, so too did her interactions with her teacher, slowly beginning to change in tone. In November he instructed her to go in 'any time & see if he has a few minutes to spare'. By the end of 1941 her previously shy tutor was 'very chatty', in January 1942 'very talkative', and by March 'very merry!'

Doreen playing her cello 'Perky' and the piano, *c.*1942.

What Doreen had perhaps not realised was that the man she met in 1941 was looking for a new direction. Just two years before, in 1939, William had renounced his entire catalogue of works. He felt that his musical style needed overhauling, and gave up his career as a flautist to focus exclusively on finding his new compositional path. And it seems that his desire for change extended to his private life, too. His relationship with Doreen became increasingly friendly, despite the fact that he was already married to Olive Pull – a pianist he had met in the 1920s when they were both students at the Academy – and was father to two young boys. When they had got engaged, Olive was emerging as a promising performer and had tentatively begun to try her hand at composition as well. But marriage put an end to her career. All that remains of her compositions are some manuscripts stuffed into a tattered Harrods bag which lives in the archive named after her husband.

If Doreen had known that Olive had put aside her career for William, it might have warned her against getting romantically involved with her new teacher, seventeen years her senior and already famous. But beyond the fact that he was married, Doreen had no way of knowing the details of William's private life. And even if she had, it might not have stopped her. She was not a worldly wise nineteen-year-old. With her curly dark hair and loveably lopsided smile she was, in her own way, a beautiful woman and had received attention from men both in her hometown and at the Academy. But William was her first serious love affair. Doreen was impressionable, and like any hard-working student she desired approval from her tutors. She clearly admired William – almost to the point of worship – and showed none of the reservations that Rebecca had when approached by her older teachers.

Their relationship became more and more intimate, with William continuing to pursue her over the next couple of years. Over the course of 1942 Doreen's feelings towards him grew more affectionate. In October, she was disappointed to find him absent – 'Couldn't find Mr Alwyn so no lesson – very sad!', and a few days later, 'Mr Alwyn not there again. Wonder what's the matter?' The tone of her comments shifted just perceptibly from professional admiration to mild infatuation. On a particularly hot day in June she noticed that he gave her lesson in just 'his shirt sleeves', and two days later he was 'terribly sweet! most helpful & very chatty'.

Throughout the summer Doreen took him new compositions regularly, and William was delighted with her progress, putting her pieces forward for inclusion in student showcase concerts. By the autumn, their student–teacher relationship had shifted to something more like close colleagues. William now brought new pieces that interested him to her lessons, asking Doreen for her opinion on them, sometimes playing her his own music as well. In November she gave a snapshot of their newly intimate dynamic: 'Practised in Room 27 while Mr Alwyn had his lunch. He played me some Grieg folk tunes – was in a very sweet mood!' This scene – one at the piano, the other listening – was to become a familiar one, the musical bedrock for their relationship. Over the coming years Doreen and William would become each other's muses, critics, confidantes and closest friends.

William may have been the focus of her attention, but Doreen had other admirers. There's an undated Valentine's Day poem from 'Philip' among her possessions, an ode to her 'beautiful eyes' which 'thrill me as the northern light', and her 'hair a gleaming brown cascade'. Presumably this came from her time at the Academy. It's difficult to tell for certain whether she had already been on dates with Philip, or whether she met him, as requested, 'on Thursday, near your gate at five o'clock'. It may have been a case of unrequited love. Or perhaps Philip became one of the many men with whom Doreen went on dates to cover her relationship with William, never revealing that her heart was already elsewhere.

William began scheduling Doreen's lessons for the end of the day, so that he had an excuse to drive her to Marylebone Station. Sometimes these lifts would include detours through Regent's Park, or covert coffees. In January 1944 Doreen wrote in a rather disgruntled tone that William 'was going to have tea with me (spent most of the lesson talking about it!) but saw Barbara and promptly shoved off!'. It was not unheard of for Academy students to have close friendships with their teachers – Dorothy often went out for dinner and concerts with John McEwen as part of a group, and Doreen would later share a house with her cello teacher from her school days, Peers Coetmore. But William's skittish behaviour – and the steady escalation of activities from teas to car drives and visits to the Royal Academy Club – suggests that this was not the kind of friendship he had in mind.

On one of these outings, William finally made his move. Years later, Doreen remembered the start of the affair:

Once we ventured as far as Hendon and I think it was here that he said 'Will you come away with me for a weekend?'

Then I said 'How soon and where?' But this did not happen until July. William went to Stevenage where his son Jonathan was at school and so he said he would take him out to lunch and establish the role of attentive father. I went down by train in the evening and having signed in we met in the hotel quite by accident, had dinner together and then planned which bedroom we should meet in – his not mine. It was a wonderful night and next day we left by car together and spent a happy few hours in the hay under a haystack. 'She has straws in her hair, she's as mad as a hatter' – I don't remember the next verse. We collected sandwiches from a nearby pub and ate them in the straw. Then alas it was time to return to London.

Their life of passion and secrecy had begun. Doreen had to learn to keep her feelings hidden – even, sometimes, from herself. Her diaries simply stop in May 1944.

o   o   o   o

Tucked away in Woking, Ethel faced bereavement after bereavement. After the devastating loss of Virginia, Betty Balfour, one of her oldest friends, died in 1941. She was followed by Ethel's niece Hilda Venn, who died of cancer in 1942, and then her old amour Winnaretta in 1943. Ethel's relationship with her had been full of fights, reconciliations and scandals, but they remained close until the day she died. 'My heart is so full of gratitude for all you put in my life,' Winnaretta wrote to her, 'your music, your incomparable singing, your wit, even your bouts of anger . . . I think of you so much, darling.'

And yet, throughout her final years, Ethel kept up her stalwart attitude. Right through 1940 and 1941 she was seen by her neighbours striding around Woking, taking the country air. She was desperately frustrated that her physical infirmities prevented her from volunteering for service as she had during World War I, leaving her unable to do 'any mortal useful thing in this awful time to help'. But she still had the energy to prepare a score of her opera *The Boatswain's Mate* for broadcast in 1941, which pleased her immensely. She was thrilled when anybody took an interest in her compositions, and overjoyed when her Mass was broadcast in 1943.

Her personality little changed by her illnesses, Ethel continued to exude warmth and goodwill and, despite having to carry out all conversations with pen and paper, she struck up many new friendships in the 1940s. 'She was a titan to the very end,' one recalled, 'making light of her infirmities, laughing at her disadvantages and being ever ready to make a joke against herself.' And there was one final (slightly tongue-in-cheek) crush – Mrs Hubbard, the woman who was translating *Impressions that Remained* into French. 'She is a remarkably attractive woman,' Ethel remarked. 'I so deeply admire Mrs Hubbard's nose!!'

And yet Ethel Smyth, slayer of misogynists and defender of women's rights, eventually met her match in, of all things, a chamber pot. In February 1942, her chamber pot broke underneath her after she got up to relieve herself on a particularly cold night. Unable to pull herself up, she had to wait to be rescued by her housekeeper the next morning. The accident caused Ethel considerable injury and, suffering from concussion, she had to be taken to a nursing home by ambulance. Although she was eventually allowed back home, she now had to have an in-house carer. 'I feel very shaky & think I missed a good chance of getting out of this world with no trouble to anyone,' she confessed to her diary. Whether her legs would ever be 'good for anything again I don't know'. When Henry Wood asked to call on her, she tried to deter him, warning him that he shouldn't 'expect to find even the ghost of the old Ethel'. But, she reassured him, 'I've had a good life.'

House guests arrived despite Ethel telling them not to come 'to see what remains of your Ethel', and she was not without company in her last days. She was still receiving guests on 5 May 1944, just three days before her death. After Ethel was cremated, her ashes were scattered on 'her' golf course opposite Coign – a fitting resting place for the 'Duchess of Woking', the Golf Club's most notorious member. Obituaries struggled to summarise Ethel's extraordinary life. 'A standard-bearer has fallen,' Edith wrote, 'a perfectly delightful companion, both sympathetic and argumentative, with a gift for friendship.' What people loved and remembered above all was her personality: 'She was a great woman, who loved truth, justice, beauty, humour and life.' Another writer astutely observed that those who initially dismissed her as an 'eccentric' eventually found her only fault was to be 'a brilliantly intelligent woman who felt violently about almost everything, and did not give a fig for even the more rudimentary conventions'. But perhaps the most complete tribute came from Vita Sackville-West, Ethel's one-time competitor for Virginia's affections, in her poem 'To Ethel: May 8th 1944':

> You lived. You fully lived. In this weak age
> Perplexed and wavering, you charged your glass
> With wine not water, faith not doubt.
> Faith where you chose to fix your blinkered eyes
> What you believed, you would believe, perverse
> Nine times in ten, but never shilly-shally.

Wild welcomer of life, of love, of art,
Your hat askew, your soul on a dead level.
Rough, tough, uncomfortable, true,
Chained to the iron railings of your creed,
Strange that you should be dead.

You were marked out to meet a violent end;
You should have matched the violent young men,
Stormers of evil in all elements,
Earth, water, air and in daring mind.
They were your peers; their life, their death, were yours;
Not in a Surrey villa, of old age,
Where you who greatly lived have gently died.

AFTERMATH

The process of writing Ethel's music out of history began with her obituaries. True, many trotted out the now-standard line that she was the 'greatest woman composer of all time', still using the gendered caveat that Ethel so despised. But a number of larger articles began to chip away at her reputation. 'It was not as a musical composer that she made her strongest mark. She had a greater command of words than of notes,' they said, relegating her compositions to the position of 'a documentary appendix' to her autobiographies.

Possibly the most galling verdict on Ethel's life was that her 'chief mistake' was to have spent so much time fighting against prejudice. Commentators chastised her for having 'forgot that it is a composer's business first, last, and most of the time, to compose'. Goodness knows what Ethel would have made of this interpretation. Had she still been alive she would surely have fired off an angry letter to *The Times*. Edith remained convinced that she was in contact with Ethel's spirit, reassuring Ethel's grieving friends that she had 'heard from my people <u>Over There</u> of her <u>happy arrival</u>'. Spirit-Ethel never commented on her obituaries. Perhaps Edith decided not to trouble her with them.

But one of the most decisive nails in Ethel's coffin was the emergence of the young opera composer Benjamin Britten. Just thirty years old when Ethel died, within a year he would establish himself as 'the Golden Boy of contemporary music, immensely successful and immensely fashionable'. And Britten wanted to cast himself as the first and only British opera composer of note. He had no intention of acknowledging Ethel as a predecessor – whatever his operas may have owed to her example. Britten's music library holds a copy of *The Wreckers* among a number of Ethel's scores, and his breakthrough opera *Peter Grimes* (also about a small coastal community's response to acts of questionable morality) owes more than a passing debt to it. Nonetheless, Britten claimed that England 'has never had a tradition of native opera', despite the fact he knew full well that the Sadler's Wells Opera, which premiered *Peter Grimes*, had staged *Wreckers* only six years before.

Worse, the critics followed Britten's lead. There were a few small dissenting voices who pointed out that he was far from England's first opera composer. But a consensus formed in agreement with Britten's view that the seventeenth-century composer Henry Purcell 'was the last important international figure of English music', the brevity of his works a much-needed 'antithesis of the music which has been popular for so long in this country'. With few left to fight on its behalf, Ethel's music couldn't withstand such a comprehensive dismissal. There were a couple of concerts – her Mass was broadcast by the BBC in 1947, and ageing friends sometimes performed her chamber works – but within a few years of her death Ethel was erased almost completely from concert halls.

From now on, Britten would be the figure who dominated Britain's concert scene. He was in the right place at the right time with the right music. *Peter Grimes* premiered less than a month after VE Day, when London was in a constant state of celebration. After nearly six years of war, relief and excitement now pulsed through the capital. Colour burst back on to bomb-ravaged streets. Women dressed in their brightest clothes danced congas around bonfires; children waved British flags at street parties held in the rubble of what had once been their neighbourhoods; red, white and blue bunting hung from the windows of homes, restaurants and pubs. Before the audience for *Peter Grimes* donned their opera finery for the first time in years, a few might have sipped their morning tea from the VE commemorative cups that some neighbourhoods made for their street parties, bearing pictures of Stalin, Churchill and Roosevelt 'United for Victory' in blue and gold.

England was ready to rebuild – and to start afresh. In July the Labour Party was elected in a shock landslide victory, displacing the wartime Prime Minister Winston Churchill. The British voted in their millions for the creation of a welfare state. A 1942 report by the economist William Beveridge had provided a tantalising glimpse of what seemed to many like a utopian dream – from unemployment benefit to national health provision and state pensions. The Beveridge Report was overwhelmingly popular with the British public, particularly among the military and among those who did not want to return to pre-war poverty. When the Conservatives expressed doubts about implementing some of the more radical suggestions of the report, British voters expressed their disapproval at the polls. And Labour rewarded them for their faith. Over the next few years, they implemented a series of bills that constituted a seismic shift in government policy, introducing a family allowance, increasing national insurance and state pensions, tightening rent controls, and creating the National Health Service in 1948.

Britten's music was hard-edged but still energetic and melodious, set to librettos that often focused on the working classes. In this England bristling with desire for change, it seemed to be the sound of the future. The film director Wendy Toye, who later worked with Doreen, played an urchin in the *Grimes* premiere, and remembered it as part of 'truly golden years at Sadler's Wells', when 'we were young and life was exciting'. Ironically, it probably helped that Britten was a pacifist. During the war his status as a conscientious objector had won him few friends, but in the post-war years his strongly held pacifist views were in tune with those of a public who had no desire to spend another second of their lives fighting.

Peter Grimes turned Britten into an overnight celebrity. Commissions followed and record companies battled for the rights to his music. He became a wealthy man (his new Rolls-Royce provoked a copy-cat purchase by the considerably older Vaughan Williams). And then in 1946, CEMA was renamed the Arts Council of Great Britain, and granted a royal charter to provide government funding for the arts. Britten received £3,000 to fund a touring opera company, the English Opera Group, and later, £500 towards the establishment of a music festival at Aldeburgh, the main focus of which would be opera. Finally, Britain was ready for the state-funded opera that Ethel had dreamed of so many years before.

Might things have been different had Britten been a woman? Would this have been the much-needed step towards gender equality that Ethel had been forced to spend her life fighting for? Or would the critics then have expressed more ambivalence about Britten's music, as they had with Ethel's? Because for all the changes that were made in post-war Britain, one of the things that remained conservative was attitudes towards gender.

As during World War I, women's wartime employment was assumed to be temporary. And in many cases, women were quite glad to give up their wartime jobs and build a stable home with a husband and children. Mass Observation found in 1944 that 'a large majority of women factory workers look forward to settling down'. The marriage rate rose after the war and continued to rise until the 1970s. A falling birth rate had provoked governmental panic, prompting a Royal Commission on Population to provide recommendations to encourage women to have children. The 1945 Family Allowances Act aimed to offer some motivation, providing a non-means-tested benefit for every second and subsequent child. And with equal pay a distant dream, women were rarely paid the same as men, which gave them less incentive to stay in their jobs. Structurally, the post-war environment was designed to encourage women out of the workplace and into the home.

The gendered war propaganda of World War II was even more extreme than that of World War I. Stereotypes of women were weaponised: they were painted as the madonnas waiting at home, saintly, for their men to return; as syphilitic whores who soldiers were warned to stay away from while on duty; as gossips whose loose tongues cost lives; or as helpless victims of the rape and abuse that would follow an Allied defeat. The essence of these caricatures lingered on in the conservative women's magazines that flew off shelves in their millions through the late 1940s, their covers demanding of readers 'Do you deserve the man you dream of?', with articles offering diet tips and cleaning advice.

Doreen may have enjoyed dipping into these magazines in her rare spare moments, but she had no intention of giving up her wartime freedoms – either in her job or her sex life. Her career was only just beginning. In 1944 she had penned her Cello Sonatina, exploiting the beautiful deep sonorities of the instrument in long, flowing melodic lines uninterrupted by the piano accompaniment. This was followed by the Piano Sonatina in 1945–6, whose fast movements whizz and snap along, full of complex rhythms and harmonies that challenge the pianist and the listener. You never quite know what the next note will be. But she manages to bring the same intensity to the central, slow movement as well. It's so powerfully introspective that it can be almost unnerving to hear, as if you're intruding on a moment that is far too private for prying ears. But once you accept the intimacy it can become like a shared meditation, the calm stillness of the music almost spiritual. It was Violet who gave the Sonatina its first performance, playing from Doreen's manuscript at the Duke's Hall in November 1946.

Doreen finished the Piano Sonatina while she was away from William – first she was on holiday with her family in Newquay, then he with his in Wales. They wrote to each other constantly, and she tried to feel close to him by listening to BBC broadcasts of his music in her holiday cottage. Their 'honeymoon period', such as it could be, had not lasted long. The difficulties of carrying out an affair with a man who was married with two children became obvious almost immediately. In William's first surviving letter to Doreen, he soundly reprimanded her for forgetting 'to write "Personal" on the envelope'. Was there an argument behind that comment, Olive picking up her husband's post to find a lengthy declaration of love in Doreen's excited scrawl? Or perhaps it was pre-emptive, delaying the inevitable, as the 'Personal' letters piled up on the doormat of their suburban home.

The curtness of William's letter set the tone for their relationship. Doreen would write to him, gushing, to say 'once again I love you.' She lamented that 'Words seem so inadequate', promising that 'I will truly try to show you with my life that I mean this with all my heart'. But his replies were always more guarded. Once, when Doreen begged for 'a real "love letter"' from him, he responded with advice about composition, comments about the weather and the hope that she would have 'time to yourself, with time for reading & relaxation'. Doreen was, unsurprisingly, disappointed. 'I did ask you for a real <u>love letter</u> – not a lecture!' The closest William got to romantic overtures was the admission that he 'Felt very dreary after leaving you'.

William tried to explain away his lack of effusion by saying he was 'self-conscious with a pen', but his earlier letters to Olive tell a different story. 'I think of you every moment and my whole life centres on your love and happiness,' he told her. 'I kiss you from the tips of your toes to the tips of your sweet breasts.' The letters are pages long, filled with sketches for Olive to show their son Jonathan. Perhaps it was guilt that stopped William from expressing himself in a similar way to Doreen. Or maybe he had initially thought of her as a casual fling, and was taken aback by the intensity of her feelings for him. For as far as Doreen was concerned, William was the heart of her existence.

If not emotionally, then at least musically William could give Doreen the support she needed. Her String Quartet No. 1, composed in 1945, made her the first woman to win the prestigious Alfred J. Clements Chamber Music Prize. The string quartet as a genre held a special place in Doreen's heart, as it had for Ethel; she thought it 'the most perfect of mediums'. Full of the ferocity and power that would become Doreen's trademark, the Quartet eventually got a broadcast with the BBC after it was accepted by the Music Advisory Panel. The BBC had expanded at such a rate that in 1933 they had set up a panel to review the vast quantities of scores submitted to them. To be broadcast on the flagship London services, a work now had to get approved by a jury of (male) composers. And they could be vicious. One piano sonata was rejected as 'Polite vicar's tea-party stuff', and a piano trio dismissed for having 'no appreciable interest either to player or listener'. Doreen, then, was doing pretty well when it was judged that there was 'no reason to exclude' her String Quartet from broadcast. William was on the Panel that year, and although he recused himself from the decision as Doreen was his student, he did say that he thought it 'as good as anything that has been written by a woman composer for a very long time'. William still saw Doreen as a 'woman' composer, rather than just a composer – and perhaps expected his colleagues to do the same. Despite the fact that women were now an increasingly regular presence in the composition classes at both the Academy and College, attitudes were slow to change.

After the String Quartet and Piano Sonatina came a flurry of song-writing including a Serenade for Voice and Piano (dedicated to William), and three songs set to texts by the popular poet Walter de la Mare. Doreen was fascinated by Vaughan Williams and his folk-music-inspired pieces, and his influence is clear in all the songs. She experimented with a whimsical, mysterious sound, weaving webs of gossamer-thin piano textures to cradle the singer's voice, plaintive but peaceful, lingering chords hanging like dew-soaked mists over the listener. Violet premiered four of these songs with the soprano Elizabeth Cooper in a concert that also included Doreen's Piano Sonatina – all her life, Doreen kept her copy of the concert programme signed by all three of them.

Doreen's biggest success of the late 1940s, however, was her first orchestral overture, *ODTAA*. The cryptic acronym referred to the adventure novel *One Damned Thing after Another* by John Masefield, and Doreen tried to capture the book's 'colour, excitement and romantic spirit of adventure'. If anything, her overture far outstrips the lacklustre novel. Her music is an explosion, the first notes bursting into life with a fire and energy that drive the piece forward relentlessly. She submitted it for consideration by the London Philharmonic Orchestra, and they considered it 'something terrific'. After the premiere in January 1947, in March Adrian Boult conducted the LPO performing it at Covent Garden, in a concert broadcast by the BBC.

In 1947 Britain was still reeling from the economic battering of war; food remained rationed, and fuel shortages were widespread. In the middle of a freezing winter, the coldest of the century, the shortages caused power cuts in February that left hungry London residents shivering in their homes, the city as dark as it had ever been during the Blitz blackouts. But music continued. Having been used as a dance hall during the war, in 1946 Covent Garden Opera House had reopened as the Royal Opera House, breathing a new lease of life into both the fading building and struggling British opera. Its lights blazed out, beacons of opulence against the grey skies of post-war London.

Wearing a new blue dress and fur coat her mother had bought her, Doreen made her way to the Opera House accompanied by one of her many admirers, the conductor Bryan Balkwill. They shared 'a cup of tea in a taxi driver's hut' before arriving at the opera, making their way up the red-carpeted foyer stairs arm in arm. But having arrived with Bryan, Doreen left with William. It must have been a peculiar evening for Bryan, having his date's tutor whisk her away from the start of the concert to the end, buying her drinks in the interval while she fielded the flocks of curious photographers and journalists who descended upon her. They would later proclaim *ODTAA* a work of 'genuine melodic invention' with 'a feeling for bright and forceful rhythms and brilliantly effective orchestration'. It was a heady night for Doreen. She was making her mark as a composer, with the man she loved and admired at her side, seeing the yellow and purple flashes of her students' college scarves that they waved for support in the audience.

THE DAILY MIRROR MARCH 10, 1947.

Her big thrill—and it's a record

DOREEN CARWITHEN, 24, in her home at Hampstead, London, is able to recapture one of the most thrilling experiences she will ever know, for she now has the recording of her overture "Odtaa," broadcast from Covent Garden.

The overture, written after only four years' experience as a composer, was played by the London Philharmonic Orchestra, under the direction of Sir Adrian Boult. Sir Adrian afterwards led her on to the concert platform to receive an ovation.

Her overture was chosen by the committee of the London Philharmonic Orchestra as being "something terrific."

Doreen pictured in the *Daily Mirror*, under the title 'Her Big Thrill – and It's a Record'.

Flushed with success, Doreen accepted William's invitation back to his house – he assured her that Olive allowed him to bring back 'as many of his students as he liked'. Only inviting Doreen, however, was clearly not what Olive had in mind. 'It was a rather sticky hour or two,' Doreen admitted, 'Olive darning socks' and the Alwyns' youngest son, Nicholas, playing at his mother's feet. 'I was obviously greatly disliked.' The beautiful fur coat earned Doreen an icy comment from Olive, who assumed it was a gift from William. After he dropped her at the station, Doreen trudged through thick snow from the Tube to the flat she shared with her sister in Finchley Road, wishing she 'had worn more sensible shoes or even boots'. It was one of the first uncomfortable experiences Doreen had with Olive, but it certainly wouldn't be the last.

o   o   o   o

With so few reminders of home around her, Rebecca was especially happy to re-establish contact with pianist James Friskin, her acquaintance from the Royal College. He still had a shy, quiet demeanour – 'farouche', as Rebecca put it – but he, like she, had come a long way from his student days. Now in his late fifties, he was no longer the nervous College timpanist. He taught piano at the Juilliard Graduate School, and was living in New York with his sister, Kate, also a music teacher. Unlike Rebecca, though, James had stopped composing. His compositional career had fizzled out, almost beginning and ending with his 1907 Piano Quintet that was labelled 'One of the most brilliant Opus Ones in existence.' He had instead prioritised teaching and playing the piano. And while he enjoyed a respectable performance career – he was best known for his sensitive Bach interpretations, and had been the first pianist to bring the *Goldberg Variations* to America – it was as a tutor that James touched the most lives. He had a caring and thoughtful dedication to his students that was completely characteristic: he routinely put others before himself almost to a fault.

James's nurturing, gentle warmth was especially welcome to Rebecca when she was feeling so isolated. They had kept in contact on and off over the years when Rebecca was in the States, but from 1942 they struck up their correspondence with renewed energy. Music was at the heart of everything they did. They sent each other articles and discussed concerts, hiding themselves from the misery of war in the comfort of pieces they both knew and loved. And in 1944 when Rebecca began to realise that she cared for James far, far more deeply than a friend, she made her first romantic overture in the form of her last viola work.

I'll Bid My Heart Be Still is a gorgeously romantic piece for her instrument and his, based on a song from James's homeland, Scotland. Unlike many of Rebecca's other works the piano and viola never seem to challenge the other, each jostling for dominance. Here the two instruments intertwine like lovers. In its own way the piece is just as theatrical as the Viola Sonata or 'The Seal Man', but the story *I'll Bid My Heart* suggests is tender, devotional. Told from the perspective of a mourning lover, the song's text concludes:

> But 'tis sweeter to fade
> In grief's gloomy shade
> Than to bloom for another than him.

There would be no fading. James responded with a musical message of his own, notes standing in for words. He wrote to her that after she had left his house, he had played the slow movement of Beethoven's *Hammerklavier* Sonata. 'Of all the music I can produce with my two hands it goes deepest with me. Perhaps it too was a sort of indirect prayer: though the direct kind has not been wanting either.'

The *Hammerklavier* movement was a complex and appropriate piece for James to pick. At moments, it can be every bit as romantic as *I'll Bid My Heart*. But there's also a hesitation — even a sense of foreboding — that occasionally surfaces, tingeing the whole with a sense of melancholy. For while James adored Rebecca, he didn't feel free to reciprocate her affections wholeheartedly. He worried that if they married, it would leave his sister Kate without a home. She taught in Massachusetts for the majority of the year, but returned to New York during the holidays to live with James. Whatever his feelings for Rebecca, James would not allow his sister to feel abandoned or displaced, *especially* when the war was making everything so uncertain.

Kate, however, was more pragmatic than James, and cared about him just as much as he cared for her. When he told his sister that he and Rebecca were in love, she of course gave her blessing to their marriage. She wanted nothing more than for her brother to find happiness, and she could see the way he lit up when he spoke about Rebecca. When they married in 1944, in a small ceremony at the Brick Presbyterian Church, it was Kate who took their wedding photograph.

The picture captures their personalities perfectly. Rebecca, just as tall as her new husband and still as glamorous as ever, looks completely at ease in her fur-collared cape, matching dress and stylish black hat. James, meanwhile, clasps his fingers together awkwardly – almost as though he's stopping himself from reaching out for Rebecca's hand – with his features casting long shadows in the late September sun. Rebecca was always more sociable and outgoing than James; even though he was nearly sixty, he still had an almost schoolboy-like 'dread of meeting' her 'host of friends', worried they wouldn't understand what she saw in him. But one of the most beautiful features of their relationship was how completely they accepted one another for who they were. Both had a tendency to be self-deprecating, and being together allowed them to sometimes glimpse themselves as the other saw them. They never manipulated or exacerbated each other's insecurities. 'I love everything about you – just as you are,' she reassured him, whether that was his chronic fear of her friends, or his habit of mashing up pies before he ate them.

Perhaps it was because they had known each other for so many years, or because they had lived alone long enough to be quite content on their own, or simply that they were old enough to know their own minds, but from the outset Rebecca and James's marriage was one built on trust, friendship and honesty. It was the kind of public, uncomplicated love that Doreen could only dream of, and for Rebecca it made the world of difference after the anguish and secrecy of her time with John Goss. When Rebecca confessed to the affair, feeling that she couldn't in good faith marry James without first presenting him with her 'many faults', James responded with unwavering certainty, expressing complete support for her. 'I should have wanted to kiss away all the pain the telling of that story must have cost you,' he told her. 'I love and honour you for the courage and greatness of soul that made you feel you must tell me about it.'

Now fifty-eight, with her dark hair flecked through with strands of grey, Rebecca was going to take the time to enjoy this nurturing relationship. She felt incomplete when they were apart. 'I love you', Rebecca told him, 'so that every time I leave you it is as though my spirit leaves my body & goes with you, while a sort of shell bearing my features walks off in the opposite direction.' They moved into an apartment on West 108th Street, a wide avenue just off Broadway that led to the Hudson River in one direction, Central Park in the other. It was perfect for James's work, just a short subway journey to the Juilliard. And in the evenings when the setting sun glinted through the large windows, sometimes James ran through chess games – one of his favourite pastimes, but not a hobby that Rebecca joined him for. She had 'too much sense' to take him on. On other nights they would listen to music together or read aloud to one another. Their life, they felt, was as perfect as it could be.

o   o   o   o

Even though she was twelve years younger than Rebecca, Dorothy was nonetheless retreating from London's musical world as Doreen was entering it. After the disappointment of the *Divertissements*, her music was rarely heard in London. Or, indeed, in any other location. She raked in under £5 in royalties from her published music in 1946–7. Britten, by contrast, made £4,185. The end of the war was a moment for her to take stock and re-evaluate. She could have moved back to London and fought for a space for her work in the new government-funded organisations – she had strong contacts with CEMA, after all, that might have paved her way to getting Arts Council funding for concerts. But after the upheaval of war and the loss of her mother, Dorothy was too tired to fight. She wanted to live quietly and peacefully, teaching and composing music that was true to her – regardless of whether it would be welcome on the new and unapologetically highbrow Third Programme launched by the BBC in 1946.

So in March, as Doreen made her debut at Covent Garden Dorothy headed to the Malvern Hills with Pookie, following the removals van carrying all their belongings to their new home, Studley House. It was a large, white house with a pleasingly romantic atmosphere about it, tucked into the hills that shielded it from the world on one side but dropped into a lush, tree-filled, sweeping view of the valley on the other.

Here, Dorothy could be isolated from the bustle and difficulties of London's concert scene. The nearest town was an hour's walk away, but footpaths from her garden led across the Hills and to St Wulstan's Catholic Church, just ten minutes from Dorothy's front door. It was a place of overwhelming peace where Dorothy could come to think, and tend to the grave of Edward Elgar, who had been buried there in 1934. Over the years Dorothy would become known to locals as the woman who tackled the precipitous pathway to the churchyard in rain and snow to leave flowers and trim the verges around Elgar's final resting place. None of them realised that she did so because his music was such an inspiration for her own.

Dorothy drew on her Land Army expertise to dig over Studley's little garden with Pookie in April, planting vegetables ready for the winter. As it had ever been, Dorothy's home was structured around her family, both dead and alive. Apart from Pookie's, the bedrooms were furnished for Dorothy's siblings and their children, ready for whenever they wanted to come and stay. The house was filled with family furniture – the piano that had once belonged to Dorothy's parents, their Turkish rug, a music cabinet that had been in the family for years, and Carlo's looking glass and dressing chest. Even after three decades, Dorothy still marked Carlo's death in her diary every year alongside, now, the death dates of Viola and Charles Edward as well.

Dorothy's life took on a new rhythm: she commuted to the Royal Academy to teach on Mondays and Thursdays, attended and gave concerts on the weekends, and on her days off she and Pookie went to the cinema in Great Malvern. Studley House gave Dorothy the stability she needed to weather the rejections coming from London. Towards the end of the war she had finished the Violin Sonata set aside after Viola's death, and sent it off for consideration for performance and publication. The Sonata is one of Dorothy's most beautiful works. The slow movement is somewhere between a prayer and an elegy, perfectly balancing hope and heartbreak. It sounds like a plea from a bygone era – even more so when put in the context of the brutal, modernist music being written by so many of her contemporaries. When the Sonata was published in 1954, she dedicated it to her late friend Elsie Owen.

Predictably, the Sonata was rejected by the Committee for the Promotion of New Music, a new organisation partly funded by CEMA. Their goal was to support young composers writing in any style, and the deluge of scores they received is testament to how desperate musicians were for any outlets after the chaos of the war. The organisation was certainly true to its title; it grew to be a significant force for new music, and many of the composers they backed are now established names in British music history. But at the outset, the informal structure and opaque selection criteria meant that the all-male Executive Committee promoted and performed a surprisingly high number of their own works. William, for example, both sat on the Committee and had a flute piece on the first list of recommended works, all of which were written by men. Tired of rejection, Dorothy didn't bother sending the Sonata to the BBC. Instead the 1947 premiere was given to little fanfare in London by two women – an occasion that was no longer noteworthy, as female soloists had become commonplace. Dorothy later accompanied the same violinist in a performance of the Sonata in Birmingham in 1949. The press barely noticed the premiere, but agreed in 1949 that the piece was 'freshly attractive'.

Yet to receive their premiere, the *Three Divertissements* were suffering a similarly uninspiring fate. Behind the scenes, they had received a relatively warm reception at the BBC. In 1940 the readers' panel thought the work would be well placed in a light music programme, and again in 1945 the new readers declared all three movements had 'charm (a rarity nowadays)' and recommended them for broadcast. Thanks to wartime broadcasting changes and subsequent disruption, though, the *Divertissements* were still waiting for a first performance in 1947. They got a rehearsal by the London Philharmonic Orchestra at the end of the year, but it wasn't until 1950 that the piece finally got its premiere, with Adrian Boult conducting. To Dorothy's delight, it was selected as the only new work to be performed as part of that year's Elgar Festival, out of which would grow an Elgar Society (Dorothy would eventually sit on the Committee of the West Midlands branch from its establishment in 1973). Nonetheless, like her earlier orchestral works, the *Divertissements* were never published.

Dorothy didn't have time to advocate for her new works, though, because she was diagnosed with breast cancer just a short time after she moved to Studley. Unlike Ethel, Dorothy had never struggled with her health. This devastating news came out of the blue. Until the end of the decade, she travelled between Malvern and Cheltenham, and sometimes to Bath, for extensive rounds of radiotherapy. It was an exhausting regime. Any spare strength she had was spent on teaching. It was impossible for her to face the cut and thrust of contemporary publishing and broadcasting, which needed Ethel's brand of hard-headed relentlessness for a woman to make any headway – to say nothing of mustering the energy to write anything new. As she headed into her fifties, Dorothy needed to concentrate her efforts on recovery, thanking God every day that she had moved to a restorative place with Pookie and her family by her side.

o   o   o   o

Whenever Rebecca came home from shopping, she always stopped to chat with the doorman, Willie. They kept each other updated on the latest news from across the city, exchanging stories about family, politics, the neighbours, the election, James's students, as Willie helped the increasingly arthritic Rebecca (or 'Mrs Frisk', as he called her) with her bags. Although Rebecca was still reasonably active, by the time she married she was starting to be troubled by varicose veins and phlebitis. She was quite content not to live at the hectic pace of her thirties and forties – and to accept a little assistance carrying her acquisitions. She was, after all, only a few years off the official retirement age.

Rebecca and James's lives now revolved around one another. 'Do you know that, more & more, I feel', Rebecca told him, 'all my life has been a kind of preparation for you?' It was a pleasure for her to relax into the domesticity that she had previously put aside for her career. She decorated their home with a few choice antiques, ornaments bought on her performance tours and furniture that she had kept with her from her very first apartment. There were a few more eclectic items that came out of the habits of wartime thrift – the most conspicuous was a wire contraption that she kept by the sink to eke out as many suds as possible from soap scraps. She took time to see her many nieces, and sometimes she and James played host for old friends when they visited New York, or went to see them perform at one of the venues dotted around their home.

Composition seems to have found little place in Rebecca's new life. This wasn't for any want of encouragement on James's part. After she presented him with *I'll Bid My Heart Be Still* he asked her to 'start off again on something larger – I'd be almost willing to bet it's there if you'd only let it come out. What about another viola sonata? Please try.' But a sonata never materialised. She revised old works, and made some arrangements of other pieces, but she only ever wrote one more new composition, a song called 'God Made a Tree', in 1954. Why did Rebecca turn to religion for her last work? God had certainly never been an uncomplicated topic for her, given her family background. It has all the dramatic grit of her earlier songs, but, unusually, this one ends triumphantly. Perhaps it was Rebecca's way of laying to rest all the angst caused by her father's unrelenting atheism.

Rebecca never fully explained why she composed so little after the war. Perhaps she didn't quite know herself. 'It was a lot of personal considerations,' she told one interviewer. 'I haven't got the *vitality*. It takes a lot.' On another occasion she simply said that she 'became more interested in what my husband was doing'. But it wasn't just to do with her and James. Musical styles had changed beyond recognition from when she had first started composing. If Rebecca was 'never interested' in the musical modernism emerging before the war, she would be even less keen on the directions that modern music took towards the end of the 1940s.

Just a few blocks away from her, the composer John Cage was experimenting with composing by chance, writing pieces that dissolved the boundaries between music, sound and noise. He wrote works for radio receivers, pianos filled with objects like screws or corks to change the instrument's timbre and tone, and would become most famous for his 1952 work *4'33"* – the 'music' being all the sounds heard while the performers do not play their instruments for four minutes and thirty-three seconds. A few years later the Columbia–Princeton Computer Music Center would be founded on West 125th Street, revolutionising the study of electronic composition in the States. And it wasn't just composition that was changing. Post-war New York was the glamorous, avant-garde world of Jackson Pollock, Nat King Cole, Cary Grant and Grace Kelly. It's quite possible Rebecca felt that her music was out of step with the world she now lived in.

Instead, she turned her hand to teaching. In 1945 James had been appointed head of the piano school at the Chautauqua Institution, the New York arm of a States-wide adult education movement. Each summer on a leafy campus overlooking Lake Chautauqua, the school ran two months of classes, and while James was giving piano masterclasses and arranging recitals, Rebecca (or Mrs Friskin, as she was better known at Chautauqua) was invited to give a series of lectures about English composers. The school's daily newspaper reported that she gave an 'extremely delightful' talk, her informal style clearly appealing to the assembled class. She let them in on her meetings with Vaughan Williams ('shy, kind, modest, clumsy') and Walton ('extremely shy and silent'), and spoke, of course, about Britten, placing them as 'the three highest ranking living English composers'.

These English composer lectures were so popular that she was invited back the next year to speak again, this time with the title 'What is there in this chamber music?' Thanks partly to the fact that chamber music broadcast particularly well, small ensembles were now firmly associated with modernism and 'difficult' music. So Rebecca's classes were billed as being for those '"terrified" of chamber music', to make it 'more enjoyable and understandable'.

Having dedicated her life to chamber music, Rebecca was the perfect person to deliver the lectures. She spoke with an infectious passion and enthusiasm for the pieces she played and loved. Her own music didn't feature often, even though the publicity for the classes mentioned she was both a composer and a performer herself. The school's students performed her *Passacaglia* and 'The Seal Man' once each, but Rebecca preferred to speak about others' works. Her lectures were full of Brahms, Dvořák, Beethoven and Mozart, the repertoire she knew best.

Rebecca and James, *c.*1954.

Rebecca found herself a second home at Chautauqua. She believed, strongly, in their educational mission, and after a few years she became President of the Chautauqua Society of New York. She and James built their years around the institution, the two of them becoming a familiar sight, strolling hand in hand between classes on the Institution's close-clipped lawns.

o   o   o   o

As it became clear that Doreen might have a promising life as a composer ahead of her, her friends strongly encouraged her to go and study abroad for a while. It was certainly good advice. Travelling to study and perform was something of a rite of passage for serious composers, especially for women. As Ethel had found out in Leipzig and Rebecca in America, travel both opened up new ideas and expanded their address books. There was an abundance of options. At the Royal College, Vaughan Williams was sending his students across the globe: at his suggestion Elizabeth Maconchy went to Prague, and Grace Williams to Vienna – both built reputations as concert composers that would far outstrip Doreen's – and Peggy Glanville-Hicks ventured to Paris to study with world-famous pedagogue Nadia Boulanger. Peggy's ballets and operas would later be performed across the world.

Doreen's relationship with William, however, blinkered her (and perhaps, also, him) to the possibilities that foreign study might offer. She was 'happy with William', believing that 'he gave me all the advice I needed then and I knew I could learn a lot more from him'. And he seems to have done little to dissuade her from her decision. The problem was that although William was famous, he was not at the forefront of new music in England, let alone internationally. He wrote romantic music that had its fair share of devoted audiences, but it seemed old-fashioned next to the ferocity of Britten's work. Doreen's music *had* that spark, a dangerous energy that

William's didn't, that a different tutor might have nurtured more comprehensively. Had she studied with somebody like Vaughan Williams, who knows what her music would have sounded like. William, though, wore his self-described 'loner' badge with pride. When his symphonies received mediocre reviews he wrote off the criticism, saying that the works 'will be looked at in future as being something quite distinct in the evolution of the symphony'. While Doreen may have had much to learn from William, he was unlikely to help her unlock the doors of Europe's concert halls, socially or stylistically.

If Doreen wanted to be a concert composer, choosing to stay in England was probably a colossal mistake. But had she studied abroad she might never have made her way into films. William indisputably excelled in film music, which was one of the few areas in which tonal music could still be unambiguously successful. Over the course of William's career he scored more than seventy films, and by the end of World War II he was recognised as one of Britain's leading film composers, having written for everything from spy thrillers and biopics to documentaries. And Doreen, having spent much of her childhood and teenage years in the cinema, was fascinated by film music. William encouraged her to score short films in her lessons, and it was immediately obvious that she had a knack for it.

Doreen's rise from expressing an interest in film music to becoming a film composer was meteoric. Women composing for films was extremely rare. In 1946 the forty-year-old Elisabeth Lutyens became the first woman to score a British documentary; she would be followed by Grace Williams (also in her forties), who scored her first feature in 1949. In the same year that Lutyens's documentary was released, Doreen joined the ranks of these pioneers when, at just twenty-four years old, she became the only woman selected for the Rank Fellowship, an apprenticeship run by Britain's largest production company, training composers and conductors to work in film.

Doreen (left) and her sister Barbara graduating from the
Royal Academy in the 1940s.

The Rank Organisation was a curious phenomenon. For years,
Hollywood movies had dominated British cinemas. This caused
considerable consternation among British politicians and cultural
leaders, who feared mass Americanisation of British culture as a
result of Hollywood's enormous influence. Various tactics were tried
to ameliorate its impact, including the introduction of a quota system in 1927, mandating that 5 per cent of cinema screen time should
be devoted to British films. When this proved unsuccessful, resulting in a glut of low-quality 'quota quickies', the quota was raised in
the 1930s to 20 per cent. And yet among the twenty million Brits
who headed to the movies every week in the 1930s, there was still an

agreed consensus that American films were 'far superior to British ones on every point'.

Into this world stepped the most unlikely saviour, entrepreneur J. Arthur Rank. He came from a milling family and knew nothing about films whatsoever, but as a fervent Christian he hoped that the cinema might be a powerful tool for spreading Christian values and morals. So he began buying up film studios and cinema chains. It's debatable whether he achieved his evangelical goals, but he nonetheless went on to fund some of the most successful British films of the early twentieth century. World War II and its aftermath only increased Rank's monopoly on the British film industry, his production company turning out propaganda films and popular features including Laurence Olivier's *Henry V* (1944) and David Lean's *Brief Encounter* (1945). Doreen joined Rank at the peak of its powers, in the same year that it finally succeeded in making British films more popular than American ones for the first and only time in British box office history.

Working in the Rank studio at Denham almost unimaginably accelerated the pace of Doreen's life. Composers usually only had a few weeks, if not days, to complete and record their score, so the music department worked at a breakneck speed. Initially Doreen was assigned all kinds of duties, mostly copying out the musicians' parts and persuading composers to sign on for films (although she was especially excited to deliver Laurence Olivier his tea and iced buns while he was filming *Hamlet*). Scouting a composer for the documentary *The Dim Little Island*, the studio sent Doreen to Vaughan Williams with instructions to wear her 'prettiest hat', and after a long tea with the composer and his cat (who got the first slice of cake), Doreen eventually ended up working with him on the resulting film.

Alongside administrative work sometimes tinged with sexism, Doreen soon started uncredited ghost composing and from there was given her first solo credit in 1948 for a short, forty-minute drama called *To The Public Danger*, about the perils of drink driving. The theme played to her strengths, allowing her to write truly gripping music that is both powerful and terrifying, and that drives the film to its apotheosis: a car crash that kills three of the four main characters. The film's music director, Muir Mathieson, was delighted with the result, and commissions began pouring onto Doreen's desk.

The Studio sent her work at an exhausting pace. In 1948–9 alone, Doreen scored nine documentary films. Each commission began with several run-throughs of the film with the music director, and sometimes the director and producer as well, to decide what kind of music was needed where, and for how long. Doreen had to get used to working as part of a team with an extremely specific brief, because 'Every point is discussed in the greatest detail – even to the actual shape of the themes to be used, and the orchestration of the score.' By the end of the sessions she would leave with the exact number of seconds of music she had to compose. Her stopwatch was always with her to check the timings – at the viewings, while she wrote, and in the final recording sessions. 'A bar or two too many or too few and the whole effect is ruined.'

It was a whirlwind existence. When Doreen was composing for a deadline she wrote through the night, fuelled by a combination of cigarettes, alcohol and caffeine. And she loved it. It may have been tiring, but it was also a life of glamour and excitement that gave her the opportunity to be close to William, who worked at Denham Studios too. They would cross each other's paths at the studios and go to premiere after-parties together, giving Doreen an excuse to wear the beautiful dresses that she loved so much and that were completely impractical during the day, when she might need to sprint across the studio at any moment to deliver a last-minute edit to the orchestra.

Terrified of public exposure, both William and Doreen went to great lengths to hide their affair from their colleagues. For Doreen it was not particularly difficult – she had plenty of other suitors. When Britten's *Peter Grimes* ran at Covent Garden, it was the conductor John Hollingsworth who took her to see it, not William. Doreen thought John 'a handsome man', and she was perfectly aware that the whole music department were rooting for them to get together. When he finally asked her to the opera, 'Everyone made a note of it and wrote it in their diaries and counted the days until John took Doreen to the opera!' She certainly enjoyed attending the production on the arm of an attractive man, dancing the night away afterwards in the ballroom of the fashionable Gargoyle Club in Soho, sipping cocktails under the gold-leaf ceiling. But John was never a romantic consideration. Doreen had no interest in anyone other than William.

William and Doreen would never have stolen a furtive kiss in the tea breaks, but he could at least take the opportunity to drive her to the station after work. Their companionable setup was short-lived, though. One day in 1948, Olive unexpectedly dropped in to the studio to hear some of her husband's music being recorded. She was furious to find Doreen at the session assisting the conductor, sitting in the recording booth, cup of tea in hand as always. William somehow managed to smooth over the situation and it passed without too much scandal. From then on, though, each began to avoid the studio when they knew the other was there, however inconvenient it was for Doreen's career.

Awkward though these altercations were, for Doreen they were never as painful as the long stretches of time that she and William had to spend apart. In 1949, just a few months before his forty-fourth birthday, William had to have a high-risk throat operation. There was only a 50 per cent chance that he would survive. Nothing could comfort Doreen. William told her 'not to worry or to try to phone his family', and for over three weeks, she had an agonising wait to find out whether he had survived the operation. Every day, she picked up the newspaper praying that she wouldn't hear about her lover's death from an obituary. To fill the hours of waiting she 'worked and worked and felt myself getting more and more ill'. With no end in sight and unable to confide in her friends and family, Doreen felt powerless, anxious and completely, utterly alone.

LOVE AND HEARTBREAK

On 25 August 1952, Doreen stepped from the cloying cacophony of Kensington Gore into the familiar cool of the Royal Albert Hall foyer. She was there for the public premiere of her Piano Concerto, making her way through the stalls to take her seat next to a friend, conductor Basil Cameron. Now twenty-nine, she was still as striking as ever with her curly hair framing her slim face, but she cut a somewhat different figure to the exuberant, jolly young woman who had revelled in her plaudits at Covent Garden just five years before. Doreen was thinner now, and stress, cigarettes and late nights were leaving their mark on her gaunt cheeks. She smiled and nodded at Basil's chitchat, only half-listening as she glanced distractedly around the Hall, secretly looking for William even though she knew he would not be there.

After weeks of waiting, Doreen had eventually managed to find out through other students that William had at least survived his throat operation. But when he finally paid her a quick visit, it was only to tell her that the family was going to the Scilly Isles for him to recover. He disappeared again, leaving her alone. This was the pattern of their lives throughout the 1950s. And Doreen had no close support network to see her through. During her time at the Academy she had lived briefly with her cello teacher, Peers, then with her sister Barbara and another friend, but now she lived on her own in a small flat in Maida Vale.

In many ways, this living arrangement suited Doreen well. She was an intensely private person who valued solitude, and she could see William whenever he had a spare moment. Nonetheless, there was little to distract her from her own thoughts in the evenings, when she missed him the most. She was supremely grateful for the 'killing' film deadlines, which stopped her from wallowing. When her days and nights were filled with work she could almost deceive herself that she was the sole focus of William's attention, and that he arrived only when she had time to see him. But it was always a short-lived fantasy. His divided loyalties were abundantly obvious on the occasions that meant the most to Doreen, which he stayed away from either to avoid angering Olive, or because of other family commitments.

William's absence aside, the 1952 Prom was one of the most exciting events of Doreen's career. She was the only woman to have a work performed all season, and the Concerto had already received an effusive reception after its broadcast premiere the previous year. The BBC Advisory Panel deemed her 'genuinely musical', and reviewers responded well to Doreen's ability to write 'a big tune in the late-Romantic vein'. As one critic put it, 'there exists in these tonally trying times a numerous audience for this kind of music'. Doreen managed to marry melody with the spiky, angular harmonies associated with modern music, creating something that both sounded progressive and had widespread appeal.

There's something almost industrial about the Concerto's opening movement: the orchestra hammers out chords that are melted down into a smooth, fluid theme that spreads from the piano to the strings. This is music that suggests images, scenes – it's obvious that Doreen was a born film composer. The jewel of the Concerto, though, is the slow movement. There's very little accompaniment – it's practically a duet between the piano and a solo violin, communicating something raw and desperate, the two instruments seeming to cry out pleadingly to one another.

For Doreen's music, if not for her personal life, these were years of promise. She was composing prolifically – in 1951–2 the BBC's Advisory Panel considered six of her works: the Violin Sonata, *Five Diversions for Wind Quintet*, Four Preludes for Piano, String Quartet No. 2, an overture called *Bishop Rock* and her 1946 song

'The Ride-by-Nights'. They got a markedly mixed response. The most modern-sounding, the String Quartet No. 2 (1950), was immediately approved by the panel as 'an excellent effort' and would be awarded a Cobbett Prize. The *Diversions*, too, were accepted and broadcast in 1953 and 1954.

But the gap between the highbrow tastes of the advisory panel and the majority of listeners was broadening. Most of the BBC's audiences liked dance music and ballads, and those who listened to classical music usually preferred canonic composers like Beethoven or light contemporary works, finding the avant-garde, atonal and experimental difficult to stomach. Critics praised Doreen's *Diversions* for managing to 'steer a well-defined course between the experimental and the congenial types of modern composition', but it only just scraped through the Panel's assessment. They considered it 'light music' – not serious and avant-garde, but 'competent, amusing, frothy and imaginative'. It eventually got a spot on the Third Programme's 'New Music' programme in September 1953. Doreen's compositions that were neither light nor avant-garde fared very poorly indeed. The Sonata was 'poverty-stricken', 'The Ride-by-Nights' a 'tawdry affair'.

Bishop Rock was one of Doreen's most electrifying works, inspired by the lighthouse that stands on the westernmost point of the Isles of Scilly. Her score conjures up the roar of the Atlantic and the lighthouse's flashing beam as it guides ships away from danger. The overture is immediately arresting, and received excellent reviews after it was chosen to open the Birmingham Proms – but the panel dismissed it as 'arid note-spinning'.

Luckily, on this occasion Doreen had supporters who could advocate for her work. Regional services were not answerable to the Advisory Panel, so in 1953 the BBC's Northern Orchestra broadcast *Bishop Rock* on the North of England Home Service, and the conductor begged the Panel to reconsider. He assured them that the orchestra had been greatly impressed by the overture, and enough momentum gathered behind the scenes that the Panel's decision was eventually overturned. *Bishop Rock* was ultimately broadcast on London's highbrow Third Programme for the first time in 1954.

Alongside all this concert work, Doreen was still regularly composing for films. The versatility needed for the range of films she scored was astonishing. In 1949 she composed for her first full-length feature, *Boys in Brown*, a drama set in a borstal for juvenile offenders, starring Dirk Bogarde and Richard Attenborough. It gave her the opportunity to write a particularly exciting chase scene, her agitated score perfectly evoking the panic Attenborough's character feels when he realises that he will be caught for the crime he has committed. On the other end of the spectrum, she produced tranquil, pastoral music for a promotional travel documentary called *East Anglian Holiday*, her score romanticising the footage of local fens, fruits and flowers.

Doreen's biggest challenge came in 1953. On 2 June, Britain woke up to rain and a public holiday. A buzz of excitement swept across the country. Bunting was hung out, trestle tables stretched for metres down the centre of streets, sandwiches and cakes were spread out on newly laundered cloths – the government even granted a few special licences for roasting oxen – as Britain awaited the coronation of Queen Elizabeth II. Before the street parties could begin in earnest, however, anybody who wasn't in the crowd lining London's streets to see the procession hurried round to the nearest house with a television set to watch the ceremony. The announcement that the coronation would be broadcast sent the number of television licences rocketing. Even though sets were bulky, small-screened and still in black and white, more than twenty million people worldwide watched the coronation, and a further twelve million listened on the wireless.

With some food rationing still in place – it would not be fully abolished until July 1954 – and coming out of a winter in which fog and floods had killed thousands, Britons were desperate for a reason to celebrate. The coronation, and the fact that the new monarch was a woman, seemed to mark a turning point. Her reign was heralded as a 'new Elizabethan Age', and many thought that the announcement that Edmund Hillary and Tenzing Norgay had reached the summit of Mount Everest, falling as it did on coronation day, was a sign that Britain's fortunes were changing.

The film industry was as eager as any to capitalise on coronation fever, so as Britain headed out to party, studios rushed to compile the day's footage into documentary films for as quick a cinema release as possible, giving just a few hours' turnaround. Pathé and British Gaumont News were competing against each other to hit the cinemas first. Thanks to the rise of television and more people having disposable income to spend on a number of pastimes, cinema audiences had been slowly declining since the war, falling from 1.6 billion in 1946 to 1.2 billion in 1955. The coronation was bound to be one of the few big-ticket items of the year, but cinema-goers would probably only watch one film. It was worth thousands of pounds to the studio to have the most efficient and reliable team – and Doreen was commissioned by Pathé.

On the days running up to the coronation, while everyone else was baking cakes and buying television sets, Doreen was in the recording studio with Adrian Boult, putting together the music for Pathé's film. She arranged music by Elgar and Walton for the title sequence and the Trooping of the Colour, and composed original material to accompany the opening scenes and to link between the pre-filmed documentary footage and music recorded live at Westminster Abbey. Doreen felt 'honoured to be asked as such a prestige film could have had any composer they liked'. Pathé were rewarded for their faith in her. Ultimately, their film screened first, at 11 a.m. on 3 June – British Gaumont's wasn't released until the 4th – and it won a BAFTA Certificate of Merit. It wasn't just shown at cinemas, but was also screened at live stage shows, including at the Ritz, the 'most successful' stage show that the hotel had 'ever run'.

o   o   o   o

Far away from the bustle of central London street parties, Dorothy was among the millions who flocked to see the coronation films. An ardent supporter of the monarchy, she always marked significant royal dates in her diary, and headed out to a fete to celebrate on the day itself. Her hectic teaching schedule prevented her from going to the cinema immediately – she taught in Cheltenham on Mondays, Birmingham on Tuesdays, at the Royal Academy on Wednesdays, and private students at Studley for the rest of the week – but she managed to find a gap between pupils a fortnight later.

The coronation festivities were a welcome reprieve from the health worries that now dominated Dorothy's life. She was intermittently bedridden with lumbago, and had to undergo several cancer operations, the most serious of which kept her in hospital for a month. Hospital trips and doctor's visits were numerous: sore throats kept Dorothy awake for days, and rashes came out as reactions to her radiotherapy.

Even when Dorothy was well, Pookie's various ailments kept the doctors at Studley. When Dorothy wasn't teaching, she was tending to her. On the days when Dorothy was recovering from radiotherapy she often had to rescue Pookie from falls in the garden, or from tumbles out of bed in the small hours of the morning. Only rarely did Dorothy ask for assistance. When they were both too ill to care for one another, she hired somebody in to help. For the most part, though, they muddled through together, bottling raspberries from Studley's small orchard and bailing water out of the dining room, which always flooded whenever the weather turned.

With so much disruption, Dorothy inevitably composed less. Despite the encouragement of friends who instructed her to 'WRITE MUSIC' and not 'get ill any more. You've had your quota,' throughout the whole of the 1950s she wrote very little at all. In 1954 and 1955, though, she mustered the energy to write two large works:

her Piano Sonata and *Adagio and Caprice* for Violin and Piano. They are two astonishingly heartfelt works. The Sonata is gently nostalgic, opening with a simple unison theme that never once seems to lose control, even when it becomes a tempest whirling over the entire keyboard. Nothing overstays its welcome. All three movements are brief and sparse – Dorothy says only what she needs to say.

Of course Dorothy tried to secure performances and publications, but both of the publishers to whom she sent the Sonata manuscript declined to even look at the score, as they were too 'overwhelmed with manuscripts'. The *Adagio and Caprice* fell into oblivion, and was never published or performed. The Sonata, too, remains unpublished, but Dorothy gave the premiere herself at Birmingham Town Hall. It would have to wait another thirty years for its broadcast premiere, and for its second performance.

It wasn't just Dorothy's new works that were suffering. Throughout the early 1950s her old pieces – even those that had once been popular, like *Spindrift* and *Rosalind* – were discontinued by their publishers. Her works were slowly falling from the repertoire completely. Perhaps if she had been aggressively self-promotional she might have been able to turn the tide. But without an exceptional intervention, it would be difficult for Dorothy to find a place in a musical world that had changed while she had chosen not to. The atonal music she had heard in 1914 had already left her feeling alienated, and by the 1950s she also had to contend with serialism, which went even further from the music she enjoyed. Serialism involved structuring music around a numerical set, or 'series', of pitches – and sometimes also dynamics, timbres and rhythms. British composers were grimly divided about serialism. William voiced the beliefs of many when he complained that it 'replaces composition with applied mathematics'.

Serialism had been around in Europe for some time, but as always the British were slow to adopt continental ideas. It wasn't until the 1950s that British composers began to take serialism seriously –

apart from Elisabeth Lutyens, who was a seasoned serialist. Her music featured in a groundbreaking concert of serial and atonal music in January 1956, held by a group calling themselves 'New Music Manchester' (named such because the majority studied in the city). The group positioned themselves as the instigators of a much-needed professionalisation of British music, which they considered to be governed by dilettantism and lack of ambition, falling far behind developments in Europe. Their music was perceived as aggressive, muscular and male, replacing early twentieth-century decadence that was both feminine and effeminate, florid and romantic in style. As one put it bluntly years later, 'That's what I am – I'm very masculine.'

It's little coincidence that this stereotype of macho modernism (which belied the more complex realities about the group and their music) became so dominant amid increasing homophobia in Britain. Until 1967, homosexual acts between men were illegal in England and Wales – and remained so in Scotland until 1980, and until 1982 in Northern Ireland. Throughout the 1950s arts institutions were rife with homophobia, quite possibly fuelled by jealousy of the many prominent gay men in classical music: the best-known today are Britten and his partner Peter Pears, composer Michael Tippett, and indeed Peter Maxwell Davies of the Manchester group. In 1955 the music director of the Arts Council announced that he was launching a 'campaign against homosexuality in British music', declaring that 'The influence of perverts in the world of music has grown beyond all measure. It if is not curbed soon, Covent Garden and other precious musical heritages could suffer irreparable harm.' It was a dangerous and difficult time to be gay in Britain.

Belligerent reassertion of heterosexual norms also had a negative impact on the perception and portrayals of women. The generation coming of age in the 1950s and 1960s had to handle just as many prejudices and stereotypes as Ethel, Rebecca and Dorothy had, if not more so. When Elisabeth Lutyens was interviewed by the *Daily*

Mirror in 1950 the focus was not on her music, but on how she balanced her children and her job. Composer Ruth Gipps, born in the same year as Doreen, was branded a 'housewife composer' (many critics insisted on using her married name, 'Mrs Baker'), and when she conducted Beethoven's Ninth Symphony, an outraged journalist blustered that 'A woman is no more expected to conduct it than build a Great Boulder Dam'. After the war, Rebecca had optimistically forecast that Ethel's outspoken approach was no longer necessary because women 'weren't up against very much'. Sadly, whatever her reasoning, British newspaper commentary suggested otherwise. Nor were statistics in favour of Rebecca's argument: for a decade after Doreen's Concerto, only eight works by women were played at the Proms.

In this climate, it's unsurprising that Dorothy's music was banished from the most prestigious concert stages. She did keep performing herself, giving the occasional recital in Birmingham, Cheltenham, Letchworth and the Malvern area. These concerts kept her spirits up throughout her most difficult periods. They were the highlights of her year, and she marked each of them with little flags in her diary. At a rate of about one big recital a year, though, her income from performance was practically non-existent. Her money came almost entirely from teaching, occasionally supplemented by renting out the top of Studley's orchard to a nearby farmer.

The event that earned the most flags in her diary, though, was her first driving lesson, at the age of sixty-three. Unlike Rebecca, who never took to driving, Dorothy loved being behind the wheel, always taking the hilly scenic routes and tackling corners at speed – and driving gave her independence. In 1958 she bought a Ford that she named Freddie, and he appears more than nearly anybody else in her diaries afterwards. She noted every belt repair and battery recharge. Thanks to Freddie, Dorothy and Pookie could escape into the countryside for picnics, leaving behind – even if just for a moment – illness and disappointment.

Dorothy on holiday with Freddie.

o   o   o   o

For Rebecca, too, the 1950s were a time of relative scarcity as far as performances of her music were concerned. Her Viola Sonata got a single BBC broadcast in 1951, with her friend Kathleen Long at the piano. Other than that, there were a few amateur performances and a couple of professional recitals, but there was nothing like the abundance of the 1920s and 1930s. She also sometimes got mentioned as a footnote to James, who even in his seventies still commanded reviews announcing him to be a pianist of 'phenomenal excellence'.

Rebecca seemed relatively unfazed by the drop in interest around her compositions. She hadn't stopped believing in her music, or her abilities as a composer. She simply loved her new life, teaching at Chautauqua and living with James. Perhaps she considered herself to have retired. Certainly both of them were getting frail enough that they sometimes hired maids to help with the laundry, cleaning and cooking. The antiquated kitchen made cooking something of an obstacle course; they kept the original 1924 appliances, including a gas stove that risked creating a fireball whenever it was turned on. But when she was mobile Rebecca handled it easily, and enjoyed this reminder of her early years in London.

Rebecca and James got into the habit of spending summers in England, visiting all of Rebecca's old friends. Coming from New York's broad streets and ample supplies of food and fuel, post-war London must have been quite a shock. While Britain was still rebuilding, America was entering a period of post-war economic expansion, the 'Golden Age of Capitalism'. Britain would routinely be about five years behind America on all the latest technologies, from televisions and cars to the atomic bomb.

In culture, too, Britain began to follow America more – over the course of the decade Hollywood blockbusters, Broadway musicals and rock 'n' roll began to saturate British culture, accelerating the dwindling interest in classical music. It wasn't until the 1960s that British culture started making appreciable waves in the States. These disparities caused huge anxieties and tensions in British politics. In 1947, Labour's Foreign Secretary had blustered that 'We regard ourselves as one of the powers most vital to the peace of the world and we still have our heroic part to play', but this was so much empty rhetoric covering a deep insecurity that continues to shape British politics, even today. In the 1950s Britain's imperial power was clearly diminishing, demonstrated most trenchantly by the 1956 Suez Crisis.

Of all Rebecca's London friends, she was happiest to see May. They resumed their shopping trips in all their favourite haunts. In old age Rebecca was as stylish as ever, and delighted in picking out exquisite antiques, clothes for James and fabrics for herself. She no longer followed the latest fashions but opted instead for a timeless, classic elegance, and was usually photographed in dark dresses and strings of pearls.

Now in her seventies, May still performed occasionally, but a lot of her time was swallowed up by the Mostly Musicians Club. The tone of the Club had changed, though. The clientele, once England's foremost composers, were now more old guard than avant-garde. Seventy-nine-year-old Vaughan Williams, for example, was by now *the* establishment figure from his generation. Rebecca attended the premiere of his final completed opera at Covent Garden in 1951 and wrote home to James that it was 'quite a moving occasion', the opera house packed to the rafters with all their old friends, letting out 'a perfect roar' when Vaughan Williams 'finally appeared'.

Vaughan Williams kept composing right up until his death in 1958, an event that shook the musical establishment. Tributes poured in from across the country, and the crowds at his memorial service filled Westminster Abbey. As one critic put it, 'Vaughan Williams has exercised such a wide influence for so long, and his music has summed up so often the mood of a decade' that it felt like the end of an era. He had been so closely associated with a pastoral, folk-inspired sound that it would be almost impossible for anybody with a comparable style to follow him. Even among Vaughan Williams's students, those who sounded least like him made the biggest mark on British music.

Also passing with much less fanfare in 1958 was Ethel's centenary. By this time, a narrative about her life had become more or less established. She had been an important historical figure because 'she was the first woman to acquire anything like a man's technique of composition', but mostly, she was a cautionary tale, who 'lived out too much of her originality in her tumultuous life and had too little to spare for her music'. This was not helped by a set of radio comedies featuring a 'composeress' called Hilda Tablet, clearly modelled at least in part on Ethel. Among other things, it sent up Ethel's many and varied interests, Hilda declaring that music was really only her 'fourth' love. Hilda Tablet proved such a popular character that she spawned a number of spin-offs, including a comedy about her all-woman opera *Emily Butter*, set in a department store, that depicted 'the whole of English womanhood'.

It wasn't the first time that Ethel had provided the inspiration for an amusing but slightly cruel caricature – she had been deeply hurt in the 1890s by her thinly veiled appearance in a satirical novel by one of her friends, worrying that it would contribute to the tendency to ridicule and belittle her. This was certainly true in the 1950s, compacted by a general feeling that Ethel's 'fighting' generation and women's suffrage were old news, almost an embarrassment.

However, when Ethel's music *was* programmed and audiences were allowed to make up their own minds, she still got largely positive responses. The BBC broadcast a number of works for her centenary, including *The Boatswain's Mate*, for which they distributed a questionnaire to gauge audience reactions. 'Shades of Hilda Tablet seemed to have hovered in the minds of several listeners,' their report admitted, but many were 'surprised by its unexpected quality', describing it as 'fresh and vital'.

Ethel's reputation as a 'character' was compounded by her regular appearances in memoirs written by old acquaintances – she provided such reliable anecdotal material that she could hardly be left out. But the most significant book for Ethel's legacy was the first full-length biography of her in 1959, written by her friend Christabel Marshall, who went by the male pen-name Christopher Marie St John.

Ethel had long admired St John's writing, but it was nonetheless unexpected when she gave her all her notes, letters and diaries –

everything except her correspondence with H. B. Perhaps Ethel had always hoped that St John would take it upon herself to write a biography. It took the writer several years to get to grips with the sheer volume of material that Ethel left behind, but her eventual book was a genuine attempt to evaluate Ethel's life and career, providing a counterweight to the caricatures and dismissals. Certainly the Ethel that St John portrays is devoted to composition, and a serious and significant figure of English music.

Nonetheless, the biography had some significant shortcomings – among which were a number of errors, omissions and undisclosed alterations of facts. Furthermore, St John was a less adept musician than writer, and besides, Ethel left her music manuscripts to a different woman whom she befriended later in life, and who contributed just one chapter to St John's book. As a result, Ethel's compositions were often mentioned almost in passing. Her personal life provided the biography's main substance, which quite likely aggravated the perception that Ethel 'put her genius into her life, and only her talent into her work'. Even if enthused readers had wanted to explore the pieces mentioned, so few of her major works had been published, and almost none recorded, that it would have been close to impossible for all but the most persistent individuals to get hold of any of her music. St John provided a comprehensive portrait of Ethel as a person, but it would be for future writers to try to make sense of Ethel as a composer.

o   o   o   o

One thing was for certain: the long lifespan of Ethel anecdotes demonstrated how truly unusual she was for her time. When Doreen was faced with gender prejudice, she reacted quite differently to Ethel. She never publicly confronted her patronising newspaper coverage, or wrote tracts defending women's right to work. She preferred to deal with problems privately and quietly.

Her most overt mutiny came when she discovered that she was being paid less than a male colleague who was writing a similar amount of music to her for the same documentary series. Equal pay had been at the forefront of feminist agendas for decades with an Equal Pay Campaign Committee set up in 1944, but in the 1950s it was still a distant dream. Doreen confronted the producer. His response was to laugh, and ask her 'Don't you think you're doing very well for a woman?' She didn't get a pay rise. Nor did she complain again.

Doreen's confrontations were rarely this direct, even though she continued to have gender-based issues over pay and representation. Despite all her work on the coronation film *Elizabeth Is Queen*, when the credits rolled she was billed as Adrian Boult's assistant, not as the composer. And she found it impossible to get an agent to represent her when the Rank Apprenticeship finished. Although she continued to receive commissions, she had nobody to negotiate contracts for her. She had to rely on the Composers' Guild to give her legal advice. They tried to steer her away from the most exploitative contracts, even if they couldn't help her to secure a fairer wage. 'I was not going to be bullied,' Doreen insisted. 'But it was like that all the time.'

Film work continued to roll in through the 1950s. Doreen produced a rip-roaring score for the otherwise entertainingly cheesy 1954 film *The Men of Sherwood Forest*, and found a much more fruitful collaboration with the choreographer, dancer and director Wendy Toye. In the male-dominated film world Wendy was quite an exception, and remarked that her pre-existing fame as a dancer and West End director opened doors. Had she 'come up through the technical ranks in the studio, I probably wouldn't have been treated in the way I was'. Muir had enticed Doreen onto Wendy's first film with the promise that it would be 'a straightforward job', only requiring a few minutes of original score and reorchestrating an existing suite. Doreen was a little suspicious, thinking it sounded 'simple, too simple, and knowing Muir I should have known there was far more work in it than was at first apparent', but she signed up for it anyway.

Working with Wendy was wholly different to anything Doreen had experienced before. Rather than bringing the composer in at the last moment, Wendy built the film around the music, planning it 'long before shooting begins'. The resulting film, *The Stranger Left No Card*, won the award for the Best Short Fiction Film at Cannes. It's a peculiar movie perhaps best described as a fantastical thriller. Doreen had to make an arrangement of a rhapsody by Hugo Alfvén – in her hands the piece sits perfectly between repetitively jovial and claustrophobically maddening, 'representing the Stranger's thoughts'. It establishes a disquieting mood that sets up the film's twist, revealing the Stranger to be not an eccentric and harmless magician, but a coolly calculating murderer who will escape from his crime scene unobserved, having discarded his magician's disguise.

Wendy and Doreen seemed to have a genuine rapport. Their collaborations are easily among Doreen's most convincing films. She went on to score Wendy's episode of the horror trilogy *Three Cases of Murder*, and her delightful Christmas comedy *On the Twelfth Day*, which was nominated for a Best Short Subject Oscar. Doreen's *Three Cases* music is thoroughly spine-tingling, bringing suspense and unease into the short, macabre tales. *On the Twelfth Day* was a completely different prospect. Wendy both directed and starred as an Edwardian lady whose suitor gives her all the gifts in the song 'The Twelve Days of Christmas', filling her house until they escape together in a hot air balloon, leaving her despairing butler to deal with the 184 birds and party of lords, ladies, milkmaids, pipers and drummers. She made the most of being able to shoot in colour, hiring a designer who constructed a flamboyant, whimsical set with strong overtones of brightly coloured Edwardian candies.

Unusually, music carries the entire film – there is no dialogue, harking back to silent movies. Doreen combined original music with arrangements of Christmas carols, always keeping the 'Twelfth Day' song at the centre. The resulting score is seamless, and Doreen described it as 'the hardest I ever wrote' because everything was so precisely choreographed. 'I have occasionally on other films, worked in thirds of seconds, but this one dealt in quarters and even sixths of seconds!' The whole thing was shot in just three weeks, the live animals causing complete chaos as painted cows and flocks of dyed pink doves roamed the studio. 'Everyone on the set – both human and animal – enjoyed themselves enormously,' Doreen enthused, 'and entered into the spirit of this fantasy with tremendous zest.'

This was exactly the kind of distraction that Doreen needed to keep her from fretting about William. A decade into their affair, it was by now quite clear that he was not intending to leave Olive. Instead he lived a 'double life', taking his older son to his university interviews and hosting dinners with Olive in the week, then escaping on weekends and free evenings to be with Doreen. He kept a journal through 1955 and 1956 that shows just how distressed and confused he was. An overwhelming feeling of guilt comes through on nearly every page, and he admits that even in his diary he cannot 'tell the whole truth and nothing but the truth' because 'I fear to hurt those that I dearly love.'

His marriage to Olive was stretched to breaking point but he clearly still cared for her. He could not simply forget their shared lives. 'We began our married life with Olive's Bechstein [piano] as our only asset,' he reminisced, 'and I still find it next to impossible to compose without the feel of it near me.' And yet although Doreen's name never appears in the journal, this is only because he sometimes substituted Olive's name for hers, or neglected to mention that Doreen was with him on long holidays across the country.

Under the strain of this dual existence William started drinking heavily. Terrified that his alcoholism would bring back his throat problems or create some new ailment, Doreen tried to do everything she could to reduce the amount he drank, always watering down the whiskeys he had at her flat. Later, he would admit that Doreen had been his 'salvation'. But saving William came at Doreen's expense. She chain-smoked to try to handle her stress and forgot to eat, getting so thin that her sister Barbara could almost close her 'hands around her waist'. William dealt with his problems by avoiding them, burying himself in his work. Doreen found it much harder to compartmentalise her life. Right at the moment when her career was reaching new heights with her regular work on critically acclaimed prize-listed films, she was spending all her energy on William.

Whenever they were apart, Doreen sent increasingly desperate letters to him. 'I cannot live without you,' she told him. 'You have become more than part of my life – you are part of me. I <u>know</u> you love me but we seem to have arrived at an impossible situation, and I dread the future.' There were moments when she was more reserved, saying that even if he decided to stay with Olive for good, 'At least I have loved and been loved and have known true happiness and contentment.' But these were few and far between. She was unable to hide the fact that when they were not together she felt 'a very real physical pain' that could be 'almost unbearable'. More than anything else she wanted him to return to her 'still wanting me loving me as much as I love & need you'.

William's hesitation was just as horrible for Olive. Doreen was a determined person who knew what she wanted, and didn't seem to have any qualms about breaking up the Alwyns' marriage. Olive knew full well that William's long absences were spent with Doreen, not least because he kept a photograph of his lover in his wallet that Olive found and confronted him over. She tried to issue ultimatums, once banning William from seeing Doreen for six weeks. Doreen was distraught, but refused to let him go. 'I drove my car up to North Square to see if the light was on in his study or bedroom and was his car outside?' Or she would call his club on the off-chance he was there to snatch a few moments' conversation. And he, in turn, always returned to Maida Vale: 'a rattle of the keys in my door and there he was'.

William would later maintain that 'the reason our marriage failed completely' was because Olive was 'madly jealous' of his career. But it seems much more complicated than that. Aside from the fact that Olive still appeared to love William and wanted to fight for the relationship, she probably resented him tearing apart their family after she had given up so much for him. Olive had put aside any ambitions she had as a musician to raise their children and support William. It must have been especially galling that he was now on the verge of leaving her for a woman who had the kind of career she had once dreamed of.

Olive's sacrifices and sadness linger unspoken and unacknowledged in all William's descriptions of his marriage. Clearly he was unhappy, but he rarely admitted what Olive gave for him. 'She had her baby – I didn't want to have a baby at all,' he wrote. 'I would have liked to be promiscuous.' William had a vision of his ideal self as a hedonist bohemian that Olive simply didn't fit. He criticised her for being 'a frightful prude about sex', and her friends for being 'the *dullest* people you could possibly imagine'. Doreen, on the other hand, posed naked for William to take photographs, sometimes wearing wigs, sometimes as herself. She much better fitted the life he wanted to lead. He found with her all the passion and sensuality that he felt was missing with Olive.

Doreen, however, was only half of the woman who William was attracted to. In public, she was Doreen Carwithen, composer. But in all her letters to William, she went by her middle name, 'Mary'. Doreen was splitting herself into two identities, professional and private. And Mary was prepared to do anything, put aside everything, discard Doreen completely for William's sake. For now these two identities were equally balanced, but it couldn't continue forever. Eventually, either Doreen or Mary would subsume the other.

DUSK

It was on one of their illicit driving holidays that William and Doreen first came to Blythburgh. There was, on the surface at least, little remarkable about the small village built on tidal marshland. It had once, perhaps, been an important Norman trading town, sitting as it does on the banks of the River Blyth. By 1960 it had a population of around three hundred, and its focal point was the medieval Holy Trinity Church, nicknamed the 'Cathedral of the Marshes', where many of Britten's works were performed. On summer days birdwatchers flocked to the village for the rare species attracted to the marsh muds which, in the winter, stretch out endlessly, the flat waters reflecting the rolling grey clouds blown inwards from the Suffolk coast so that sky and earth merge seamlessly.

Blythburgh's bleak tranquillity and hints of long-lost history proved an irresistible combination for Doreen and William. It couldn't have been more different from London. Riding on a post-war wave of affluence, the capital was modernising at a pace that neither composer was really comfortable with. Doreen was still only thirty-eight – and although she had never been one to follow the latest trends, had she been with a different man she might have enjoyed the Italian-style espresso bars in newly popular areas like Soho, and the boutique stores that would make sixties London an unrivalled fashion destination.

As it was, William seemed much older than his fifty-five years, and regarded contemporary London with a kind of horror. He disdained serialism, and Rodgers and Hammerstein musicals, and when the Beatles arrived he would disdain them, too. He was committed to his own ideals of beauty. Throughout the fifties, when the rest of London was turning to Jackson Pollock, Mark Rothko and Pop Art, William had accumulated an impressive collection of Pre-Raphaelite paintings. Their dreamlike, idealised depictions of historical scenes were hideously unfashionable at the time, but William loved their 'spiritual sensuality'. He took Doreen on a pilgrimage to lay flowers at the grave of Dante Gabriel Rossetti, the Pre-Raphaelite closest to William's heart perhaps because he was both a poet and artist, modelling the Romantic polymath that William aspired to be.

Relations with Olive were not getting any less fraught. William was still drinking heavily, and Doreen just wanted to escape from the lies and fights and anxiety. Blythburgh seemed the perfect place to hide away from the world. Leaving behind her teaching jobs, Doreen bought a small cottage on Chapel Road for £825. It had five rooms, no bathroom and barely enough space in the kitchen to cook, but she was quite content. The bedroom had a view over the estuary, and she could make do by bathing in a small tin bath. Besides, she was not planning on having anybody but William stay in her sanctuary. She had always been relatively self-sufficient and liked living on her own. And most importantly, uprooting to Suffolk paved the way for William to follow her.

After seventeen years of leading two lives, William finally had to choose. His children were now fully grown and living away from home, so on 19 April 1961 he left Olive and his family for the last time. Doreen called it 'E-Day', the date 'written on my heart'. They wrote to Doreen's parents, finally breaking their silence about the relationship. 'I hope you will understand and not underrate the distress of mind of both of us before taking this step,' William told them. 'Doreen has always respected my feelings and has loyally kept in the background.' They welcomed William without hesitation, simply grateful to finally have an explanation for Doreen's increasingly poor health.

For Olive, too, 19 April was no doubt differently unforgettable. William never told her that he was leaving. He simply upped and left, taking nothing with him from their thirty-two-year marriage but a few scores and some of his Pre-Raphaelite paintings. He claimed that he left it to his doctor to break the news to Olive. She immediately called her elder son, Jonathan, who remembered her being 'hysterical. She went downhill all the way. It broke her heart.' Olive led a lonely life after William left her, never remarrying. She and William only glimpsed each other again once, at their son Nicholas's wedding.

From the moment that William stepped into the Blythburgh cottage, Doreen Carwithen became Mary Alwyn. She changed her name by deed poll and began wearing a wedding ring even though they wouldn't marry legally until 1975, in a small ceremony with just a few friends and a cake that Mary bought herself. It was far less a companionship of equals than James and Rebecca's marriage; from the day of the elopement, Mary structured her existence solely around her partner. When Olive kept the Bechstein on which he liked to compose, it was Mary who sorted the situation, hiring a piano tuner to improve their instrument while he fumed and despaired. By the end of the year William was overwhelmed by stress and had a nervous breakdown that he believed would leave him unable to compose. Mary nursed him back to health, coaxing him into playing daily piano duets with her. Just a few weeks later, he was well enough to complete his Movements for Piano.

Settling into her new domestic role, Mary set about finding them a more hospitable place to live. The decrepit and poorly equipped cottage only heightened their elopement's sense of against-all-odds-romanticism, and they ambitiously christened it 'Lark Rise' after the autodidact Flora Thompson's semi-autobiographical novels about her rural upbringing, William perhaps wanting to identify with the writer's self-made success. Nonetheless, after a few months they began to tire of the lack of heating and having to wash in the sink. After weeks of unsuccessful house-hunting, they decided to build their own. They could construct a home that suited their needs perfectly. It would be a dream house.

Mary and William.

Mary turned the same energy that she had once used for composing to what would become the second Lark Rise. They bought a plot opposite the cottage, and building began in 1962. Having never gardened before, she read up on roses and planned out the acre-and-a-half grounds in detail. She oversaw the foundations being laid, and liaised with the architect. But reality fell short of the ideal. The freezing winter of 1962 delayed building, and problems dogged the project for two years. When the Alwyns finally moved into Lark Rise in February 1964, they were accompanied by carpenters, a plumber and builders fixing the heating that clanged 'like a ship's engine'. The stunning view over the marshes was marred by 'a garden of mud like a rough sea'.

Over the coming months, problems were slowly ticked off Mary's checklist. A local farmer turfed the garden for her, and she began landscaping. She selected 'tall trees and shrubs with attractive flowers', and finished off the garden with William's 'Naked Ladies', a group of Italian statues that they had bought on one of their holidays. In went the teal carpets, the walls were painted pale pink and double glazing was fitted throughout the house.

With the builders finally gone, Lark Rise was almost eerily silent. Elisabeth Lutyens was one of William's closer friends, becoming relatively friendly with Mary by association. The three had a peculiar relationship – William advocated for Elisabeth's work, not Mary's, to be performed at Benjamin Britten's Aldeburgh Festival – and the two women never seem to have developed a close friendship. By contrast, Elisabeth and William wrote to each other regularly, and she became one of the privileged few invited to stay at Lark Rise. She thought it was

> like an enchanted castle of fairy-story origin, with Mary as a 'sleeping beauty' to be awakened by you, her prince. [. . .] One saw the wind stir the trees – but heard nothing; the birds hop about, making no noise. It was as if everything was under a spell – a spell of love, but a spell which admitted no outside interference.

Others were less polite. Jonathan Alwyn, whose relationship with his father became increasingly strained after William's separation from Olive, described it as being 'like visiting Gormenghast, the holy of holies. If you so much as hiccuped they would frown.'

Their dream home was, in truth, a shrine to William. Mary maintained perfect conditions for him to work. He created, while she busied herself by copying out parts, typing up his manuscripts and hassling conductors and record labels on his behalf. She identified herself with him so much that at one point she began writing her notebooks *as* William. It reads like a fantasy of what she hoped to be for him. She is the perfect critic: when she gives feedback William realises, 'As usual she is right and I alter the phrase to her judgement.' The typed scripts she brings him are 'perfect as usual'. While second-wave feminism was sweeping across the UK and US with revolutionary critiques of the idea that 'true feminine fulfillment' came from being a housewife and mother, Mary was embodying a fifties ideal.

The transition from Doreen to Mary coincided almost exactly with the move to the second Lark Rise. Doreen penned her final compositions in 1964: a set of Six Little Pieces for cello and an orchestral work called *Suffolk Suite*, which was a commission from Framlingham College, a local boys' school. She had lost none of her ability to craft a taut, engaging score. The suite includes sonic portraits of important Suffolk landmarks – the jovial, almost pompous finale depicts the twelfth-century fortress Framlingham Castle – but, overall, it gives an idea of what the county meant to Doreen. She revisited her *East Anglian Holiday* music for the second movement, 'Orford Ness', the sweeping melodies and slow harp accompaniment evoking the gentle lines of the mud-flats and reed marshes, and the graceful movements of the birds that inhabit them. It was a highly idealised depiction – Orford Ness is a shingle spit that was used for military testing during both world wars and atomic weapons testing afterwards, but there's no hint of laboratories and control towers in Doreen's suite. As with so many things in Doreen's life, she saw the Ness through rose-tinted spectacles, showing only what she wanted to see. The whole suite is full of hope. Not a single note ruffles the overriding impression of peace and happiness. It was a utopian farewell. Royalty attended Doreen's last premiere, at the opening of Framlingham College's concert hall. Doreen Carwithen stepped out on to the stage for her final bow. Mary Alwyn returned home to Lark Rise with William.

o   o   o   o

With her continual trips in and out of hospital, Dorothy little expected to outlive all of her family except her brother Alfred. Her younger sister Sis died in 1956, followed by Pookie in 1960. For all Dorothy's sixty-two years Pookie had been like a second mother to her. Even though she had never been able to hear a note of Dorothy's music she had supported her without question, adopting an almost parental conviction that anything her charge produced would be wonderful. She had been such a stalwart fixture of Dorothy's life that when she passed it felt as though a vital part of Dorothy, a part that kept her optimistic and alive, simply faded away.

Even in her darkest moments, though, Dorothy flatly refused to lose 'her zest for life'. She busied herself with anything that stopped her from wallowing. In the months after Pookie's death she took a long holiday with her sister Winkie, Freddie carrying them to the Lake District, Scotland, Yorkshire, Durham and Wiltshire. She had to drop the majority of her regular teaching because of her health, and replaced lessons with projects and hobbies like repainting Studley House, or watching musicals at the cinema. By the 1960s televisions were ubiquitous in England, so cinema trips became rare events – attendance had plummeted to 327 million visits a year by 1965. Musicals and James Bond films dominated the decade. Unlike William, Dorothy absolutely loved the colour and flamboyance of big-budget musicals. Among her favourites were *My Fair Lady*, *Mary Poppins* and *The Sound of Music*. And she wasn't alone. In 1965, 1966 and 1968 *The Sound of Music* soundtrack outsold the Beatles, the Rolling Stones, Bob Dylan, Tom Jones, Simon & Garfunkel, Otis Redding and Diana Ross & the Supremes to become the UK's best-selling album in each year. Pop may have been dominating teenagers' lives, but a solid proportion of Britain, like Dorothy, still enjoyed ballads and sing-along musical numbers that harked back to the music hall.

The most absorbing of Dorothy's new hobbies was archery. She took up the sport in 1961 to build strength in her arms and back

after all her operations, and warmed to it immediately. After a fortnight she delightedly recorded that she had hit her first gold, the
innermost ring of the target, and for the rest of the decade Fridays
and Sundays were archery days. She frequently brought home tour-
nament prizes, making her, as a niece put it, one of the club's 'more
surprising' high scorers.

As always, above all else Dorothy's 'deep and abiding Faith' gave
her purpose. For decades she and her brother Clifford had been active
members of the Society of St Gregory, a Catholic group founded in
1929 to promote lay participation in the liturgy, so Dorothy was well
prepared for the Church's significant changes in the sixties. In an
attempt to modernise and reach out to Catholics worldwide, the
Second Vatican Council of 1962–5 agreed that the Catholic Church
should encourage more congregational participation in the liturgy –
which, naturally, the Society of St Gregory actively supported.

To encourage this a series of subtle changes was made to the liturgy, including allowing Mass to be given in the vernacular instead of
in Latin. Musically, this meant that new Mass settings were needed.
Dorothy had been turning her attention to religious composition for
a while – she wrote a *Missa Simplex* in Latin for a local school in 1959
alongside other sacred works – and in 1964 she completed her first
Mass in English, *A Simple Mass for the People*, commissioned by the
Gregorian Institute of America in Ohio. A number of other Masses
and choral works followed, including *A Mass for Ampleforth, Four
Anthems for Our Lady* and *A Short English Mass for Congregation*.

Dorothy's religious music found a global audience in a way that
her secular music never had. Her Masses, motets and anthems
were sung in Britain, America and South Africa. In 1968 alone, her
Short English Mass sold 1,630 copies worldwide. As highbrow classical music audiences were embracing complexity, the simplicity of
Dorothy's religious settings was the basis of their wide appeal. As
one magazine enthused, she used 'a melody which takes its rhythm
from the words as spoken' and she always composed with amateur

singers in mind, ensuring that her music could be sung by any congregation.

While Dorothy's Catholic music was enjoying an autumn flowering, her concert works had all but disappeared. Her last orchestral outing during her lifetime was in 1960. Hoping to raise awareness of contemporary women composers, a young conductor called Kathleen Merritt led an all-woman programme at the Wigmore Hall that placed Dorothy alongside five of her colleagues. But, Kathleen hastened to add, 'I am not a feminist'; the newspapers noted approvingly that she has 'none of the alarming if admirable trappings of women who fight for women's causes', and also promoted music by living male composers. In early 1960s Britain, 'feminism' still had derogatory connotations, and professional women often distanced themselves from it to avoid dismissal or scorn. It wasn't quite enough to save Kathleen's concert, though. The performance was merely 'serviceable enough in a home-spun way', and critics complained about the lack of atonal and serial music. 'It was as decorous as one always supposes a gathering of ladies to be.'

Dorothy did not rise to attitudes like this. Instead, she amused herself by collecting critical jargon that she felt ascended to truly risible levels of pretentiousness. (A particular favourite, that she jotted down on a scrap of paper, was 'The tightly controlled application of the aleatoric principle of indeterminacy is both simpler & intellectually more honest than Stockhausen's logarithmic methods for creating sprays of sound.') She was assisted by her nieces, who posted anything they thought would make her laugh. And when Dorothy had enough, she strung them together to make nonsense poetry.

Despite all her ailments, Dorothy kept herself young at heart by surrounding herself with younger people. She kept teaching for the Royal Academy right up until 1970, when she turned seventy-two. And even then, she still gave some private tuition. 'Every lesson began with tea and biscuits,' her final student remembered. 'The china was beautiful and the biscuits were disgusting – exceptionally soggy.' Lessons were technically one hour long, but Dorothy would often run over, pleased to have the company and happy to feel useful. Her non-teaching hours were devoted to her numerous nieces and nephews. Of all of them, two of Alfred's children, Merryn and Columb, spent the most time at Studley, laughing at the nutcrackers that Dorothy kept in the sitting room and hoovering up her dreadful soggy biscuits. Dorothy couldn't have known it in 1970, but the nephew and niece who had rolled down her garden slopes as children were the future of her music. Without Merryn and Columb, very few of her scores would have survived at all.

o   o   o   o

Like Dorothy, Rebecca spent much of her time with younger and younger people as she aged. After twenty-three happy years of marriage, James passed away from a heart attack in 1967, leaving eighty-one-year-old Rebecca alone in New York. 'My heart aches for you,' Dora wrote to her. 'I only hope that in Time it will be a comfort to you to know how you transformed his life & made his happiness.' Perhaps Rebecca would have briefly considered moving back to Britain as Dora was still living in London, but the majority of her family lived in the States. She now had a veritable fleet of great-nieces and nephews, most of whom, confusingly, were named Eric, Hans, Rebecca or some variant on Joseph. Rebecca had remained close to her tight-knit family, and did not want to move so far away when her own mobility was steadily decreasing. So she chose to stay in the New York apartment where she and James had been so happy.

To make it less lonely she took in a series of female piano students from the Juilliard School as lodgers. Hearing them practise and listening to their School news reminded Rebecca of James and kept her from brooding. In the weeks after his death Rebecca busied herself by fulfilling the wishes of his will. Generous until the end, he had left provision for two scholarships for students in financial hardship to be set up in his name, one at Juilliard and one at the Royal College. Rebecca arranged for these to be put in place and then began sorting the music scores he had left behind, now worth a small fortune. True to James's memory, she did not keep them, but donated them to a local community music college.

Some of the more unexpected guests among the parades of people coming in and out of Rebecca's apartment were feminist academics and musicians. By the 1970s, second-wave feminism in America had started to see some of its greatest legal and social successes, including the passing of the Equal Pay Act in 1963 and *Roe v. Wade*, which legalised abortion, in 1973. Women's studies began to be institutionalised in universities, largely growing out of literature departments; the first Women's Studies programme opened at San Diego State College in 1970, and the ensuing decade saw the publication of many of the classics of feminist literature, from Germaine Greer's *The Female Eunuch* to bell hooks's *Ain't I A Woman: Black Women and Feminism*. This explosion of interest brought young academics to Rebecca's doorstep, as they put together sources that would adequately acknowledge women's place in music history. For musicologists had quickly excised Rebecca from the record. The first time Rebecca had an entry in the *Grove Dictionary*, in the 1928 edition, she had an article calling her a 'composer and viola-player', with a brief biography and list of all her major works. But her entry in the *New Grove Dictionary*, eventually published in 1980, read in its entirety: 'English viola player and composer, wife of James Friskin.'

Where Ethel might have waded into the fray, providing potential biographers with as much information as they could stomach, Rebecca was much more guarded. She consented to a number of interviews but kept up a tongue-in-cheek, self-deprecating tone in all of them – in her first big interview for WQXR she described the 1919 Coolidge Competition as 'that one little whiff of success that I've had in my life', joking that at times she had thought herself '*terribly* important'. Nonetheless, she received enough attention that by the mid-seventies it was clear that second-wave feminism could, potentially, mark an important turning point for her music.

One of the main barriers to Rebecca's inclusion in dictionaries and histories was a complete lack of knowledge about her unpublished works. She had always been extremely selective about what she chose to publish, and with her unpublished scores in her own possession, it was almost impossible to get an understanding of her full output. So in 1976 she worked with a PhD student called Christopher Johnson, who had come into her life as the husband of a great-niece, to put together a thematic catalogue of her complete *oeuvre* as part of his doctoral coursework.

It was, to put it mildly, an onerous task. Rebecca kept her manuscripts in a large, old-fashioned music cabinet, and while they were kept neatly, there was no sense of chronology. Average student efforts were jumbled alongside later works like the Trio, that blazing fire of modern music. Together, Rebecca and Christopher began sifting through the trays of scores to try to piece them into some kind of timeline, using her diary wherever possible to assign accurate dates. For some pieces it was impossible to be precise – on the front of these scores, there are still Rebecca's pencilled-in dates with a question mark after them.

Perhaps it was the flurry of interest in her music that prompted Rebecca to follow in Ethel's footsteps and write a memoir. Or it may have been a way of remembering James, honouring his hope that she would write one last big piece – but this time she worked in words instead of notes. She focused on telling the story of her adolescence, partly using the writing as a way to meditate on some of her more conflicted feelings about her father, and rethink her relationship with him. 'Nowadays, people who dabble in psychoanalysis sometimes maintain that a relationship like Papa's and mine shows that the father is in love with his daughter. But', she added as a caveat, 'psychoanalysis didn't exist when I was a girl; or if it did I had never heard of it.' Nonetheless, Joseph's behaviour was troubling enough that she needed to ask the question – and she couldn't help but wonder.

Besides what Rebecca consciously chose to tell about herself, the unpublished, typed manuscript also reveals an enormous amount about both her and James. They were inveterate recyclers, so when she handed her notes to a niece to type up, she typed on the back of circulars that had been kept as spare paper. Ethel, Dorothy and Doreen were all staunch Conservatives – Dorothy was still attending Conservative meetings in the 1970s – but Rebecca was wholeheartedly on the left of the political spectrum. She and James were generous with their time and money, hoping to leave the world a more equal place than they had found it. Between them, they were on the mailing lists for the World Wildlife Fund, National Council of Negro Women, Quaker societies, anti-war campaigns, fundraisers for émigré composers displaced by war, education programmes, environmental groups – and more. Rebecca kept up a keen interest in politics up until her death; when the Watergate scandal broke she watched avidly on her television, calling her great-nephew Christopher to mull over the latest developments.

Rebecca died, quietly, in October 1979, at the age of ninety-three. The memoir – her final composition – lay, mid-revision, on her desk, watched over by a small bronze tiger that she had brought back from her Asia tour. Unlike Ethel, who was granted obituaries in all the major newspapers, Rebecca's passing prompted little fanfare. The *New York Times* carried a short notice mentioning her Coolidge Competition successes. Her death went entirely unmarked by the British papers.

She had, however, lived long enough to see the first ripples of what would become tidal waves of change, bringing her music to a new generation of listeners. Besides the academic interest in her work, in 1977 Rebecca sat in the audience to witness her Sonata receive its first highly publicised professional performance in decades, at the

Alice Tully Hall in New York. The response was mainly one of shock. 'Had she not been a woman composer', the *New York Times* admitted, 'Miss Clarke might be heard more today.' By way of thanks, Rebecca composed a short, four-bar token of gratitude for the violist, and wrote her own programme note for the recital. Reflecting on the Sonata's history, she recalled that some people believed it impossible for a woman to have composed it. She responded in her characteristically understated way: 'I take this opportunity to emphasize that I do indeed exist.'

The real watershed moment came in 1980, with the Sonata's first recording. It put Rebecca's music on the radio – and not just in the UK and the US. The recording itself came from a Czech label. Again, the piece provoked a combination of delight and surprise, getting extremely laudatory reviews in the British press. It took a few years for Rebecca's music to really gain traction – and early write-ups were littered with mistakes, from misspellings of work titles to a persistent myth that she had composed nothing since 1925 – but by 1986 the Sonata had established a firm foothold in the viola repertory. It became so popular that one critic even complained that Rebecca was 'over-played' which, while a wild exaggeration, does reflect something true about the piece's meteoric rise. It is now one of the better-recorded works ever written by a woman, and most violists will at some point play it. But it really was just the Sonata that became well known. The Trio, *Passacaglia* and a select number of songs also made their way on to programmes, but Rebecca's 1941 ballad *Binnorie*, for example, didn't get its recording premiere until 2020. Even for classical music aficionados, many of her works remain sufficiently unfamiliar that they can still have 'the startling force of a discovery', as one 1980 critic put it.

Ethel, too, experienced a small second-wave feminist renaissance, but her path was much more convoluted. If anything, Rebecca was helped by relative anonymity – her music was allowed to stand for itself. But by the 1980s many critics and performers believed they already knew everything they needed to about 'the almost self-parodying Ethel Smyth' who was 'rarely taken seriously'. Her life was still a continual source of fascination, exacerbated by the publication of Virginia Woolf's diaries and letters from the late 1970s onwards. Virginia's deliciously cruel caricatures did nothing to help Ethel's reputation as 'an old battleaxe who wore tweeds and funny hats'. Although she was the subject of another biography and numerous academic articles, often focused on her sexuality, her music surfaced more rarely. And when it did, reviews were mixed, frequently trotting out tired tropes about Ethel or about women's composition more broadly.

Really, Ethel had to wait until the 1990s for substantial recognition as a serious composer, which largely came thanks to the conductor Odaline de la Martínez. Building on Ethel's work, she had become the first woman to conduct a complete Proms concert in 1984, and in 1994 conducted and recorded the Proms premiere of *The Wreckers*. The performance was 'a revelation'. 'The sheer brilliance of the writing, the sheer power of the execution of the idea, are apparent right from the opening bars of the overture,' the critics enthused. Martínez has continued to champion Ethel as a composer first and foremost, subsequently recording her Serenade, Concerto, *The Boatswain's Mate* and *Fête Galante*.

For Dorothy, though, the 1980s brought no such rediscovery. From 1968, the combined impact of repeated serious operations and musical rejections finally began to take its toll. For the first time ever, she confided to her diary that she was 'Very depressed'. These bouts of depression became more frequent, and her health problems were becoming so debilitating that in 1977, when she turned seventy-nine, she decided to leave Studley for Perrins House, a nursing home in Malvern. She spent much of the year clearing out her home, deciding which pieces of furniture should go into storage to pay for her nursing bills, and which few, treasured items would come with her to the small room overlooking the Malvern Hills.

She drafted in Merryn and Columb to help her sort through everything – tables needed to be sold, her china packed away and her Bechstein transferred to a former student's home in London. But no provision was made for her music. As the final items made their way from the house, Merryn came across Dorothy in her bedroom, surrounded by all her manuscripts. 'I heard her just saying "It's hopeless, who's going to want this? Nobody is going to want it. Come on",' Merryn remembered. And then Dorothy began tearing her life's work in two, planning to burn the lot. With astonishing presence of mind, Merryn dived in with a box, telling her that she would take all the unwanted manuscripts out to burn herself. Dorothy put everything in – everything except the four works that were so dear to her that she couldn't bear to part with them, even in her lowest moment: *Lamia*, *Koong Shee*, *The Rock* and the Piano Concerto. Those manuscripts went with her to Perrins, where she kept them in a box at the end of her bed.

Merryn kept every single scrap that Dorothy had intended to destroy. But because the manuscripts were in such disarray, unsorted and uncatalogued, some slipped through Merryn's net. Many of Dorothy's chamber works turned up decades later, in an old radiogram that had previously been put in storage. Some are still being discovered in Merryn and Columb's home, in the boxes that they eventually inherited from Studley. Others are thought lost for good – although they may, like some of Dorothy's other 'lost' works, be unearthed in some file or cabinet somewhere.

Dorothy was in the wrong place at the wrong time for second-wave feminism. Her life was not as extraordinary as Ethel's, her music not as modernist as Rebecca's – and as a Catholic, conservative, single woman, she didn't fit the profile that feminists were then prioritising. And even if curious musicians had wanted to play her works, the majority were unpublished, and the published works mostly out of print. The most determined performers would have had difficulty getting hold of scores. So Dorothy heard only one more broadcast of her music before she died. In 1981, she was delighted to hear her Piano Sonata get its broadcast premiere on Radio 3 in a programme also including some of William's piano music – he and Mary were certainly listening, two hundred miles away in Blythburgh. But no repeat performances followed.

Even though Dorothy rarely composed in her final years, the impulse had not disappeared. She wrote one last piece while at Perrins: a short piano piece for the left hand called *Zapateado*, composed for a fellow pianist at the nursing home. She also sketched a seventeen-bar-long *Frivolous Air on a Ground Bass*, in memory of her old tutor John McEwen. Perhaps she had considered working it up into a full piece, but it never happened.

Towards the end of 1981, on one of her visits to Alfred's house, Dorothy sat at his piano – something she had not done in years. And she played, for hours, all the pieces that she had loved as a young pianist and that had made her famous. Chopin, Schumann, Liszt, her own pieces; her fingers still knew the patterns, after all those years. Merryn and Columb opened the windows, and a small crowd gathered outside on the street, listening to Dorothy give her final concert. 'I think she knew that she was coming to the end of her life,' Merryn recalled. 'In a way the performance was her farewell to us.' Just a few weeks later, Dorothy died from pneumonia on 12 January 1982, aged eighty-three. In one of her last diary entries, she simply wrote: 'Cold got me down.'

o   o   o   o

Mary Alwyn was far too wrapped up in William to try to reap any benefits from 1970s feminism. When academics came to the house to interview him about his music, she never mentioned that she, too, had once been a famous composer, called Doreen Carwithen. Similar to Dorothy, though, her urge to compose had not faded entirely – just been suppressed. Shortly before her fifty-third birthday in 1975 she composed another cello work, called *Seascapes*, and sent it off to Oxford University Press. In what must have felt like fate pushing her back to focus on William, the Press promptly lost the score. They wouldn't guarantee publication even if she rewrote the work from her sketches, so she didn't bother. The complete first draft remains, unpublished, in the Cambridge University Library. But when William composed his own *Seascapes* in 1980, perhaps inspired by the same source as Mary, his set of four songs was both published and performed.

Doreen (centre right) with William (far right), her sister Barbara (left),
Dulcie (centre left), and Barbara's children.

Eloping with Mary seems to have extinguished William's creative inhibitions. From the mid-1960s until his death, he created a number of works on sexual themes that he had, perhaps, felt that he simply could not tackle while with Olive. After he had watched police recover a woman's body from the Blythburgh marshes near their house, he penned a novel that combined autobiography with an imagined relationship with the drowned woman. She is objectified and sexualised: at one point she stands in front of a mirror, 'cups her breasts in her hands and presses her nipples against the glass, flattening their tips against the glass'. Publishers declined the book. Undeterred, William followed this up with several poetry collections, also rejected. Refusing to take no for an answer, Mary self-published them through a local printer.

The projects that consumed William throughout the 1960s and 1970s, however, were two operas, *Juan or the Libertine* and *Miss Julie*. Despite Mary's best efforts, *Juan* (based on the story of Don Juan) was not performed. For *Miss Julie*, Mary managed to negotiate a BBC broadcast in 1977. William would later claim that the opera was 'hailed as a masterpiece' and couldn't believe that opera companies weren't jumping to stage it, but the reality was more muted. William had adapted the libretto from a play by the deeply misogynist Swedish playwright August Strindberg, whose vitriolic views about women saturate the text. Critics damned his romanticisation of Strindberg's chilling misogyny – which Mary had not seemed to object to. It was mostly thanks to her that *Miss Julie* was recorded in 1983 and received its stage premiere in 1997.

When William wasn't composing or writing he was painting, often with Mary as his muse in varying states of undress. A photograph of a naked Mary sat on his desk as inspiration, showing only her torso, and he worked surrounded by statues of naked women. His paintings adorned Lark Rise; one musician admitted that he 'was rather nonplussed by the nude paintings of an already elderly Mary on the sitting room wall', gazing down at him as he tried to make light conversation over scones and tea. On sunny days William took his paints out to Blythburgh's banks or the beach at Southwold to paint the landscape, sometimes including Mary as she sat and read. In 1979 Mary orchestrated an exhibition of his art at a local gallery. Two paintings sold.

Mary as painted by William, given to her as a birthday gift.

Of all the things that irked William – and there were many – one of the most pressing was the fact that he had never been on the Honours List. Nothing peeved him as much as the feeling that his talents were going unrecognised. When being interviewed by a biographer he explained that 'I keep on using the word "brilliant", but I can't think of any other word because I had quite exceptional gifts.' 'All my colleagues of my age (and less than my standing) have collected their knighthoods and CBE's,' he complained in 1976. 'But not even a "red brick" university has considered me worthy of an honorary degree.' This was a persistent thorn in his side, which made the honours a priority for Mary. Throughout the 1970s she rallied support from his colleagues, and succeeded in getting him a CBE in 1978 – which was deemed a 'disappointment' because it wasn't a knighthood. She kept up a tireless campaign: just before his seventy-seventh birthday, William finally got his much-wanted honorary doctorate, from the University of Leicester.

Mary would have made William immortal if she could. But good health was the one thing that it was not in her gift to give, however hard she tried to keep him well rested and free from stress. In 1981 he suffered his first stroke, shortly after Olive's death in a nursing home, and was rushed to Norfolk and Norwich Hospital. Mary accompanied him, living in a nearby hotel for the duration of his hospital stay. She visited him every day, and having to leave in the evenings made them so miserable that a friend bought walkie-talkies to allow them to speak to one another. Mary simply couldn't bear the thought that she might not find out for hours if he took a turn for the worse overnight. These days were so painful to remember that when Mary recalled them later for William's biographer, she wrote in the present tense, reliving every moment – and then scored out her writing with thick, heavy lines, as though the act of scratching out her words might be able to erase them from her memory, too.

That time William pulled through, but in 1985 he was returned to hospital in Southwold, with a brain tumour and a shadow on one of his lungs. Mary knew he was nearing the end. Never one for public displays of emotion, she busied herself preparing funeral arrangements and obituaries, making herself as useful to William as she could be until his last moments. On 11 September 1985, Mary

said I would talk to him and I did, saying that he had put up a splendid fight but now he should relax and give in. He seemed to understand and I put my arms round him and he seemed comforted and more peaceful [. . .]. It was nearly midnight when he took one large deep breath and that was the end.

o   o   o   o

For twenty-five years, Mary's days had been the same. She made William tea in the mornings, coffee in the afternoons, and sat with him in the evenings listening to records. Without William, Mary had no purpose. She kept everything at Lark Rise as it was when he died – his clothes still hanging in the wardrobes, his desk still laid out as though he might return at any moment, cigarette in hand, to start a new composition. By 1986 she was, as a friend put it, 'hitting bottom', on medication for persistent migraines, struggling with depression and at points contemplating suicide.

It was Mary's old friend from the Academy, Violet, who was her rock through these miserable years. She knew only too well the pain of losing a partner, her husband having died in 1967. Now a music teacher, she distracted Mary with weekly phone calls, in which she told her about her students, and they updated each other about their cats (Violet always had more than four; Mary was more restrained). They organised holidays that became the highlight of Mary's calendar. They travelled the world together, setting off for destinations as diverse as New Zealand, Canada, Cyprus, Egypt, Israel, Madeira, Portugal and France – sometimes they took Mary's electric blue

VW Golf, nicknamed 'Blue Bird'. The most memorable trip was to Norway, where they visited the house of the composer Edvard Grieg, who had been a favourite of William and Mary's. 'It was a magical voyage', Mary remembered, with 'constant views of snow-capped mountains.'

But perhaps the thing that helped Mary's grief the most was feeling as though she was securing William's posthumous legacy. In his will he had left funds to promote his own work, so Mary established a William Alwyn Foundation to ensure that he would receive recordings and performances. She collected together his correspondence and papers to make an archive that would go to Cambridge University Library when she died. She poured money into an enormous project on the Chandos label, overseeing the recording of his complete symphonies and numerous other works which, as when he was alive, were admired by a small devoted group. Nobody would do the same for her after her death.

Mary sometimes fought William's corner with a virulence that could be counter-productive – she lost many friends and poten-tial musical allies over what she perceived to be slights against her beloved husband. Once someone fell short of the adoration she felt was William's due she cut them out of her life entirely with the cry 'He's out!' At times there was a sense of desperation about her behaviour. Perhaps her desire to succeed on William's behalf was made all the more urgent because she had given up her career for his: she *had* to make him a success, otherwise what had her sacrifice been for?

For even as Mary turned sixty-five, there was still a little of Doreen Carwithen left in her. Perhaps she could only resurface once William had died. Those friends who knew that Doreen Carwithen existed encouraged her to compose again, hoping she would 'turn your thoughts again to your own creative side which I guess you have neglected because of being such a wonderful support to Bill and working on his behalf'. And, tentatively, she did. By 1987 she was 'into a period of creativity', working on nothing less than a Symphony, an Oboe Concerto, a Romance for Cello and Orchestra and her String Quartet No. 3. And three years later, as part of the Chandos project recording William's works, she allowed her own Piano Concerto, *Bishop Rock* and *ODTAA* to be recorded.

Having never mentioned her compositions to anyone who visited Lark Rise, she finally played some of her own music to those who had been coming to the house for years to see William, and who were completely unaware that Doreen existed. They were bowled over by it. Consistent across all their accounts of hearing Mary play Doreen's music for the first time is a feeling of complete shock – not only that she had been a composer at all, but also that she wrote the kind of music that she did. They would never have guessed that quiet, careful Mary, who they knew for slipping discreetly into William's shadow, could have composed the fiery, energetic music that they now heard blaring from her speakers. 'There is still time for you to make a mark again in this field if you have the urge,' one friend reassured her.

A CD of her String Quartets and Violin Sonata followed in 1998, lauded as 'a passionate outpouring, strong and purposeful'. She went to the recording session, but it was an odd event – she seemed to hover between being Doreen and Mary. Doreen would have thrown herself into proceedings, but instead the composer whom the quartet met was 'a remote, even unapproachable figure, sometimes offering a word of advice or pointing out a discrepancy'. William's biographer drove her to and from the venue, and she confided to him that she 'didn't have much confidence in the pieces she had written so many years before'.

Perhaps she might have been more content with her new pieces, but she never got the chance to finish them. In December 1999, Mary was found in Lark Rise by the police, who had been called by a worried local tradesman unable to get a response at her door. Like William so many years before her, she had suffered a stroke, and was transferred to hospital to recover. She would spend her final years in a nursing home, only occasionally returning to Lark Rise for day visits. Once, she was treated to a birthday concert in the living room looking out over the marsh. It was one of the rare occasions when she dropped her inscrutable demeanour, and was 'visibly moved' to hear her own music again, in the room that held such happy memories of her life with her husband.

Mary took her cat, Tabitha, with her to her penultimate residence, the Manor Farm care home in Kessingland. She was given a small room that looked quite similar to Dorothy's, except that hers was 'made smaller by the constant muddle of books and unsorted papers that littered it', and otherwise contained only 'a sink and single bed and cupboards'. She earned something of a reputation as a difficult resident: she bought Sky Sports to watch cricket, turned up to full volume; if other residents roamed into her space she would repel them with her walking stick; she gave nurses she disliked rude nicknames; and when she needed to attend a Chandos session, she demanded (unsuccessfully) that she be carried to the studio by helicopter. But Mary could still be 'a lovely lady' when she wanted to, and always had plenty of visitors. As well as old musician friends and everybody she knew through their interest in William's work, her sister Barbara came to see her, as did Barbara's son Mark, who entertained Mary no end by whizzing her along the corridors in her wheelchair.

Violet, though, never got to visit. Just a short while after Mary's stroke Violet was diagnosed with cancer, and died quickly afterwards, in April 2000. Her passing left Mary reeling from 'inconsolable grief', compounded by Tabitha being run over in the same month. 'It seemed too much to bear,' she thought. 'First my darling Tabitha and then my dearest friend V.' Violet had been one of the few people left who had known both Mary and Doreen. She could even remember Doreen before William, and she had been her most constant musical supporter. Violet knew Doreen's music in a way that not even her family did – Doreen was so used to keeping secrets from her family that Barbara didn't find out that her sister had scored films until after her death. Mary wasn't just losing a friend. She was losing a part of her past to which nobody else had access.

Doreen Carwithen never gave up on her music. She had confided to a friend that her desire to compose 'was beginning to return', even if illness ultimately prevented her from finishing her last works. When she died from a second stroke on 5 January 2003, her obituaries remembered her as 'a substantial creative personality in her own right'. As she came to the end of her life, she set a friend straight. 'I am not Mary,' she told him. 'I am Doreen.'

EPILOGUE

Every morning I listen to BBC Radio 3's Essential Classics programme. And over the past few years, they've been playing more music by women. There's been a noticeable increase even in the time that I've been writing this book. This morning, as I write, they're playing Doreen's *Bishop Rock*, something that would have been unlikely even a few years ago, and impossible before 1996 because no commercial recording existed. On Twitter, people are responding enthusiastically to her music. It's a 'phenomenal piece', one listener says. There's a sense of incredulity among posters – how is this music not better known? Who was this woman? What did she write? What was she like?

This is such a familiar experience. When this music is played and heard, audiences love it and are curious to find out more. Conductor Rebecca Miller has been instrumental in resurrecting and recording Dorothy's music, and in 2019 she brought some of her orchestral pieces to the public for the first time since the 1950s, conducting the Southbank Sinfonia. The pieces were met with enthusiasm from both players and audience. They responded to Dorothy's 'really inventive, imaginative music, quite unique in its style', she says. And overwhelmingly, when given an opportunity to hear this music, people want to know: 'Where has this woman been all our lives?'

Surely, our musical world can only be richer for putting this music onto programmes and into histories. And it feels as though the tides might be changing for the women of *Quartet*. When Odaline de la Martínez conducted Ethel's *The Wreckers* in 1994, the performance was faced with a fair amount of resistance. This came mainly from those who 'had never heard of Smyth except in her life as a suffragette', she recalls, but who nonetheless prejudged the music, dismissing it as 'Women's Institute stuff'. Now, thirty years later, Odaline has recorded most of Ethel's major works. In 2022, *The Wreckers* was staged by both Glyndebourne Opera in the UK and Houston Grand Opera in the USA; a recording of *The Prison* has made Ethel a Grammy-winning composer; and a world premiere recording of *Der Wald* is soon to be released. I previewed sections of this book at a festival dedicated entirely to Doreen for her centenary, nearly everything Rebecca composed has now been recorded, and Rebecca Miller is preparing a recording of Dorothy's orchestral music.

Yet I can't help but feel some trepidation. Because it seems that even when women composers experience a renaissance, it is only too brief and their works soon disappear again for another century or more. As Odaline puts it, interest flares up for as long as women are 'creating headlines', and then dies down again. And when Rebecca Miller has conducted music by women, she's found that 'in general people do still critique music by women composers more harshly'.

It shows in the statistics. Classical music today has a gender problem. Only 8.2 per cent of orchestral concerts worldwide feature works by women. A meagre 1.8 per cent of music played by top US orchestras is written by women. And it's not just composers who are sidelined. American orchestras today are made up on average of only 37 per cent women, and fewer than 10 per cent of these orchestras have been conducted by a woman.

Sometimes the language used to describe music by women is *still*, frankly, breathtaking – all too uncomfortably reminiscent of the kind of press that Ethel faced in the nineteenth century. Clara Schumann's music is, according to one journalist, 'embarrassingly banal' and Fanny Mendelssohn's 'bloody awful'. Both, apparently, were only famous because they 'traded on their surnames' (ignoring the fact that Clara was a celebrated pianist long before she married). Perhaps we could dismiss this as an isolated case, but if we turn to another author in another paper, we find Louise Farrenc introduced with the disclaimer that her music needs no 'special pleading'. And so it continues. No wonder we still hear so few works by women.

If the women of *Quartet* are to stay in our concert halls, rather than briefly reappearing in a passing phase, we need to secure everything that denied them longevity in the first place – publications, performances, recordings, histories. Speaking passionately about guaranteeing Ethel's place in music's future, Odaline tells me that 'our duty is to make the scores available, letting people know it's there, making the recordings available, making the music available. That's the only way.' And that is, partly, the reason that I wrote this book. I am too used to walking into bookshops and seeing biographies of women writers, women artists – but when I reach the music section I am confronted only by the names of men. And so long as women remain unusual and exceptional, they cannot be the familiar or the favourite.

I love the warhorses of classical music, the Beethovens and Bachs. I do not want their music to disappear. But their pieces cannot mean all things to all people. I also love Florence Price's *Fantasie Nègre No. 3*, for example, but it's only possible for me to know this because of pianist Samantha Ege, who recorded the piece for the first time, having recovered the incomplete score in an archive. All her work is dedicated to researching and performing women composers, and she will soon be playing Doreen's Concerto in Arkansas. Samantha says that she does this work because 'some of us do not always find our artistic voice in the scores that we are given to learn and to listen to as music students. Some of us do not always find our stories reflected in the regularly programmed works of the concert hall. Some of us seek musical sounds that speak to us more personally and directly.' And she finds this direct communication in Doreen's music. She was drawn to the Concerto because it 'seemed to tell so much of my story'.

For me, too, when I hear and play Doreen's music, or tell her story, I feel a powerful sense of belonging. She and I are such different people with different lives and desires and beliefs. And yet there is still something that I recognise in the music written by every woman in *Quartet* – as Samantha puts it, something that makes me feel as if 'the music has been with me my whole life'. I can only hope that this book will have introduced someone, somewhere, to a piece of music that gives them this sensation of kinship and, perhaps, acceptance. And with performers who love this music advocating for it, recording it and sharing it, I am looking to the future with optimism. Maybe, a century after Ethel wrote that women's music was squashed by the 'temptation to pretend that women are non-existent musically', their time has come.

ACKNOWLEDGEMENTS

All books are the work of a multitude, and especially so this one since it was written during a pandemic in the midst of lockdowns. I am indebted to all the individuals and institutions who made this book possible by providing online services, guidance and research assistance that allowed me to write remotely. To mention but a few: Tom Dale and Tigger Burton at the Oxford Music Faculty Library; Thomas Henderson at Durham University Library and Collections; Margaret Jones at the Cambridge University Library; Conor Kerr and Louisa Costelloe at Queen's University Belfast Special Collections; Stacey Krim at the Martha Blakeney Hodges Special Collections and University Archives; Eve Leckey at the Brewster-Peploe Archive; Juli McLoone at the University of Michigan Library; Louise North, Els Boonen and Katie Ankers at the BBC Written Archives Centre; Chamisa Redmond at the Library of Congress; Robert Winckworth at UCL Library Special Collections, and Andrea Tiffany and Jonathan Davies who provided research assistance.

All unpublished material and images appear courtesy of the Elisabeth Lutyens Trust; Ethel Smyth Estate; Edith Somerville Estate; Syndics of Cambridge University Library; Vaughan Williams Charitable Trust; William Alwyn Foundation; the Literary Executors of the Herbert Howells Trust; British Broadcasting Corporation; Mirrorpix; Getty Images; the National Portrait Gallery; British Library Board; Museum of London; Surrey History Centre; The Women's Library at LSE; London News/Mary Evans Picture Library; New York Public Library; Starr Brewster; Andrew Palmer; Merryn and Columb Howell; Jenni Carwithen; Pookie Blezard; and Christopher Johnson. I am grateful to Cambridge University

Library, Queen's University Belfast Special Collections & Archives, the Brewster-Peploe Archive, Martha Blakeney Hodges Special Collections and University Archives, BBC Written Archives Centre, New York Public Library and University of Michigan Library for permitting me to reproduce material from their archives. And my personal thanks must additionally go to Christopher Johnson, Rebecca Clarke's copyright holder; Merryn and Columb Howell at the Dorothy Howell Trust; Andrew Knowles of the William Alwyn Foundation; Doreen's niece, Jenni; and Margaret Jones at Cambridge University Library, for their unfailing personal support for this book, and for the countless hours they have dedicated to helping me work through material, proofread, fact-check and ideas-bounce. The tea and biscuits have also been inordinately welcome. From the bottom of my heart, thank you.

Because I am writing about women who lived so recently, it has been a privilege to speak to many of their friends, family and colleagues, as well as those who never met them but are still connected to their lives in some way. I am extremely grateful to Toby Appel, Mark Chivers, Giles Davies, Dr Sophie Fuller, Daniel Grimwood, Duncan Honeybourne, Michael Jones, Chris Kingham and Alan Rose, Colin Macdonald and David Hickman, Sandy Macfarlane, Odaline de la Martínez, Rebecca Miller, Brian Murphy, Berendina Norton, Andrew Palmer, Jill Teasley, Peter Tootill and John Turner for giving their time and expertise to help with my research.

My colleagues have invariably shaped this book through their years of guidance and support. In particular, my thanks go to Professor Daniel M. Grimley, Professor Jonathan Cross, Professor Douglas Shadle, Hannah Millington, Dr Amy Zigler, Gabriella di Laccio, Dr Flora Willson, Dr Anna Beer, Dr Helen Castor, Dr Nathan Waddell, Professor Natasha Loges, Dr Chris Dromey, Sholto Kynoch, John Andrews, Joshua Ballance and the New London Orchestra, Kristine Pommert, Paul Arnold and Caroline Donne. I must also thank my students, who have kept me questioning and supplied me with biscuits, and those writers whose work has profoundly shaped this book, especially: Marcia Citron, Suzanne G. Cusick, Ellie M. Hisama, bell hooks, Marian Wilson Kimber, Hermione Lee, Susan McClary, Erika Rappaport, Alex Ross, Elizabeth Wood and Mari Yoshihara. In a slightly different vein, thanks are due to many folks on Twitter for being so supportive, generous and a constant beacon in the Twitter gloom (even if we have crossed over to real life), especially @deeplyclassical, @DrDavidVernon, @Adrian_Specs, @francesmlynch, @LucySetonW, @mikeirons12 and @sarahfritzwritr.

Writing this book has been a pleasure and a joy from start to finish, and it wouldn't have been so without my phenomenal agent and editor, John Ash and Ella Griffiths. Thank you both for believing in this book, showing me what it could be, and guiding me from being a person with ideas to a writer. I can't express enough gratitude for your unfailing enthusiasm, patience, encouragement, advice, surprise books and chocs and copious pots of tea. Heartfelt thanks also go to the incredible team at Faber, including Josephine Salverda, Laura Hassan, Lauren Nicoll, Jess Kim, Fiona Smith and my (incredibly patient!) copy-editor Kate Hopkins. Thank you to Sarah Ereira for the index and to Tom Etherington for a cover image that I adore.

Finally, but by no means least, my friends and family have supported this book from the start. My first thanks must go to those who have generously become impromptu readers and research assistants: Anita Sonawane, Ben Knowles, Tom Nash and Dr Pamela Bickley. Numerous friends have lent me their expertise and time, including Dr Bernadette Young, Dr James Donaldson, Mark Scott and Revd Helena Bickley-Percival. Dr Samantha Ege has not only proofread and ideas-bounced, but been an inspiration and a tireless source of support both personally and professionally. Ellie Hoolahan is the Ethel to my Edith. Helena (again) has been my rock and guide. Natasha Robinson and David Jeffrey have been there for me when I needed it most. Others who have variously raged and enthused with me about the weirdest research rabbit holes, past and present, include Alex Kirri, Alex Millington, Alyx Brett, Amber and Andrew Trask, Anna Schmidtmann, Becky, Owen and Tarn Cotton-Barratt, Carson Becke, Cayenna Ponchione-Bailey, Conrad Cotton-Barratt and Stephanie Crampin, David Newman, Eric Laitenberger, Giulia Monducci, James Trickey, Jason Weir, Lora Dimitrova, Leo Mercer, Owen Hubbard, Percy Bickley-Percival, Romy Minko, Sam Bruce, Sebastian Wedler and Simon Brackenborough. My thanks go to my family, who are entirely responsible for my love of music and of writing, and who gave me the confidence to write this in the first place. And lastly, to my wonderful husband, Dr Seb Farquhar, who can somehow muster enthusiasm about my work even under the most trying circumstances. Oh, and Mr Dog. Can't forget Mr Dog.

IMAGE CREDITS

ABBREVIATIONS AND ARCHIVES

ABBREVIATIONS USED

ATWO	*As Time Went On*
CETD	Charles Edward Travel Diary
CJ	Christopher Johnson
DC	Doreen Carwithen
DH	Dorothy Howell
DHT	Dorothy Howell Trust
EMW	Elizabeth Mary Williamson
ENS	Emma 'Nina' Smyth
EP	Emmeline Pankhurst
ES	Ethel Smyth
ESC	Elizabeth Sprague Coolidge
FPE	*Female Pipings in Eden*
H. B.	Henry Bennet Brewster
HMT	Hochschule für Musik und Theater, Leipzig
JB	Julia Brewster
LOC	Library of Congress
MB	Maurice Baring
MBH	Martha Blakeney Hodges Special Collections & University Archives
MEP	Mary Elizabeth Ponsonby
NYPL	New York Public Library
QUB	Special Collections & Archives, Queen's University Belfast
RC	Rebecca Clarke
SFdP	San Francesco di Paola/Brewster-Peploe Archive, Florence
UML	University of Michigan Library
VGW	Violet Gordon Woodhouse
VSW	Vita Sackville-West
VW	Virginia Woolf
WA	William Alwyn
WAA	William Alwyn Archive
WHN	*What Happened Next*

ARCHIVES USED

BBC Written Archives Centre

The Henry W. and Albert A. Berg Collection of English and American Literature, The New York Public Library, Astor, Lenox and Tilden Foundations

Bibliothèque Nationale de France

The Bodleian Library

The British Library

Durham University Library and Collections

Hochschule für Musik und Theater, Leipzig

Library of Congress

Martha Blakeney Hodges Special Collections & University Archives, University Libraries, The University of North Carolina at Greensboro

San Francesco di Paola/Brewster-Peploe Archive, Florence

Special Collections & Archives, Queen's University Belfast

University College London Special Collections

University of Michigan Library

William Alwyn Archive, Cambridge University Library

SELECT BIBLIOGRAPHY

BOOKS AND PERIODICAL ARTICLES

Thomas Beecham, *A Mingled Chime: Leaves from an Autobiography* (London: Hutchinson, 1944)

Thomas Beecham, 'Dame Ethel Smyth (1858–1944)', *Musical Times*, Vol. 99/4 (Jul. 1958)

Amy Helen Bell, *Murder Capital: Suspicious Deaths in London, 1933–53* (Manchester: Manchester University Press, 2015)

Anne Olivier Bell (ed.), *The Diary of Virginia Woolf* (London: Hogarth Press, 1977–1984)

Corinne E. Blackmer and Patricia Juliana Smith (eds), *En Travesti: Women, Gender Subversion, Opera* (New York: Columbia University Press, 1995)

Harry Brewster, *Out of Florence: From the World of San Francesco di Paola* (London: Bloomsbury, 2000)

Harry Brewster, *The Cosmopolites: A Nineteenth-Century Family Drama* (Norwich: Michael Russell Publishing, 1994)

Alden V. Brown, 'The Grail Movement to 1962: Laywomen and a New Christendom', *US Catholic Historian* Vol. 3/3 (1983), pp. 149–66

Susan Budd, *Varieties of Unbelief: Atheists and Agnostics in English Society, 1850–1960* (London: Heinemann Educational Books, 1977)

Julia Katharine Bullard, *The Viola and Piano Music of Rebecca Clarke* (PhD Thesis, University of Georgia, 2000)

Antoinette Burton, *Burdens of History: British Feminists, Indian Women and Imperial Culture, 1865–1915* (Chapel Hill, NC: University of North Carolina Press, 2000)

Vincent James Byrne, *The Life and Works of Dorothy Howell* (MSt Thesis, University of Birmingham, 2015)

Barbara Caine, *English Feminism, 1780–1980* (New York: Oxford University Press, 1997)

Lionel Carley (ed.), *Delius: A Life in Letters* (Cambridge, MA: Harvard University Press, 1983–8)

Doreen Carwithen, *Violet Graham Cole (31.1.1923 – 3.10.2000)* (unpublished manuscript)

Rebecca Clarke, *I Had A Father Too: or, The Mustard Spoon* (unpublished manuscript)

Rebecca Clarke, 'The Woman Composer – Then & Now', 1945 lecture manuscript repr. *Morpheus* (Oxford: Oxford University Press, 2002)

Violet Graham Cole, *Memoirs* (unpublished manuscript)

Louise Collis, *Impetuous Heart: The Story of Ethel Smyth* (London: William Kimber, 1984)

Patrick Cory, 'Obituary: Dorothy Howell 1898–1982', *Royal Academy of Music Magazine* (Spring 1983)

David Cox, *The Henry Wood Proms* (London: BBC, 1980)

Elizabeth Crawford, *The Women's Suffrage Movement: A Reference Guide 1866–1928* (London: Routledge, 1999)

Liane Curtis (ed.), *A Rebecca Clarke Reader* (Bloomington: Indiana University Press, 2004)

Kathleen Dale, 'Ethel Smyth's "Prentice Work"', *Music & Letters* Vol. 30/4 (1949), pp. 329–36

Hadassah F. Davis, *Dreams and their Consequences: A Memoir of the Bentwich Family, 1880–1922* (Providence, RI: Pafnuty Press, 2003)

Jeremy Dibble, *Charles Villiers Stanford: Man and Musician* (New York: Oxford University Press, 2002)

Wheeler W. Dixon (ed.), *Re-Viewing British Cinema, 1900–1992: Essays and Interviews* (Albany: State University of New York Press, 1994)

Jennifer Doctor, *The BBC and Ultra-Modern Music, 1922–1936: Shaping a Nation's Tastes* (Cambridge: Cambridge University Press, 1999)

Jessica Douglas-Home, *Violet: The Life and Loves of Violet Gordon Woodhouse* (London: Harvill Press, 1996)

David Duff, *Victoria Travels: Journeys of Queen Victoria between 1830 and 1899, with Extracts from Her Journal* (London: Muller, 1970)

Christopher E. Ellis, *The Choral Anthems of Alice Mary Smith: Performance Editions of Three Anthems by a Woman Composer in Victorian England* (PhD Thesis, Ball State University, 2014)

Betty Friedan, *The Feminine Mystique* (New York: W. W. Norton & Co., 1963)

J. A. Fuller-Maitland (ed.), *The Grove Dictionary of Music and Musicians* 2nd ed. (London: Macmillan & Co., 1904–10)

Martin Gilbert, *The First World War: A Complete History* (Electronic Edition: RosettaBooks, 2014)

Adrian Gregory, *The Last Great War: British Society and the First World War* (Cambridge: Cambridge University Press, 2008)

Jill Halstead, *Ruth Gipps: Anti-Modernism, Nationalism, and Difference in English Music* (Aldershot: Ashgate, 2006)

Amanda Harris, 'The Smyth–Brewster Correspondence: A Fresh Look at the Hidden Romantic World of Ethel Smyth', *Women and Music: A Journal of*

Gender and Culture Vol. 14 (2010), pp. 72–94

Rev. H. R. Haweis, *Music and Morals* (New York: Harper & Brothers, 1872)

George Henschel, *Musings and Memories of a Musician* (London: Macmillan & Co., 1918)

Margaret R. Higonnet, with Jane Jenson, Sonya Michael and Margaret Collins Weitz (eds), *Behind the Lines: Gender and the Two World Wars* (New Haven and London: Yale University Press, 1987)

Jocelyn Hillgarth and Julian Jeffs (eds), *Maurice Baring: Letters* (Wilby: Michael Russell, 2007)

Joseph Holbrooke, *Contemporary British Composers* (London: Cecil Palmer, 1925)

Meirion Hughes, *The English Musical Renaissance and the Press 1850–1914: Watchmen of Music* (Aldershot: Ashgate, 2002)

Aldous Huxley (ed.), *The Letters of D. H. Lawrence* (London: William Heinemann, 1932)

Christopher St John, *Ethel Smyth: A Biography* (London: Longmans, Green & Co., 1959)

Christopher Johnson, *Rebecca Clarke, Viola-Player and Composer: A Life* (unpublished manuscript, 2020)

Sylvia Kahan, *Music's Modern Muse: A Life of Winnaretta Singer, Princesse de Polignac* (Rochester, NY: University of Rochester Press, 2003)

Elizabeth Kertesz, *Issues in the Critical Reception of Ethel Smyth's Mass and First Four Operas in England and Germany* (PhD Thesis, University of Melbourne, 2001)

Paul Kildea, *Benjamin Britten: A Life in the Twentieth Century* (London: Allen Lane, 2013)

Lisa A. Kozenko, 'Aeolian Hall, 1912–1927: "A Building Without Precedent"', *The Gotham Center for New York City History*, https://www.gothamcenter. org/blog/aeolian-hall-1912-1927-a-building-without-precedent.

William M. Kuhn, *Henry & Mary Ponsonby: Life at the Court of Queen Victoria* (London: Gerald Duckworth & Co., 2002)

Hermione Lee, *Virginia Woolf* (London: Vintage, 1997)

Rachel Lumsden, '"The Music Between Us": Ethel Smyth, Emmeline Pankhurst, and "Possession"', *Feminist Studies*, Vol. 41/2 (2015), pp. 335–70

Ross McKibbin, *Classes and Cultures: England, 1918–1951* (Oxford: Oxford University Press, 1998)

Robert Mackay, 'Leaving out the Black Notes: The BBC and "Enemy Music" in the Second World War', *Media History* Vol. 6/1 (2000), pp. 75–80

Sam Manning, *Cinemas and Cinema-Going in the United Kingdom: Decades of Decline, 1945–65* (London: University of London Press, 2020)

Sharon Marcus, *Between Women: Friendship, Desire, and Marriage in Victorian England* (Princeton, NJ: Princeton University Press, 2007)

Rhiannon Mathias, *Lutyens, Maconchy, Williams and Twentieth-Century British Music: A Blest Trio of Sirens* (Farnham: Ashgate, 2012)

Ian Maxwell, *Ernest John Moeran: His Life and Music* (Woodbridge: Boydell & Brewer, 2021)

Hannah Millington, '"1910": Ethel Smyth's Unsung Suffrage Song', *The Musicology Review* Vol. 10 (2021), pp. 55–76

Donald Mitchell, Philip Reed and Mervyn Cooke (eds), *Letters from a Life: The Selected Letters of Benjamin Britten* Vol. 3 (1946–1951) (London: Faber & Faber, 2004)

Paul Moeyes, *Siegfried Sassoon: Scorched Glory: A Critical Study* (London: Macmillan, 1997)

Sue Morgan and Jacqueline de Vries (eds), *Women, Gender, and Religious Cultures in Britain, 1800–1940* (Abingdon: Routledge, 2010)

Brian Murphy, *A Pure Flame: A Preface to the Life and the Work of William Alwyn* (Rochester, MI: Honors College, Oakland University, 2000)

Francis Neilson, *My Life in Two Worlds* (Appleton, WI: C. C. Nelson Publishing Co., 1952)

Rosa Newmarch, *Tchaikovsky: His Life and Works* (London: Grant Richards, 1900)

Kate Nichols and Sarah Victoria Turner (eds), *After 1851: The Material and Visual Cultures of the Crystal Palace at Sydenham* (Manchester: Manchester University Press, 2017)

Nigel Nicolson (ed.), *The Letters of Virginia Woolf* (London: Hogarth Press, 1975–94)

Andrew Palmer (ed.), *Composing in Words: William Alwyn on His Art* (London: Toccata Press, 2009)

Vivian Perlis, 'The Futurist Music of Leo Ornstein', *Notes* Vol. 31/4 (Jun. 1975), pp. 735–50

Martin Pugh, *Women and the Women's Movement in Britain 1914–1959* (Basingstoke and London: Macmillan, 1992)

June Purvis, *Emmeline Pankhurst: A Biography* (London: Routledge, 2002)

June Rockett, *Held in Trust: Catholic Parishes in England and Wales 1900–1950* (London: St Austin Press, 2001)

Paul Rodmell, *Charles Villiers Stanford* (Aldershot: Ashgate, 2002)

Sarah Rothenberg, '"Thus Far, but No Farther": Fanny Mendelssohn-Hensel's Unfinished Journey', *Musical Quarterly*, Vol. 77/4 (1993), pp. 689–708

Philip Rupprecht, *British Musical Modernism: The Manchester Group and Their Contemporaries* (Cambridge: Cambridge University Press, 2015)

Stanley Sadie (ed.), *New Grove Dictionary of Music and Musicians* (London: Macmillan, 1980)

Dominic Sandbrook, *The Great British Dream Factory: The Strange History of our National Imagination* (London: Penguin, 2016)

J. J. Scarisbrick (ed.), *History of the Diocese of Birmingham, 1850–2000* (Strasbourg: Éditions du Signe, 2008)

Elaine Showalter, *The Female Malady: Women, Madness, and English Culture, 1830–1980* (London: Virago, 1987)

Osbert Sitwell, *Left Hand, Right Hand!* (Boston: Atlantic Monthly Company, 1944)

Ethel Smyth, *A Final Burning of Boats, etc.* (London: Longmans, Green & Co., 1928)

Ethel Smyth, *As Time Went On* (London: Longmans, Green & Co., 1936)

Ethel Smyth, *Beecham and Pharaoh* (London: Chapman & Hall, 1935)

Ethel Smyth, *Female Pipings in Eden* (London: P. Davies, 1933)

Ethel Smyth, *Impressions That Remained* (London: Longmans, Green & Co., 1919)

Ethel Smyth, *Inordinate Affection: A Story for Dog Lovers* (London: Cresset Press, 1936)

Ethel Smyth, *Maurice Baring* (London: William Heinemann, 1938)

Ethel Smyth, *Streaks of Life* (London: Longmans, Green & Co., 1921)

Ethel Smyth, *What Happened Next* (London: Longmans, Green & Co., 1940)

W. B. Stephens (ed.), *A History of the County of Warwick: Volume 7, the City of Birmingham* (London: Archibald Constable, 1964)

Caroline E. M. Stone (ed.), *Another Side of Ethel Smyth: Letters to Her Great-Niece, Elizabeth Mary Williamson* (Edinburgh: Kennedy & Boyd, 2018)

Marie Stopes, *Married Love* (London: A. C. Fifield, 1919)

Jan G. Swynoe, *The Best Years of British Film Music, 1936–1958* (Woodbridge: Boydell Press, 2002)

Jill Teasley, *Chronicle of the Life and Work of Doreen Carwithen* (Dissertation: Lewis & Clark College, Portland, 2000)

R. Larry Todd (ed.), *Mendelssohn and his World* (Princeton, NJ: Princeton University Press, 1991)

Laura Trevelyan, *A Very British Family: The Trevelyans and their World* (London: I. B. Tauris, 2012)

Michael Trott (ed.), *Half-Century: The Elgar Society, 1951–2001* (Rickmansworth: Elgar Editions, 2001)

Martha Vicinus, *Intimate Friends: Women Who Loved Women, 1778–1928* (London and Chicago: University of Chicago Press, 2006)

Benjamin Wolf, 'The SPNM 1943–1975: A Retrospective', *Musical Times* Vol. 154/1925 (2013), pp. 47–66

Elizabeth Wood, 'On Deafness and Musical Creativity: The Case of Ethel Smyth', *Musical Quarterly* Vol. 92/1/2 (2009), pp. 33–69

Elizabeth Wood, 'Performing Rights: A Sonography of Women's Suffrage',
    Musical Quarterly Vol. 79/4 (Winter 1995), pp. 606–43
Henry Wood, *My Life of Music* (London: Victor Gollancz, 1938)
Adrian Wright, *The Innumerable Dance: The Life and Work of William Alwyn*
    (Woodbridge: Boydell Press, 2008)
Amy Zigler, '"What a Splendid Chance Missed!": Dame Ethel Smyth's *Der Wald*
    at the Met', *Opera Journal* Vol. 54/2 (2021), pp. 109–63

NEWSPAPER ARTICLES (BY DATE)

Damian Thompson, 'There's a good reason why there are no great female
    composers', *The Spectator*, 16 Sept. 2015
Caroline Donald, 'Fascinating Rhythms', *Sunday Times*, 13 Sept. 2015
Tom Service, 'Symphony Guide: Louise Farrenc's Third', *Guardian*, 24 Jun. 2014
'Doreen Carwithen', *Independent*, 18 Jan. 2003
Geoffrey Norris, 'Classical CD of the week', *Daily Telegraph*, 31 Jan. 1998
Wilfrid Mellers, 'Masters, originals and also-rans', *Times Literary Supplement*, 1
    Nov. 1996
Simon Heffer, 'Force-10 gale of musical drama', *Daily Telegraph*, 2 Aug. 1994
Desmond Shawe-Taylor, 'Songs of England', *Sunday Times*, 14 Jun. 1981
Barry Millington, 'Songmakers' Almanac', *The Times*, 8 Aug. 1978
'Rewarding Program Assembled by Toby Appel for Viola Recital', *New York
    Times*, 4 Apr. 1977
Michael Kennedy, 'One woman and the English music machine', *Daily Telegraph*,
    24 Jun. 1967
Wendell Margrave, 'Friskin at 75 is Phenomenal', *Evening Star* (Washington,
    DC), 17 Mar. 1961
J. E., 'Women Make Music', *Sunday Times*, 24 Apr. 1960
Donald Mitchell, 'Too Decorous Women Composers', *Daily Telegraph*, 19 Apr. 1960
Martin Cooper, 'Distaff Staves', *Daily Telegraph*, 6 Feb. 1960
'Women Composers of Today', [unknown newspaper and day], 1960
Charles Thomas Osborne, 'Dame Militant', *Times Literary Supplement*,
    6 Mar. 1959
'Centenary Concert', *The Times*, 31 Oct. 1958
Martin Cooper, 'Music's English Genius', *Daily Telegraph*, 27 Aug. 1958
'Two Centenaries that Raise an Old Question', *The Times*, 11 Apr. 1958
Margaret Lane, 'Women on the March', *Daily Telegraph*, 12 Apr. 1957
'Music Chief Leads Big Campaign Against Vice', *People*, 24 Jul. 1955
M. Montagu-Nathan, 'Radio in Retrospect', *Musical Opinion*, Nov. 1953
Ernest Bradbury, 'Mr John Goss', *The Times*, 20 Feb. 1953

'World of Music: Doreen Carwithen's Concerto', *The Stage*, 28 Aug. 1952

J. F. W., 'A Birmingham Composer. Recital by Dorothy Howell', *Birmingham Post*, 10 May 1949

'Summer Schools Notes', *Chautauquan Daily* Vol. 71/8, 8 Jul. 1947

Ralph Hill, 'A New Woman Composer', *Daily Mail*, 3 Mar. 1947

'Mrs Friskin Gave Delightful Talk on Composers at DAR', *Chautauquan Daily* Vol. 70/30, 3 Aug. 1946

'Celebrated Pianist Is New Head of Piano Department', *Chautauquan Daily*, Vol. 69/10, 12 Jul. 1945

'Ethel Smyth. To Fight or to Work?', *The Times*, 9 Jun. 1944

Compton Mackenzie, 'Editorial: Ethel Smyth', *Gramophone*, Jun. 1944

Edith Somerville, 'Obituary. Dame Ethel Smyth', *The Times*, 31 May 1944

'Obituary. Dame Ethel Smyth', *The Times*, 10 May 1944

'Greatest Woman Composer Dead', *Evening Telegraph*, 9 May 1944

Alfred Frankenstein, 'Argentina's Composers Make Debut', *San Francisco Chronicle*, 7 Aug. 1942

'Professor guilty – but insane', *Evening Standard*, 10 Feb. 1941

'Concert and Opera. Bombing of the Queen's Hall in London – Musical Activity Goes On', *New York Times*, 1 Jun. 1941

'Refugees' £1 for Philharmonic', *Daily Telegraph*, 21 May 1941

F. B., 'Queen's Hall Audiences', *Daily Telegraph*, 17 Aug. 1940

'Promenade Concerts', *The Times*, 12 Aug. 1940

'Music and the Arts', *The Times*, 17 Jun. 1940

'Mr. & Mrs. F. Clarke's Golden Wedding', *Bucks Herald*, 28 May 1937

L. R. B., 'Bristol Musical Club. A Trio by Rebecca Clarke', *Western Daily Press*, 28 May 1936

William McNaught, *Evening News*, 5 Feb. 1935

L. R. B., 'Bristol Musical Club', *Western Daily Press*, 28 Sept. 1933

'Sweet Songs', *The Era*, 17 Jun. 1931

'Classified Advertising', *Daily Telegraph*, 2 May 1931

'Notes and News', *Woman's Leader and the Common Cause*, 13 Mar. 1931

'Dame Ethel Smyth and Brewster's "Prison"', *Truth*, 4 Mar. 1931

'Unveiling Ceremony', *Woman's Leader and the Common Cause*, 14 Mar. 1930

'Police Band Plays Suffragettes' War March', *Daily Mail*, 7 Mar. 1930

'The Whiteleaf High School', *Bucks Herald*, 4 Jan. 1929

'Viola recital at Ealing Green', *Acton Gazette*, 16 Nov. 1928

E. K., 'London Concerts. New Work by Miss Dorothy Howell', *Daily Telegraph*, 8 Oct. 1928

E. G. P., 'The Last "Prom"', *Daily Herald*, 8 Oct. 1928

'Three Choirs Festival', *Gloucester Citizen*, 8 Sept. 1928

'New Experiments in Music', *The Times*, 5 Jul. 1927

R. C., 'Dame Ethel Smyth', *Daily Mail*, 29 Aug. 1927

'Bournemouth Music Festival', *The Times*, 23 Apr. 1927

H. A. S., 'New Quartet. Organisation of Great Promise', *Westminster Gazette*,
    5 Feb. 1927

'BBC Chamber Concert', *The Times*, 16 Jun. 1926

'Chenil Chamber Concerts', *Daily Telegraph*, 16 Jun. 1926

Douglas Marcel Booth-Frazier, 'Correspondence: Stourbridge and Music',
    County Express, 26 Dec. 1925

'Songs by John Goss', *West Sussex Gazette*, 29 Oct. 1925

'A Woman Composer', *Western Mail*, 24 Oct. 1925

'Wireless Music', *Daily Mail*, 24 Oct. 1925

R. C., 'Entente Cordiale', *Daily Mail*, 23 Jul. 1925

'Royal College of Music', *The Times*, 23 Jul. 1925

'An English Mass', *Daily Telegraph*, 9 Feb. 1924

'Dame Ethel Smyth's Mass', *The Times*, 8 Feb. 1924

'Music 30 Years Neglected. Dame Ethel Smyth's Mass in D', *Daily Mail*,
    8 Feb. 1924

Adrian Boult, 'An English "Mass" Waiting Recognition', *Daily Telegraph*,
    26 Jan. 1924

Richard Aldrich, 'New Music Heard as Festival Ends', *New York Times*,
    30 Sept. 1923

A. K., 'Brilliant Girl Composer: Five Recalls for Miss Dorothy Howell', *Daily
    News*, 24 Aug. 1923

'Dorothy Howell: Woman Composer at the "Proms"', *Yorkshire Post*, 20 Aug. 1923

'Fête Galante', *The Times*, 5 Jun. 1923

'West Lindsey Musical Festival', *Lincolnshire Echo*, 28 Apr. 1923

W. H. Haddon Squire, 'Rebecca Clarke Sees Rhythm as Next Field of
    Development', *Christian Science Monitor*, 9 Dec. 1922

M. M. S., 'Women Composers on London Programs', *Christian Science Monitor*,
    23 Nov. 1922

'A New Trio', *Daily Telegraph*, 6 Nov. 1922

'Pictures of Festival', *Leeds Mercury*, 2 Oct. 1922

'The "Chronicle" Causerie', *Sevenoaks Chronicle and Kentish Advertiser*, 22 Jan. 1922

'The Woes of a British Woman Composer', *Daily Mail*, 10 Jan. 1922

'Woman's Music Scorned', *Daily Mail*, 10 Jan. 1922

'Music of the Week', *Daily Herald*, 22 Oct. 1921

E. E., 'Promenade Concerts: A Willow Pattern Ballet', *Pall Mall Gazette*,
    21 Oct. 1921

Ernest Newman, 'The Week in Music', *Manchester Guardian*, 6 Oct. 1921

'Miss Winifred Christie's Recital', *Daily Telegraph*, 30 May 1921

'Composer's Odd Training', *Belfast Telegraph*, 28 Apr. 1921

'Are Women Necessary to English Music: Dr Ethel Smyth Angry About Orchestra Decision', *Birmingham Daily Gazette*, 22 Nov. 1920

Damaris, 'Talk of the Town', *Pall Mall Gazette*, 8 Nov. 1920

'New Songs and Ballads', *Daily Telegraph*, 19 Jun. 1920

'A Viola Sonata', *Daily Telegraph*, 2 Jun. 1920

Douglas Buchanan, 'How a Woman's Government Would Work', *Daily Mirror*, 13 Feb. 1920

'Miss Clarke Interprets Her Own Compositions', *New York Tribune*, 17 Jan. 1920

'Miss Ethel Smyth's Memoirs', *The Spectator*, 10 Jan. 1920

Feste, 'The Musician's Bookshelf', *Musical Herald*, 1 Dec. 1919

Ernest Newman, 'Dr Ethel Smyth's Autobiography', *Observer*, 23 Nov. 1919

Tobias Matthay, 'Children's Music and the British Composer', *Daily Telegraph*, 8 Nov. 1919

Orlo Williams, 'Miss Ethel Smyth's Memoirs', *Times Literary Supplement*, 23 Oct. 1919

Richard Aldrich, 'Chamber Music Given on Mountain', *New York Times*, 26 Sept. 1919

R. O. M., 'Promenade Concerts', *The Athenaeum*, 19 Sept. 1919

'A Gifted Birmingham Girl', *Birmingham Daily Gazette*, 13 Sept. 1919

'A Girl Musical Genius', *Daily Mirror*, 13 Sept. 1919.

'English Strauss', *Daily Sketch*, 13 Sept. 1919

'New Composer', *Pall Mall Gazette*, 11 Sept. 1919

'Our Girl Composer: Blue Eyes, Bobbed Hair – and Fame: Her First Work at 9', *The Globe*, 11 Sept. 1919

R. C., 'Two New Musicians', *Daily Mail*, 12 Mar. 1919

H. B. Dickin, 'Piano Recitals', *Unknown Paper*, 11 Mar. 1919

'Capacity House Gives Rapturous Aloha to Artists', *Honolulu Advertiser*, 2 Nov. 1918

'Second Recital of Selinsky Quintet Scores New Success; Hall Again Jammed to Doors', *Honolulu Star-Bulletin*, 2 Nov. 1918

'Music Lovers Welcome Famous Musicians', *Honolulu Advertiser*, 20 Oct. 1918

'Selinsky Quintet Opens Honolulu's First Season of Chamber Music in Brilliant Success to Packed House', *Honolulu Star-Bulletin*, 19 Oct. 1918

'Noted Musicians Engaged for the Selinsky Quintet', *Honolulu Star-Bulletin*, 7 Aug. 1918

Colin McAlpin, 'Germany: Her Music', *Musical Times* (Aug. 1916)

'New Yorkers Fleeing City to Escape the Dreaded Infantile Paralysis', *Courier-Journal*, 11 Jul. 1916

Ernest Newman, '"The Spirit of England": Edward Elgar's New Choral Work',
 Musical Times, May 1916

'Philharmonic Conerts', *Liverpool Daily Post*, 23 Mar. 1916

'The Boatswain's Mate: Operatic Joking à la Wagner and Strauss', *The People*,
 30 Jan. 1916

'English Opera', *Sheffield Daily Telegraph*, 29 Jan. 1916

'Lady Composer and Conductor', *Aberdeen Journal*, 29 Jan. 1916

'The Boatswain's mate', *Hull Daily Mail*, 29 Jan. 1916

B. C., 'W. W. Jacobs to Music', *Daily Mail*, 29 Jan. 1916

'The Boatswain's Mate: Dr Ethel Smyth on Her New Opera', *Westminster
 Gazette*, 27 Jan. 1916

Ernest Newman, 'English Music and English Humour', *Birmingham Daily Post*,
 27 Dec. 1915

'New Works at the Promenades', *Truth*, 1 Sept. 1915

'English Music', *The Times*, 19 Jun. 1915

'Hallé Concert', *Daily Citizen*, 26 Feb. 1915

Ernest Newman, 'The War and the Future of Music', *Musical Times*, Sept. 1914

Ethel Smyth, 'Venus, the Bishops, and a Moral', *The Suffragette*, 1 May 1914

'The Musical Works of Dr Ethel Smyth', *Musical Times* Vol. 54/840 (1913)

Ethel Smyth, 'Women Musicians: A New Quality of Sound', *Times of India*
 (reprint of article from *Daily Telegraph*), 23 Dec. 1913

'Women in Orchestras', *The Common Cause*, 24 Oct. 1913

Ethel Smyth, 'First Performance of Arnold Schönberg's "Gurre-Lieder"',
 The Suffragette, 14 Mar. 1913

'Music: Mr Dunhill's Chamber Concert', *The Times*, 3 Mar. 1913

Ethel Smyth, '"The Rose Cavalier": Opera by Richard Strauss', *The Suffragette*,
 21 Feb. 1913

F. V. K., 'Composer and Suffragist', *The Suffragette*, 15 Nov. 1912

'The Birmingham Musical Festival', *Musical Times*, Vol. 53/837 (Nov. 1912)

'Society of Women Musicians', *Musical Times*, Vol. 52/822 (Aug. 1911)

'Some Press Opinions', *Votes for Women*, 7 Apr. 1911

'Miss Smyth's Concert', *Daily Telegraph*, 3 Apr. 1911

'Brilliant At Home at the Little Theatre', *Votes for Women*, 27 Jan. 1911

'Music: Four New Choral Works', *Observer*, 30 Oct. 1910

'London Choral Society', *Daily Telegraph*, 27 Oct. 1910

'Lady Composer's Opera', *Bradford Weekly Telegraph*, 2 Apr. 1909

'The Maud Powell Trio', *Evening Times* (Grand Forks, ND), 29 Jan. 1909

Gertrude Mary Kangley, 'Equal Suffrage for Women', *Seattle Republican*,
 11 Dec. 1908

'A Remarkable Tribute', *Eastern Evening News*, 17 Nov. 1906

'"Der Wald's" Composer', *Colfax Gazette*, 26 Jun. 1903

'Woman in Music: Miss Ethel Smyth Talks about Her Art and Work', *New York Tribune*, 6 Feb. 1903

Common Chord, 'Key-Notes', *The Sketch*, 30 Jul. 1902

'A New English Opera. "Der Wald" at Covent Garden', *The Globe*, 19 Jul. 1902

'New Opera's Great Success', *Pall Mall Gazette*, 19 Jul. 1902

'Miss E. M. Smyth's "Fantasio"', *The Queen*, 9 Jul. 1898

G. B. Shaw, 'Miss Smyth's Decorative Instinct', *World*, 25 Jan. 1893

'Dramatic and Musical Gossip', *Referee*, 22 Jan. 1893

'London Correspondence', *Birmingham Daily Post*, 19 Jan. 1893

'Royal Choral Society', *Standard*, 19 Jan. 1893

'Interview', *Women's Penny Paper*, 24 Dec. 1892

'Mr Manns' Benefit Concert', *The Times*, 28 Apr. 1890

'Music', *Daily News*, 28 Apr. 1890

'Women as Composers', *Musical Times and Singing Class Circular* Vol. 28/528 (1887), pp. 80–2

'The Feminine in Music', *Musical Times and Singing Class Circular*, Vol. 23/476 (1882)

'The Great Handel Festival at the Crystal Palace', *Musical Times and Singing Class Circular*, Vol. 8/173 (1857), pp. 71–4

SELECT DISCOGRAPHY

DOREEN CARWITHEN

James Gilchrist and Nathan Williamson, *One Hundred Years of British Song Vol. 2*
(Somm SOMMCD 0636, 2021)

Daniel Grimwood, *Alwyn and Carwithen: Piano Works* (Edition Peters EPS007,
2019)

Fenella Humphreys and Nathan Williamson, *Violin Sonatas* (Lyrita SRCD359,
2017)

Mark Bebbington, Richard Jenkinson and Innovation Chamber Ensemble,
Concertos for Piano & Strings (Somm SOMM254, 2014)

Sorrel String Quartet, Lydia Mordkovitch and Julian Milford, *Violin Sonata,
String Quartets 1 & 2* (Chandos CHAN 9596, 1998/2013)

Gavin Sutherland and BBC Concert Orchestra, *The Film Music of Doreen
Carwithen* (Vocalion CDLX 7266, 2012)

Howard Shelley, Richard Hickox and London Symphony Orchestra, *Doreen
Carwithen: Piano Concerto, Bishop Rock, ODTAA, Suffolk Suite* (Classics
CHAN 10365X, 2006)

REBECCA CLARKE

Dana Zemtsov and Anna Fedorova, *Silhouettes* (Channel CCS42320, 2020)

Gryphon Trio, *Clarke – Ravel: The End of Flowers* (Analekta AN29520, 2018)

Raphael Wallfisch and John York, *Rebecca Clarke: Music for Cello & Piano* (Lyrita
SRCD354, 2016)

Philip Dukes, Sophia Rahman, Daniel Hope and Robert Plane, *Rebecca Clarke*
(Naxos 8557934, 2007)

Geoffrey Webber and the Choir of Gonville & Caius College, Cambridge,
Rebecca Clarke: The Complete Choral Music (ASV DCA 1136, 2003)

Patricia Wright, Jonathan Rees and Kathron Sturrock, *The Cloths of Heaven:
Songs & Chamber Works by Rebecca Clarke* (Guild GMCD7208, 2000)

Josef Kod'ousek and Květa Novotná, *Benjamin Britten, Rebecca Clarke, Henry
Eccles: Compositions for Viola and Piano* (Supraphon 1111 2694, 1980)

DOROTHY HOWELL

Rumon Gumba and BBC Philharmonic, *British Tone Poems Vol. 2* (Chandos CHAN 10981, 2019)

Duncan Honeybourne, *A Hundred Years of British Piano Miniatures* (Naxos GP789, 2018)

Danny Driver, Rebecca Miller and BBC Scottish Symphony Orchestra, *The Romantic Piano Concerto 70: Beach, Chaminade & Howell* (Hyperion CDA68130, 2017)

Lorraine McAslan and Sophia Rahman, *Dorothy Howell: Chamber Music* (Dutton CDLX7144, 2005)

ETHEL SMYTH

Douglas Bostock and Südwestdeutsches Kammerorchester Pforzheim, *British Music for Strings Vol. 3* (CPO 5554572, 2021)

Mannheim String Quartet, *Smyth: String Quartet and String Quintet* (CPO 9993522, 2021)

James Blachly, Sarah Brailey, Dashon Burton and Experiential Orchestra and Chorus, *The Prison* (Chandos CHSA5279, 2020)

Odaline de la Martínez, Lucy Stevens, Elizabeth Marcus and Berkeley Ensemble, *Dame Ethel Smyth: Songs and Ballads* (Somm SOMMCD0611, 2020)

Maier Quartet, *Rendezvous: Leipzig* (dB Productions DBCD197, 2020)

Lionel Handy and Jennifer Hughes, *British Cello Works* (Lyrita SRCD383, 2019)

Odaline de la Martínez and Lontano Ensemble, *Fête Galante* (Retrospect Opera RO007, 2019)

Sakari Oramo and BBC Symphony Orchestra and Chorus, *Dame Ethel Smyth: Mass in D and Overture to 'The Wreckers'* (Chandos CHSA5240, 2019)

Tasmin Little and John Lenehan, *Tasmin Little Plays Clara Schumann, Dame Ethel Smyth & Amy Beach* (Chandos CHAN 20030, 2019)

Odaline de la Martínez and Lontano Ensemble, *The Boatswain's Mate* (Retrospect Opera RO001, 2018)

Odaline de la Martínez, Huddersfield Choral Society and BBC Philharmonic Orchestra, *The Wreckers* (Retrospect Opera RO004, 2018)

Smyth: Chamber Music & Songs Vols. 1–4 (Troubadisc TRO-CD 01403, 10405 and 01417, 2012)

Liana Serbescu, *Ethel Smyth: Complete Piano Works* (CPO 9993272, 2000)

Odaline de la Martínez, Sophie Langdon, Richard Watkins and BBC Philharmonic, *Smyth: Serenade in D & Concerto for Violin, Horn and Orchestra* (Chandos CHAN 9449, 1996)

EXPLORE OTHER COMPOSERS IN *QUARTET*

Sir John Barbirolli, *Elgar: Orchestral Works* (Warner Classics 9029643842, 2022)

Trio Chausson, *Fanny & Felix Mendelssohn* (Mirare MIR594, 2022)

Peter Cigleris, Gareth Hulse, Duncan Honeybourne and Tippett Quartet, *Dedication: Ruth Gipps* (Somm SOMMCD 0641, 2021)

Peter Cigleris, Deian Rowlands, Ben Palmer and BBC National Orchestra of Wales, *Rediscovered* (Signum SIGCD656, 2021)

Vladimir Jurowski, Sarah Connolly, Robert Dean Smith and Berlin Radio Symphony Orchestra, *Mahler: Das Lied von der Erde* (Pentatone PTC5186760, 2020)

Isata Kanneh-Mason, *Romance: The Piano Music of Clara Schumann* (Decca 4850020, 2019)

Samantha Ward, Murray McLachlan, Charles Peebles and Royal Liverpool Philharmonic Orchestra, *Dora Bright & Ruth Gipps: Piano Concertos* (Somm SOMM 0273, 2019)

Rumon Gamba and BBC National Orchestra of Wales, *Ruth Gipps: Symphonies Nos. 2 and 4, Song for Orchestra and Knight in Armour* (Chandos CHAN 20078, 2018)

Trio Karénine, *Fauré, Ravel & Tailleferre* (Mirare MIR376, 2018)

Elena Sartori, Allabastrina and La Pifarescha, *Francesca Caccini: La liberazione di Ruggiero dall'isola di Alcina* (Glossa GCD 923902, 2017)

Tippett Quartet, *Alwyn: String Quartets Nos 10–13* (Somm SOMM 0165, 2017)

Seiji Ozawa and Staatskapelle Dresden, *Richard Strauss: Salome* (Philips 4321532, 1994/2015)

Myra Hess, *The Art of Myra Hess* (Heritage HTGCD260, 2013)

Richard Hickox and City of London Sinfonia, *Grace Williams: The Dancers* (Chandos CHAN 9617, 2013)

Robert King, The King's Consort and Choir of The King's Consort, *I Was Glad: Sacred Music by Stanford & Parry* (Vivat VIVAT 101, 2013)

Khatia Buniatishvili, Paavo Järvi and Orchestre de Paris, *Khatia Buniatishvili plays Chopin* (Sony 88691971292, 2012)

Harriet Cohen, *Harriet Cohen: Complete Solo Studio Recordings* (APR APR7304, 2012)

Quatuor Danel, Francette Bartholomée and Daniel Blumenthal, *Debussy: Quatuor, Trio, Danses* (Fuga Libera FUG595, 2012)

Roderick Williams and Iain Burnside, *The English Song Series Vol. 22: Benjamin Britten* (Naxos 8572600, 2012)

Yuja Wang, Claudio Abbado and Mahler Chamber Orchestra, *Yuja Wang Plays Rachmaninov* (DG 4779308, 2011)

Janine Jansen, Daniel Harding and Mahler Chamber Orchestra, *Tchaikovsky: Violin Concerto* (Decca 4780651, 2008)

Vaughan Williams: The Lark Ascending (Decca CFMFW43, 2008)

Goldner String Quartet and Piers Lane, *Bloch: Piano Quintets* (Hyperion CDA67638, 2007)

Herbert von Karajan and Berliner Philharmoniker, *Stravinsky: The Rite of Spring* (1964–5/2007)

The Summerhayes Piano Trio, *English Romantic Trios* (Meridian 5015959447825, 2007)

Vernon Handley, Barry Wordsworth, Manoug Parikian, London Symphony Orchestra and London Philharmonic Orchestra, *Elizabeth Maconchy: Selected Works* (Lyrita SRCD288, 2007)

James Weeks, Exaudi and Endymion, *Elisabeth Lutyens: Chamber & Choral Works* (NMC NMCD124, 2006)

Angela Malsbury, Howard Shelley and London Mozart Players, *Alice Mary Smith Symphonies and Andante for Clarinet and Orchestra* (Chandos CHAN 10283, 2005)

Janice Watson, Catherine Wyn-Rogers, Toby Spence, Neal Davies and Steuart Bedford, *The English Song Series Vol. 8: Liza Lehmann* (Naxos 8557118, 2004)

Jacqueline du Pré and Daniel Barenboim, *Brahms, Chopin & Franck Cello Sonatas* (Warner 5862332, 2004)

Pierre Boulez and Berlin Philharmonic, *Ravel: Daphnis et Chloé and La Valse* (DG E4470572, 1995)

Ralph Kirshbaum, *Bach: Cello Suites* (Erato 5616092, 1994)

NOTES

I have used Christian names for the four main composers in *Quartet*, and for their close friends, as this is how they would have referred to one another. For less intimate acquaintances, I have used surnames.

For all correspondence and diary entries I have retained original spelling and punctuation, however idiosyncratic.

PRELUDE

2 *enormous eagerness [. . .] positively glitter*: VW Diary, 23 Oct. 1930. Anne Olivier Bell (ed.), *The Diary of Virginia Woolf* Vol. 3 1925–1930 (London: The Hogarth Press, 1980), p. 325.

2 *indomitable & persistent*: VW Diary, 25 Aug. 1930. Ibid., p. 313.

2 *the greatest woman*: 'Police Band Plays Suffragettes' War March', *Daily Mail*, 7 Mar. 1930.

3 *the most objectionable*: Elizabeth Crawford, *The Women's Suffrage Movement: A Reference Guide 1866–1928* (London: Routledge, 1999), p. 641.

3 *Ethel used to*: VW to Quentin Bell, 3 Dec. 1933. Nigel Nicolson (ed.), *The Sickle Side of The Moon. The Letters of Virginia Woolf Vol. 5: 1932–1935* (London: The Hogarth Press, 1979), p. 256.

3 *let women*: ES to DH, 2 Jan. [1930]. All correspondence and personal material relating to DH held at DHT.

4 *all have*: 'Women as Composers', *Musical Times and Singing Class Circular*, Vol. 28/528 (1 Feb. 1887), pp. 80–2, p. 81.

4 *to blazes*: Martin Cooper, 'Distaff Staves', *Daily Telegraph*, 6 Feb. 1960.

9 *the faults*: Ethel Smyth, *Impressions That Remained* Vol. 2 (London: Longmans, Green & Co., 1919), p. 239.

10 *the first woman*: VW to ES, 24 Dec. 1940. Nigel Nicolson (ed.), *Leave the Letters Till We're Dead: The Letters of Virginia Woolf* Vol. 6 1936–1941 (London: The Hogarth Press, 1994), p. 453.

11 *if the world*: ES, *Impressions* Vol. 2, pp. 6–7.

13 *If nothing but*: Ethel Smyth, 'Venus, the Bishops, and a Moral', *The Suffragette*, 1 May 1914.

13 *the best civilizing*: Antoinette Burton, *Burdens of History: British Feminists*,

Indian Women and Imperial Culture, 1865–1915 (Chapel Hill, NC: University of North Carolina Press, 2000), p. 11.

13 not just for: Sarah Amos quoted ibid., p. 3.

13 See ES to EP, 18 Dec. 1913; undated Feb. 1914; 2 Mar. 1914; 3 Apr. 1914. All letters ES to EP at Ethel Mary Smyth Letters, MSS 0119, Martha Blakeney Hodges Special Collections and University Archives, University Libraries, University of North Carolina at Greensboro. See also Ethel Smyth, Beecham and Pharaoh (London: Chapman & Hall, 1935).

18 end of the: DC to WA, Tuesday night, undated. WAA. All correspondence between DC and WA at WAA.

19 my mother: ES quoted Osbert Sitwell, Left Hand, Right Hand! (Boston: Atlantic Monthly Company, 1944), p. 316.

20 I wonder: ES to H. B., 6 Oct. 1892, quoted Ethel Smyth, As Time Went On (London: Longmans, Green & Co., 1936), p. 156.

20 Lesbianism?: VW to ES, 28 Sept. 1930. Nigel Nicolson (ed.), A Reflection of the Other Person: The Letters of Virginia Woolf Vol. 4 1929–1931 (London: Hogarth Press, 1978), p. 159.

20 an analysis of: VW to ES, 24 Dec. 1940. Nigel Nicolson (ed.), Leave the Letters Till We're Dead: The Letters of Virginia Woolf Vol. 6 1936–1941 (London: The Hogarth Press, 1994), p. 453.

20 a sexual: Martha Vicinus, Intimate Friends: Women who Loved Women, 1778–1928 (London and Chicago: University of Chicago Press, 2006), xix. On relationships between Victorian women see also Sharon Marcus, Between Women: Friendship, Desire, and Marriage in Victorian England (Princeton: Princeton University Press, 2007).

21 I very definitely: Ethel Smyth, A Final Burning of Boats, etc. (London: Longmans, Green & Co., 1928), pp. 15–16.

21 temptation to pretend: ibid., p. 38.

ETHEL

23 would have melted [. . .] would have been: Ethel Smyth, Impressions That Remained Vol. 1 (London: Longmans, Green & Co., 1919), p. 48.

24 a tragic figure: ibid., p. 50.

24 large enough: ibid., p. 52.

24 When Ethel: Emma (Nina) gave birth at 5 Lower Seymour Street.

26 decorated in 1861: My thanks to Mark Scott for establishing that John Smyth was awarded a military Order of the Bath.

27 flattered vanity: ES, Impressions Vol. 1, p. 117.

28 to whom: ibid., p. 68.

28 *uncastrated cat*: VW to ES, 14 Aug. 1932. Nicolson, *Letters* Vol. 5, p. 89

28 *being caught by*: VW to Quentin Bell, 14 May 1930. Nicolson, *Letters* Vol. 4, p. 171.

29 *agony of love*: ES, *Impressions* Vol. 1, p. 73.

29 *shallow heart*: poem in British Library Add MS 46861.

29 *a new world*: ES, *Impressions* Vol 1, p. 85.

31 *moral health*: Rev. H. R. Haweis, *Music and Morals* (New York: Harper & Brothers, 1872), p. 47.

32 *1857 rendition*: VW to ES, 14 Aug. 1932. Nicolson, *Letters* Vol. 5, p. 89.

33 *Christabel Pankhurst was*: June Purvis, *Emmeline Pankhurst: A Biography* (London: Routledge, 2002), p. 75.

33 *the mystery*: Pietro Scudo, quoted in 'The Feminine in Music', *Musical Times* Vol. 23/476 (1882), p. 522.

34 *These expeditions*: ES, *Impressions* Vol. 1, p. 112.

35 *exceedingly fair*: 'Interview', *Women's Penny Paper*, 24 Dec. 1892.

35 *under the sod*: ES, *Impressions* Vol. 1, p. 124.

36 *most of*: ibid., p. 51.

36 *the revelation*: ibid., p. 124.

37 *widely considered*: Elaine Showalter, *The Female Malady: Women, Madness, and English Culture, 1830–1980* (Virago: London, 1987), p. 61.

37 *LEIPZIG!!*: ES to ENS, 28 Jul. 1877. All letters ES to ENS at HMT.

39 *so pure*: ES to ENS, 21 Dec. 1877. HMT.

39 *I sometimes*: ES to ENS, 12 Aug. 1877. HMT.

39 *Every day I*: ES to ENS, 19 Aug. 1877. HMT.

40 *sole unmarried*: ES to ENS, 13 Feb. 1887. HMT.

40 *a nun*: ES, *A Final Burning*, p. 27.

41 *always remain*: Abraham Mendelssohn to Fanny Mendelssohn, 16 Jul. 1820, quoted Sarah Rothenberg, '"Thus Far, but No Farther": Fanny Mendelssohn-Hensel's Unfinished Journey', *Musical Quarterly*, Vol. 77/4 (1993), pp. 689–708, p. 689.

41 *disgrace all*: Fanny Mendelssohn to Felix Mendelssohn, Jul. 1846, quoted Nancy B. Reich, 'The Power of Class: Fanny Hensel', in *Mendelssohn and his World* ed. R. Larry Todd (Princeton: Princeton University Press, 1991), pp. 86–99, p. 94.

42 *an exquisite*: ES to EP, 18 Dec. 1913. MBH.

42 *cerebral excitement*: ES to ENS, early Feb. 1878. HMT. My thanks to Dr Bernadette Young for helping me to understand Ethel's illnesses, and the treatments that she received.

43 *deep &*: ES to ENS, 9 Sept. 1877. HMT.

43 *I came*: ES to ENS, c. 26 Oct. 1877. HMT.

43 *commotion*: ES, *Impressions* Vol. 1, p. 177.

44 *if she reflected*: ibid., p. 178.

44 *with a*: Richard Specht, quoted ibid., p. 193.

44 *our little circle*: Sir George Henschel, *Musings and Memories of a Musician* (London: Macmillan & Co., 1918), pp. 175–6.

45 *staring at*: Smyth, *Impressions* Vol. 1, p. 264.

46 *dear face*: ibid., p. 205.

47 *aethereal quality*: ES, *Impressions* Vol. 1, p. 192.

47 *as no one*: ES to VW, 16 Aug. 1930. Berg Coll. MSS Woolf: Smyth, Ethel Mary. 84 ALS. Henry W. and Albert A. Berg Collection of English and American Literature, New York Public Library, Astor, Lenox and Tilden Foundations. All letters ES to VW at NYPL.

47 *the very tenderest*: ibid., p. 204.

47 *I often*: Lisl to ES, 15 Jul. 1878, quoted ES, *Impressions* Vol. 2, p. 19.

SERENADE

49 *contact with*: ES, *Impressions* Vol. 2, p. 53.

49 *Here, Da Vinci*: Harry Brewster, *Out of Florence: From the World of San Francesco di Paola* (London: Bloomsbury, 2000), p. 1.

50 *He asked her*: Harry Brewster, *The Cosmopolites: A Nineteenth-Century Family Drama* (Norwich: Michael Russell Publishing, 1994), pp. 26–7.

50 *what a poor*: Lisl to ES, 14 Aug. 1878, quoted ES, *Impressions* Vol. 2, p. 21.

50 *she flies:* Lisl to ES, 24 Sept. 1879, quoted ibid., p. 25.

50 *extraordinary views on*: ibid., p. 63.

51 *Julia was*: ibid., p. 64.

51 *one must*: ibid., p. 90. Emphasis original.

51 *My God*: ibid., p. 38.

52 *I sometimes*: Lisl to ES, 19 Oct. 1884, quoted ibid., p. 117.

52 *a kind*: Lisl to ES, 11 Jan. 1884, quoted ibid., p. 117.

52 *the gentlest*: ibid., p. 64.

52 *Our roots*: ibid., p. 127.

53 *I will do*: H. B. to JB, Jun. 1884, quoted Amanda Harris, 'The Smyth–Brewster Correspondence: A Fresh Look at the Hidden Romantic World of Ethel Smyth', *Women and Music: A Journal of Gender and Culture* Vol. 14 (2010), pp. 72–94, p. 81.

53 *You know*: JB to ES, Jun. 1884. Unpublished letters between ES, JB and H. B. held at SFdP.

54 *Your strength*: ES to JB, Jun. 1884. SFdP.

54 *The poem would*: H. B. to ES, 19 Jul. 1884. SFdP.

54 *I never*: ES to H. B., 16 Jul. 1884. SFdP.

54 *not even*: ES to H. B., 12 Aug. 1884. SFdP.

55 *three civilizations*: H. B. to ES, 17 Aug. 1884. SFdP.

55 *I mean*: ES to H. B., 6 Aug. 1884. SFdP.

55 *blame neither*: ES, *Impressions* Vol. 2, p. 127.

55 *felt as if*: Lisl to ES, 27 Jan. 1884. Ibid., p. 118.

56 *Every turn*: ibid., 127.

57 *fight for you*: H. B. to ES, 17 Aug. 1884. SFdP.

57 *It is all*: ES to H. B., 1884, quoted in Brewster, *The Cosmopolites*, p. 123.

57 *I do not*: ES to H .B., 12 Aug. 1884. SFdP.

58 *My mistaken reading*: ES, *Impressions* Vol. 2, p. 133.

58 *No – it cannot*: ibid., p. 130.

58 *nothing is more*: Ethel Smyth, *Inordinate Affection: A Story for Dog Lovers* (London: The Cresset Press, 1936), p. 82.

60 *spasm upon spasm*: Ethel Smyth, '"The Rose Cavalier": Opera by Richard Strauss', *The Suffragette*, 21 Feb. 1913.

60 *originalities and*: Pyotr Ilyich Tchaikovsky, quoted Rosa Newmarch, *Tchaikovsky: His Life and Works* (London: Grant Richards, 1900), p. 194.

61 *two straws*: ES, *Impressions* Vol. 2, p. 209. See also Laura Trevelyan, *A Very British Family: The Trevelyans and Their World* (London: I. B. Tauris, 2012).

61 *something in*: ES to Nelly Benson, quoted Louise Collis, *Impetuous Heart: The Story of Ethel Smyth* (London: William Kimber, 1984), p. 47.

61 *By one*: ES, *Impressions* Vol. 2, p. 219.

61 *Now all was*: ibid., p. 225.

62 *burned like a*: ibid., p. 227.

63 *all carnal*: Mary Benson diary, 1 Oct. 1896, quoted Vicinus, p. 95.

63 *outside patient*: ES to Mary Benson, 16 Oct. 1892, quoted ES, *ATWO*, p. 145.

63 *if the men*: ES, *Impressions* Vol. 2, p. 238.

63 *an unquenchable*: Ethel Smyth, *Streaks of Life* (London: Longmans, Green & Co., 1921), p. 31.

63 *the easiest*: ibid., p. 6.

64 *the kindest*: ibid., p. 18.

64 *many a*: Joachim to ES, 22 Mar. 1888, quoted ES, *Impressions* Vol. 2, p. 172.

64 *devoid of*: ibid., p. 162.

64 *deadly dull*: ibid., p. 164.

64 *the tremendous*: Vernon Lee, quoted ES, *ATWO*, p. 295.

65 *an amusing*: ES, quoted Kathleen Dale, 'Ethel Smyth's Prentice Work', *Music & Letters* Vol. 30/4 (1949), pp. 329–36, p. 331.

65 *hard modern*: Henry James, quoted Kate Nichols and Sarah Victoria Turner (eds), *After 1851: The Material and Visual Cultures of the Crystal Palace at*

Sydenham (Manchester: Manchester University Press, 2017), p. 1.

66 *English music*: Joseph Bennett reviewing Parry's Symphony in G, 4 Sept. 1882, quoted Meirion Hughes, *The English Musical Renaissance and the Press 1850–1914: Watchmen of Music* (Aldershot: Ashgate, 2002), p. 41.

66 *great success*: ES, *Impressions* Vol. 2, p. 227.

67 *a vigour*: 'Mr Manns' Benefit Concert', *The Times*, 28 Apr. 1890.

67 *anticipated in*: 'Music', *Daily News*, 28 Apr. 1890.

67 *from the*: 'Music', *Illustrated London News*, 14 Nov. 1863, quoted Christopher E. Ellis, *The Choral Anthems of Alice Mary Smith: Performance Editions of Three Anthems by a Woman Composer in Victorian England* (PhD Thesis, Ball State University, 2014), p. 30.

REBECCA

71 *rivers of*: Rebecca Clarke, *I Had A Father Too: or, The Mustard Spoon* (unpublished manuscript, privately held by Christopher Johnson), p. 19. All material from the memoir quoted courtesy of Christopher Johnson.

71 *truthful, affectionate*: ibid., p. 21.

71 *something eager*: ibid., p. 11.

71 *striking [. . .] features*: ibid., p. 6.

72 *an exhilarating*: ibid., p. 7.

72 *Can it*: ibid., p. 8.

73 *cried with*: ibid., p. 11.

73 *stimulate our*: ibid., 27.

73 *an uneasy*: ibid., p. 17.

73 *by far*: ibid., p. 16.

73 *all warmth*: ibid., p. 16.

74 *pleasant untrained*: ibid., p. 10.

74 *It was not*: ibid., p. 33.

74 *sometimes really painfully*: ibid., p. 23.

74 *the naughtiest*: ibid., p. 26.

74 *despotism*: ibid., p. 28.

74 *appealed to*: ibid., p. 28.

75 *made out of*: ibid., p. 39.

75 *a dark*: ibid., p. 34.

75 *the special*: ibid., p. 33.

76 *I was*: ibid., p. 34.

76 *only a*: ibid., p. 39.

76 *was like*: ibid., p. 48.

77 *we were*: ibid., p. 21. On the prevalence of atheism, see Susan Budd, *Varieties*

of Unbelief: Atheists and Agnostics in English Society, 1850–1960 (London: Heinemann Educational Books, 1977), pp. 5–6.

77 *a bitter*: ES, *Impressions* Vol. 2, pp. 266–7.

78 *leaden reluctance*: Ethel Smyth, *What Happened Next* (London: Longmans, Green & Co., 1940), p. 34.

78 *unearthly [. . .] a visitant*: ES, *Impressions* Vol. 2, p. 216.

79 *the strongest*: ibid., p. 77.

78 *You won't*: Specht, quoted Elizabeth Kertesz, *Issues in the Critical Reception of Ethel Smyth's Mass and First Four Operas in England and Germany* (PhD Thesis, University of Melbourne, 2001), p. 191.

79 *sweetest, most entrancing*: ES, *Streaks of Life*, p. 99.

80 *delighted with this*: ibid., p. 100.

80 *the presence of*: ibid., p. 107.

80 *School was*: RC, *Father*, p. 79. CJ.

80 *Rebecca would*: ibid., p. 47.

80 *came from*: ibid., p. 41.

81 *marble-topped*: ibid., p. 56.

81 *were going up*: ibid., p. 53.

81 *repurposing and*: CJ, private correspondence with the author.

82 *gawky, shy*: RC, *Father*, p. 79. CJ.

82 *of being jolted*: ibid., p. 109.

82 *everything I did*: ibid., p. 111.

82 *an extra skin*: ibid., p. 112.

82 *desperation [. . .] all the*: ibid., p. 111.

83 *ardour*: ibid., p. 68.

83 *would get an*: ibid., p. 104.

83 *was fast becoming*: ibid., p. 105.

83 *strutting around*: ibid., p. 98.

A CHANGING WORLD

85 *I hardly*: 'Interview', *Women's Penny Paper*, 24 Dec. 1892.

85 *incapable of*: Sarah Grand, *The Modern Man and Maid*, quoted in Barbara Caine, *English Feminism, 1780–1980* (New York: Oxford University Press, 1997), p. 135.

86 *seldom perceived*: ES, *WHN*, p. 200.

87 *the Press*: ES, *ATWO*, p. 172.

87 *distinctly original*: 'London Correspondence', *Birmingham Daily Post*, 19 Jan. 1893.

87 *modern and singularly*: 'Royal Choral Society', *Standard*, 19 Jan. 1893.

87 *Why will so*: 'Dramatic and Musical Gossip', *Referee*, 22 Jan. 1893, quoted Kertesz, p. 176.

87 *If you take*: G. B. Shaw, 'Miss Smyth's Decorative Instinct', *World*, 25 Jan. 1893, quoted ibid., p. 174.

88 *evidence of*: ES, *ATWO*, p. 47.

88 *an opera*: ES, *WHN*, p. 76.

89 *fashion my*: ES, *ATWO*, p. 44.

89 *the whole*: ibid., p. 182.

89 *She appeals*: ES to H. B., 1 Feb. 1893. SFdP.

90 *hectoring manner*: MEP to Vernon Lee, 1893, quoted William M. Kuhn, *Henry & Mary Ponsonby: Life at the Court of Queen Victoria* (London: Gerald Duckworth & Co., 2002), p. 231.

90 *inscriptions carved*: ibid., p. 3.

90 *No eye:* Thomas Moore, 'Come o'er the Sea'.

90 *interruptions without*: MEP to Arthur Ponsonby, 12 Aug. 1891, quoted Kuhn, p. 229.

90 *gentle tenderness*: MEP to Vernon Lee, 1893, quoted ibid., p. 231.

90 *wanted [. . .] as much*: ES to Mary Benson, 24 Aug. 1893, quoted ES, *ATWO*, p. 227.

90 *I often*: ibid., p. 222.

90 *my love*: ES to H. B., 1 Apr. 1893, quoted Harris, p. 89.

91 *obscurely grateful*: H. B. to ES, 17 Apr. 1893. Quoted ibid.

91 *in no human*: ES, *ATWO*, p. 90.

91 *at arms length*: ES to MEP, quoted Collis, p. 68.

91 *There is a*: ES to MEP, quoted ES, *WHN*, p. 145.

91 *I love my*: ES to MEP, quoted Collis, p. 72.

91 *matrimonial bickerings*: ES, *WHN*, p. 23.

91 *written with immense*: ES, *ATWO*, p. 213.

91 *Ethel recycled*: See Elizabeth Wood, 'The Lesbian in the Opera: Desire Unmasked in Smyth's *Fantasio* and *Fête Galante*', *En Travesti: Women, Gender Subversion, Opera* ed. Corinne E. Blackmer and Patricia Juliana Smith (New York: Columbia University Press, 1995), pp. 285–305, at pp. 291–3.

92 *first woman to:* VW to ES, 24 Dec. 1940. Nicolson, *Letters* Vol. 6, p. 453.

92 *Darling, I am*: ES to H. B., 7 Dec. 1897, quoted ES, *WHN*, p. 143.

93 *Never in my*: RC, *Father*, p. 96. CJ.

94 *a dazzling experience*: ibid.

95 *our English music*: Douglas Marcel Booth-Frazier, 'Correspondence: Stourbridge and Music', *County Express*, 26 Dec. 1925.

95 *a large patch*: RC, *Father*, p. 97. CJ.

96 *an unknown mystery*: ibid., p. 87.

96 *a momentary shiver*: ibid., p. 142.

96 *devastatingly dull*: ibid., p. 81.

97 *the time*: ibid., p. 114.

97 *full of*: 'Miss E. M. Smyth's "Fantasio"', *The Queen*, 9 Jul. 1898.

97 *one of*: ES, *ATWO*, p. 204.

98 *everlastingness of*: H. B., 'Argument', *Der Wald* (London: Schott & Co., 1902).

98 *a perpetual*: ES, *WHN*, p. 7.

99 *wistful human*: ES, *Inordinate Affection*, p. 27.

99 *dynasty*: ibid.

99 *a weakness*: ES, *WHN*, p. 30.

99 *whether the*: Ethel Smyth, 'Dame Ethel Smyth Talks Politics in 1937', BBC Archives. https://www.bbc.co.uk/sounds/play/p02kygyx.

100 *composing Amazon*: S. K. Kordy. 'London, in der Season', *Neue Zeitschrift für Musik* Vol. 98/39, 17 Sept. 1902. Quoted Kertesz, p. 162.

100 *The work*: D. Warte, 'Erstaufführungen', *Deutsche Bühnen-Genossenschaft*, 18 May 1902. Quoted ibid., p. 140. Kertesz translates 'Das Werk der englischen Komponistin' as 'The work of the [female] English composer'. I have translated it instead as 'The work of the English composeress'.

100 *must fight*: ES to H. B., quoted ES, *WHN*, p. 210.

101 *A couple*: Sullivan's was *Ivanhoe* in 1891, and Stanford had both *Shamus O'Brien* in 1896, which ran for one hundred performances, and *Much Ado about Nothing* in 1901.

101 *one of*: ES, *WHN*, p. 204.

101 *a strange*: Francis Neilson, *My Life in Two Worlds* (Appleton, WI: C. C. Nelson Publishing Co., 1952), p. 208, p. 213.

102 *I can't*: MEP, quoted Collis, p. 82.

102 *a really fine*: 'A New English Opera. "Der Wald" at Covent Garden', *The Globe*, 19 Jul. 1902.

102 *original opera of*: 'New Opera's Great Success', *Pall Mall Gazette*, 19 Jul. 1902.

102 *a distinct and*: ibid.

102 *the most modern*: Common Chord, 'Key-Notes', *The Sketch*, 30 Jul. 1902.

103 *a duty*: 'Woman in Music: Miss Ethel Smyth Talks about her Art and Work', *New York Tribune*, 6 Feb. 1903. For a full discussion of *Wald*'s American reception, see Amy Zigler, '"What a Splendid Chance Missed!": Dame Ethel Smyth's *Der Wald* at the Met', *The Opera Journal* Vol. 54/2 (2021), pp. 109–63.

104 *the young woman*: '"Der Wald's" Composer', *Colfax Gazette*, 26 Jun. 1903.

104 *as out of*: ES, *WHN*, p. 221.

107 *I am certain*: ES to Winnaretta de Polignac, 1904, quoted Sylvia Kahan, *Music's Modern Muse: A Life of Winnaretta Singer, Princesse de Polignac* (Rochester, NY: University of Rochester Press, 2003), p. 134.

107 *in nomine W*: ES to Augustine Bulteau, 16 Oct. [1906 or 1907], quoted ibid., p. 161. As well as meaning 'in the name of', 'in nomine' can also refer to a piece of music where multiple lines cross and intertwine around a single, continuous melody. Possibly Ethel meant to invoke this double meaning.

107 *to be separate*: ES to Augustine Bulteau, 4 Sept. 1908, quoted ibid., p. 155.

107 *in spite of*: ES to Augustine Bulteau, 16 Oct. [1906 or 1907], quoted ibid., p. 161.

108 *I feel*: ES, quoted Collis, p. 86.

108 *Safely delivered*: ES to H. B., 31 May 1904, quoted ES, *WHN*, p. 254.

108 *conquers you*: MB to Vernon Lee, 10 Jan. 1908, quoted Jocelyn Hillgarth and Julian Jeffs (eds), *Maurice Baring: Letters* (Wilby: Michael Russell, 2007), p. 75.

111 *first reaction*: RC, *Father*, p. 117. CJ.

112 *cried my*: ibid., p. 118.

113 *Suddenly a new*: ibid., p. 119.

113 *felt a responsibility*: ibid., p. 120.

113 *the result was*: ibid., p. 121.

114 *Everything connected:* ES to Augustine Bulteau, 16 Oct. [1906 or 1907]. Nouvelles Acquisitions françaises, Bibliothèque Nationale de France, Paris. 15727:71–72.

114 *moment in the*: ES, *WHN*, p. 261.

116 *exceptionally nasty*: Alfred Heuß, 'Zur Opernsaison 1906/1907', *Leipziger Kalender* (1908), quoted Kertesz, p. 155.

117 *a composer of*: Bruno Walter, quoted 'The Musical Works of Dr Ethel Smyth', *Musical Times* Vol. 54/840 (1913).

118 *must love happily*: H. B. to ES, unknown date, quoted Smyth, *WHN*, p. 295.

120 *to hope as*: ibid., 309.

120 *unearthly*: ibid., p. 312.

120 *one of the*: 'A Remarkable Tribute', *Eastern Evening News*, 17 Nov. 1906.

121 *my H. B. Requiem*: ES to EMW, Mar. 1925, Caroline E. M. Stone (ed.), *Another Side of Ethel Smyth: Letters to her Great-Niece, Elizabeth Mary Williamson* (Edinburgh: Kennedy & Boyd, 2018), p. 38.

121 *like a quiet*: ES, *WHN*, p. 320.

123 *Birmingham had a*: Reverend John Sharp, 'II. The Diocese of Birmingham, 1850–2000', *History of the Diocese of Birmingham, 1850–2000*, ed. J. J. Scarisbrick (Strasbourg: Éditions du Signe, 2008), p. 11.

123 *around 400,000*: 'The Growth of the City', in *A History of the County of Warwick: Volume 7, the City of Birmingham*, ed. W. B. Stephens (London: Archibald Constable, 1964), pp. 4–25. *British History Online* http://www.british-history.ac.uk/vch/warks/vol7/pp4-25 [accessed 22 December 2021].

123 *derogatory nicknames*: June Rockett, *Held in Trust: Catholic Parishes in England and Wales 1900–1950* (London: St Austin Press, 2001), p. 12.

124 *where Charles Edward had been baptised*: Incidentally, while J. R. R. Tolkien lived in Edgbaston he worshipped at the church to which Dorothy's first school was attached.

124 *the country continues*: David Duff, *Victoria Travels: Journeys of Queen Victoria between 1830 and 1899, with Extracts from Her Journal* (London: Muller, 1970), p. 26.

126 *as though Winkie*: Charles Edward Travel Diary (CETD). DHT.

126 *wore black*: Merryn Howell, private conversation with the author.

126 *noble mountains*: CETD. DHT.

127 *exactly what I*: CETD. DHT.

129 *the most idiotic*: Thomas Beecham to Frederick Delius, 17 Jun. 1908. Lionel Carley (ed.), *Delius: A Life in Letters* Vol. 1 1862–1908 (Cambridge, MA: Harvard University Press, 1983), pp. 356–7.

129 *the one and*: Beecham to Delius, 29 Mar. 1909. Ibid., p. 20.

129 *one of the*: Thomas Beecham, *A Mingled Chime: Leaves from an Autobiography* (London: Hutchinson, 1944), p. 118.

130 *the midst*: 'Music: Four New Choral Works', *Observer*, 30 Oct. 1910.

130 *almost brutal*: 'London Choral Society', *Daily Telegraph*, 27 Oct. 1910.

131 *Violet from Ethel*: ES to VGW, quoted in Jessica Douglas-Home, *Violet: the Life and Loves of Violet Gordon Woodhouse* (London: Harvill Press, 1996), p. 108.

131 *one of*: 'Lady Composer's Opera', *Bradford Weekly Telegraph*, 2 Apr. 1909.

131 *among the most*: 'Ethel Smyth', *Grove Dictionary of Music and Musicians* Vol. 4 ed. J. A. Fuller-Maitland (London: Macmillan & Co., 1908), 2nd ed., p. 490.

132 *The clergy were*: Carmen M. Mangion, 'Women, religious ministry and female institution-building', Sue Morgan and Jacqueline de Vries (eds), *Women, Gender, and Religious Cultures in Britain, 1800–1940* (Abingdon: Routledge, 2010), pp. 72–93, p. 79.

134 *the greatest*: Ethel Smyth Diary, 14 May 1926. Ethel Smyth Collection, amso02, Diaries 1917–1942, Special Collections, University of Michigan Library. All extracts from ES Diaries at UML, unless otherwise stated.

135 *make some*: RC, *Father*, p. 144. CJ.

135 *a refuge*: ibid.

136 *the temperament*: ibid., p. 152.

136 *a possibility*: Stanford to Joseph Clarke, 1 Jan. 1908. Provided by Christopher Johnson. Rebecca is sometimes identified as the first woman Stanford taught, but both Katharine Ramsay and Marion Scott had previously studied with him, from 1892 to 1895 and 1896 to 1904 respectively. Paul Rodmell, *Charles Villiers Stanford* (London: Ashgate, 2002), p. 351.

136 *a sort*: Sidney Peine Waddington quoted in Jeremy Dibble, *Charles Villiers Stanford: Man and Musician* (New York: Oxford University Press, 2002), p. 135.

137 *always so*: RC, *Father*, p. 171. CJ.

137 *I was*: ibid., p. 159.

138 *everything would*: ibid.

138 *the apple*: ibid., p. 154.

139 *right in the*: ibid., p. 158.

139 *great domed*: ibid., p. 159.

139 *a fish out*: ibid.

139 *inviting Vaughan Williams*: Vaughan Williams gamely agreed to conduct despite, as he put it, knowing very little Palestrina 'or the traditions as to how he should be sung'. Characteristically, he suggested that this would allow them to 'make up a tradition of our own!'. RVW to Beryl Reeves, 12 May 1910. British Library, available digitally at http://vaughanwilliams.uk, VWL364. Reproduced by permission of the Vaughan Williams Charitable Trust.

139 *moody and*: RC, *Father*, p. 156. CJ.

140 *as goodnatured*: ibid., p. 158.

140 *a happy*: ibid., p. 159.

141 *quite an adventure*: ibid., p. 174.

142 *Don't kick*: ibid., p. 176.

FREEDOM

144 *a watershed*: RC, *Father*, p. 181. CJ.

145 *Huxleys, Galsworthys*: Margery Bentwich quoted in Hadassah F. Davis, *Dreams and their Consequences: A Memoir of the Bentwich Family, 1880–1922* (Providence, RI: Pafnuty Press, 2003), p. 35.

145 *greatly impressed*: RC, *Father*, Handwritten additional notes p. 15. CJ.

146 *helping hand*: ibid., handwritten notes p. 11.

146 *meant fame*: ibid.

146 *Don't she*: ibid.

147 *self-possession*: 'The Maud Powell Trio', *The Evening Times* (Grand Forks, ND), 29 Jan. 1909. May's cello was an eighteenth-century instrument built by Domenico Montagnana. It was given to her by a donor, and would have cost the equivalent of millions of pounds to replace.

147 *an enormous rally*: Gertrude Mary Kangley, 'Equal Suffrage for Women', *The Seattle Republican*, 11 Dec. 1908.

148 *a fad*: ES to EP, 15 Sept. 1910. MBH.

148 *indifference tinged*: Ethel Smyth, *Female Pipings in Eden* (London: P. Davies, 1933), p. 191.

149 *be a more*: ES to EP, 15 Sept. 1910. MBH.

149 *to work alongside*: Teresa Billington, quoted Purvis, pp. 67–8.

149 *bright eyes*: ES, *FPE*, p. 191.

149 *like a stringed*: ibid., p. 195.

150 *She was seen*: Purvis, pp. 98–9.

150 *an even more*: ES, *FPE*, p. 188.

152 *all the spirit*: 'Brilliant At Home at the Little Theatre', *Votes for Women*, 27 Jan. 1911.

152 *wonderful*: ES, *FPE*, p. 201.

153 *the second song*: For a detailed analysis of the genesis of '1910', see Hannah Millington, '"1910": Ethel Smyth's Unsung Suffrage Song', *The Musicology Review* 10 (2021), pp. 55–76.

153 *the concert would*: 'Miss Smyth's Concert', *Daily Telegraph*, 3 Apr. 1911.

154 *the product . . . virile*: 'Some Press Opinions', reprint of comment in the *Pall Mall Gazette*, *Votes for Women*, 7 Apr. 1911.

154 *foreheads pressed*: ES, *FPE*, p. 194.

155 *with the nightingales*: Aileen Preston, quoted Purvis, p. 163.

156 *she neither*: Thomas Beecham, 'Dame Ethel Smyth (1858–1944)', *Musical Times*, Vol. 99/4 (Jul. 1958), p. 364.

157 *mentally unstable*: Crawford, p. 641. For more details on Emmeline's arrest, see Purvis, 182.

158 *top music-teaching*: Bantock was Principal of the Birmingham and Midland Institute of Music and Peyton Professor of Music at the University of Birmingham.

158 *obliged to state*: 'The Birmingham Musical Festival', *Musical Times*, Vol. 53/837 (Nov. 1912), p. 724.

160 *centre for the*: 'Society of Women Musicians', *Musical Times*, Vol. 52/822 (Aug. 1911), p. 535.

160 *prejudice against*: Rebecca Clarke, 'The Woman Composer – Then & Now'; 1945 lecture manuscript repr. *Morpheus* (Oxford: Oxford University Press, 2002), p. 15.

160 *has nothing to*: W. H. Haddon Squire, 'Rebecca Clarke Sees Rhythm as Next Field of Development', *Christian Science Monitor*, 9 Dec. 1922.

160 *about as much*: RC, 'The Woman Composer', p. 14.

162 *slunk into*: Rebecca Clarke quoted in 'Musicologist Ellen D. Lerner interviews Rebecca Clarke, 1978 and 1979', *A Rebecca Clarke Reader*, ed. Liane Curtis (Bloomington: Indiana University Press, 2004), p. 214.

163 *blend of*: Ethel Smyth, 'Women Musicians: A New Quality of Sound', *The Times of India*, repr. letter from the *Daily Telegraph*, 23 Dec. 1913.

163 *Sir Henry's*: 'Women in Orchestras', *The Common Cause*, 24 Oct. 1913.

163 *that was considered*: RC quoted in 'Musicologist Ellen D. Lerner', p. 214.

163 *showed remarkable skill*: 'Music: Mr Dunhill's Chamber Concert', *The Times*, 3 Mar. 1913.

165 *heavenly*: DH to parents, 8 Feb. 1914. DHT.

165 *most perfect*: DH to parents, undated letter from Ladies' Room, Royal Academy. DHT.

165 *a marvel*: DH to parents, undated letter Tuesday morning from RAM. DHT.

165 *things are most*: DH to parents, 1 Feb. 1914. DHT.

165 *I can't*: DH to parents, 18 Jan. 1914. DHT.

166 *a sleeky-haired*: DH to parents, undated letter from Ladies' Room, Royal Academy. DHT.

166 *full of promise*: Sadly, this was not to be for the Livens siblings. Both were committed to asylums in the 1930s, as their mother had been before them. They remained in institutional care until their deaths. Duncan Honeybourne, liner notes to *A Hundred Years of British Piano Miniatures* (Naxos GP789, 2018).

166 *immensely*: DH to parents, undated letter Wednesday 1914. DHT.

166 *heavenly*: DH to parents, 8 Feb. 1914. DHT.

167 *I have never*: DH to parents, 30 Mar. 1914. DHT.

167 *rather liked*: Rebecca Clarke Diary, 18 Oct. 1919. Unpublished, held privately by CJ. All extracts from the diary quoted courtesy of Christopher Johnson.

167 *brush up*: Ethel Smyth, 'First Performance of Arnold Schönberg's "Gurre-Lieder"', *The Suffragette*, 14 Mar. 1913.

168 *sufferers of*: *Daily Mail*, 28 Mar. 1914 quoted Vivian Perlis, 'The Futurist Music of Leo Ornstein', *Notes* 31/4 (Jun. 1975), pp. 735–50, p. 739.

168 *a notable tribute*: F.V. K., 'Composer and Suffragist', *The Suffragette*, 15 Nov. 1912.

169 *wrung in a sort*: Smyth, 'First Performance'.

169 *Mountains of male*: ES to EP, 19 Dec. 1913. MBH.

170 *death on the*: Ethel Smyth, 'On the Road', *Three Songs* (Leipzig: Universal Edition, 1913).

170 *Sing thy song*: Ethel Smyth, 'Possession', *Three Songs* (Leipzig: Universal Edition, 1913).

170 *during sleepless nights*: ES, *FPE*, p. 213.

172 *heartrending to*: ibid.

172 *Don't make*: ibid., p. 214.

172 *patience and*: ES to EP, 18 Dec. 1913. MBH.

173 *her blessing*: ES, *FPE*, 216.

173 *obsessed her*: Emmeline Pethick-Lawrence, quoted Purvis, p. 251.

174 *loathsome*: ES to EP, 18 Dec. 1913. MBH.

174 *making the boatswain*: ES to EP, 26 Dec. 1913. Quoted Elizabeth Wood, 'Performing Rights: A Sonography of Women's Suffrage', *Musical Quarterly* Vol. 79/4 (Winter 1995), pp. 606–43, p. 629.

174 *a great lighthouse*: ES to EP, 29 Dec. 1913. MBH.

175 *come to bring*: ES to EP, 9 May 1914. MBH.

175 *I have touched*: ES to EP, 14 Jun. 1914. MBH.

175 *the ghost of*: ES, *FPE*, p. 235.

WAR (1)

178 *Such are the*: *Daily Mail* editorial 12 Aug. 1914, quoted Adrian Gregory, *The Last Great War: British Society and the First World War* (Cambridge: Cambridge University Press, 2008), p. 48.

178 *emotional solidarity*: Ernest Newman, 'The War and the Future of Music', *Musical Times* (Sept. 1914), pp. 571–2, p. 572.

178 *went into a*: Arthur Bliss, letter in *Pall Mall Gazette*, 11 Oct. 1916, quoted Paul Moeyes, *Siegfried Sassoon: Scorched Glory: A Critical Study* (London: Macmillan, 1997), p. 86.

179 *unpleasant heaped-up*: Colin McAlpin, 'Germany: Her Music', *Musical Times* (Aug. 1916), pp. 363–4, p. 363.

179 *our bestial foe*: Ernest Newman, '"The Spirit of England": Edward Elgar's New Choral Work', *Musical Times* (May 1916), pp. 235–9, p. 235.

179 *one of the best*: 'English Music', *The Times*, 19 Jun. 1915.

179 *simple and unpretentious*: 'New Works at the Promenades', *Truth*, 1 Sept. 1915.

179 *English music has*: 'Philharmonic Concerts', *Liverpool Daily Post*, 23 Mar. 1916.

180 *give up labelling*: 'The Boatswain's Mate: Dr Ethel Smyth on her New Opera', *Westminster Gazette*, 27 Jan. 1916.

180 our own *lady*: 'Hallé Concert', *Daily Citizen*, 26 Feb. 1915. Emphasis mine.

180 *a landmark*: 'Lady Composer and Conductor', *Aberdeen Journal*, 29 Jan. 1916. See also 'English Opera', *Sheffield Daily Telegraph*, 29 Jan. 1916.

180 *amuse them*: Ernest Newman, 'English Music and English Humour', *Birmingham Daily Post*, 27 Dec. 1915.

180 *Wagnerian stuffing*: 'The Boatswain's Mate: Operatic Joking à la Wagner and Strauss', *The People*, 30 Jan. 1916.

180 *palms and minarets*: B. C., 'W. W. Jacobs to Music', *Daily Mail*, 29 Jan. 1916.

180 *clever and modern*: 'Lady Composer and Conductor', *Aberdeen Journal*.

180 *intensely human*: 'The Boatswain's Mate', *Hull Daily Mail*, 29 Jan. 1916.

181 *could no more work*: ES to EP, August 1914, quoted Collis, p. 145.

181 *plunge into*: ES, *ATWO*, p. 1.

183 *war in heaven*: D. H. Lawrence to Lady Ottoline Morrell, 9 Sept. 1915, Aldous Huxley (ed.), *The Letters of D. H. Lawrence* (London: William Heinemann, 1932), p. 253.

183 *Pleasant all*: DH to parents, 12 Jun. 1915. DHT.

183 *among the 478,893*: Martin Gilbert, *The First World War: A Complete History* (Electronic Edition: RosettaBooks, 2014), p. 82.

183 *no end of*: DH to parents, 23 Sept. 1914. DHT.

184 *the Hard-to-please*: DH to parents, Jun. 1915. DHT.

184 *patent rag-time*: DH to parents, 16 Jul. 1915. DHT.

184 *ripping, topping*: DH to parents, 7 Oct. 1914. DHT.

186 *simply screamed*: DH to her mother, Wednesday 1916 (undated). DHT.

187 *Jelly was a*: Such was the power of the legends surrounding Jelly that it came as less of a surprise than it perhaps should have done when she claimed that during a séance Robert Schumann's spirit had told her of the existence of his Violin Concerto, a work that was previously thought lost. Many communications with Schumann's ghost later, the score was finally located in the Prussian State Library. Jelly, companion to the devil and the dead, finally gave the Concerto its UK premiere in 1938.

189 *the Dreaded Infantile*: 'New Yorkers Fleeing City to Escape the Dreaded Infantile Paralysis', *Courier-Journal*, 11 Jul. 1916. For more detail on this trip, see Christopher Johnson, *Rebecca Clarke, Viola-Player and Composer: a Life* (unpublished manuscript, 2020), Word files.

190 *Possibly Clarke's soaring*: This interpretation is suggested in Johnson, *Rebecca Clarke*.

192 *She did not*: ES, *FPE*, p. 237.

192 *Life is*: MB to ES 20 Sept. 1916, quoted in Christopher St John, *Ethel Smyth: A Biography* (London: Longmans, Green & Co., 1959), p. 265.

194 *Far from being*: see Martin Pugh, *Women and the Women's Movement in Britain 1914–1959* (Basingstoke and London: Macmillan, 1992); Caine, *English Feminism*; and Margaret R. Higonnet, with Jane Jenson, Sonya Michael and Margaret Collins Weitz (eds), *Behind the Lines: Gender and the Two World Wars* (New Haven and London: Yale University Press, 1987).

195 *the first*: Advertisement for the Aeolian Hall, quoted in Lisa A. Kozenko, 'Aeolian Hall, 1912–1927: "A Building Without Precedent"', *The Gotham Center for New York City History* [Accessed 12 Jan. 2022] https://www.gothamcenter.org/blog/aeolian-hall-1912-1927-a-building-without-precedent.

196 *one of*: 'Noted Musicians Engaged for the Selinsky Quintet', *Honolulu Star-Bulletin*, 7 Aug. 1918.

196 *finest evening*: 'Selinsky Quintet Opens Honolulu's First Season of Chamber Music in Brilliant Success to Packed House', *Honolulu Star-Bulletin*, 19 Oct. 1918.

196 *great, dark*: 'Music Lovers Welcome Famous Musicians', *Honolulu Advertiser*, 20 Oct. 1918.

197 *pioneer*: 'Capacity House Gives Rapturous Aloha to Artists', *Honolulu Advertiser*, 2 Nov. 1918.

197 *sonority with*: 'Second Recital of Selinsky Quintet Scores New Success; Hall Again Jammed to Doors', *Honolulu Star-Bulletin*, 2 Nov. 1918.

198 *glare of*: RC Diary, 23 Mar. 1919. CJ.

198 *beautiful roads*: ibid., 24 Mar. 1919.

198 *perhaps evoking*: Johnson also makes this connection in Johnson, *Rebecca Clarke*.

198 *a great cause*: RC to Elizabeth Sprague Coolidge, 28 Sept. 1918. Elizabeth Sprague Coolidge Foundation Collection, Music Division, Library of Congress.

199 *beginning to get*: RC Diary, 3 Apr. 1919. CJ.

199 *a negligée of*: ibid., 11 Jun. 1919.

200 *hardly believe*: ibid., 11 Jul. 1919.

200 *awful things*: DH to parents, 20 May 1916. DHT.

201 *shrapnel, high explosive*: Carlo Howell War Diary, 26 Aug. 1915. DHT.

201 *simply melted*: DH to parents, [June] 1917. DHT.

204 *You must not run*: Tobias Matthay to DH, 23 Mar. 1919. DHT.

204 *Apart from*: John Blackwood McEwen to Charles Edward, 20 Sept. 1919. DHT.

204 *46 men*: Vincent James Byrne, *The Life and Works of Dorothy Howell* (MSt Thesis, University of Birmingham, 2015), p, 24.

205 *a very encouraging*: R. C., 'Two New Musicians', *Daily Mail*, 12 Mar. 1919.

205 *showed a real*: H. B. Dickin, 'Piano Recitals', *Unknown Paper*, 11 Mar. 1919, DHT.

209 *one of the*: 'Our Girl Composer: Blue Eyes, Bobbed Hair – and Fame: Her First Work at 9', *The Globe*, 11 Sept. 1919.

209 *the very antithesis*: 'English Strauss', *Daily Sketch*, 13 Sept. 1919.

209 *a little facile*: 'New Composer', *Pall Mall Gazette*, 11 Sept. 1919.

209 *shake herself free*: R. O. M., 'Promenade Concerts', *The Athenaeum*, 19 Sept. 1919.

211 *an enthusiastic belief*: 'A Girl Musical Genius', *Daily Mirror*, 13 Sept. 1919.

211 *English Strauss*: 'English Strauss', *Daily Sketch*, 13 Sept. 1919.

211 *exceptional for*: Henry Wood, *My Life of Music* (London: Victor Gollancz, 1938), p. 400.

211 *made such*: Henry Wood to DH, 13 Sept. 1919. DHT.

211 *all musical London*: 'A Gifted Birmingham Girl', *Birmingham Daily Gazette*, 13 Sept. 1919.

212 *well in time*: By comparison, the soprano Aino Ackté had commissioned a piece from Sibelius in 1911 – by 1912 she was still waiting, and by 1913 completely furious. Sibelius wrote her a piece to a different libretto as a gesture of appeasement, but the work she had originally commissioned never materialised. A composer who delivered their works on time was nothing short of gold dust.

212 *as big a*: ES Diary, 17 Jul. 1923. UML.

212 *greatly appreciated*: Raymond Rose to DH, 26 Nov. 1919, quoted Byrne, p. 46.

213 *heavenly*: RC Diary, 19 Aug. 1919. CJ.

213 *A red-letter*: ibid., 24 Aug. 1919.

213 *really is incredible*: ibid., 27 Aug. 1919.

214 *did not play*: ibid., 25 Sept. 1919.

214 *the elfish*: Herbert Peyser, *Musical America*, quoted Julia Katharine Bullard, *The Viola and Piano Music of Rebecca Clarke* (PhD Thesis, University of Georgia, 2000), p. 37.

214 *had unquestionably*: Richard Aldrich, 'Chamber Music Given on Mountain', *New York Times*, 26 Sept. 1919.

216 *splendid notices*: RC Diary, 27 Jan. 1920. CJ.

216 *genius*: 'Miss Clarke Interprets Her own Compositions', *New-York Tribune*, 17 Jan. 1920.

217 *one of the*: Orlo Williams, 'Miss Ethel Smyth's Memoirs', *Times Literary Supplement*, 23 Oct. 1919.

217 *perfect sincerity*: Ernest Newman, 'Dr Ethel Smyth's Autobiography', *Observer*, 23 Nov. 1919.

217 *the psychology*: 'Miss Ethel Smyth's Memoirs', *The Spectator*, 10 Jan. 1920.

217 *Those of us*: Feste, 'The Musician's Bookshelf', *Musical Herald*, 1 Dec. 1919.

217 *organise our*: Douglas Buchanan, 'How a Woman's Government Would Work', *Daily Mirror*, 13 Feb. 1920.

218 *I don't know*: ES to Edith Somerville, 15 Jul. 1918. All correspondence between Ethel and Edith is held at the Special Collection & Archives, Queen's University Belfast, MS17/878.

218 *I have had*: ES diary, 12 Nov. 1919. UML.

219 *That such a*: ES to Edith, 31 Oct. 1919. QUB.

220 *If I thought*: ES to Edith, 11 Jul. 1920. QUB.

220 *so happy*: ES to Edith, 19 Dec. 1919. QUB.

223 *arguing that in*: Tobias Matthay, 'Children's Music and the British Composer', *Daily Telegraph*, 8 Nov. 1919.

224 *If a thing*: ES to DH, 10 Sept. 1921. DHT.

225 *There were a*: The women with songs at the Proms were: Liza Lehmann, Ethel Barns, Teresa del Riego, Molly Carew, Dorothy Forster, Désirée MacEwen, Maude Valerie White, Ethel Angless, Katie Moss, Alma Goetz and Florence Aylward. Radclyffe Hall also wrote the text for another song, 'To-day I heard the cuckoo call', sung on the Last Night. The composer is unknown, but it may have been arranged by Hall's partner Mabel Batten. https://www.bbc.co.uk/events/e3cxn3.

225 *note of originality*: 'Music of the Week', *Daily Herald*, 22 Oct. 1921.

225 *was the most*: Rebecca Clarke to Elizabeth Sprague Coolidge, 1919.

226 *distinctly clever*: 'A Viola Sonata', *Daily Telegraph*, 2 Jun. 1920.

226 *no novel outlook*: E. E., 'Promenade Concerts: A Willow Pattern Ballet', *Pall Mall Gazette*, 21 Oct. 1921.

226 *use and abuse*: 'Miss Winifred Christie's Recital', *Daily Telegraph*, 30 May 1921.

226 *distinguished work*: 'New Songs and Ballads', *Daily Telegraph*, 19 Jun. 1920.

226 *expert refurbishing*: Ernest Newman, 'The Week in Music', *Manchester Guardian*, 6 Oct. 1921.

226 *Couldn't help*: RC Diary, 9 Jul. 1920. CJ.

227 *everybody enthusiastic*: ibid., 30 Jun. 1920.

228 *jolly*: ibid., 26 Apr. 1921.

228 *something almost like*: RC, *Father*, p. 135. CJ.

228 *Dismayed about*: RC Diary, 11 Jun. 1921. CJ.

229 *really quite*: ibid., 2 Oct. 1921.

230 *Thank you*: ES to Edith, 7 Jun. 1920. QUB.

230 *raining blood*: ES to Edith, 3 Jul. 1920. QUB.

231 *when I*: ES to Edith, 1 Jul. 1920. QUB.

231 *music spirit*: ES to Edith, 17 Oct. 1920. QUB.

231 *is the core*: ES to Edith, 5 Jul. 1920. QUB.

232 *to discipline*: 'Composer's Odd Training', *Belfast Telegraph*, 28 Apr. 1921.

232 *huge combs*: Damaris, 'Talk of the Town', *Pall Mall Gazette*, 8 Nov. 1920.

232 *increase the*: Marie Stopes, *Married Love* (London: A. C. Fifield, 1919), xi.

233 *a cruel*: 'Are Women Necessary to English Music: Dr Ethel Smyth Angry about Orchestra Decision', *Birmingham Daily Gazette*, 22 Nov. 1920.

233 *typical Edith*: Edith to ES, 25 Jan. 1921. QUB.

234 *die of boredom*: Edith to ES, 28 Feb. 1921. QUB.

234 *the 'crust'*: Edith to ES, 23 Dec. 1921. QUB.

THE ROARING TWENTIES

235 *Don't bother your:* John Blackwood McEwen to Howell, 30 Aug. 1923. DHT.

235 *to pester*: ES to DH, 8 Nov. 1921. DHT.

235 *Don't think for*: ES to DH, 15 Nov. 1921. DHT.

235 *You must cling*: ES to DH, 15 Nov. 1921. DHT.

236 *talk for most*: 'Dorothy Howell: Woman Composer at the "Proms"', *Yorkshire Post*, 20 Aug. 1923.

237 *Imagination was*: 'West Lindsey Musical Festival', *Lincolnshire Echo*, 28 Apr. 1923.

238 *full of life*: A. K., 'Brilliant Girl Composer: Five Recalls for Miss Dorothy Howell', *Daily News*, 24 Aug. 1923.

238 *without a shred*: ES Diary, 15 Dec. 1921. UML.

238 *all impulse to*: ibid., 2 Jul. 1919.

240 *not only the*: 'The "Chronicle" Causerie', *Sevenoaks Chronicle and Kentish Advertiser*, 22 Jan. 1922. oo *musical prophet without*: 'The Woes of a British Woman Composer', *Daily Mail*, 10 Jan. 1922.

240 *a musical genius*: ES Diary, 14 Jan. 1922. UML.

240 *When the time*: ibid., 23 Apr. 1922. UML.

240 *For 30 years*: 'Woman's Music Scorned', *Daily Mail*, 10 Jan. 1922.

240 *Wearing a dazzling*: 'Pictures of Festival', *Leeds Mercury*, 2 Oct. 1922.

241 *Now it's done*: ES Diary, 15 May 1922. UML.

241 *it is going*: Edith to ES, 17 Apr. 1922. QUB.

241 *frequently on the*: 'Fête Galante', *The Times*, 5 Jun. 1923.

241 *I've written a*: ES Diary, 20 Feb. 1923. UML. Elizabeth Wood presents a detailed analysis showing how themes in *Entente* relate to Smyth's childhood in 'On Deafness and Musical Creativity: The Case of Ethel Smyth', *Musical Quarterly* Vol. 92/1/2 (2009), pp. 33–69.

242 *really brilliant*: M. M. S., 'Women Composers on London Programs', *Christian Science Monitor*, 23 Nov. 1922.

242 *a frank disciple*: 'A New Trio', *Daily Telegraph*, 6 Nov. 1922.

243 *getting quite pleased*: RC Diary, 13 Nov. 1922. CJ.

244 *to cool off*: ibid., 30 Dec. 1922.

244 *danced the New*: ibid., 31 Dec. 1922.

244 *Brilliant green*: ibid., 10 Jan. 1923.

244 *Glorious scenes*: ibid., 4 Mar. 1923.

244 *Most beautiful thing*: ibid., 4 Feb. 1923.

244 *a small but*: ibid., 6 Feb. 1923.

244 *general indifference*: ibid., 21 May 1923.

244 *a splendid success*: Hong Kong. ibid., 17 Apr. 1923.

244 *native instruments*: ibid., 28 Feb. 1923.

245 *I have missed*: ibid., May 1923.

245 *felt as though*: ibid., 19 May 1923.

245 *most enthusiastic*: 16 Jun. 1923.

245 *fine-looking chaps*: ibid., 17 Jul. 1923.

245 *Am so glad*: ibid., 28 Aug. 1923.

245 *some of my*: RC to ESC, 12 Aug. 1923. LOC, Elizabeth Sprague Coolidge Box 33, Folder 12.

247 *inform, educate and entertain*: Broadcasting: Copy of Royal Charter for the continuance of the British Broadcasting Corporation (2016). (http://downloads.bbc.co.uk/bbctrust/assets/files/pdf/about/how_we_ govern/2016/charter.pdf)

247 *It is all*: ES to DH, 28 Jan. 1937. DHT.

248 *when a guide*: Joseph Holbrooke, *Contemporary British Composers* (London: Cecil Palmer, 1925).

248 *three lesser-known*: Some works by Herbert and Woodforde-Finden are (very rarely) performed today, but Clayton's *Summer in the Woods* Overture has never been recorded.

248 *The finest thing*: ES Diary, 30 Jun. 1927. UML.

248 *profound generalizations*: 'Bournemouth Music Festival', *The Times*, 23 Apr. 1927.

249 *new or*: Jennifer Doctor, *The BBC and Ultra-Modern Music, 1922–1936: Shaping a Nation's Tastes* (Cambridge: Cambridge University Press, 1999), p. 92.

250 *colourful and*: 'Chenil Chamber Concerts', *Daily Telegraph*, 16 Jun. 1926.

250 *musicianly and*: 'BBC Chamber Concert', *The Times*, 16 Jun. 1926. Rebecca's *Chinese Puzzle* was also played in the Spring Concert series, but was not broadcast.

251 *power and*: Adrian Boult, 'An English "Mass" Waiting Recognition', *Daily Telegraph*, 26 Jan. 1924.

251 *novelty of*: 'An English Mass', *Daily Telegraph*, 9 Feb. 1924.

251 *extraordinarily beautiful*: 'Dame Ethel Smyth's Mass', *The Times*, 8 Feb. 1924.

251 *British musical leaders*: 'Music 30 Years Neglected. Dame Ethel Smyth's Mass in D', *Daily Mail*, 8 Feb. 1924.

251 *glorious resuscitation*: ES Diary, 29 Mar. 1924. UML.

252 *this death might*: ibid., 8 Jul. 1928.

252 *There never was*: ibid., 5 Aug. 1923.

252 *Often in the*: ibid., 12 Jun. 1925.

252 *Nothing can*: ibid., 3 Jun. 1925.

252 *probably be the*: ibid., 21 Jun. 1925.

252 *When I first*: EMW to ES, 22 Aug. 1928. Stone, p. 78.

254 *capital idea for*: 'Royal College of Music', *The Times*, 23 Jul. 1925.

254 *the homeliest little*: R. C., 'Entente Cordiale', *Daily Mail*, 23 Jul. 1925.

254 *a stream of*: ES Diary, 4 Aug. 1925. UML.

254 *I shall never*: ibid., 22 Dec. 1925.

254 *just to see*: ibid., 31 Dec. 1925.

255 *quips and outbursts*: R. C., 'Dame Ethel Smyth', *Daily Mail*, 29 Aug. 1927.

255 *delighted [. . .] everything comes*: ES Diary, 25 Mar. 1926. UML.

255 *this perpetual*: ibid., 5 Mar. 1928.

255 *their reception was*: 'Three Choirs Festival', *Gloucester Citizen*, 8 Sept. 1928.

256 *Ethel conducted*: In the same concert Ethel's old friend Bruno Walter conducted the Overture from *The Boatswain's Mate*, and the second act of *The Wreckers*.

256 *Some of her*: Richard Aldrich, 'New Music Heard as Festival Ends', *New York Times*, 30 Sept. 1923.

256 *very depressed*: RC Diary, 29 Sept. 1923. CJ.

256 *it is very*: ibid., 30 Sept. 1923.

256 *The chief thing*: RC to ESC, 7 Oct. 1923. LOC, Elizabeth Sprague Coolidge Box 33, Folder 12.

257 *Trying to write*: RC Diary, 23 Nov. 1923. CJ.

257 *reflective of*: 'A Woman Composer', *Western Mail*, 24 Oct. 1925.

257 *bold modern*: 'Wireless Music', *Daily Mail*, 24 Oct. 1925.

258 *Funny, cracked*: RC Diary, 25 Dec. 1925. CJ.

258 *very very gifted*: ES to EMW, 31 Dec. 1925. Stone, p. 53.

258 *a perfect darling*: ibid.

258 *followed up and*: 'Musicologist Ellen D. Lerner', *A Rebecca Clarke Reader*, pp. 207–10.

259 *a new organisation*: H. A. S., 'New Quartet. Organisation of Great Promise', *Westminster Gazette*, 5 Feb. 1927.

262 *a basket*: 'Mr & Mrs F. Clarke's Golden Wedding', *Bucks Herald*, 28 May 1937.

265 *of wireless fame*: 'Viola recital at Ealing Green', *Acton Gazette*, 16 Nov. 1928.

265 *strangely quiet, reserved*: 'Robert Sherman Interviews Rebecca Clarke about Herself', *A Rebecca Clarke Reader*, p. 178. You can hear the broadcast interview online at 'Rebecca Clarke 90th Birthday', NYPR Archive Collections 84556, https://www.wnyc.org/story/rebecca-clarke-90th-birthday.

266 *had to turn*: Clarke Diary, 4 Nov. 1921. CJ.

266 *people to go*: ibid., 14 Jul. 1925.

267 *simply beautifully*: ibid., 31 Dec. 1924.

267 *very jolly*: ibid.

267 *pleasant light*: 'Songs by John Goss', *West Sussex Gazette*, 29 Oct. 1925.

267 *earnestly and*: 'Sweet Songs', *The Era*, 17 Jun. 1931.

268 *laugh at*: ibid.

268 *gentle, modest*: Ernest Bradbury, 'Mr John Goss', *The Times*, 20 Feb. 1953.

268 *This street*: DH, *The Rock*, manuscript score. DHT.

269 *a forceful*: E. G. P., 'The Last "Prom"', *Daily Herald*, 8 Oct. 1928.

269 *an advance*: E. K., 'London Concerts. New Work by Miss Dorothy Howell', *Daily Telegraph*, 8 Oct. 1928.

270 *Mrs Pankhurst was*: ES to DH, 2 Jan. 1930. DHT.

270 *a strange*: 'Unveiling Ceremony', *Woman's Leader and the Common Cause*, 14 Mar. 1930.

271 *spinster*: 'Dorothy Howell', *City of York* Departure Log, 8 Aug. 1932.

271 *counteract in the*: Jacques van Ginneken, 'The Grail as a Young Woman's Movement: Aims, Methods, and Basic Idea' quoted Alden V. Brown, 'The Grail Movement to 1962: Laywomen and a New Christendom', *US Catholic Historian* Vol. 3/3 (1983), pp. 149–66, p. 150.

272 *indispensable but unattributed*: The programme states that 'The music has been written specially for this production, choirs have been trained, artists of every kind have given their services, and all are happy to work with the lovely anonymity that characterises the Grail'. John G. Vance, 'Introduction', *The Hound of Heaven* Programme (1936), xii. Durham University Library and Collections, UC/P39/9.

272 *Oh! don't I*: ES to DH, 28 Jan. 1937. DHT.

273 *if not with*: DH to ES, undated. DHT.

273 *a brisk tramp . . . a bluff*: VW Diary, 21 Feb. 1930. Bell, *Diary* Vol. 3, pp. 290–2.

274 *a general look*: VW to ES, 12 Oct. 1940. Nicolson, *Letters* Vol. 6, p. 439.

274 *has a vein*: VW Diary, 21 Feb. 1930. Bell, *Diary* Vol. 3, p. 291.

274 *If you only*: VW to ES, 30 Jan. 1930. Nicolson, *Letters* Vol. 4, p. 130.

274 *I did love*: ES to VW, 2 May 1930. NYPL.

275 *might concisely*: Vita Sackville-West, 'Ethel Smyth, the Writer', quoted St John, *Ethel Smyth*, p. 246.

276 *a very genuine*: VW Diary, 6 Jul. 1930. Bell, *Diary* Vol. 3, p. 308.

276 *a game old*: VW Diary, 16 Jun. 1930. Ibid., p. 306.

276 *in her spotted*: VW Diary, 2 Feb. 1932. Anne Olivier Bell (ed.), *The Diary of Virginia Woolf* Vol. 4 1931–1935 (London: The Hogarth Press, 1982), p. 69.

276 *it would be*: VW Diary, 20 Aug. 1930. Bell, *Diary* Vol. 3, p. 313.

276 *at once hideous*: VW to Quentin Bell, 14 May 1930. Nicolson, *Letters* Vol. 4, p. 171.

276 *Ethel Smyth is*: VW to Vanessa Bell, 11 Apr. 1930. Ibid., p. 156.

276 *or she'll come*: VW to VSW, 19 Mar. 1932. Nicolson, *Letters* Vol. 5, p. 36.

276 *every instant will*: VW to VSW, 4 Mar. 1930. Nicolson, *Letters* Vol. 4, p. 148.

276 *I think you*: ES to VW, 30 Jul. 1932. NYPL.

277 *my old uncastrated*: VW to ES, 14 Aug. 1932. Nicolson, *Letters* Vol. 5, p. 90.

277 *Tell them*: Ethel Smyth and H. B. Brewster, *The Prison* (London: J. Curwen & Sons, 1930), p. 7.

277 *as a fly*: ES Diary, 11 Aug. 1930. UML.

278 *I have never*: ibid., 11 Aug. 1930.

278 *is as good*: ibid., 22 Aug. 1930.

278 *a swathed satin*: VW Diary, 4 Feb. 1931. Bell, *Diary* Vol. 4, pp. 9–10.

279 *the John affair*: RC Diary, 15 Jul. 1928. CJ.

279 *with instructions*: ibid., 25 Dec. 1928.

281 *fire and devotion*: *Rotterdam Courant* quoted in 'Classified Advertising', *Daily Telegraph*, 2 May 1931.

281 *powerful and pungent*: L. R. B., 'Bristol Musical Club', *Western Daily Press*, 28 Sept. 1933.

282 *a creative talent*: L. R. B., 'Bristol Musical Club. A Trio by Rebecca Clarke', *Western Daily Press*, 28 May 1936.

282 *an emerging modernist*: The three pieces were: Two Motets for Double Chorus, broadcast 15 Mar. 1935; Concerto for Viola and Orchestra, 4 Feb. 1938; String Quartet No. 3, 7 Oct. 1938.

283 *No lipstick, silk*: William McNaught, *Evening News*, 5 Feb. 1935, quoted Rhiannon Mathias, *Lutyens, Maconchy, Williams and Twentieth-Century British Music: A Blest Trio of Sirens* (Farnham: Ashgate, 2012), p. 48.

283 *embossed brass*: Jill Teasley, *Chronicle of the Life and Work of Doreen Carwithen* (Dissertation: Lewis & Clark College, Portland, 2000), p. 5.

284 *slumber song*: 'The Whiteleaf High School', *Bucks Herald*, 4 Jan. 1929.

285 *either excruciatingly hideous*: 'New Experiments in Music', *The Times*, 5 Jul. 1927.

286 *Peers Coetmore*: Ian Maxwell, *Ernest John Moeran: His Life and Music* (Woodbridge: Boydell & Brewer, 2021), p. 235. Peers Coetmore married the composer Ernest John Moeran in 1945.

287 *little evidence*: 'Dame Ethel Smyth and Brewster's "Prison"', *Truth*, 4 Mar. 1931.

287 *Both Ethel Smyth*: Article from the *New Statesman*, quoted Collis, p. 187.

287 *had its composer*: Article from the *New Statesman*, quoted 'Notes and News', *Woman's Leader and the Common Cause*, 13 Mar. 1931.

287 *The story of*: ES Diary, 28 Feb. 1931. UML.

288 *'Serious' classical music*: See Ross McKibbin, *Classes and Cultures: England, 1918–1951* (Oxford: Oxford University Press, 1998), pp. 465–7.

288 *I wonder how*: VW to ES, 9 Jul. [1940]. Nicolson, *Letters* Vol. 6, p. 404.

288 *the BBC agreed*: They did not, however, consent to broadcasting a speech Ethel gave at one of the concerts. In an internal memo marked 'VERY URGENT', engineers were instructed to cut the broadcast before listeners could get 'even [...] the impression that she is about to make a speech'. Internal Memo, 6 Jan. 1934. BBC Written Archives Centre, RCONT1 Dame Ethel Mary Smyth Artist, 910, File 2 1934–1935.

288 *deafening us*: VW to Quentin Bell, 10 Jan. 1934. Nicolson, *Letters* Vol. 5, p. 269.

289 *sordid crumby*: VW Diary, 4 Mar. 1934. Bell, *Diary* Vol. 4, p. 203.

289 *who but Ethel*: VGW, 4 Mar. 1934. Quoted Douglas-Home, p. 240.

289 *It was my*: ES Diary, 9 Dec. 1937.

290 *These spectacular*: ES to EMW, 6 May 1938. Stone, p. 333.

290 *the biggest*: Smyth Diary, 20 Sept. 1938. UML.

291 *so powerless*: ibid., 9 Oct. 1938.

291 *Everything rushed*: ibid., 23 Oct. 1938.

291 *inevitable*: ibid., 26 Aug. 1939.

292 *unproductive mouth*: RC, quoted 'Musicologist Ellen D. Lerner', p. 212.

WAR (II)

295 *While the BBC*: Robert Mackay, 'Leaving out the Black Notes: the BBC and "enemy music" in the Second World War', *Media History* Vol. 6/1 (2000), pp. 75–80.

296 *Thank God*: Henry Wood, quoted David Cox, *The Henry Wood Proms* (London: BBC, 1980), p. 135.

296 *not a little*: F. B., 'Queen's Hall Audiences', *Daily Telegraph*, 17 Aug. 1940.

297 *principalities and*: 'Promenade Concerts', *The Times*, 12 Aug. 1940.

298 *from lovely old*: 'Refugees' £1 for Philharmonic', *Daily Telegraph*, 21 May 1941.

298 *had sheltered*: VW to ES, 11 Sept. 1940. Nicolson, *Letters* Vol. 6, p. 429.

298 *all windows*: VW to ES, 20 Sept. 1940. Ibid., p. 432.

298 *an island sea*: VW to ES, 14 Nov. 1940. Ibid., p. 444.

299 *secretly terrified*: ES, quoted Collis, p. 203.

299 *screaming howling*: VW to Quentin Bell, 12 Dec. 1933. Nicolson, *Letters* Vol. 6, p. 239.

299 *Virginia comes off*: VW to ES, 9 Jul. 1940. Ibid., p. 404.

299 *Why shouldnt you*: VW to ES, 24 Dec. 1940. Ibid., p. 453.

300 *so much of*: VW to ES, 12 Jan. 1941. Ibid., pp. 459–60.

300 *but it darkens*: ES to VW, 2 Mar. 1941, quoted Collis, p. 203.

300 *I do feel*: ES to VW, unknown date, quoted ibid., p. 203.

300 *Leonard showed me*: VW to ES, 12 Oct. 1940. Nicolson *Letters* Vol. 6, p. 439.

300 *convinced we shall*: VW to ES, 12 Oct. 1940. Ibid.

300 *ever so many*: VW to ES, 1 Feb. 1941. Ibid., pp. 465–7.

301 *You have given*: ES to VW, 4 Feb. 1941. Ibid., p. 470.

301 *damnable*: VW to ES, 10 Mar. 1941. Ibid., p. 478.

301 *Later perhaps*: ES to Vanessa Bell, 11 Apr. 1941. Quoted Hermione Lee, *Virginia Woolf* (London: Vintage, 1997), p. 763.

301 *She was*: ES to Henry Wood, 25 Apr. 1941, quoted Collis, p. 204.

301 *very boring*: Doreen Carwithen Diary, 24 Jun. 1940. All DC diaries held at WAA.

302 *practised furiously*: ibid., 15 Jun. 1941.

302 *those few*: ibid., 8 Sept. 1941.

302 *very nice crowd*: ibid.

303 *Thank God*: ibid., 9 Sept. 1941.

303 *rang up*: ibid., 17 Sept. 1941.

304 *Just listen*: Doreen Carwithen, *Violet Graham Cole (31.1.1923 – 3.10.2000)* (unpublished manuscript).

304 *if we ever*: ibid.

304 *we sat together*: ibid.

304 *We discovered*: ibid.

305 *faint-red angry*: Ed Murrow, 'London after Dark', *CBS*, 21 Sept. 1940.

305 *clouds of white*: 'Concert and Opera. Bombing of the Queen's Hall in London – Musical Activity Goes On', *New York Times*, 1 Jun. 1941.

305 *we can project*: Rebecca Clarke, handwritten notes on Officers of the United States Section of the International Society for Contemporary Music to Clarke, undated (August–September 1942). Quoted Johnson, *Rebecca Clarke*.

307 *very unpretentious*: RC to Alfred Frankenstein, 23 Jun. 1942. Quoted ibid.

307 *the most important*: Alfred Frankenstein, 'Argentina's Composers Make Debut', *San Francisco Chronicle*, 7 Aug. 1942.

308 *my mind will*: Rebecca Clarke, handwritten notes on ISCM correspondence. Quoted Johnson, *Rebecca Clarke*.

308 *puckered from*: Rebecca Clarke, 'Wilton', *Observations*, no. 69. Quoted ibid.

309 *rather than ask*: 'Professor guilty – but insane', *Evening Standard*, 10 Feb. 1941. See also Amy Helen Bell, *Murder Capital: Suspicious Deaths in London, 1933–53* (Manchester: Manchester University Press, 2015), p. 68.

310 *splendid*: Elizabeth Poston to Howell, 28 Mar. 1941. DHT.

310 *include your most*: Elizabeth Poston to Howell, 20 Mar. 1941. DHT.

310 *provide opportunities for*: 'Music and the Arts', *The Times*, 17 Jun. 1940.

311 *all they should*: Phyllis Osborne (CEMA) to Howell, 14 Sept. [early 1940s]. DHT.

311 *throw yourself down*: Violet Graham Cole, *Memoirs* (unpublished manuscript).

312 *her heavy shoes*: DC, *Violet*.

312 *He is very*: DC Diary, 10 Oct. 1941. WAA.

312 *a gift for*: ibid., 17 Oct. 1941.

312 *a 'flair'*: ibid., 24 Oct. 1941.

313 *any time*: ibid., 14 Nov. 1941.

313 *very chatty*: ibid., 29 Nov. 1941.

313 *very talkative*: ibid., 6 Jan. 1942.

313 *very merry!*: ibid., 10 Mar. 1942.

314 *Couldn't find*: ibid., 29 Oct. 1942.

314 *Mr Alwyn not*: ibid., 3 Nov. 1942.

314 *his shirt sleeves*: ibid., 23 Jun. 1942.

314 *terribly sweet!*: ibid., 25 Jun. 1942.

315 *Practised in Room*: ibid., 9 Nov. 1942.

315 *beautiful eyes*: Undated Valentine's letter from Philip. WAA. Alternatively, Margaret Jones suggested that 'Philip' might be a pseudonym adopted by William, given his love of nicknames and alter-egos. However, the handwriting is subtly different to William's – perhaps he altered his writing to stay 'in character', but it seems more likely that Doreen had other suitors besides him.

315 *was going to*: DC Diary, 13 Jan. 1944. WAA.

316 *Once we ventured*: Doreen Carwithen Notebooks. All DC Notebooks at WAA.

317 *My heart is*: Winnaretta to ES, December 1940, quoted Collis, p. 87.

317 *any mortal useful*: ES to VW, unknown date, quoted Collis, p. 203.

317 *She was a*: Kathleen Dale, 'A Personal Recollection' in St John, p. 238.

317 *She is a*: ES Diary, 3 Dec. 1940.

318 *I feel very*: ES Diary, 3 Feb. 1942.

318 *good for anything*: ES Diary, 11 Apr. 1942.

318 *expect to find*: ES to Henry Wood, 28 Feb. 1942, quoted Collis, p. 205.

318 *to see what*: ES to Henry Wood, 5 Jun. 1942, quoted ibid., 205.

318 *A standard-bearer*: Edith Somerville, 'Obituary. Dame Ethel Smyth', *The Times*, 31 May 1944.

318 *She was a*: Compton Mackenzie, 'Editorial. Ethel Smyth', *Gramophone*, Jun. 1944.

318 *a brilliantly intelligent*: Edward Sackville-West, 'Ethel Smyth as I Knew Her', St John, p. 252.

AFTERMATH

321 *greatest woman*: 'Greatest Woman Composer Dead', *Evening Telegraph*, 9 May 1944.

321 *It was not*: 'Obituary. Dame Ethel Smyth', *The Times*, 10 May 1944.

321 *a documentary appendix*: 'Ethel Smyth. To Fight or to Work?', *The Times*, 9 Jun. 1944.

321 *chief mistake*: ibid.

321 *heard from my*: Edith Somerville to Phyllis Williamson, 22 May 1944. Stone, 372.

321 *the Golden Boy*: Paul Kildea, *Benjamin Britten: A Life in the Twentieth Century* (London: Allen Lane, 2013), p. 309.

322 *has never had*: ibid., p. 282.

322 *was the last*: Britten, quoted ibid., p. 264.

322 *VE commemorative cups*: See Imperial War Museum EPH 4372, tea cup with propaganda sticker.

323 *truly golden years*: Wendy Toye, quoted 'Complete History', Sadler's Wells website. https://www.sadlerswells.com/about-us/our-story/complete-history [Accessed 13 Dec. 2021].

324 *a large majority*: 'Will the Factory Girls Want to Stay Put or Go Home?', *Mass Observation*, 8 Mar. 1944.

325 *Do you deserve*: *Woman's Own*, 27 Jun. 1947.

325 *to write 'Personal'*: WA to DC, 21 Jul. 1945. WAA.

326 *once again I*: DC to WA, Sunday 11.30 [undated]. WAA.

326 *a real 'love'*: DC to WA, 9 Aug. 1957. WAA.

326 *time to yourself*: WA to DC, 13 Aug. 1957. WAA.

326 *I did ask*: DC to WA, 15 Aug. 1957. WAA.

326 *Felt very dreary*: WA to DC, 31 Jul. 1945. WAA.

326 *self-conscious*: WA to DC, 6 Aug. 1957. WAA.

326 *I think of*: WA to Olive Pull, 3 Jun. 1934. WAA.

326 *I kiss you*: WA to Olive Pull, 10 Jun. 1934. WAA.

326 *the most perfect*: DC Diary, 31 Jul. 1986. WAA.

327 *Polite vicar's*: BBC Music Advisory Panel Report on Franz Holford Piano Sonata in B flat Minor. BBC Written Archives Centre, Music Reports R27/586, 1928–1954, Hol–How.

327 *no appreciable interest*: BBC Music Advisory Panel Report on Dulcie Holland Trio for Piano, Violin and Cello. BBC Written Archives Centre, Music Reports R27/586, 1928–1954, Hol–How.

327 *no reason*: Edmund Rubbra, BBC Music Advisory Panel Report on Doreen Carwithen String Quartet No. 1. BBC Written Archives Centre, Music Reports R27/558, Doreen Carwithen.

327 *as good as*: William Alwyn, BBC Music Advisory Panel Report on Doreen Carwithen String Quartet No. 1. BBC Written Archives Centre, Music Reports R27/558, Doreen Carwithen.

328 *colour, excitement*: Thomas Russell, notes to *ODTAA*, London Philharmonic Orchestra Programme, 2 Mar. 1947.

328 *something terrific*: Teasley, p. 16. Intriguingly, there was a women's literary society at Girton College, Cambridge also named Odtaa. It is unlikely Doreen could have known about this connection, though – unless she had been reading Virginia Woolf's *A Room of One's Own*, part of which came from a talk that Virginia gave to the Odtaa society.

328 *cup of tea*: DC Notebooks. WAA.

328 *genuine melodic invention*: Ralph Hill, 'A New Woman Composer', *Daily Mail*, 3 Mar. 1947.

329 *as many of*: DC Notebooks. WAA.

330 *Olive darning*: ibid.

330 *farouche*: RC, *Father*, p. 154. CJ.

330 *One of the*: ibid., p. 155.

331 *But 'tis*: Thomas Pringle, 'I'll Bid My Heart Be Still'.

331 *Of all*: James Friskin to RC, 5 May 1944. CJ.

332 *it was Kate*: Johnson, *Rebecca Clarke*.

332 *dread of meeting*: Friskin to RC, 30 Jul. 1944. CJ.

332 *I love everything*: RC to Friskin, 31 Jul. 1944. CJ.

333 *many faults*: RC to Friskin, 20 Jul. 1944. CJ.

333 *I should have*: Friskin to RC, 16 Aug. 1944. Quoted Johnson, *Rebecca Clarke*.

333 *I love you*: RC to Friskin, Sunday morning [undated]. CJ.

333 *too much sense*: 'Celebrated Pianist is New Head of Piano Department', *Chautauquan Daily*, Vol. 69/10, 12 Jul. 1945.

334 *Britten, by contrast*: Kildea, p. 293.

335 *a music cabinet*: Dorothy's music cabinet was eventually given as a wedding gift to one of her students.

336 *William, for example*: Benjamin Wolf, 'The SPNM 1943–1975: a Retrospective', *Musical Times* Vol. 154/1925 (2013), pp. 47–66, pp. 48–51.

336 *freshly attractive*: J. F. W., 'A Birmingham Composer. Recital by Dorothy Howell', *Birmingham Post*, 10 May 1949.

336 *charm (a rarity)*: Gordon Jacob, BBC Music Advisory Panel Report on Dorothy Howell *Divertissements*, BBC Written Archives, Music Reports R27/586, 1928–1954, Hol–How.

336 *an Elgar society*: Michael Trott, *Half-Century: The Elgar Society, 1951–2001* (Rickmansworth: Elgar Editions, 2001), pp. 4–5, p. 28.

337 *the doorman, Willie*: CJ, private correspondence with the author.

337 *Do you know*: RC to Friskin, 24 Aug. 1944. CJ.

338 *a wire contraption*: CJ, private correspondence with the author.

338 *start off again*: Friskin to Clarke, 5 May 1944. CJ.

338 *It was a*: Clarke, quoted in 'Robert Sherman', pp. 176–7.

338 *became more*: 'Musicologist Ellen Dr Lerner', p. 211.

338 *never interested*: ibid., p. 212.

339 *extremely delightful*: 'Mrs Friskin Gave Delightful Talk on Composers at DAR', *Chautauquan Daily* Vol. 70/30, 3 Aug. 1946.

340 *'terrified' of chamber*: 'Summer Schools Notes', *Chautauquan Daily* Vol. 71/8, 8 Jul. 1947.

341 *happy with William*: DC Notebooks. WAA.

342 *loner*: William Alwyn, '*Winged Chariot*' in Andrew Palmer (ed.), *Composing in Words: William Alwyn on his Art* (London: Toccata Press, 2009), p. 31.

342 *will be looked*: William Alwyn, quoted Adrian Wright, *The Innumerable Dance: The Life and Work of William Alwyn* (Woodbridge: The Boydell Press, 2008), p. 120.

342 *In 1946*: Elisabeth Lutyens scored the 1946 documentaries *Jungle Mariners* and *The Way from Germany*, and the Rank film *Penny and the Pownall Case* (starring Christopher Lee) in 1948. Grace Williams's 1949 film was *Blue Scar*, which predated Doreen's *Boys in Brown* by only a few months.

344 *far superior to*: Mass Observation 1937 study, quoted Dominic Sandbrook, *The Great British Dream Factory: The Strange History of our National Imagination* (London: Penguin, 2016), p. 22.

344 *entrepreneur J. Arthur*: Sandbrook, p. 30.

344 *prettiest hat*: DC, quoted Wright, p. 109.

345 *Every point is*: DC, Lecture on Film Music for Furzedown College, 1956. WAA. Doreen had previously given a talk about film composition for 'Film Time' on the BBC, broadcast on the Home Service 21 Aug. 1952, in which

she addressed prejudice against women composers. DC, Lecture on Film Music: Insert for 'Film Time', 1952. WAA.

346 *a handsome man*: DC Notebooks. WAA.

346 *Everyone made*: ibid.

346 *not to worry*: DC, quoted Wright, p. 122.

LOVE AND HEARTBREAK

350 *killing*: 'Interview with Doreen Carwithen, 2 July 1997' in Jan G. Swynoe, *The Best Years of British Film Music, 1936–1958* (Woodbridge: Boydell Press, 2002), p. 220.

350 *genuinely musical*: Lennox Berkeley, BBC Music Advisory Panel Report on Doreen Carwithen Piano Concerto. BBC Written Archives Centre, Music Reports R27/558, Doreen Carwithen.

350 *a big tune*: 'World of Music: Doreen Carwithen's Concerto', *The Stage*, 28 Aug. 1952.

350 *There exists*: M. Montagu-Nathan, 'Radio in Retrospect', *Musical Opinion*, Nov. 1953.

351 *an excellent effort*: Benjamin Frankel, BBC Music Advisory Panel Report on Doreen Carwithen String Quartet No. 2. BBC Written Archives Centre, Music Reports R27/558, Doreen Carwithen.

351 *steer a well-defined*: Montagu-Nathan, 'Radio in Retrospect'.

351 *competent, amusing*: Norman Fulton, BBC Music Advisory Panel Report on Doreen Carwithen *Five Diversions for Wind Quintet*. BBC Written Archives Centre, Music Reports R27/558, Doreen Carwithen.

351 *poverty-stricken*: BBC Music Advisory Panel Report on Doreen Carwithen Sonata for Violin and Piano. BBC Written Archives Centre, Music Reports R27/558, Doreen Carwithen.

351 *tawdry affair*: H. Crop-Jackson, BBC Music Advisory Panel Report on Doreen Carwithen 'The Ride-by-Nights'. BBC Written Archives Centre, Music Reports R27/558, Doreen Carwithen.

351 *arid note-spinning*: BBC Music Advisory Panel Report on Doreen Carwithen *Bishop Rock*. BBC Written Archives Centre, Music Reports R27/558, Doreen Carwithen.

352 *The announcement*: Sandbrook, p. 45.

353 *falling from 1.6 billion*: Sam Manning, *Cinemas and Cinema-Going in the United Kingdom: Decades of Decline, 1945–65* (London: University of London Press, 2020), p. 51.

353 *honoured to be*: DC, quoted Wright, p. 110. She was paid £250 for the film.

353 *most successful*: ABC News, Aug. 1953, quoted Manning, p. 57.

354 *WRITE MUSIC*: Herbert Howells to DH, 26 Apr. 1952. DHT. Reproduced by kind permission of the Literary Executors of the Herbert Howells Trust.

355 *overwhelmed with*: Augener to DH, 13 Sept. 1958. See also J. W. Chester to DH, 7 Oct. 1958. DHT.

355 *replaces composition*: William Alwyn, 'The Musical Opinions of Doctor Crotch', in Palmer, p. 250.

356 *New Music Manchester*: The musicians most associated with New Music Manchester were Harrison Birtwistle, Peter Maxwell Davies, Alexander Goehr, John Ogdon and Elgar Howarth. For more information about the group and their 1956 concert, see Philip Rupprecht, *British Musical Modernism: The Manchester Group and their Contemporaries* (Cambridge: Cambridge University Press, 2015).

356 *That's what I*: Harrison Birtwistle, quoted Caroline Donald, 'Fascinating Rhythms', *Sunday Times*, 13 Sept. 2015.

356 *Until 1967*: When the Wolfenden Report, recommending the decriminalisation of homosexual acts, was published in 1957, it was rejected by Parliament.

356 *a campaign against*: Steuart Wilson and Walford Davies, quoted 'Music Chief Leads Big Campaign against Vice', *People*, 24 Jul. 1955. Quoted Donald Mitchell, Philip Reed, Mervyn Cooke (eds), *Letters from a Life: The Selected Letters of Benjamin Britten* Vol. 3 (1946–1951) (London: Faber & Faber, 2004), p. 7.

357 *A woman is*: Francis Martin, 'The Night Mrs Baker Made History', *Everybody's Weekly*, 16 Mar. 1957. Quoted Jill Halstead, *Ruth Gipps: Anti-Modernism, Nationalism, and Difference in English Music* (Aldershot: Ashgate, 2006), p. 41.

357 *weren't up against*: RC, 'The Woman Composer', p. 15.

357 *occasionally supplemented*: Howell Diary, 14 Nov. 1959. DHT.

359 *phenomenal excellence*: Wendell Margrave, 'Friskin at 75 is Phenomenal', *Evening Star* (Washington, DC), 17 Mar. 1961.

359 *about five years behind*: The US carried out its first nuclear test in 1945, Britain in 1952; similarly by 1954, 56 per cent of Americans owned a TV, but it took until 1959 for 58 per cent of Brits to possess one.

359 *We regard ourselves*: Ernest Bevin, quoted Sandbrook, p. 219.

360 *quite a moving*: RC to Friskin, 27 Apr. 1951. Quoted Johnson, *Rebecca Clarke*.

360 *Vaughan Williams has*: Martin Cooper, 'Music's English Genius', *Daily Telegraph*, 27 Aug. 1958.

360 *she was the*: 'Two Centenaries that Raise an Old Question', *The Times*, 11 Apr. 1958.

360 *lived out too*: 'Centenary Concert', *The Times*, 31 Oct. 1958.

361 *Hilda Tablet*: Elisabeth Lutyens was another of the models for Hilda, and

was so unimpressed that she apparently considered legal action against the author, Henry Reed. The broadcasts ran through the 1950s.

361 *the whole of: Emily Butter: An Occasion Recalled*, broadcast 25 Feb. 1958 on the Third Programme. Text was by Henry Reed, music by Donald Swann.

361 *a satirical novel*: The work was E. F. Benson's *Dodo* trilogy. Ethel was widely acknowledged as the model for the composer Edith Staines.

361 *almost an embarrassment*: see for example Margaret Lane, 'Women on the March', *Daily Telegraph*, 12 Apr. 1957.

361 *Shades of Hilda*: BBC Written Archives Centre, R27/1,695/1, Audience Response Report LR/58/731, 9A, 1958. Those who disliked it complained that 'the militant suffragette was too obvious', rendering the opera 'a trivial affair'.

361 *written by*: St John was also a playwright and suffragette, who lived in a *ménage à trois* with the actress Edith Craig (daughter of Ellen Terry) and the artist Clare ('Tony') Atwood.

362 *except her correspondence*: St John, xviii. Ethel gave her H. B. letters to his grandson, and as a consequence of this division, even though St John relied heavily on Ethel's published memoirs, H. B. occupies a relatively insignificant part of her biography.

362 *put her genius*: Charles Thomas Osborne, 'Dame Militant', *Times Literary Supplement*, 6 Mar. 1959.

363 *Don't you think*: DC, quoted Swynoe, p. 228. The Sex Discrimination Act was not passed until 1975.

363 *I was not*: ibid., p. 228.

363 *come up through*: Wendy Toye, quoted Wheeler W. Dixon (ed.) *Re-Viewing British Cinema, 1900–1992: Essays and Interviews* (Albany: State University of New York Press, 1994), p. 127.

363 *a straightforward job*: Article for *The Sound Track*, unknown date [1952?], pp. 351–2. WAA.

364 *simple, too simple*: ibid.

364 *long before shooting*: ibid.

364 *Best Short Fiction Film*: Jean Cocteau was on the judging panel and hailed it as a masterpiece. Dixon, p. 130.

364 *representing the Stranger's*: Article for *The Sound Track*. WAA.

365 *the hardest I*: Swynoe, p. 226.

365 *I have occasionally*: DC, Lecture on *On the Twelfth Day*. WAA.

365 *double life*: WA, quoted Brian Murphy, *A Pure Flame: A Preface to the Life and the Work of William Alwyn* (Rochester, MI: Honors College, Oakland University, 2000), p. 27.

365 *tell the whole*: WA 30 Nov. 1955, 'Ariel to Miranda', in Palmer, p. 131.

365 *We began our*: WA 11 Oct. 1955, ibid., p. 120.

366 *salvation*: WA, quoted Murphy, p. 28.

366 *hands around her*: Barbara Carwithen, quoted Wright, p. 182.

366 *I cannot live*: DC to WA, Saturday 15 Feb. Unknown year. WAA.

366 *At least I*: DC to WA, Friday evening. Unknown date. WAA.

366 *very real physical*: DC to WA, 9 Apr. 1958. WAA.

366 *still wanting me*: DC to WA, Tuesday night, unknown date. WAA.

366 *I drove my*: DC quoted Wright, p. 123.

367 *the reason our*: WA, quoted Murphy, p. 26.

367 *She had her*: WA, quoted Wright, p. 52.

367 *the* dullest *people*: WA, quoted Murphy, p. 30.

DUSK

370 *spiritual sensuality*: WA, quoted Wright, p. 144.

370 *written on my*: DC, quoted Murphy, p. 35.

370 *I hope you*: WA to the Carwithens, 23 Apr. 1961. Quoted Wright, p. 279.

371 *hysterical*: Jonathan Alwyn, quoted Wright, p. 182.

372 *like a ship's*: DC, quoted Murphy, p. 15.

372 *a garden of*: DC, quoted Wright, p. 188.

373 *tall trees and*: DC, quoted Wright, p. 185.

373 *like an enchanted*: Elisabeth Lutyens to WA, 5 Oct. 1973. WAA.

373 *like visiting Gormenghast*: Jonathan Alwyn, quoted Wright, p. 190.

374 *As usual she*: DC, quoted Wright, p. 239.

374 *true feminine fulfillment*: Betty Friedan, *The Feminine Mystique* (New York: W. W. Norton & Co., 1963), p. 18.

375 *her zest for*: Patrick Cory, 'Obituary: Dorothy Howell 1898–1982', *Royal Academy of Music Magazine* (Spring 1983).

375 *327 million visits*: Manning, p. 51.

376 *more surprising*: DH papers. DHT.

376 *deep and abiding*: Manning, p. 51.

376 *A Mass for Ampleforth*: Byrne dates the *Mass for Ampleforth* to 1967, but Howell's diary places its completion date before December 1966. It was published a year later.

376 *1,630 copies*: Dorothy Howell's royalty statement from Ascherberg, Hopwood & Crew for 1968. DHT.

376 *a melody which*: *Church Music*, Vol. 2/24 (Apr. 1968).

377 *I am not*: J. E., 'Women Make Music', *Sunday Times*, 24 Apr. 1960.

377 *none of the*: ibid.

377 *serviceable enough*: 'Women Composers of Today', [unknown newspaper and day], 1960. Clipping held at DHT.

377 *It was as*: Donald Mitchell, 'Too Decorous Women Composers', *Daily Telegraph*, 19 Apr. 1960.

377 *Every lesson*: Berendina Norton, private correspondence with the author.

378 *My heart aches*: Dora Clarke to RC, 22 Mar. 1967. Provided by CJ.

379 *English viola player*: 'Rebecca Clarke': Stanley Sadie (ed.), *New Grove Dictionary of Music and Musicians* Vol. 4 (London: Macmillan, 1980), p. 448.

379 *that one little*: Clarke, quoted in 'Robert Sherman', p. 171.

380 *Nowadays, people*: RC, *Father*, p. 149. CJ.

381 *Rebecca's passing*: 'Rebecca Clarke', *New York Times*, 19 Oct. 1979.

382 *Had she not*: 'Rewarding Program Assembled by Toby Appel for Viola Recital', *New York Times*, 4 Apr. 1977.

382 *I take this*: 'Rebecca Clarke's 1977 Program Note on the Viola Sonata', *A Rebecca Clarke Reader*, p. 226.

382 *Sonata's first recording*: Josef Koďousek & Květa Novotná, *Benjamin Britten, Rebecca Clarke, Henry Eccles: Compositions for Viola and Piano* (Supraphon 1111 2694, 1980).

382 *over-played*: Wilfrid Mellers, 'Masters, Originals and Also-rans', *Times Literary Supplement*, 1 Nov. 1996.

382 *better-recorded works*: Presto Music, a record catalogue site, lists more than thirty recordings of the Sonata. However, to put into context the idea that Rebecca's music was at any point 'over-played', just one of Beethoven's Piano Sonatas, the 'Moonlight', has more than nine hundred listings.

382 *the startling*: Desmond Shawe-Taylor, 'Songs of England', *Sunday Times*, 14 Jun. 1981.

383 *almost self-parodying*: Barry Millington, 'Songmakers' Almanac', *The Times*, 8 Aug. 1978.

383 *an old battleaxe*: Michael Kennedy, 'One Woman and the English Music Machine', *Daily Telegraph*, 24 Jun. 1967.

383 *a revelation*: Simon Heffer, 'Force-10 Gale of Musical Drama', *Daily Telegraph*, 2 Aug. 1994.

383 *Very depressed*: DH Diary, 16 Aug. 1968. DHT.

384 *I heard her*: Merryn Columb, private interview with the author.

385 *I think she*: ibid.

385 *Cold got me*: DH Diary, 18 Dec. 1981. DHT.

387 *cups her breasts*: William Alwyn, *All Things Corruptible*. Quoted Wright, p. 203.

387 *hailed as*: WA quoted ibid., p. 243.

387 *premiere in 1997*: Mary would have been delighted by *Miss Julie*'s more positive recent reception. Chandos released a recording in 2020 which got a warm critical welcome – with noticeably few comments about the libretto.

Sakari Oramo and BBC Symphony Orchestra, Alwyn: *Miss Julie* (Chandos CHAN5253, 2020)

387 *was rather nonplussed*: John Turner, quoted ibid., p. 256. William also approached other local women to sit for him.

389 *I keep on*: WA, quoted Murphy, p. 13.

389 *All my colleagues*: WA to Bernard Barrell, Jul. 1976, quoted Wright, p. 254.

389 *disappointment*: ibid., p. 255. It was Elisabeth Lutyens who first tried to put William forward for an honorary degree, in 1973.

390 *said I would*: DC, quoted Wright, p. 265.

390 *hitting bottom*: Brian Murphy to DC, 7 Jan. 1986. WAA.

390 *suicide*: Andrew Palmer, private correspondence with the author.

391 *It was a*: DC, *Violet*.

391 *turn your thoughts*: William Blezard to DC, 20 Sept. 1985. WAA.

392 *into a period*: William Blezard to DC, 8 Nov. 1987. WAA.

392 *There is still*: William and Joan Blezard to DC, 22 Dec. 1990. WAA.

392 *a passionate outpouring*: Geoffrey Norris, 'Classical CD of the week', *Daily Telegraph*, 31 Jan. 1998.

392 *a remote, even*: Wright, p. 275.

393 *visibly moved*: ibid., p. 273.

393 *made smaller by*: ibid., p. 273.

393 *a lovely lady*: Kim Hammond, quoted Wright, p. 268.

393 *inconsolable grief*: Wright, p. 273.

393 *It seemed too*: DC, *Violet*.

394 *was beginning to*: William Blezard to DC, 22 Dec. 1990. WAA.

394 *a substantial creative*: 'Doreen Carwithen', *Independent*, 18 Jan. 2003.

394 *I am not*: DC, quoted Wright, p. 189.

EPILOGUE

395 *really inventive*: All quotes by Rebecca Miller from a private interview with the author, 10 Mar. 2022.

395 *had never heard*: All quotes by Odaline de la Martínez from a private interview with the author, 9 Mar. 2022.

396 *embarrassingly banal*: Damian Thompson, 'There's a Good Reason Why There Are No Great Female Composers', *The Spectator*, 16 Sept. 2015.

397 *special pleading*: Tom Service, 'Symphony Guide: Louise Farrenc's Third', *Guardian*, 24 Jun. 2014.

397 *some of us*: All quotes by Dr Samantha Ege from a private interview with the author, 10 Mar. 2022.

398 *temptation to pretend*: Smyth, *A Final Burning*, p. 15.

INDEX

Numbers in *italic* refer to pages with illustrations.

Frankfurt Opera House, 175
Friskin, James: appearance, 138, 330, *340*; career, 330, 339, 358–9; character, 138, 330; Chautauqua Institution, 339, 341; death, 378; marriage, 332–3, 337–8, 359, 371; political views, 381; relationship with Rebecca, 330–3; summers in England, 359; will, 378–9; works, 138, 330
Friskin, Kate, 330, 332

Garrett, Rhoda, 56
Geistinger, Marie, 43–4
Gipps, Ruth, 357
Girton College, 32, 89, 118
Glanville-Hicks, Peggy, 341
Gloucester Cathedral, 251
Glyndebourne Opera, 396
Godfrey, Dan, 248, 270
Gordon Woodhouse, Violet, 128–31, 289
Goss, John, 267–8, 278–9, 333
Goss, Mabel, 267, 278, 279
Graham, Violet: cats, 390; death, 393; friendship with Doreen/Mary, 11, 304, 390, 393–4; musical education, 304; piano performances, 11, 312, 325, 327; piano playing, 304; prizes, 304; wartime activities, 311–12
the Grail society, 271–2
Grieg, Edvard, 391
Grove Dictionary of Music and Musicians, 131, 379

Hallé Orchestra, 233
Harty, Hamilton, 233
Hawaii, Rebecca's concerts, 196–7, 245
Haweis, Reverend Hugh Reginald, 31
Hayward, Marjorie, 163, 242, 259, *280*
Herbert, Muriel, 248
Herzogenberg, Heinrich von, 45–6, 49
Herzogenberg, Lisl von: appearance, 47; character, 47; death, 89; musical career, 47; relationship with Ethel, 45–7, 51–2, 55–8, 64, 89, 90; sister Julia, 49, 50–2, 57–8
Hess, Myra, 109, *110*,

Hildebrand, Adolf von, 49–50
Hildebrand, Irene von, 49–50
Hildegard von Bingen, 10
His Majesty's Theatre, 129
Hollingsworth, John, 346
Holloway Prison, 3, 156, 172, 175
Holmès, Augusta, 92
Houston Grand Opera, 396
Howard, Ernest, 145
Howell, Alfred (brother of Dorothy), 124, *125*, 271, 375, 378, 385
Howell, Carlo, 124, *125*, 183, 200–2, 203, 204, 271, 335
Howell, Charles Edward (father of Dorothy): appearance, *125*; career, 124, 126, 158; death, 270–1, 335; family life, 124, 127–8; marriage, 124; musicianship, 123, 127, 128; religion, 123, 124, 132; son Carlo's death, 201–2; support for Dorothy's musical career, 157–9, 204; travels, 126–7
Howell, Clifford (brother of Dorothy), 124, *125*, 132, 376
Howell, Columb (nephew of Dorothy), 15–16, 378, 384–5
Howell, Dorothy: appearance, 6–7, *17*, 123, *125*, 127, *133*, *185*, 201, 209, *210*, 249, 250, *358*; archery, 375–6; BBC job offer, 309; birth, 124; broadcast premiere of Piano Sonata, 385; broadcasting work, 246–50, 272, 310; brother Carlo's death, 201–2, 204, 271, 335; car (Freddie), 357, *358*, 375; career, 6, 204–5, 212, 216, 236, 250, 272, 309–10, 334, 354, 357; career plans, 134–5, 204; CEMA concerts, 310–11, 334; character, 3, 6, 186–7, 211–12, 214; childhood, 13, 123–8, 285; commission for songs, 212; composing, 157–8, 159, 184, 202, 221–2, 269, 271, 309, 335, 354–5, 385; composing music for children, 158, 223–4, 236–7, 272; conducting offer, 235; death, 9, 385; diary, 16, 335, 354, 357, 383, 385; *Divertissements* premiere, 336; education, 16, 131–4, 157, 159; Elgar Society, 336; Elgar's

Woolf, Virginia: appearance, *275*; character, 275–6; correspondence with Ethel, 19, 277, 298, 299–301, 383; death, 276, 300–1, 316; diary, 276, 298, 383; on Ethel, 28, 274, 276, 278, 288–9, 383; on Ethel and Emmeline, 3; first meeting with Ethel, 273–4; listening to Ethel's music, 278, 289; relationship with Ethel, 20, 28, 274–7, 287, 298–9; relationship with Vita, 275–6, 318; wartime, 298; women's wartime employment, 324; works, 274, 288

World War I: anti-German activities, 188; Armistice Day, 194; bombing raids, 182–3, 200, 294; deaths, 201–2, 229; declaration, 177–8; Dorothy's activities, 182; effects on musical life, 178–9, 205, 233; Ethel's pro-war stance, 179–80; Ethel's war work, 181–2, 192, 216, 317; gas attacks, 188; gendered war propaganda, 193–4; German Spring Offensive,

194; Rebecca in America, 188–9, 200; spiritualism, 218–19; trenches, 182; volunteers, 183; Women's Land Army, 193; women's wartime employment, 324

World War II: Air Raid warnings, 304; Blitz, 293–4, 297, 298, 306, 328; British film industry, 344; conscientious objectors, 323; declaration, 291; Doreen's experiences, 292, 301, 304; Dorothy's war work, 291, 293, 308–9, 311, 335; effects on musical life, 294–8, 335; flying bombs (V-1s and V-2s), 311–12; gendered war propaganda, 324–5; German raids, 298–9; Rebecca in America, 292, 294, 305–6, 307–8, 331; VE-Day, 322; Women's Land Army, 291, 293, 308–9, 311; women's wartime employment, 324

Ysaÿe, Eugène, 83